Business Process Driven Database Design

with Oracle PL/SQL

(Edition II)

Rajeev Kaula

Contents

Preface

Business Process driven Database Design with PL/SQL (Edition II) extends the previous edition with updated content along with review questions and problem-solving exercises. A new database has been added to provide more problem-solving skills. The textbook embraces a fresh approach to database design. It outlines database design from a business perspective that is rooted in the concept of a business process. Unlike traditional texts that generally outline database design from an application perspective, this book takes a broader approach that dovetails how the concept of a business process that is utilized for business operations can also be the foundation for database design. Such an approach ensures a more robust and integrated database structure that is more closely aligned with business goals and objectives.

The textbook also extends the understanding of database beyond standalone SQL. This extension is through the integration of business logic with database design thereby enabling better support for enterprise applications. The incorporation of business logic facilitates the threading of SQL with logic constructs thereby providing a richer understanding of database manipulation and utilization. In a way, business process driven database design encapsulates both facets of a database – its structure and business logic manipulation to provide a wholesome understanding and processing of organizational data.

This book is for anyone (student or professional) who desires to understand database design in a way that is more business-oriented. It can also be used as a textbook in a level 1 or level 2 database design course. Database design as outlined in the book involves the modeling of business operations through entity-relationship (ER) and relational models. The extension of database design through business logic processing is provided through database stored program units. The inclusion of business logic as part of database design in a way also supports Oracle's thick database paradigm. Such a paradigm emphasizes the placement of procedural logic to implement business activities or functions in a database such that they are securely hidden from outside of the database entities.

The book covers essential concepts of business process modeling with business rules, conceptual modeling with ER diagrams, relational model with SQL, and database programming to ensure proper implementation of business logic. Oracle's primary database language PL/SQL is introduced to develop database program units that can support business rules and business logic. The topics are explained in a simplified way through tutorials and many examples for a reader to quickly grasp the material. It is written in a hands-on style for any student or professional to expand their knowledge of database design from a fresh perspective.

Structure of the book

The book consists of nine chapters and four appendixes. Chapter 1 introduces database and its features. Chapter 2 covers conceptual modeling with the entity-relationship model. Chapter 3 introduces database design with business process modeling and business rules concepts. The chapter outlines the transformation of business rules into ER model. Chapter 4 introduces essential relational model concepts and SQL along with the transformation of ER model into database tables. Chapter 5 covers more detailed SQL. Chapter 6 introduces Oracle's PL/SQL language that is extended with database program units coverage in Chapter 7. Chapter 8 introduces PL/SQL web features through the PL/SQL Web Toolkit. Chapter 9 outlines the business logic aspect of database design through PL/SQL. Appendix A lists the first database Superflex Apartment tables, while Appendix B provides the SQL script for installing the database tables. Appendix C lists the second database Outdoor Clubs & Product tables, while Appendix D provides the SQL script for installing the database tables.

Prerequisite

The book presumes no prior background in database, but some understanding of structured programming logic is recommended to discern business logic implementation with PL/SQL. To practice the examples in the book the following software should be installed: (i) Software diagraming software like Oracle SQL Developer Data Modeler (free download from www.oracle.com), Microsoft Visio, ConceptDraw Diagram, and so on for ER diagraming, (ii) Oracle Express Edition (XE) DBMS (free download from www.oracle.com), and (iii) Oracle SQL Developer (free download from www.oracle.com) for working with SQL and PL/SQL languages. Oracle XE should be installed first followed by Oracle SQL Developer.

Using the book

Details on the topics covered in the book are listed in the table of contents. To get the most out of the book it is strongly recommended that anyone reading the book practice the chapter examples. To practice the book ER diagraming examples, use any of the diagraming software listed above or any other similar software. To practice the book SQL and PL/SQL examples, use (copy) the SQL script in Appendix B and Appendix D to install the two textbook databases.

Chapter 1. Introduction to Database

Databases have long played a critical role in enterprise applications ranging from desktop and web systems to emerging mobile systems. Nearly all enterprise systems and applications interact with relational databases. Relational databases have become the standard for enterprise data. However, as businesses view their operations in terms of business processes, enterprise applications built on relational databases need to be more business processes-centered. As a consequence, database design and development has to move from being application-driven to become business process-driven.

This chapter introduces the topic of database with a description of its features, along with an overview of the software that manages the database environment. Since database software is separated from business applications, the nature of database access by business applications in the context of Oracle's thick database paradigm is explained followed by the database development process.

Database Features

A database is a repository of data on business activities. Essential features that define a database environment include integrated data, reduced data duplication, and program/data duplication.

Shared and Integrated Data

The data stored in a database repository is integrated and shared from an organizational perspective. Data integration involves combining the data utilized for various business operations into a unified and uniform representation. This means that for example data pertaining to sales order in Marketing is combined with shipping and inventory data in Production, along with invoice and payment data in Accounting. Such integration enables an application in Production to access correct information from Accounting on a sales order, and if changes are made in Production on the sales order, then other functional areas or applications can get the updated information.

Reduced Data Duplication

Since the data in a database is integrated, there is less duplication of information. Data on various business activities or things of significance like sales order, customer, employee, etc. need to be recorded only once. As data is recorded once, there are fewer problems pertaining to accuracy, reliability, and integrity of data across an organization. Reduced data duplication also ensures that business rules and constraints are uniformly and consistently enforced across business operations.

Program/Data Independence

Data in a database is structured and modeled independently of how it will be accessed by application programs. This separation of applications from their data in a database, provides flexibility in the development of applications. Applications can be modified without a corresponding change in the data that they will process. Also, data in database can be modeled on how the business activities are performed irrespective of whether there is an application to support a business activity. This feature minimizes the impact of data format changes on applications. Further, any modification in database is instantly available to all applications.

The concept of data independence eventually led to the development of the three-level ANSI-SPARC framework for database software design as shown in Figure 1-1. The objective of the three-level framework is to separate the users or business application view of the database from the way that it is physically stored on a storage device. It consists of external level, conceptual level, and internal level.

The external level defines the user or application view of the database. It is tailored to the user or business application data requirements. The conceptual and the internal level represent the entire database. The conceptual level describes the logical structure of database and is independent of how the data is physically stored on a storage device. This logical structure is also referred to as schema or conceptual schema. The internal level specifies how the conceptual schema is stored on a storage medium like a hard disk. The internal level representation is also referred as internal schema and can include specification of files, indexes, and other data structures.

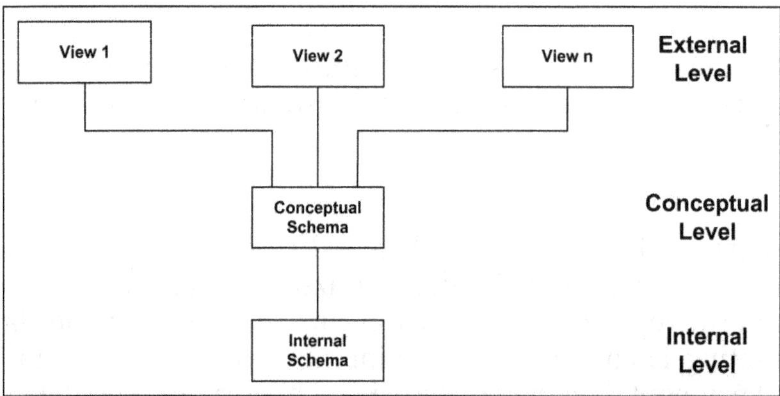

Figure 1-1: Three-level Framework for Database Software Design

The three-level framework provides many benefits for database and business application development.

- It allows for separate customized application views. This means that each user or business application can access the same data, but have different customized views of it.
- It hides the physical storage details from users or business application. This means that users and business applications do not have to deal with physical database storage details. They should be allowed to work with the data itself, without concern for how it is physically stored.
- The database administrator (DBA) should be able to change the database storage structures without affecting the views or the conceptual schema.

Database Management Systems (DBMS) Software

A database management system (DBMS) is a software that controls the development, maintenance, and use of a database repository. DBMS software have evolved over time from the initial versions offering just efficient storage and retrieval of data to the current versions that offer a broad and complex set of features like data dictionary, support for application languages, Web access, concurrent access, XML support, security management, and so on. The increasing complexity of DBMS software has necessitated the need of database administrators (DBAs) and other specialists to manage its working.

DBMS software utilizes data modeling concepts for structuring and retrieval of data. Most of the widely used DBMS software currently are based on the relational model for data storage and retrieval. As organizations increasingly view data as a business asset, data in DBMS has become the pivot for efficient running of business applications with organization-wide impact. To facilitate effective development of business applications, enterprise DBMS software follow the three-level ANSI-SPARC framework of Figure 1-1.

A DBMS software stores and manages data on a storage device like hard disk. It stores two categories of data as shown in Figure 1-2. One category consists of definitions of data items for business activity and subjects like sales order, customer, employee, location, etc.. The other category consists of values assigned to the defined data items. The category that consists of definitions of data items is called as *metadata*, and often referred as *data dictionary*.

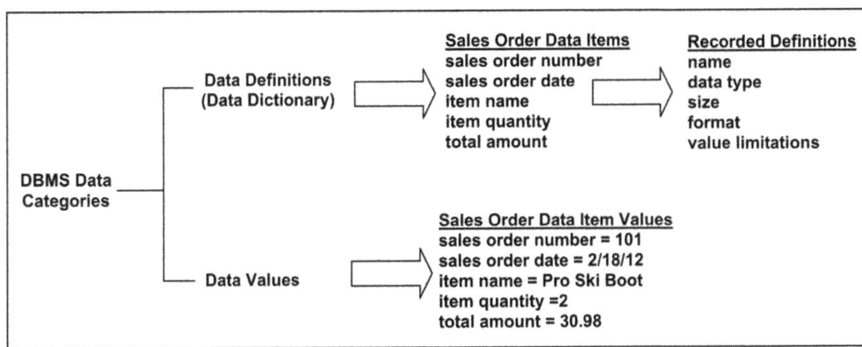

Figure 1-2: Category of Data in DBMS

For example, suppose information about sales order has to be recorded in the database. The data dictionary storage will consist of the definition of this business subject name i.e. sales order, along with the definition of different data items that will be part of sales order like sales order number, sales order date, item name, item quantity, and total amount. The values taken by the various data items in sales order will now be the other category of data. These values are then manipulated by business applications. In general, a data dictionary besides recording data definitions, also records relationship definitions, security specifications, along with information on data origin, usage, and format.

Some of the major components or subsystems of the DBMS software are DBMS engine, data definition subsystem, data manipulation subsystem, and data administration subsystem (shown in Figure 1-3). Each of the subsystem is described briefly:

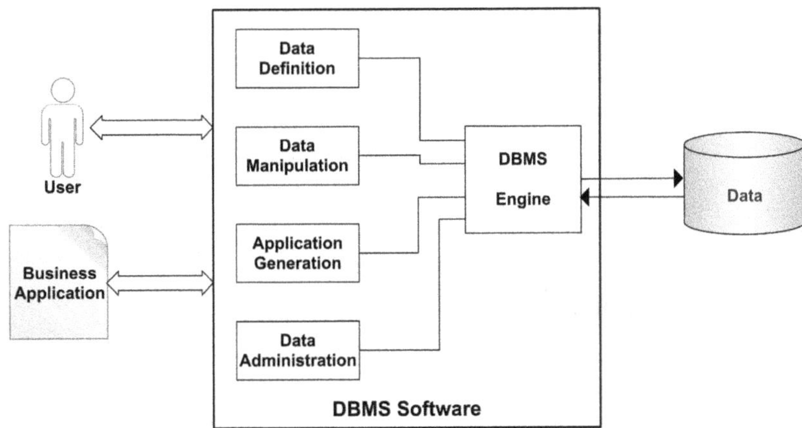

Figure 1-3: DBMS Subsystems

DBMS Engine

DBMS engine accepts logical requests from various other DBMS subsystems, and converts them into physical equivalents for access to a storage device like hard drive.

Data Definition Subsystem

Data Definition subsystem enables the creation of the structure of the database and the associated data dictionary. It allows the creation and maintenance of tables, relationships, and constraints.

Data Manipulation Subsystem

Data manipulation subsystem enables the retrieval and manipulation of data in database. It includes tools like SQL, report generator, and query-by-example (QBE).

Application Generation Subsystem

Application generation subsystem contains facilities to develop transaction-intensive applications like data entry screens, and programming language interfaces including DBMS specific database languages like PL/SQL.

Data Administration Subsystem

Data administration subsystem ensures the administration of the overall database environment through the software. It consists of features like backup and recovery, security management, query optimization, concurrency control, and change management.

Business Application Interaction with DBMS

As all business applications utilize DBMS software to store and retrieve data, there are two general frameworks that specify how applications interact with the DBMS. One framework is referred to as the client-server framework as shown in Figure 1-4(a). In the client-server framework, the business applications reside on the client machines, while the DBMS is on a separate machine referred to as a database server. Users interact through a GUI (Graphical User Interface) with the business application. The business application interacts with the database server over a network through the database language SQL. The database server is shared among client applications. The client applications request the database server to retrieve or manipulate data. The database server locates and processes the data, and returns the results back to the application.

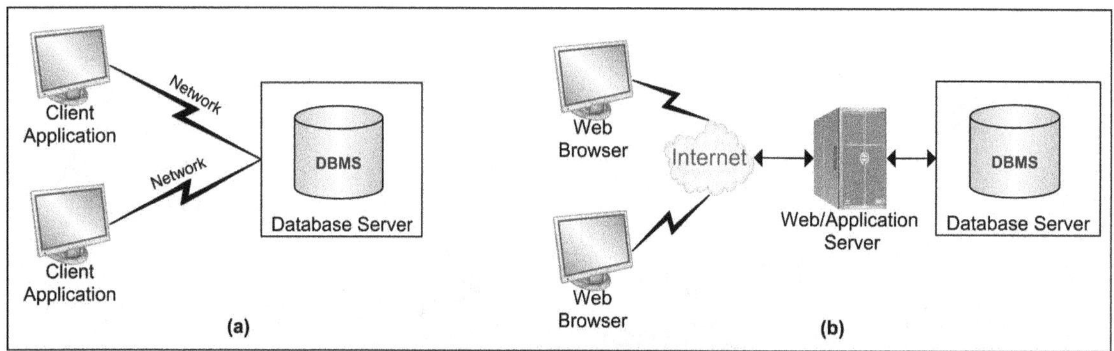

Figure 1-4: Frameworks for Application Interaction with DBMS

The second framework as shown in Figure 1-4(b) is referred as a Web framework. In this framework, the business applications are hosted on a separate machine referred as a Web server.

Users interact with their applications through a Web browser. The Web server processes the business application, and as part of processing interacts with the database server over a network through the database language SQL. The applications on the Web server request the database server to retrieve or manipulate data. The database server locates and processes the data, and returns the results back to the Web server, which then formats the output for display in the Web browser.

To handle the increasing complexity of Web applications, the Web framework is often extended with the inclusion of another server between the Web server and the database server called an application server. The application server houses the business application logic and also handles the interaction with the database server.

A business application interacts with the database server in two ways as shown in Figure 1-5.

- In the first approach, the business application directly accesses the SQL Engine in the database server for all retrieval and manipulation of data. For example, an application written in Visual Basic or PHP directly communicates with the database server through its application logic using the database language SQL for retrieval and manipulation of data. This interaction is often referred as Inline SQL.
- In the second approach, business rules and business logic reside on the database server in the form of stored program units. Data retrieval and manipulation by the SQL Engine is now handled by the stored program units API (application program interface). As database is shared among business applications, these stored program units are also shared among business applications. The business applications now complements their direct interaction with the database server by involving stored program units. Utilization of stored program units for application development enhances database processing for applications.

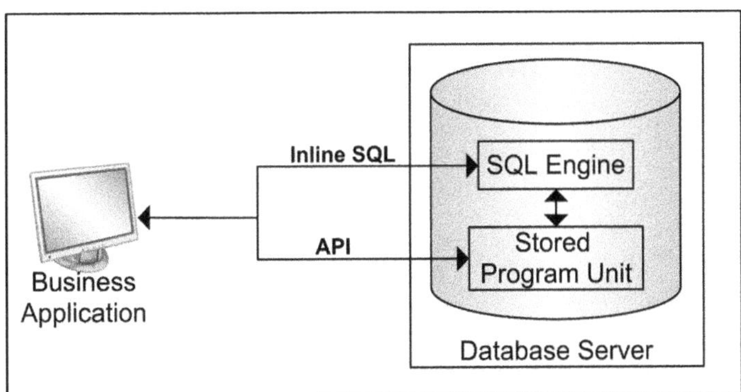

Figure 1-5: Nature of Database Interaction by Applications

Stored program units facilitate a data-centric approach toward business applications. It is also referred as thick database paradigm by Oracle. Thick database paradigm emphasizes the placement of procedural logic to implement each business activity or function securely hidden from outside-of-the-database entities, thereby enabling an organization to better handle changes in the business environment.

For instance, suppose an organization has developed a business application in C# language, but for some reason now plans to migrate the application to Java language. Re-writing the entire application including the implementation of all the business logic is costly and time-consuming. However, if the organization follows a data-centric thick database paradigm approach that involves good data modeling, wherein most of the business logic is implemented at the database level through stored program units, the migration will take less time, as most of the business rules affecting business logic are already taken care by the database. Besides, stored program units can greatly reduce the amount of traffic going back and forth over the network and improve database server security by preventing SQL injection (a technique to maliciously exploit applications that use client-supplied data in SQL statements) attacks.

Database Development Process

Database development is a systematic process involving a series of phases from concept to design to implementation, with the goal of developing an operational database for business applications and business processes in an organization. These phases as depicted in Figure 1-6 are conceptual data modeling, logical data modeling, and physical database design. The conceptual data modeling and logical data modeling phases are concerned with the logical representation of information, while the physical database design phase is concerned with the implementation of information on storage medium. These phases are described now.

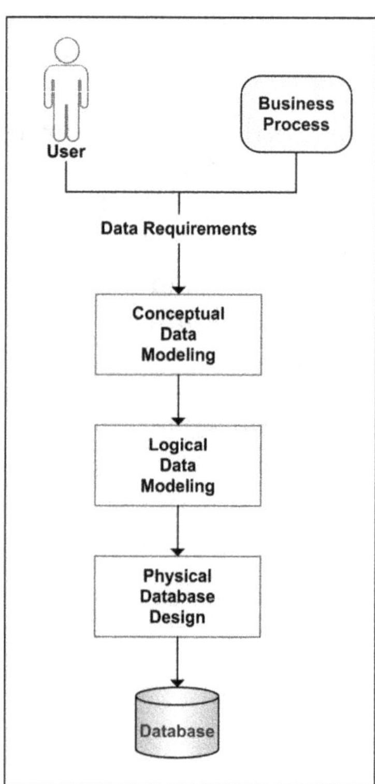

Figure 1-6: Database Development Phases

Conceptual Data Modeling

This phase transforms the business rules and associated data requirements of users, applications, and business processes into a conceptual data model such as Entity Relationship (ER) model. Conceptual data models are representations of business rules that map business data and its utilization during business operations. Conceptual model creates such maps in the form of entity types and relationships. Specifically, it describes the things of significance to an organization (entity types), about which it is inclined to collect information, and the characteristics (attributes) and associations between such pairs of those entity types (relationships). Figure 1-7 shows a part of an ER model of an apartment rental business process. The rectangles (Apartment and Rental) represent entity types, while the labeled line (Rents) represents relationship. Data requirements are expressed through interviews with users, documentation of existing systems or business processes, review of prevailing guidelines, information sources, and questionnaires. The ER model is not tied to implementation details.

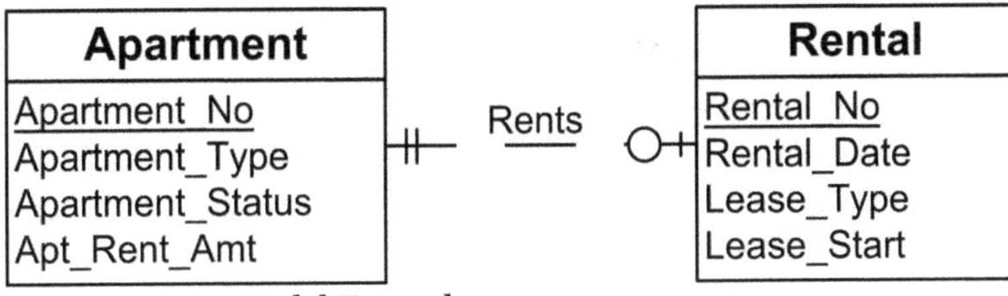

Figure 1-7: ER Model Example

Logical Data Modeling

This phase transforms the ER model of conceptual data modeling phase into a structure for implementation on a commercial DBMS. The focus is not on efficient implementation on the DBMS. The attempt in this phase is to refine the ER model for implementation. Since most of the commercial DBMS are based on the relational model, the logical data modeling phase usually produces a relational data model. Consequently, the ER model is transformed into a relational model.

Physical Database Design

The physical database design is concerned with the efficient implementation of the logical model on the storage medium like hard disk. Besides implementation of relational model structures, this phase also considers performance improvements, storage, and access methods and structures.

The database development process oftentimes is not performed in isolation. It is conducted along with activities in the systems analysis, systems design, and systems implementation phases of systems development process. The conceptual data modeling phase is part of the systems analysis phase. The logical data modeling phase is part of the systems design phase, while the physical database design phase is completed during systems design and system implementation phases.

Database Design Approaches

There can be two approaches to database design and development. The first approach is application driven, while the second approach is business process driven. Both approaches are explained now.

Application driven Database Design

Database design is often perceived from the perspective of application development and tied to systems development life cycle and its variants. The structure of database and the processing of business operational logic involving database is tied to the application. Even though with the development of three-level ANSI framework database structure was separated from application, processing of business logic was still perceived from the perspective of individual applications. In this approach, the conceptual and logical database design is often determined through application requirements. As shown in Figure 1-8 (a), business logic processing involving database is still handled through the application in the form of inline SQL.

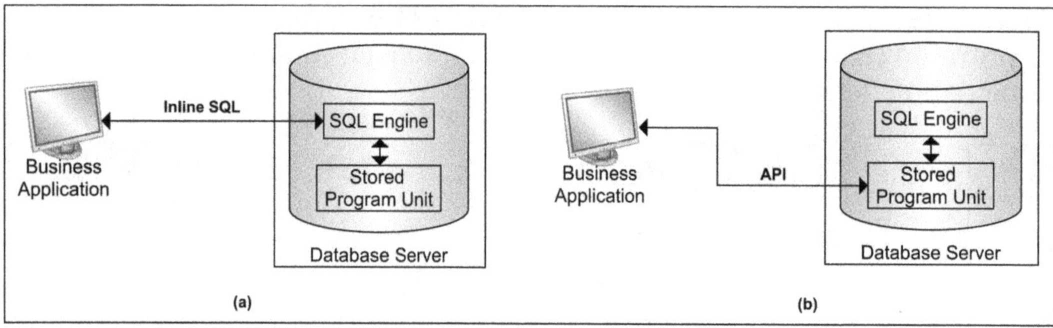

Figure 1-8: Application driven Database Design

A variant of this approach is Oracle's thick database paradigm. Thick database paradigm emphasizes the placing of the procedural or business logic to implement each business activity or function securely hidden from outside-of-the-database applications. In other words, thick database paradigm moves the business logic that is associated with database from applications to stored program units inside the DBMS. In this environment, applications interact with stored program units as shown in Figure 1-8 (b) for business logic processing through stored program unit API.

Business Process driven Database Design

With the development of the Internet and its accompanying global marketplace, businesses largely adopted enterprise systems like ERP to handle business operations. Enterprise systems utilized the concept of business process to automate business operations as the business process approach provided a mechanism to map business operations with information technology. In this environment business process operational guidelines were streamlined in the form of business rules. While these guidelines (or business rules) were largely independent of business applications or information technology, they facilitated identification of the data (entity types) utilized by the business process along with how it is handled or processed (business logic).

As a business process may involve one or more applications to complete the operational task, database structure and associated business logic need not be tied to individual applications. Instead, it should be separated from the application. Database structure and associated business logic should now be specified independently within the context of business processes. Database development will commence with the conceptual and logical design of the database followed by its associated business logic through interaction with business process specifications. In this approach (Figure 1-9) business application interacts with stored program units in the database to execute business logic.

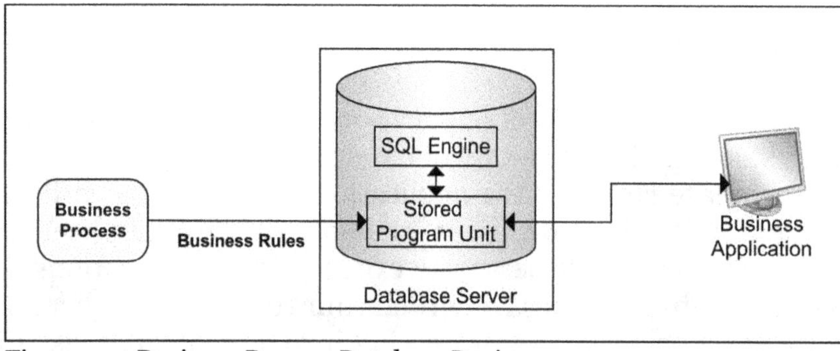

Figure 1-9: Business Process Database Design

Business process-driven database design approach (i) allows applications to focus more on user interface (UI) and other features, and (ii) provide the flexibility to work across different levels of interface like desktop, Web, mobile, and cloud. This approach also tweaks Oracle's thick database paradigm from a database design perspective such that the database structure and business logic affecting the database can be developed and implemented inside the DBMS independent of the applications.

Review Questions

1. List the various features of database.
2. Describe the concept of data independence.
3. What is the objective of three-level ANSI-SPARC architecture for database software design.
4. Describe the levels of the three-level ANSI-SPARC architecture for database software design.
5. What is the purpose of database management system (DBMS) software.
6. Describe data dictionary.
7. Describe the subsystems of DBMS.
8. What are the frameworks that facilitate business application interaction with DBMS.
9. Describe conceptual data modeling.
10. Describe logical data modeling.

Review Exercises

1. The data stored in a database repository is integrated and ________ from an organizational perspective.
2. Data in a database is structured and modeled __________ of how it will be accessed by application programs.
3. The objective of the three-level architecture is to separate the __________ view of the database from the way that it is physically stored on a storage device.
4. The conceptual level describes the logical _________ of data.
5. The _______ ________ accepts logical requests from various other DBMS subsystems, and converts them into physical equivalents for access on a storage device like hard drive.
6. In the client-server framework the business __________ reside on the client machines, while the __________ is on a separate machine referred as a database server.
7. In the Web framework, business applications are hosted on a separate machine referred as a _______ Server.
8. _________ data models are maps of business data and their relationships.
9. The ________ data modeling phase usually produces a relational data model.

Chapter 2. Introduction to Data Modeling

Entity-relationship (ER) modeling provides a visual approach to create an abstract and conceptual representation (diagram) of business data or information related to business operation. It is the primary technique to perform data modeling during the conceptual data modeling phase of the database development process. It facilitates a visual representation of the data model thereby providing for more effective communication with the organization in understanding its operations. Due to its visual representation, it is easy to understand. While the ER model is not tied to data implementation details or how data may change, it can be easily transformed through well-defined rules into a relational model.

This chapter outlines the fundamentals of conceptual data modeling through the entity-relationship diagram. It provides the basic skills of ER modeling. As there are many ER modeling notations, the book focuses on the Crow Foot notation. The transformation of the ER model into a relational model is outlined in a later chapter.

Entity Relationship (ER) Model

ER modeling approach models the utilization of data by business as specified through business rules or business guidelines into (i) categories referred to as entity types and (ii) associations among entity types referred to as relationships. An entity type represents any logical collection of data of interest to an organization. So an entity type can represent anything that an organization needs to store in the database. Technically, it is a term given to a collection of data that represents facts and constraints pertaining to the entity as expressed through relevant business rules. For example, "customer" can be the name of an entity type that represents a collection of data on various characteristics and facts about a customer (like customer name, address, email, and so on) that are important to a business. These characteristics of an entity type are referred to as attributes. From the customer example, customer name, address, email are attributes of the customer entity type. A similar rationale applies to other entity types in business like employee, product, sales order, and so on.

Relationships indicate the use of data during business operations. Such use of data is identified through an understanding of business rules that impact business operations. Relationships are names given to semantic expressions that represent the utilization of data during business operations. From a data modeling standpoint relationships reflect association among entity types. For instance, "a customer places a sales order" is a very common business rule representing business interaction with customers. However, from a data modeling standpoint, it implies that if "customer" and "sales order" happen to be entity types, then, there will be a relationship between these two entity types.

As far as naming of entity types and relationships are concerned, in a loose sense, natural language semantics can be utilized. Entity types correspond to nouns, while relationships are verbs or prepositional phrases connecting nouns. From this perspective, one can abstract an entity-relationship diagram as a collection of business rule sentences.

Diagram Symbols

Entity-relationship diagrams have symbols to represent entity types, attributes, and relationships. Entity types are represented by a rectangle with two sections, wherein the name of the entity type appears in the top section of the rectangle. Attributes are listed in the lower section of the rectangle. Every entity type has an entity identifier, often referred to as the primary key. Figure 2-1 shows an entity type Rental with four attributes. The primary key of the rental entity type is Rental_No.

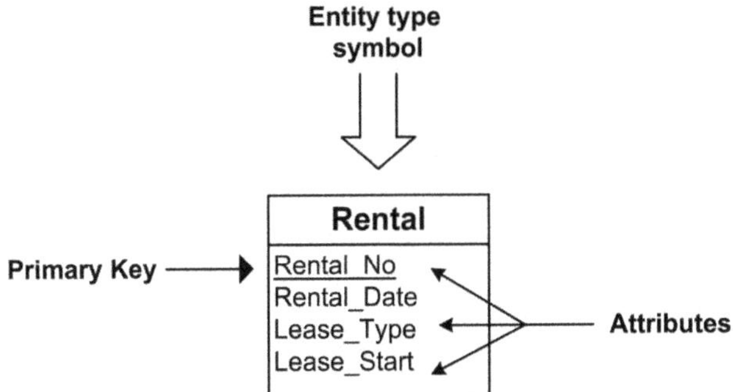

Figure 2-1: Entity Type Diagram Entries

The primary key or entity identifier is associated with the concept of entity instances. Entity instances are values collectively taken by attributes for each distinct value of the primary key. Technically, entity instances are referred to as entities. Often times entities and entity types are used interchangeably. Figure 2-2 shows three entity instances for entity type Rental. In the figure, each instance has a unique value of the primary key Rental_No.

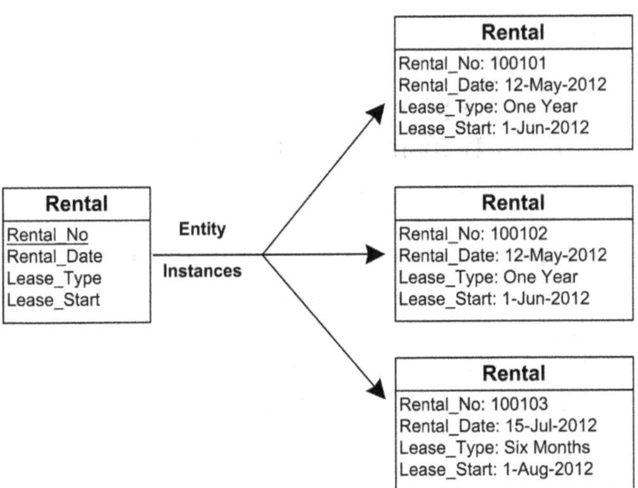

Figure 2-2: Entity Instance Example

Relationships in ER diagrams are bi-directional solid, dotted, or hyphenated lines connecting entity types. Often times relationships are named. The relationship name appears above the relationship line. In general, the relationship names should be as close as possible to the semantic expression of the business operation. Figure 2-3 shows a relationship between Rental entity type and Staff entity types in an apartment rental business. The relationship name "Facilitates" implies that every rental is facilitated by some staff (employee).

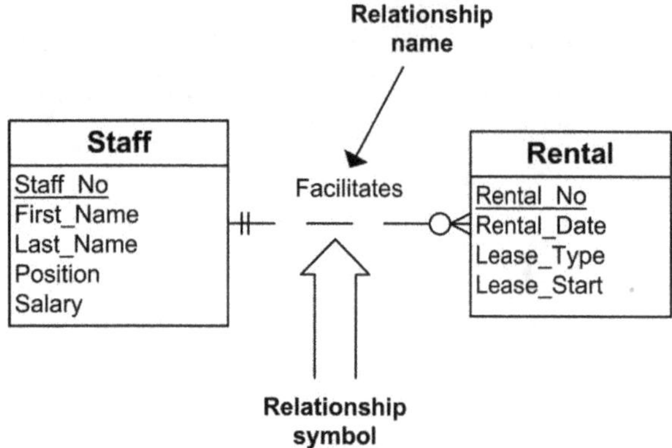

Figure 2-3: Relationship Representation

Relationship Cardinality

Relationships have constraints referred to as cardinality that specify the number of entity instances that participate in a relationship. Cardinality specification is classified into two categories: minimum cardinality and maximum cardinality. Minimum cardinality is the minimum number of entity instances of both entity types that participate in a relationship, while maximum cardinality is the maximum number of entity instances of both entity types that participate in the relationship. Cardinality specifications are expressed in both directions of a relationship.

To explain cardinality specifications, consider Figure 2-4. The figure shows entity instances for Rental and Staff entity types of Figure 2-3. In the figure, the Rental entity instances containing Rental_No 100101 and Rental_No 100102 are facilitated by the Staff entity instance containing Staff_No SA200, while the Rental entity instance containing Rental_No 100103 is facilitated by Staff entity instance containing Staff_No SA240. Staff entity instance with Staff_No SA220 has not facilitated any rental. So, from the entity instance relationship diagram one can conclude that:

(i) At a minimum, every Rental entity instance will be associated with a Staff entity instance, while a Staff entity instance may not be associated with a Rental entity instance. This indicates the minimum cardinality of the relationship.

(ii) At a maximum, a Rental entity instance is associated with only one Staff entity instance, while a Staff entity instance is associated with one or more Rental entity instances. This indicates the maximum cardinality of the relationship.

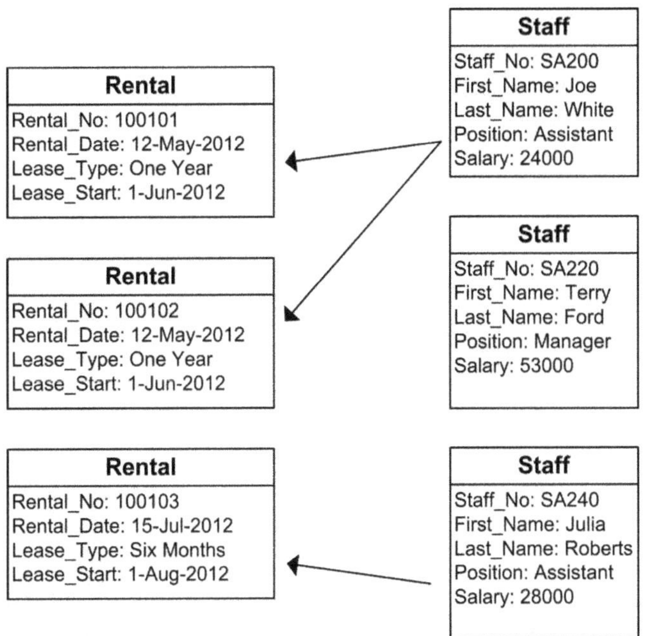

Figure 2-4: Entity Instance Relationship Example

Minimum cardinality can be expressed in two forms:

1. Zero (or optional) cardinality: Zero cardinality implies that it is possible for some entity instances to not have a relationship with an entity instance in the related entity type. Zero cardinality is also referred to as optional cardinality. Zero or optional minimum cardinality is shown by a circle symbol.
2. One (or mandatory) cardinality: One cardinality implies that it is required for each entity instance to have a relationship with some entity instance in the related entity type. One cardinality is also referred to as mandatory cardinality. One or mandatory minimum cardinality is shown by a vertical bar symbol.

Maximum cardinality can be expressed in two forms:

1. One cardinality: One cardinality implies that an entity instance can have a relationship with only one entity instance in the related entity type. One maximum cardinality is shown by a vertical bar symbol.
2. Many cardinality: Many cardinality implies that an entity instance can have a relationship with many entity instances in the related entity type. Many maximum cardinality is shown by a fork or crow's foot symbol.

Figure 2-5 shows cardinality representation with respect to the Facilitates relationship in an ER diagram. In the diagram, the minimum and maximum cardinality symbols are placed adjacent to each entity type in the relationship.

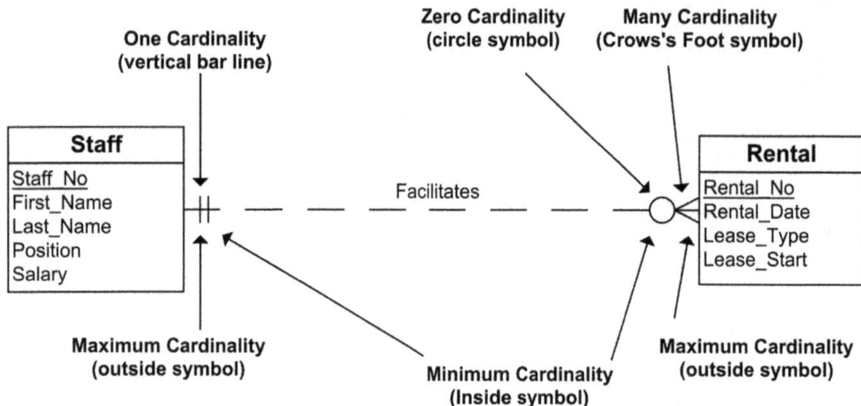

Figure 2-5: Relationship Cardinality Representation

The cardinality of an entity type is always read with respect to the minimum and the maximum cardinality specification appearing besides the related entity type on the other side of the relationship line. Figure 2-6 shows the reading of the cardinality for each entity type in a relationship.

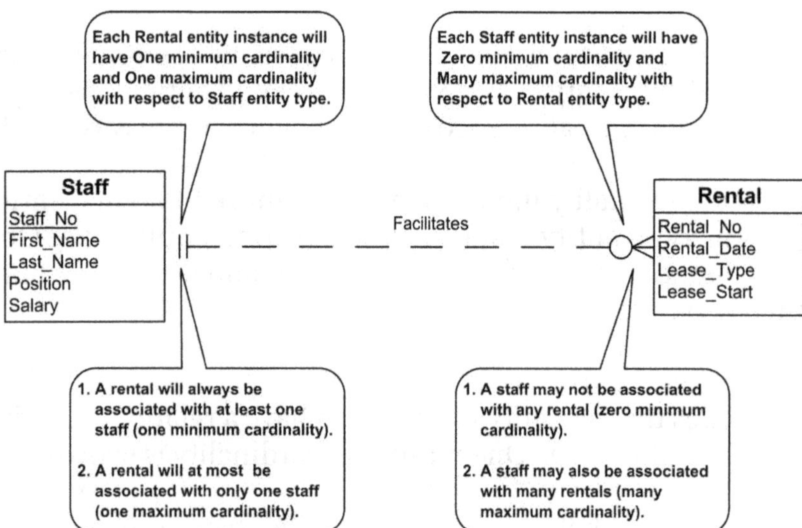

Figure 2-6: Cardinality Reference for Entity Types

Database Relationships Representation

ER model diagram shows database relationships based on how entity instances of one entity type are associated with entity instances of another entity type. As mentioned in Chapter 1, database relationships can be expressed in three forms: one-to-one (1:1), one-to-many (1:N), and many-to-many (M:N). Database relationship forms are generally based on the maximum cardinality specifications of a relationship.

One-to-One (1:1) Entity Relationship:

One-to-one (1:1) relationship exists if an entity instance of one entity type is related to only one entity instance of another entity type. Figure 2-7 shows a 1:1 relationship (Has) between Rental entity type and Apartment entity type in an apartment rental business. The maximum cardinality of the relationship implies that at a maximum one Rental entity instance will be associated with only one Apartment entity instance, and vice-versa. The minimum cardinality of the relationship implies that an Apartment entity instance may be optionally associated with a Rental entity instance, while a Rental entity instance will always be associated with an Apartment entity instance. The 1:1 cardinality is sometimes referred to as *single-valued* or *functional.*

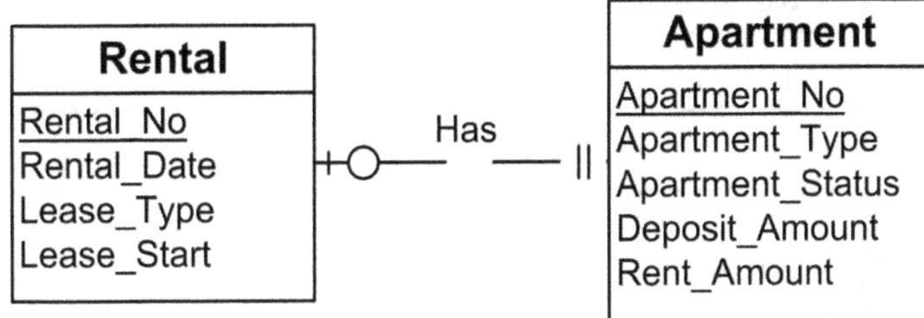

Figure 2-7: 1:1 Entity Relationship

One-to-Many (1:N) Entity Relationship:

One-to-many (1:N) relationship exists if an entity instance of one entity type is related to many entity instances of another entity type. Figure 2-5 shows the 1:N relationship (Facilitates) between Staff entity type and Rental entity type.

Many-to-Many (M:N) Entity Relationship:

Many-to-many (M:N) relationship exists if an entity instance of one entity type is related to more than one (many) entity instances of another entity type, and vice-versa. Figure 2-8 shows the M:N relationship (Files) between Rental entity type and Complaints entity type in an apartment rental business. The maximum cardinality of the relationship implies that at a maximum one Rental entity instance will be associated with many Complaints entity instances, and vice-versa. The minimum cardinality of the relationship implies that a Rental entity instance may be optionally associated with a Complaint entity instance, while a Complaint entity instance will always be associated with a Rental entity instance.

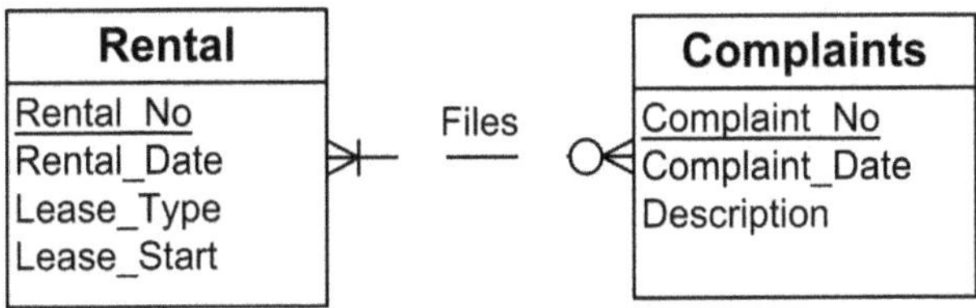

Figure 2-8: M:N Entity Relationship

Table 2-1 and Table 2-2 provide a summary of cardinality classifications.

Classification	Description
Mandatory	Minimum cardinality is one.
Optional	Minimum cardinality is zero.

Table 2-1: Cardinality Classification Summary

Classification	Description
1:1	Maximum cardinality is one in both directions.
1:N	Maximum cardinality is one in one direction, and maximum cardinality is more than one (N) in the other direction.
M:N	Maximum cardinality is more than one (N) in both directions.

Table 2-2: Cardinality Classification Summary

Identifying Relationship and Weak Entity Types

In an ER model, all attributes have single values within an entity instance. However, there are times when some attributes may have multiple values within the same entity instance. In these situations, the attributes that have multiple values are separated into another entity type, which is then designated as a weak entity type. The weak entity type is always dependent on the original entity type, as it contains attributes that essentially are part of the original entity type.

For example, consider the entity type Tenant in an apartment rental business as shown in Figure 2-9 (a). A sample entity instance of the Tenant entity type is also shown in the diagram. In the entity instance, the attributes License_No, Auto_Make, Auto_Model, Auto_Color have multiple values for the Tenant entity instance due to the fact that a tenant may have more than one automobile parked in the apartment complex. As each attribute within an entity instance can have only one value, attributes License_No, Auto_Make, Auto_Model, and Auto_Color are placed in another entity type called Tenant_Auto as shown in Figure 2-9 (b). Since the four attributes of Tenant_Auto essentially belong to the Tenant entity type, so the Tenant_Auto entity type will be dependent on the Tenant entity type. Tenant_Auto entity type now is a weak entity type with respect to Tenant entity type, and the relationship (Has) between Tenant and Tenant_Auto is referred as *identifying relationship*. Identifying relationships are always shown by solid lines.

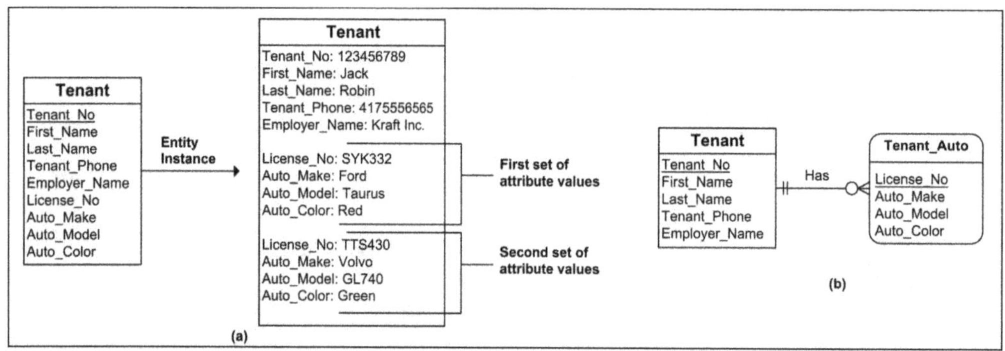

Figure 2-9: Weak Entity Type Representation

The identifying relationship is always 1:N, wherein the maximum cardinality from the original (strong) entity type to the weak entity type will always be many. Generally, the attributes within a weak entity type may not have a primary key. But, often times one (or more) attribute within the attributes may be selected as the primary key. To distinguish a weak entity type from other entity types in the ER model, often times a rounded rectangle box is utilized for its representation.

Relationship with Attributes

It is possible for database relationships to also have attributes, especially with M:N relationships. In an M:N relationship, the relationship attribute is associated with the combination of both entity types, not just one of the entity types. If an attribute is associated with only one entity type, then it should be part of that entity type and not the relationship. For example, in Figure 2-10 (a), the attribute Status is associated with the Files relationship. Hence attribute Status is associated with the combination of Rental and Complaints entity types. In other words, a Rental entity instance relationship with Complaints entity instance determines the value of the Status attribute. So, a Rental entity instance having a Rental_No attribute value of 100101 and a Complaint entity instance having Complaint_No attribute value of 10010 can have the Status attribute value Pending.

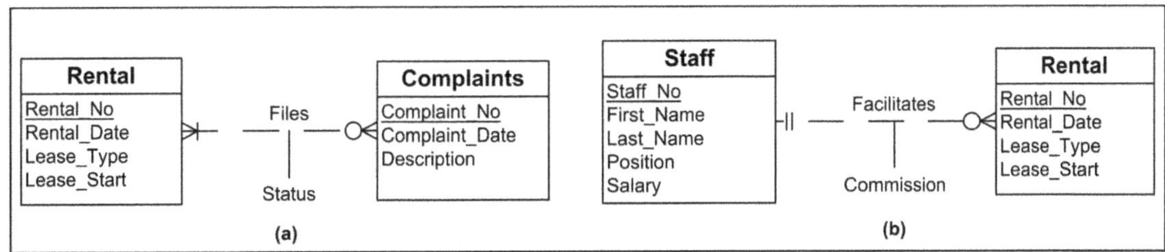

Figure 2-10: Representation of Database Relationship with Attributes

1:N relationships can also have attributes, but such specifications are much less common than M:N relationship with attributes. For example, in Figure 2-10 (b), the attribute Commission is associated with the Facilitates relationship, and hence is not in either Staff or Rental entity types. A Rental will have a commission only if it is facilitated by a Staff.

Self-Referencing Relationship

A self-referencing relationship involves association among members of the same entity type. These relationships are not common but do show important dependencies among instances of the same entity type. Figure 2-11(a) shows a self-referencing relationship Supervises involving the Staff entity type. Figure 2-11(b) shows the entity instances of the relationship. Since the relationship is 1:N, the entity instances are shown in a hierarchy, wherein the higher level Staff entity instance supervises lower-level Staff entity instances. Self-referencing relationships occur in a variety of business situations like dependency among accounts and parts.

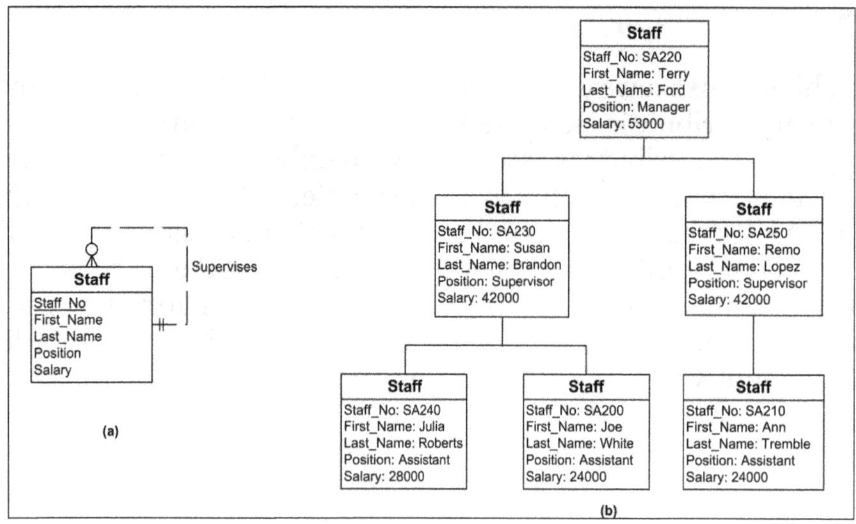

Figure 2-11: Representation of Self-Referencing Relationship

M-Way Relationship

M-Way relationships are short for multi-way relationships. These relationships involve more than two entity types. For example, the Chen ERD (which is named after Dr. Peter Chen published the landmark paper defining Entity-Relationship Model in 1976[1]) notation uses a diamond symbol to show the relationship between more than two entity types as shown in Figure 2-12(a). The Uses relationship lists suppliers and parts utilized on projects. Relationship instance in this case will specify what supplier provides what parts for what projects. In other words, each of the entity types now has a M:N relationship with each other.

The Crow's Foot notation cannot directly represent M-way relationships because the Crow's Foot notation only supports (binary) relationship between two entity types. To represent M-Way relationship, the Crow's Foot notation utilizes an *associative entity type*. An associative entity type is a weak entity that replaces an M-way relationship. The associate entity type has a 1:N relationship with the other M-Way entity types as shown in Figure 2-12(b).

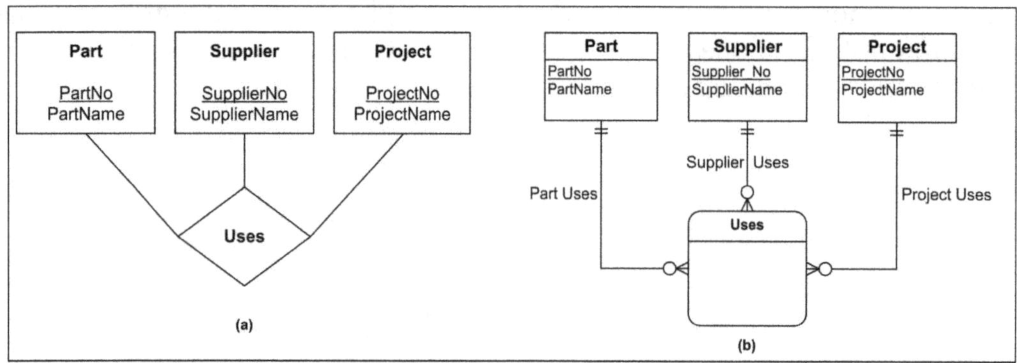

Figure 2-12: Representation of M-Way Relationship

[1] Peter Chen, "The Entity-Relationship Model: Toward a Unified View of Data," ACM Transactions on Database Systems, Vol. 1, 1976, pp. 9-36.

As an associative entity type represents an M-Way relationship (or M:N relationship among multiple entity types), it is also possible to represent M:N relationship between two entity types through an associative entity type. Figure 2-13 shows the representation of the Files relationship of Figure 2-10(a) through an associative entity type. The associative entity type Files in the diagram is a weak entity type. The Files entity type has a 1:N identifying relationship with the Rental and Complaints entity types. In other words, an M:N relationship can be converted into two identifying 1:N relationships through an associative entity type.

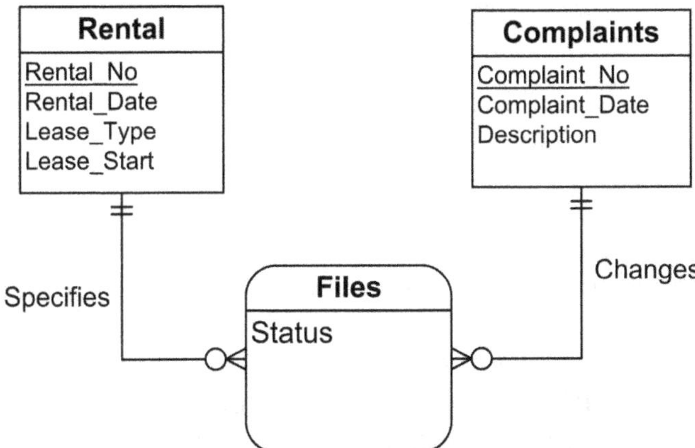

Figure 2-13: M:N Relationship with Associate Entity Type

Generalization Hierarchies

Generalization hierarchies represent a collection of entity types that are arranged in a hierarchical structure. A generalization hierarchy creates two levels of entity types. The top-level entity type is referred to as a *supertype*, while the lower-level entity types are referred to as *subtype*. The process of creating a generalization hierarchy begins by identifying common attributes among different entity types and placing (or moving) these common attributes into a supertype entity type. The entity types whose common attributes were placed in the supertype then become the subtype entity types. The supertype entity type is also referred to as a *parent* or generalized entity type, while a subtype entity type is also referred to as a *child*. The subtype entity is related to only one supertype entity type. The generalization hierarchy allows subtype entity types to show unique characteristics (attributes) of the entity that is being represented. The relationship between a supertype and subtype is also known as IS_A.

The hierarchical structure that associates the supertype and subtype entity types also provides for an *inheritance* relationship among the entity types. Inheritance characteristics of the relationship allow the subtype entities to inherit all or part of the attributes contained in the supertype entity type. One of the ideas behind the creation of a generalization hierarchy with inheritance characteristics is to allow further optimization of the data model by reducing duplication in the development of entity type structures.

Figure 2-14 shows a generalization hierarchy based on the structure of Staff and Tenant entity types in the apartment rental business. Figure 2-14(a) shows the attributes of the Staff and Tenant entity types. The common attributes of the two entity types are moved to a new supertype entity type Person in Figure 2-14(b). Once the common attributes are placed in the Person supertype, the Staff and Tenant entity types become subtype entities with unique characteristics.

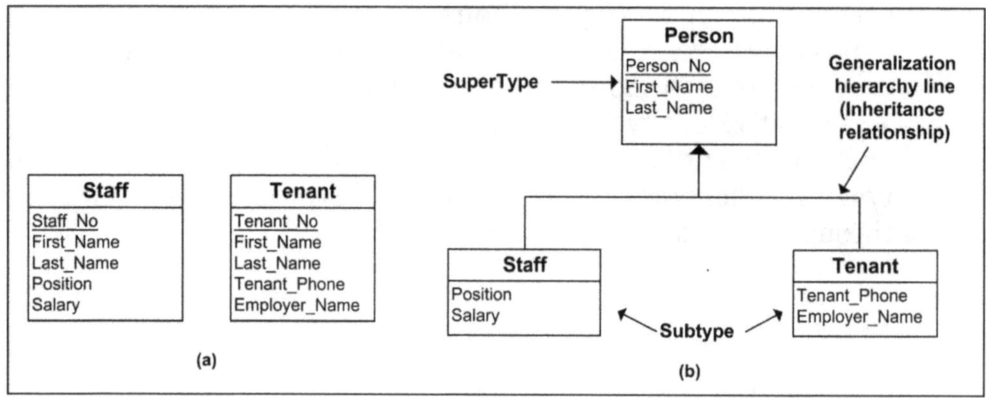

Figure 2-14: Representation of Generalization Hierarchy

Generalization hierarchies do not show the regular minimum and maximum cardinalities, because they are always the same. Instead, generalization hierarchies show a different type of cardinality that applies as a group between supertype and subtypes entity types. These generalization hierarchy cardinalities are referred to as *disjoint (D)* and *completeness (C)*[2]. Disjoint cardinality implies that a supertype entity instance can only be part of one of the subtype entity instances. In other words, the subtype entity instances are distinct. Figure 2-15(a) shows a disjoint constraint implying that a Person can either be a Staff or Tenant. Completeness cardinality implies subtypes are overlapping with supertype entity instance such that a supertype entity instance may be associated with more than one subtype entity instances. Figure 2-15(b) shows a generalization hierarchy with completeness cardinality where a Person can be both a Student and a Faculty, eg. a teaching assistant.

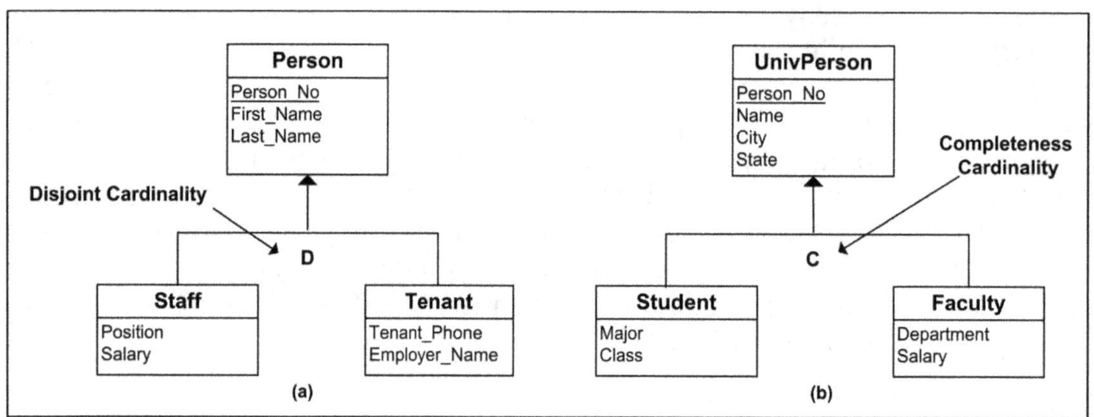

Figure 2-15: Generalization Hierarchy Cardinality Specification

Generalization hierarchies can be extended to more than one level. Figure 2-16 shows a multi-level generalization hierarchy pertaining to financial securities.

[2] The D and C symbols have been adopted from the book: Michael Mannino, Database Design, Application Development, and Administration (Third Edition), McGraw-Hill, 2007.

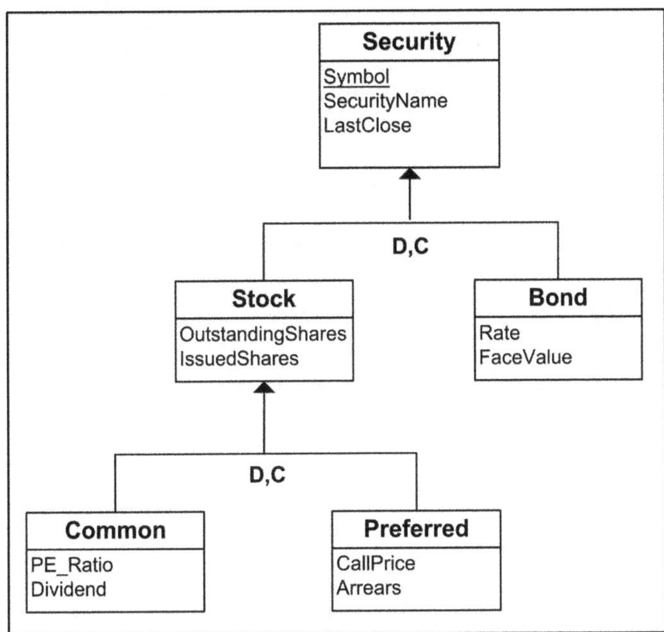

Figure 2-16: Multi-level Generalization Hierarchy

ER modeling through ER diagrams represents business rules that enable enforcement of organizational policies and thus promote proper communication among business participants. Features like entity identifier (or primary key), cardinalities, identification dependencies, generalization hierarchies are all means to interpret business policies for storage and representation.

Review Questions

1. Describe the difference between entity types and entity.
2. Describe database relationship cardinality.
3. Explain forms of minimum cardinality.
4. Explain forms of maximum cardinality.
6. Explain self-referencing relationships.
5. Describe identifying relationship and weak entity types.
7. Explain M-Way relationship.
8. Describe generalization hierarchy representation.

Review Exercises

1. ER modeling is a technique to model the utilization of data by business into ________ and ________.
2. Relationships are names given to ________ __________ that represent utilization of data during business operations.
3. The primary key or entity identifier is associated with the concept of _______ _________.
4. Cardinality specification is classified into ________ cardinality and __________ cardinality.
5. _________ relationship exists if an entity instance of one entity type is related to only one entity instance of another entity type.
6. _________ relationship exists if an entity instance of one entity type is related to many entity instances of another entity type.

7. ________ relationship exists if an entity instance of one entity type is related to more than one entity instances of another entity type, and vice-versa.
8. A ________ relationship involves association among members of the same entity type.
9. ________ relationships involve more than two entity types.
10. A ________ ________ creates two levels of entity types, with the top level entity type referred as a ________, while the lower level entity types referred as ________.

Problem Solving Exercises

2-1. Develop an ER model of a Sales Order Process as follows:

a. Start the ER diagram with Distributor and SalesOrder entity types having 1:N relationship from Distributor to SalesOrder. Choose an appropriate relationship name. The minimum cardinality for the relationship is as follows: a Salesorder is optional for the Distributor, while the Distributor is mandatory for a Salesorder. The Distributor entity type will have the following attributes: DistributorID, Name, Street, City, State, Zip, Phone, and Email. The primary key of Distributor entity type is DistributorID attribute. The SalesOrder entity type will have the following attributes OrderID, OrderDate, ShipDate, TotalAmount, Shipping. The primary key of SalesOrder entity type is OrderID attribute.
b. Extend the ER diagram of requirement a with a Customer entity type, and a 1:N relationship from Customer to SalesOrder. Choose an appropriate relationship name. The minimum cardinality for the relationship is as follows: a Salesorder is mandatory for the Customer, and the Customer is also mandatory for a Salesorder. The Customer entity type will have the following attributes: CustomerID, Name, Street, City, State, Zip, Phone, and Email. The primary key of Customer entity type is CustomerID.
c. Extend the ER diagram of requirement b with an Employee entity type, and a 1:N relationship from Employee to SalesOrder. Choose an appropriate relationship name. The minimum cardinality for the relationship is as follows: a Salesorder is optional for the Employee, while the Employee is mandatory for a Salesorder. The Employee entity type will have the following attributes: EmployeeID, Name, Street, City, State, Zip, Phone, and Email. The primary key of Customer entity type is EmployeeID.
d. Extend the ER diagram of requirement c with a self-referencing 1:N relationship involving the Employee entity type. Choose an appropriate relationship name. The minimum cardinality for the relationship is optional in both directions.
e. Extend the ER diagram of requirement d with an Item entity type, and a M:N relationship from Items to SalesOrder. Choose an appropriate relationship name. The minimum cardinality for the relationship is as follows: a Salesorder is optional for the Item, while the Item is mandatory for a Salesorder. The Item entity type will have the following attributes: ItemID, ItemName, Price, and QuantityOnHand. The primary key of Item entity type is ItemID. Add a relationship attribute Quantity to the M:N relationship.
f. Revise the ER diagram of requirement e by transforming the M:N relationship into an associative entity type with two identifying 1:N relationships.
g. List some entity instances of Distributor and SalesOrder entity types of requirement a.
h. List some entity instances of Customer entity type of requirement b.
i. List some entity instances of the Employee entity type of requirement d with a dependency diagram.

2-2. Develop an ER model of a Student Bookstore Purchase process as follows:

a. Start the ER diagram with Student and BookPurchase entity types having 1:N relationship from Student to BookPurchase. Choose an appropriate relationship name. The minimum cardinality for the relationship is mandatory in both directions. The Student entity type will have the following attributes StudentID, Name, Street, City, State, Zip, Phone, and

Email. The primary key of Student entity type is StudentID attribute. The BookPurchase entity type will have the following attributes: OrderID, OrderDate, TotalAmount, and PaymentType. The primary key of BookPurchase entity type is OrderID attribute.

b. Extend the ER diagram of requirement a with a Book entity type, and a M:N relationship from BookPurchase to Book. Choose an appropriate relationship name. The minimum cardinality for the relationship is as follows: a Book is mandatory for a BookPurchase, while the BookPurchase is optional for a Book. The Book entity type will have the following attributes: BookISBN, Title, CourseNo, and QuantityInStock. The primary key of Book entity type is BookISBN.
c. Extend the ER diagram of requirement b with a BookAuthors entity type, with an identifying relationship from Book to BookAuthors. Choose an appropriate relationship name. The minimum cardinality for the relationship is mandatory in both directions. The BookAuthors entity type will have the following attributes: FirstName and LastName.
d. Extend the ER diagram of requirement c with a Publisher entity type, and a 1:N relationship from Publisher to Book. Choose an appropriate relationship name. The minimum cardinality for the relationship is mandatory in both directions. The Publisher entity type will have the following attributes: PublisherID, Name, Street, City, State, Zip, Phone, and Email. The primary key of Publisher entity type is PublisherID.
e. List some entity instances of Student and BookPurchase entity types of requirement a.
f. List some entity instances of Book entity type of requirement b.
g. List some entity instances of BookAuthors entity type of requirement c.

2-3. Develop an ER model of an Insurance Claims process as follows:

a. Start the ER diagram with AutoPolicy and Claims entity types having 1:N relationship from AutoPolicy to Claims. Choose an appropriate relationship name. The minimum cardinality for the relationship is optional in both directions. The AutoPolicy entity type will have the following attributes: PolicyNo, YearPremium, EffectiveDate, ExpirationDate. The primary key of AutoPolicy entity type is PolicyNo attribute. The Claims entity type will have the following attributes: ClaimNo, ClaimDate, AmountClaimed, AmountPaid, ClaimStatus, and SettlementDate. The primary key of Claims entity type is ClaimNo attribute.
b. Extend the ER diagram of requirement a with a PolicyDetails entity type, and an identifying relationship from AutoPolicy to AutoPolicyDetails. Choose an appropriate relationship name. The minimum cardinality for the relationship is mandatory in both directions. The AutoPolicyDetails entity type will have the following attributes: VIN (Vehicle Identification Number), ModelYear, AutoMake, AutoModel, BodilyInjuryAmt, PropertyDamageAmt, MedicalPaymentsAmt, and UninsuredMotoristsAmt. The primary key of AutoPolicyDetails entity type is VIN.
c. Extend the ER diagram of requirement b with a HomePolicy entity type, and a 1:N relationship from HomePolicy to Claims. Choose an appropriate relationship name. The minimum cardinality for the relationship is optional in both directions. The HomePolicy entity type will have the following attributes: PolicyNo, YearPremium, EffectiveDate, ExpirationDate, DwellingAmt, PersonalPropertyAmt, PersonalLiabilityAmt, and MedicalPaymentsAmt. The primary key of HomePolicy entity type is PolicyNo.
d. Extend the ER diagram of requirement c with an Agent entity type, and a 1:N relationship from Agent to HomePolicy, and a 1:N relationship from Agent to AutoPolicy. Choose an appropriate relationship name for the two relationships. The minimum cardinality for the 1:N relationship from Agent to HomePolicy is as follows: a HomePolicy is optional for an Agent, while the Agent is mandatory for a HomePolicy. The minimum cardinality for the 1:N relationship from Agent to AutoPolicy is as follows: a AutoPolicy is optional for an Agent, while the Agent is mandatory for a AutoPolicy. The Agent entity type will have

the following attributes: AgentNo, AgencyName, Street, City, State, Zip, Phone, and Email. The primary key of Agent entity type is AgentNo.

e. Extend the ER diagram of requirement d with a Customer entity type, and a 1:N relationship from Customer to HomePolicy, and a 1:N relationship from Customer to AutoPolicy . Choose an appropriate relationship name for the two relationships. The minimum cardinality for the 1:N relationship from Customer to HomePolicy is as follows: a HomePolicy is optional for a Customer, while the Customer is mandatory for a HomePolicy. The minimum cardinality for the 1:N relationship from Customer to AutoPolicy is as follows: a AutoPolicy is optional for a Customer, while the Customer is mandatory for a AutoPolicy. The Customer entity type will have the following attributes: CustomerID, Name, Street, City, State, Zip, Phone, and Email. The primary key of Customer entity type is CustomerID.

2-4. Develop an ER model of a University course registration process as follows:

a. Start the ER diagram with Student and Course entity types having M:N relationship from Student to Course. Choose an appropriate relationship name. The minimum cardinality for the M:N relationship from Student to Course is as follows: a Student is mandatory for a Course, while the Course is optional for a Student. The Student entity type will have the following attributes StudentID, Name, Gender, DOB (Date of Birth), Status, Major, Minor, AssistantStatus, Street, City, State, Zip, Phone, and Email. The primary key of the Student entity type is StudentID attribute. The Course entity type will have the following attributes: CourseNo, Title, Department, and OfferingSemesters. The primary key of Course entity type is CourseNo attribute.

b. Extend the ER diagram of requirement b with a Faculty entity type, and a M:N relationship from Faculty to Course. Choose an appropriate relationship name for the relationship. The minimum cardinality for the M:N relationship is optional in both directions. The Faculty entity type will have the following attributes: FacultyID, Name, Gender, DOB (Date of Birth), Department, Rank, Phone, and Email. The primary key of Faculty entity type is FacultyID.

c. Extend the ER diagram of requirement b with a Staff entity type, and a 1:N relationship from Staff to Course. Choose an appropriate relationship name for the relationship. The minimum cardinality for the 1:N relationship is mandatory in both directions. The Staff entity type will have the following attributes: StaffID, Name, Gender, DOB (Date of Birth), College, Rank, Phone, and Email. The primary key of Staff entity type is StaffID.

d. Extend the ER diagram of requirement c with a generalization hierarchy containing the Employee entity type, the Faculty entity type, and the Staff Entity type. The Employee entity type is the supertype, and the Faculty and Staff are subtypes. The generalization hierarchy should have disjoint and completeness cardinality. The Employee supertype will have the following attributes: EmployeeID, Name, Gender, DOB (Date of Birth), Rank, Phone, and Email. The primary key of Employee supertype is EmployeeID. The Faculty subtype will have the following attributes: Department. The Staff subtype will have the following attributes: College.

e. Extend the ER diagram of requirement d with a generalization hierarchy containing the UniversityPerson entity type, the Employee entity type, and the Student Entity type. The UniversityPerson entity type is the supertype, and the Employee and Student are subtypes. The generalization hierarchy should have disjoint and completeness cardinality. The UniversityPerson supertype will have the following attributes: UniversityID, Name, Gender, DOB (Date of Birth), Phone, and Email. The primary key of UniversityPerson supertype is UniversityID. The Employee subtype will have the following attributes: Rank.

The Student subtype will have the following attributes: Status, Major, Minor, AssistantStatus, Street, City, State, Zip.

Chapter 3. Database Design with Business Process

Business operations are reflected through business processes and business rules, wherein a business process follows a sequence of activities necessary to complete an operational task. Business processes are documented through business process models. Essentially an organization is a collection of business processes.

Business rules by definition are guidelines that are an abstraction of the policies and practices of business activities. In a way, business rules enable business activities to accomplish business objectives and can apply to people, processes, corporate behavior, computing systems, and so on. Such guidelines also assist in the identification of entity types, attributes, constraints, database relationships, and processing rules.

Business process activities are operationalized through associated business rules. Each activity completion can involve one or more business rules. As business rules indicate what and how data enables business activities to operate, data as a consequence become integral to business process specifications and associated business logic.

Traditionally data modeling is done from the perspective of business applications. However, utilizing business process models for data modeling provides a more holistic and integrated perspective as the business process covers logically related activities that together accomplish an operational task. It enables database design independent of application and user-interface. The key to business process driven data modeling is (a) the transformation of relevant business rules that reference data that is affecting business process operations into a data model and associated database structure, and (b) converting the processing specifications in business rules to develop business logic of the business process.

This chapter provides a methodology that utilizes business process models along with business rules to develop a conceptual ER model. A short overview of business process modeling is covered next followed by business rules concepts to facilitate database design.

Business Process

A business process is a sequence of logically related and structured activities to accomplish some task associated with an organization's product or service such as processing a customer's order. It is often documented and visualized through models referred to as business process models. Since business process models show the sequence of activities required to complete a business task, these diagrams also show the workflow of how a business performs various operational tasks. As business operations are based on their business processes, such processes, in general, can be categorized into three types:

(i) business processes that accomplish operational tasks limited to a functional area like accounts payable or payroll,
(ii) business processes that accomplish operational tasks that span functional areas like sales order, and
(iii) business processes that accomplish operational tasks that span across to another organization like supply chain just-in-time manufacturing.

Technically a business process transforms a set of inputs into a set of outputs in the form of some product or service for another person or business process that can span functional areas and cross organizations. As business processes are based on how work is done in an organization, they enable a good understanding of how data impacts business activities and operations.

Business processes are documented through business process models. Such models map the sequence of work or activities being performed in order to complete an operational task. They provide a graphic description of the business process that enables an organization to focus on process interfaces, process details, analysis, and design vocabulary. Standards have been developed to model business processes. A popular standard to develop business process models is Business Process Model and Notation (BPMN).

Business Process Model and Notation (BPMN)

BPMN shows the flow of control and data (messages) along with the association of data artifacts to process activities. It simplifies the understanding of the flow of business activities and the overall business process. The current version is 2.0. BPMN's four basic elements or object categories are flow objects, connecting objects, swim lanes, and artifacts. Full details on BPMN 2.0 notations can be accessed at http://www.bpmn.org/. This chapter for simplicity covers the four essential notations for diagraming business process models to facilitate understanding its association with a database model.

1. Flow Objects

Flow objects are the main describing elements. Some of the essential flow object types shown in Figure 3-1 are described below.

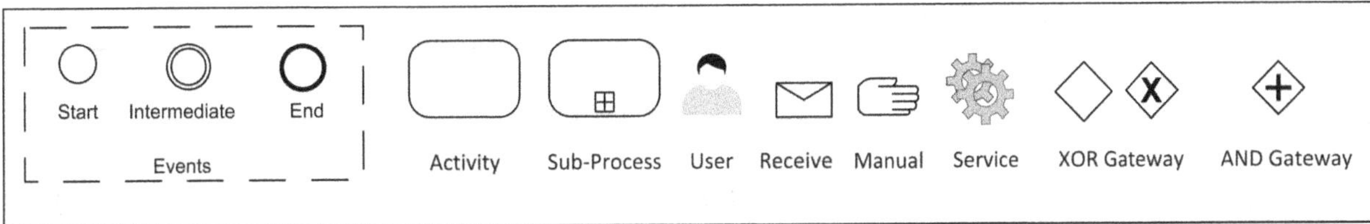

Figure 3-1: Flow Objects symbols

Flow Objects	**Description**
Events	An event is represented as a small circle and refers to something that represents the initiation or conclusion of some work. Events can be (i) *start* events that act as a trigger that starts the process and is drawn with a single narrow border; (ii) *intermediate* events that represent the state between the start and end events and are drawn with a double border; and (iii) *end* events that represent the conclusion of the process and are drawn by a single thick or bold border.

Activity	An activity is drawn with a rounded-corner rectangle. It describes the kind of work which must be done within the business process. An activity is either a task or a sub-process. A task is an activity that is atomic or cannot be further broken down. Various task types exist, like user, receive, service, and so on. A user task type activity indicates work that is done by a person with the assistance of an application. A receive task activity indicates work that is relying on an incoming message from a third party. A manual task is performed by a person without the aid of an application. A service task activity is a work that uses an automated application or web service for completion.
Sub-Process	A sub-process is an activity that can be broken down further to show more details in the form of a child-level process.
Gateway	A gateway controls process flows by splitting it into alternate paths. Gateway can be exclusive or parallel. An exclusive gateway (also referred to as XOR gateway) represents a condition and is drawn with a diamond shape that can result in forking and merging of paths. A parallel gateway (also referred to as AND-split gateway) is drawn with a + inside the diamond symbol has one input flow in and concurrent output flows out wherein the output flow activities are performed in parallel or overlap in time. Concurrent paths can also be joined later through another parallel gateway.

Table 3-1: Flow Objects Description

2. Connections

Connecting objects connect flow objects. Some of the essential connections types shown in Figure 3-2 are described below.

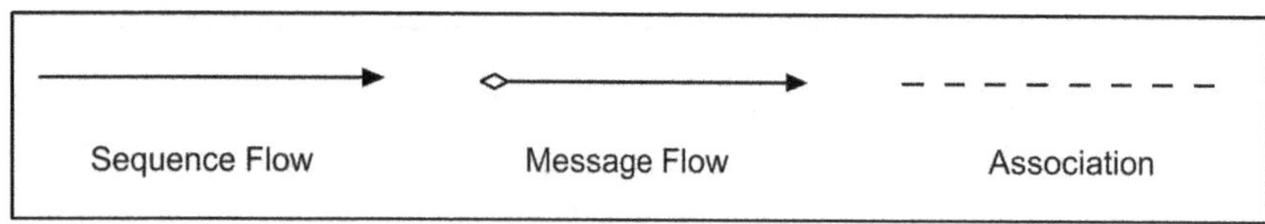

Figure 3-2: Connection symbols

Connections	Description
Sequence Flow	A *sequence flow* is drawn with a solid line and arrowhead which illustrates the order in which the activities are performed.
Message Flow	A *message flow* is drawn with a dashed line, an open diamond at the start, and an arrowhead at the end. It illustrates what messages flow across organizational boundaries. A message flow cannot be used to connect activities or events within the same pool.

Association	An *association* is drawn with a dotted line. It is used to associate an artifact or text to a flow object.
Table 3-2: Connections Description	

3. Swimlanes

Swimlanes is a visual mechanism for organizing the work flow. Some of the essential swimlanes types shown in Figure 3-3 are described below.

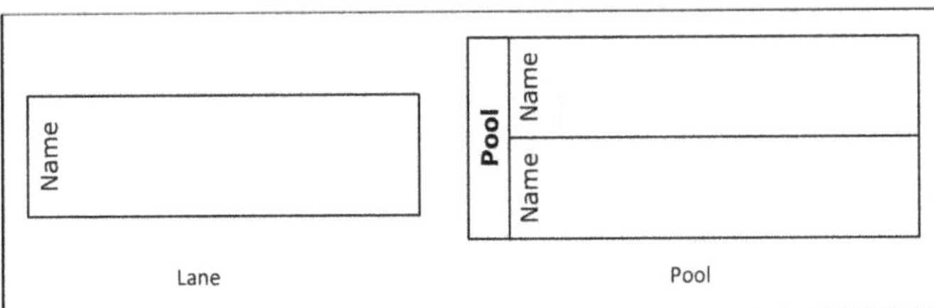

Figure 3-3: Swimlanes symbols

Swimlanes	Description
Pool	A pool represents the participants (in the form of some function or role) involved in the process. It may contain one or more lanes (like a real swimming pool).
Lane	A lane depicts activities performed within its boundaries. It may contain flow objects, connecting objects and artifacts. It is also show responsibilities for activities performed.
Table 3-3: Swimlanes Description	

4. Artifacts

Artifacts represent the inclusion of some additional information into the diagram. Some of the essential artifacts types shown in Figure 3-4 are described below.

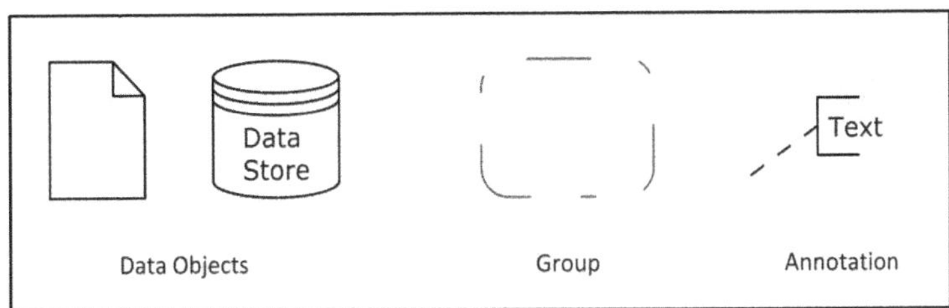

Figure 3-4: Artifacts Symbols

Artifacts	Description
Data Objects	Data objects are notations that illustrate what data is required or produced by an activity.

Group	A group is illustrated with a rounded-corner rectangle and dashed lines. It is used to group different activities but does not affect the flow in the diagram.
Annotation	An annotation is a short narrative text to enhance the understanding of the diagram.
Table 3-4: Artifacts Description	

Some general guidelines when drawing business process model diagrams:

- There should be no open arrow lines. Arrow lines have to connect one symbol to another.
- Decision symbols must show the options available.
- Roles in swimlane diagrams should only be included if they participate in the completion of some activity.
- Start and end symbols should be included to indicate the beginning and ending of the process.

Figure 3-5 below is a swimlane model of "Create Rental" business process for a hypothetical apartment complex business. The model shows the sequence of activities involved in the creation of a new apartment rental. It also includes the two roles Tenant and Front Desk play in the completion of activities. Business process models are logical. So, how and where the activities are performed is not considered. It is possible for example that the rental inquiry activity could be through a phone, or Web site, or in person. Also, Complete Rental activity can be on paper or PDF. From a data modeling perspective, logical specification is important, as it enables focusing on what data is needed to complete the activities irrespective of their eventual implementation.

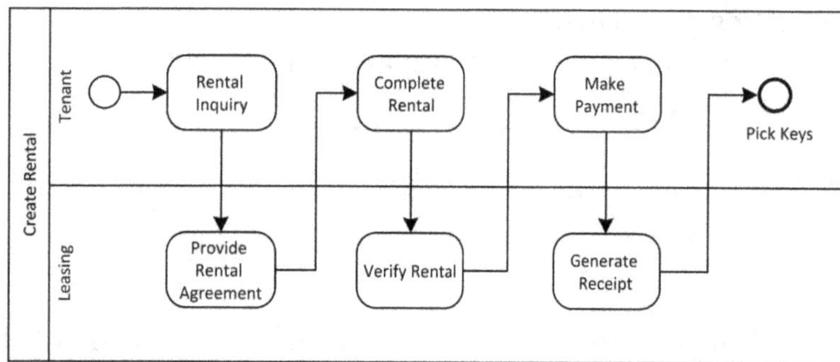

Figure 3-5: Create Rental Business Process Model

Business Rules Guidelines for Data Modeling

A business rule is a statement that defines or constrains some aspect of a business[1]. It pertains to the facts that are recorded as data and provide the constraints that govern the values of those facts. Business rules of any business process define characteristics of data that will apply to business process operations. These guidelines can be utilized to gain insight into the identification and structure of entity types, the existence of database relationships, and specifications of data model

[1] http://www.businessrulesgroup.org; D.C. Hay "Modeling Busines Rules: What Data Models Do" The Data Administration Newsletter (http://www.tdan.com), Issue 27, January 2004; Rajeev Kaula "Integrated Framework to Model Data with Business Process and Business Rules" International Journal of Database Management Systems, Vol. 8, No.6, 2016, pp. 1-12.

linked business logic. Business rules can be documented for the entire business process or documented for each activity within a business process to fine-tune the alignment of business rules with the entire business process.

There are four categories of business rules guidelines with respect to data modeling. It is possible for more than one guideline to apply as they collectively facilitate the development of the conceptual data model like ER model with respect to business process operations.

1. Definitions of business terms

   This category emphasizes the utilization of relevant business terms as a way to identify entity type or its structure and database relationships in a conceptual data model. The reference to a term is itself a business rule as it describes how people think and talk about it. Sometimes these terms may be fairly obvious through business rules that emerge from observation or documentation. Other times these terms may emerge during the modeling process when reference to some attribute in an entity type may suggest another entity type with database relationship. The following examples of business rules within the create rental business process of Figure 3-5 facilitate entity type identification.

   - A statement like "terms tenant and rental relevant for apartment complex business." Such statements imply that the business needs to record details on tenant and rental. The level of details that needs to be recorded as attributes in tenant entity type can be something that is put in rental agreement like tenant social security number, name, phone, email, and so on. Similarly, details to be recorded as attributes for rental entity type can be information in the rental agreement like rental number, rental date, type of rental, and so on. As a rental is always associated with a tenant, such association may suggest a database relationship between rental and tenant entity types.
   - Another way to identify terms and entity types relevant to a business can be detected for instance through the apartment number attribute in the rental entity type. Even though a rental is tied to an apartment number, the attribute apartment number is itself associated with other details of an apartment that are relevant to the business. These details together logically constitute another entity type that can be called apartment. So, in this case the earlier inclusion of apartment number as rental entity type attribute can be replaced with a database relationship between apartment and rental entity types.

2. Facts relating terms to each other

   This category emphasizes business rules that describe the nature of operating policies of a business process in terms of the facts that relate business terms to each other. For example, customers can place sales order is a fact. Such business rules are represented as relationships, cardinalities, attributes, and generalization structures in a conceptual data model. The following examples of business rules within the create rental business process in Figure 3-5 facilitate database relationship identification.

   - A statement like "only one tenant must sign a rental agreement to complete the rental process." This business rule represents the minimum and maximum cardinality of one pertaining to the database relationship between the tenant and rental entity types. As only one tenant will be tied to a rental and vice-versa, the minimum and maximum cardinality of one will be both ways. Such business rules in a way may also reconfirm the earlier database relationship between tenant and rental entity types as explained earlier.

3. Constraints

    This category emphasizes how guidelines in the form of business rules that specify constraints on business process behavior in some way can lead to the specification of constraints on the data pertaining to the behavior within the entity types of a conceptual data model. A constraint is a condition that determines what values an attribute or relationship can or must-have. Constraints category can be expressed either through attribute constraints, cardinality constraints, or some process business logic. The following examples of business rules within the create rental business process in Figure 3-5 facilitate constraints specification.

    - A statement like "every tenant automobile license plate number must be registered in the rental agreement." This business rule represents a value constraint on the license attribute in the tenant entity type that emphasizes that there will not be a blank value for tenants who park automobiles.
    - A statement like "a rental agreement must have only one staff associated with it." This business rule represents cardinality constraints pertaining to the relationship between staff and rental entity types. Now since staff is a term that is relevant to business process operations, so as per category one guideline it can be an entity type itself. Details on staff as recorded in the apartment complex business employment records like staff name, address, and so on can become the attributes of the entity type.

4. Derivations

    This category emphasizes how a fact in one form that is transformed into some other knowledge or derived fact to support business process operations can affect entity types in a conceptual model. Such derivations can be based on arithmetic expression or some aspect of process business logic. The following example of a business rule within the create rental business process in Figure 3-5 indicates a process business logic requirement.

    - A statement like "no apartment should be rented if there are complaints pending on the apartment." This business rule illustrates how the status of apartment complaints effects the completion of the business process. It involves data recorded in two entity types - rental and complaints. The rental entity type is associated with the recording of new rental, while the complaints entity type is associated with the recording of complaints pertaining to the apartments. The business rule binds the recording of new rental to complaints entity type such that the complaint entity type should not have any form of complaints pending with respect to an apartment before a rental can be assigned to an it. Such business rules implementation goes beyond traditional data modeling as it is associated with business logic. However, inclusion of business logic is essential for the integrity of the data model. Such business logic involve programmatic support. The most optimum approach is to utilize database program units as they can be often linked with entity types in the database. Database program units are covered in later chapters.

The above categories of business rules provide a mechanism to identify the structure of the data model and associated business logic. They assist in extracting relevant data modeling information pertaining to business operations. In nutshell, a business process model defines the scope of the data model and its business rules provide the guideline to extract information. This combination leads to a conceptual data model that is more aligned with business operations.

Transform Business Process Derived Business Rules into ER Model

Three business process scenarios of a hypothetical apartment complex business (referred to as Superflex Apartment) are now explained along with associated business rules having BR prefix. This is followed by their transformations into ER model. Through this methodology, an entity type from one business process model can be expanded with the inclusion of additional details for the same entity type from another business process model. Consequently, the transformation of all business processes at the end will reflect a comprehensive data model for all business operations.

Create Rental Business Process

This operational task deals with the sequence of activities involved in completing a rental agreement. The associated business process model is shown in Figure 3-6. This figure is a copy of Figure 3-5 earlier. Some of the business rules associated with the business process are listed in Table 3-5 below the business process diagram.

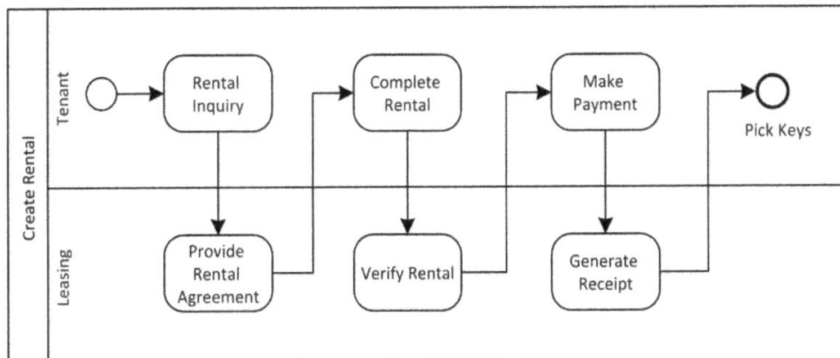

Figure 3-6: Create Rental Business Process Model

Business Rules ID	Business Rules Description
BR-1	Terms tenant, rental relevant for business process.
BR-2	Only one tenant must sign a rental agreement to complete the rental process.
BR-3	Rental lease type can be monthly or yearly.
BR-4	A monthly rental lease is 10% more than the regular yearly apartment rent.
BR-5	Rental agreement payment will include the apartment deposit amount and first month rent.
BR-6	A rental agreement must have only one staff associated with it.
BR-7	Besides regular staff, even part-time staff can facilitate rental agreements.
BR-8	Every tenant automobile license plate number must be registered in the rental agreement.
BR-9	Every tenant is allowed free parking for one registered automobile.
BR-10	No apartment should be rented if there are complaints pending on the apartment.

BR-11	Apartment complaint status can be fixed, pending, or not determined.
BR-12	All tenants must have good credit scores.
BR-13	Tenant has to provide details on all persons staying in the apartment.

Table 3-5: Create Rental Business Process Business Rules

These business rules gradually enable the creation of the conceptual ER model. Some of the finer details on attributes and relationships not referred in a business rule can also be completed through documents and observations. The transformation of individual business rules to ER model is explained below.

BR-1:

Business rule statement "terms tenant and rental relevant for business process" pertains to category 1 guideline and implies that the business needs to record details on tenant and rental. The level of details that needs to be represented as attributes in tenant entity type can be something that is put in rental agreement like tenant social security number, name, phone, email, and so on. Similarly, details on rental entity type that can be represented as attributes can be information in the rental agreement like rental number, rental date, type of rental, and so on. As a rental is always associated with a tenant, it suggests a database relationship between rental and tenant entity types. So the initial diagram will be as shown in Figure 3-7.

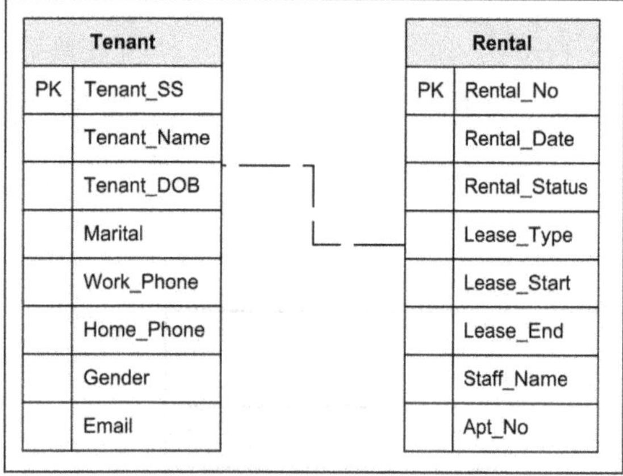

Figure 3-7: BR-1 associated initial ER model

The second aspect of identifying terms and entity types relevant to a business process can be discerned through the apartment number (Apt_No) attribute in the rental entity type. Even though a rental is tied to an apartment number, the attribute apartment number is itself associated with other details of an apartment that are relevant to the business. These details together logically constitute another entity type that can be called apartment. Details on the apartment entity type like apartment number, apartment type, rental status, and so on can be represented as attributes in the entity type. Now the earlier inclusion of apartment number as rental entity type attribute as shown in Figure 3-7 can be replaced with a database relationship between apartment and rental entity types. Through observation of the rental agreement it maybe obvious that only one apartment is referred in the rental agreement. This suggests that the minimum and maximum cardinality of apartment with rental is one. Also it is possible that an apartment may be vacant sometimes, even though the goal is to keep it rented with some rental always. This suggests that the minimum cardinality of rental with apartment is optional while the maximum cardinality is one. So the initial diagram of Figure 3-7 can be extended as Figure 3-8.

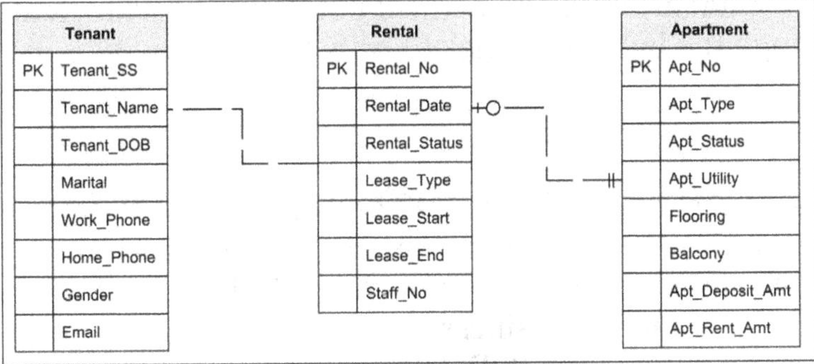

Figure 3-8: BR-1 associated refined ER model

BR-2:

Business rule statement "only one tenant must sign a rental agreement to complete the rental process" pertains to category 2 guideline that is completed during the Complete Rental activity and then enforced during the Verify Rental activity. It represents the minimum and maximum cardinality of one pertaining to the database relationship between tenant and rental entity types. As only one tenant will be tied to a rental and vice-versa, the minimum and maximum cardinality of one will be both ways. Such rules also reconfirm the earlier database relationship between tenant and rental entity types as shown in Figure 3-7 and Figure 3-8. Inclusion of these details now extends the previous version of the data model with cardinalities as shown in Figure 3-9.

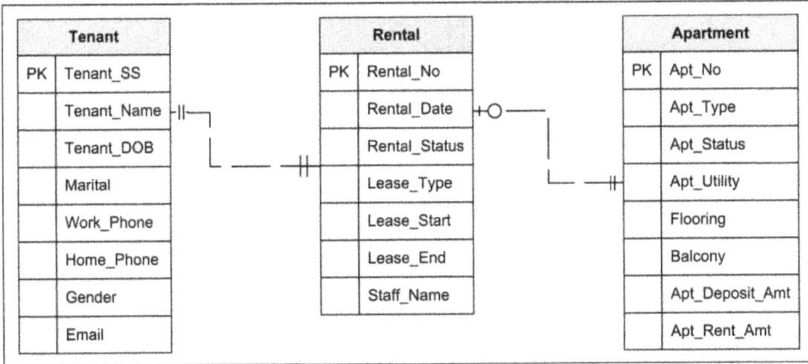

Figure 3-9: BR-2 associated ER model

BR-3:

Business rule statement "rental lease type can be monthly or yearly" pertains to category 3 guideline that implies that the values taken by lease_type attribute in rental entity type should either be monthly or yearly. This rule can be included during the transformation of the entity type into relations as a value constraint.

BR-4:

Business rule statement "a monthly rental lease is 10% more than the regular yearly apartment rent" pertains to category 3 guideline that is explained during Provide Rental Agreement activity and then checked through the business logic of Verify Rental activity.

BR-5:

Business rule statement "Rental agreement payment will include the apartment deposit amount and first month rent" pertains to category 2 guideline that is explained during the Provide Rental Agreement activity and then checked through the business logic of Verify Rental activity.

BR-6:

Business rule statement "A rental agreement must have only one staff associated with it" pertains to category 1 and 2 guidelines that are followed during the Provide Rental Agreement activity and then checked through the business logic of Verify Rental activity. Now since the term staff is itself associated with other details that could be relevant to the business process, these details together logically constitute another entity type that can be called staff. Details on the staff entity type like staff number, name, position, and so on can be represented as attributes in the entity type. Since a staff is facilitating rental agreement it implies that staff and rental entity type have database relationship. As per the business rule if only one staff assists in the handling of rental agreement, it is possible that the same staff can also assist in other rental agreements. This means that the relationship is 1:N. The minimum cardinality of staff with respect to rental will be mandatory. Similarly, the minimum cardinality of rental with staff will also be mandatory. Inclusion of these details now extends the previous version of the ER model with cardinalities as shown in Figure 3-10.

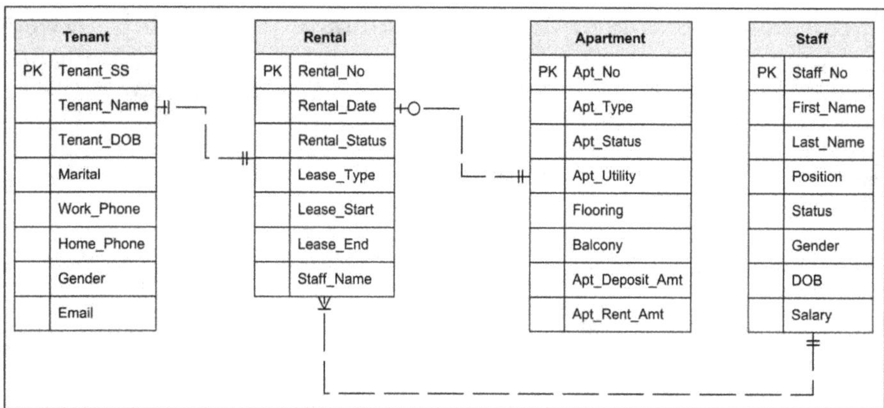

Figure 3-10: BR-6 associated ER model

BR-7:

Business rule statement "besides regular staff, even part-time staff can facilitate rental agreements" pertains to category 2 guideline that is followed during the Provide Rental Agreement activity and then checked through the business logic of Verify Rental activity.

BR-8:

Business rule statement "every tenant automobile license plate number must be registered in the rental agreement" pertains to category 3 guideline and represents a value constraint on the license attribute in the tenant entity type that emphasizes that there will not be a blank value for each tenant. As there was no license_no attribute in the tenant entity type, this rule now forces inclusion of this attribute. The rule is specified would be specified in the rental agreement. It is followed during the Complete Rental activity and then enforced through the business logic of

Verify Rental activity. This rule will extend previous model with the inclusion of additional attribute in tenant entity type as shown in Figure 3-11.

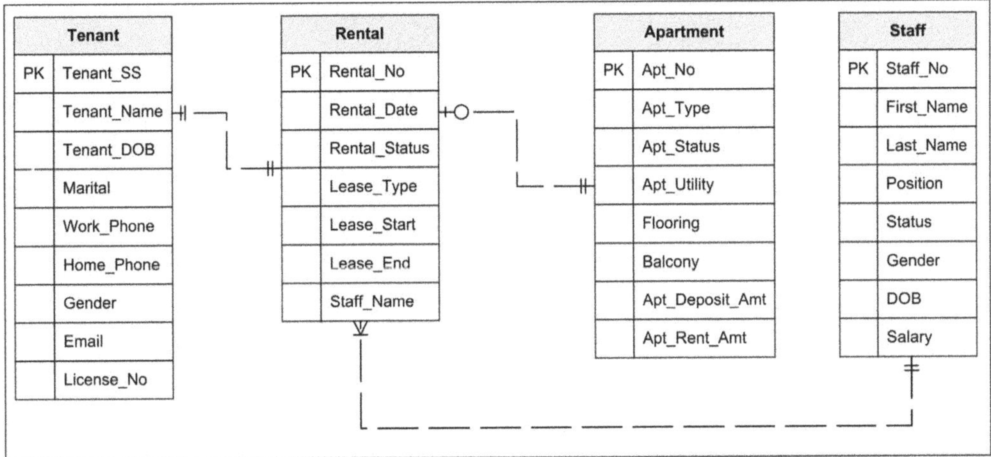

Figure 3-11: BR-8 associated ER model

BR-9:

Business rule statement "every tenant is allowed free parking for one registered automobile" pertains to category 1 and 2 guidelines. As the apartment complex would like to record details on tenant's automobile, such details can be added to the tenant entity type. However, it is possible that the tenant may have more than one automobile especially if the tenant has family. To take care of such situations, the tenant entity type should be extended through a weak entity type called as tenant_auto that allows recording of information on multiple automobiles. The weak entity type may include other relevant automobile details like automobile type, make, color, year, parking fee, and so on. The relationship between tenant and tenant_auto will be 1:N, wherein the minimum cardinality of tenant_auto will be optional as a tenant may not have any automobile. Inclusion of these details now extends the previous version of the model as shown in Figure 3-12.

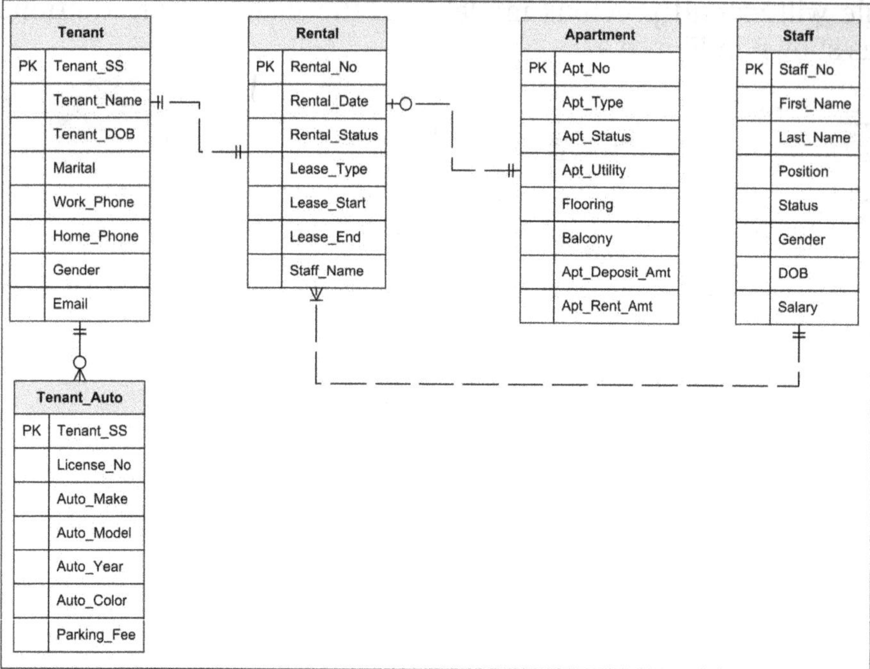

Figure 3-12: BR-9 associated ER model

BR-10:

Business rule statement "no apartment should be rented if there are complaints pending on the apartment" pertains to category 1 and 4 guidelines. It illustrates how the status of apartment complaints affects the completion of the business process. As per category 1 guideline, use of the term "complaints" implies details on complaints has relevance to business and consequently should be created as an entity type with appropriate attributes. This rule deals with data recorded in two entity types - rental and complaints. The rental entity type is associated with the recording of new rental, while the complaints entity type is associated with the recording of complaints pertaining to the apartments. The business rule binds the recording of new rental to complaints entity type such that the complaint entity type should not have any form of complaints pending with respect to an apartment before a rental can be assigned to an it. This rule will be enforced during the Verify Rental activity. However, such business rules implementation go beyond traditional data modeling as it is associated with activity business logic. However, inclusion of complaints entity type now extends the previous version of the model as shown in Figure 3-13.

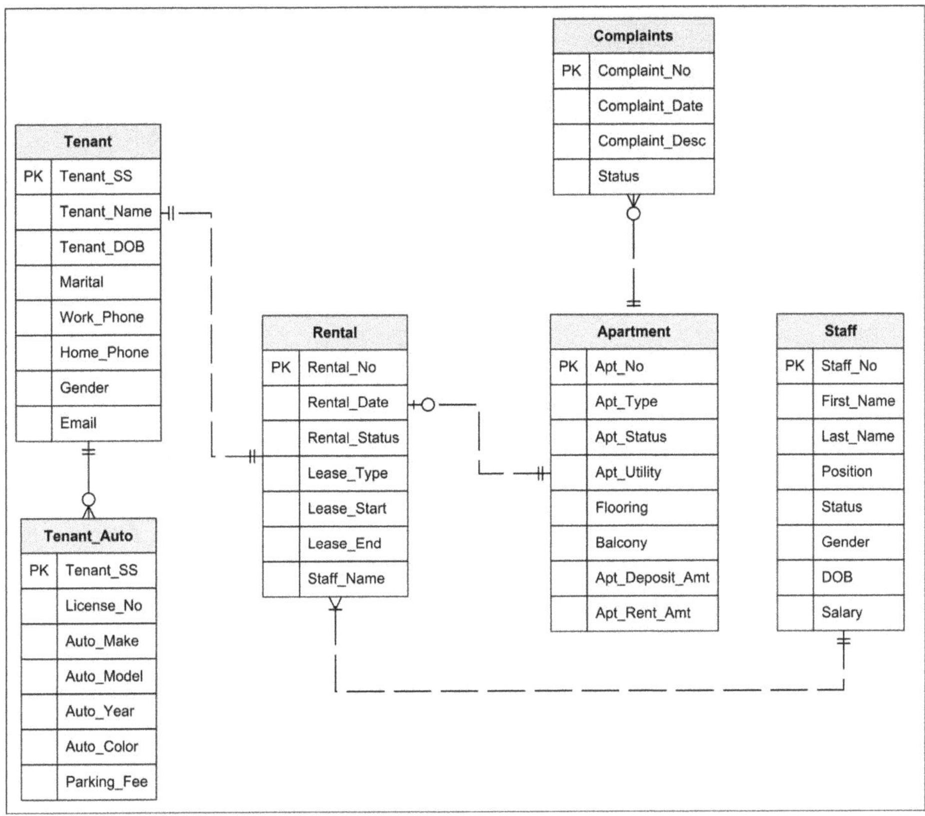

Figure 3-13: BR-10 associated ER model

BR-11:

Business rule statement "Apartment complaint status can be fixed, pending, or not determined" pertains to category 3 guideline that implies that the values taken by status attribute in rental entity type should either be fixed, pending, or not determined. This rule can be included during the transformation of the entity type into relations as a value constraint.

BR-12:

Business rule statement "All tenants must have good credit scores" pertains to category 2 guideline that involves extending the tenant entity type with attributes for credit score and the agency from which the scores are retrieved. The checking of credit scores is performed during the business logic of Verify Rental activity. Figure 3-14 now extends the previous version of the model with additional attributes in Tenant entity type.

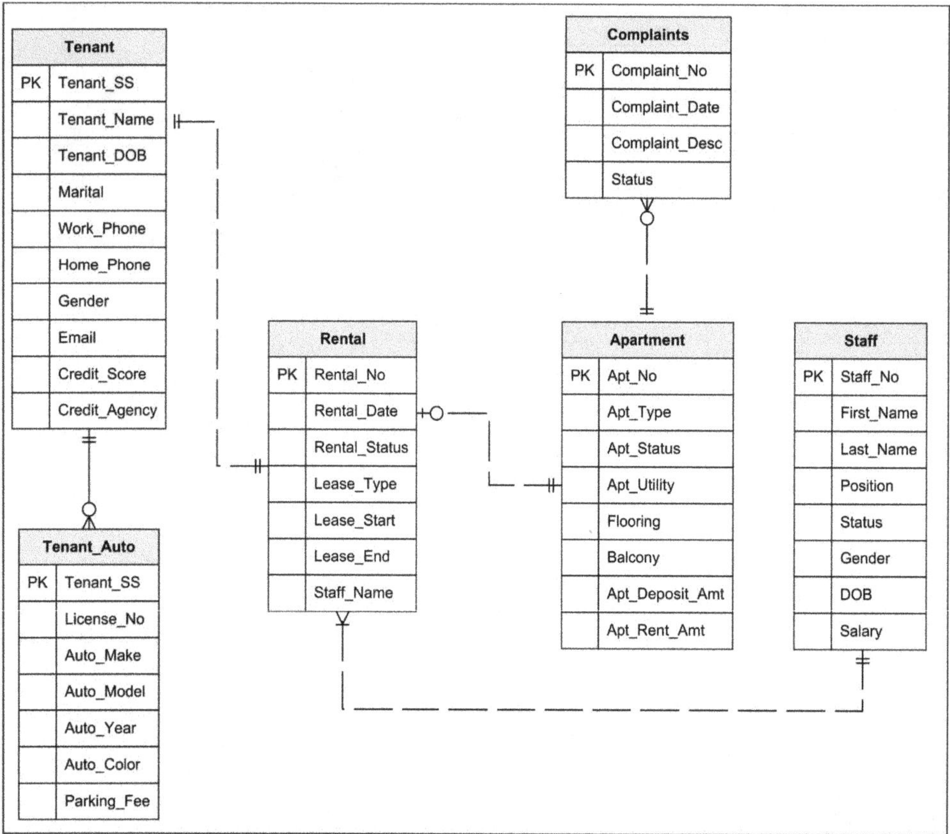

Figure 3-14: BR-12 associated ER model

BR-13:

Business rule statement "tenant has to provide details on all persons staying in the apartment" pertains to category 2 guideline. Since there may possibly be many persons staying with the tenant, a new weak entity tenant_family will be created. The relevant attributes like name, social security number, spouse, child, gender and data of birth will be included in the weak entity type. The relationship between tenant and tenant_family will be 1:N, wherein the minimum cardinality of tenant_family will be optional as it is possible for a tenant to also be single. Inclusion of these details now extends the previous version of the model as shown in Figure 3-15.

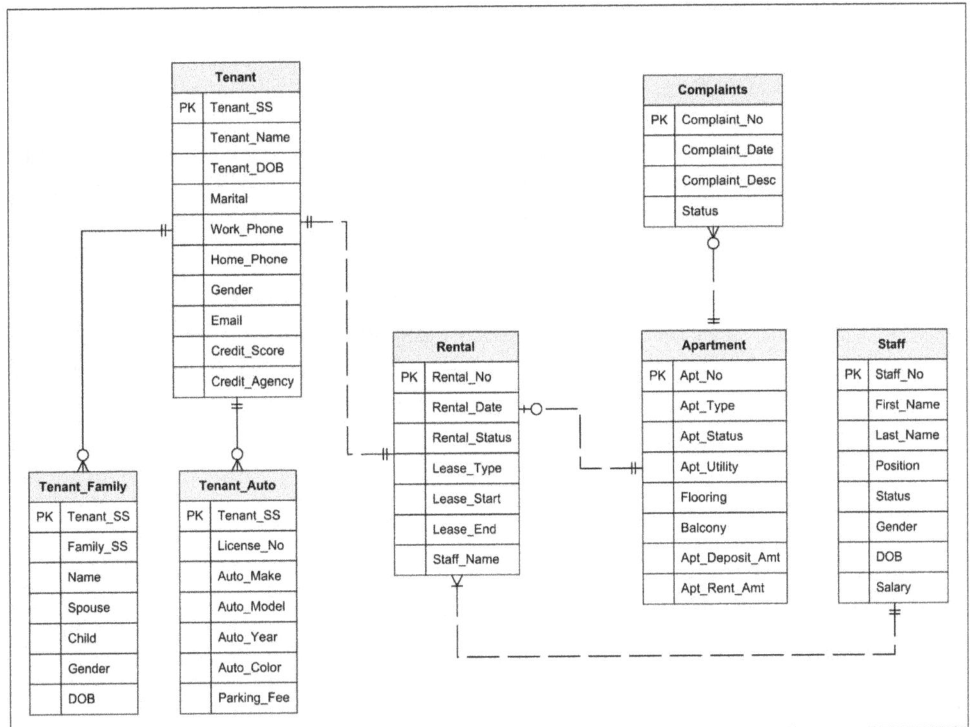

Figure 3-15: BR-13 associated ER model

Handle Rent Business Process

This operational task deals with the sequence of activities involved in handling apartment rent. The associated business process model is shown in Figure 3-16. Some of the business rules associated with the business process are listed in Table 3-6 below the business process diagram.

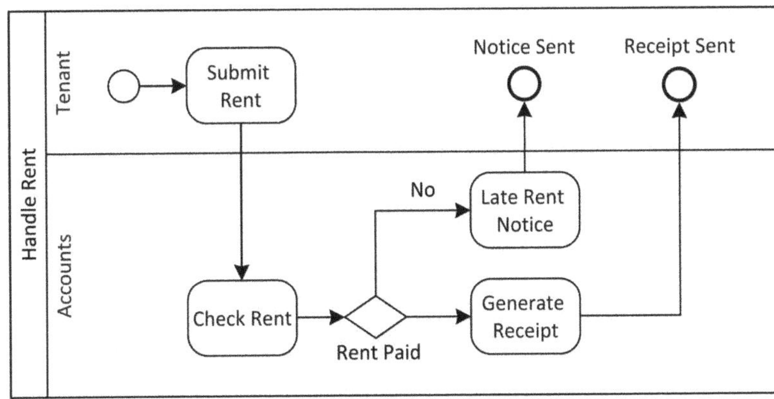

Figure 3-16: Handle Rent Business Process model

Business Rules ID	Business Rules Description
BR-14	Monthly rent receipts are sent electronically after invoice are paid.
BR-15	Rental payments can be cash, check, or credit card.

Table 3-6: Create Rental Business Process Business Rules

BR-14:

Business rule statement "Monthly rent receipts are sent electronically after invoice are paid" pertains to category 1 and 4 guidelines. As per the category 1 guideline the term invoice will have details that the business needs to record and so it has relevance to business. Consequently an entity type rental_invoice with appropriate attributes is created. From a modeling perspective, a rental entity type instance will be associated with one or more rental_invoice instances, while a rental_invoice entity type instance will be associated with only one rental instance. Inclusion of these details now extends the previous version of the model as shown in Figure 3-17. From category 4 guideline perspective, the business rule essentially refers to the business logic of Generate Receipt activity. Such business rules implementation go beyond traditional data modeling as it is associated with activity business logic.

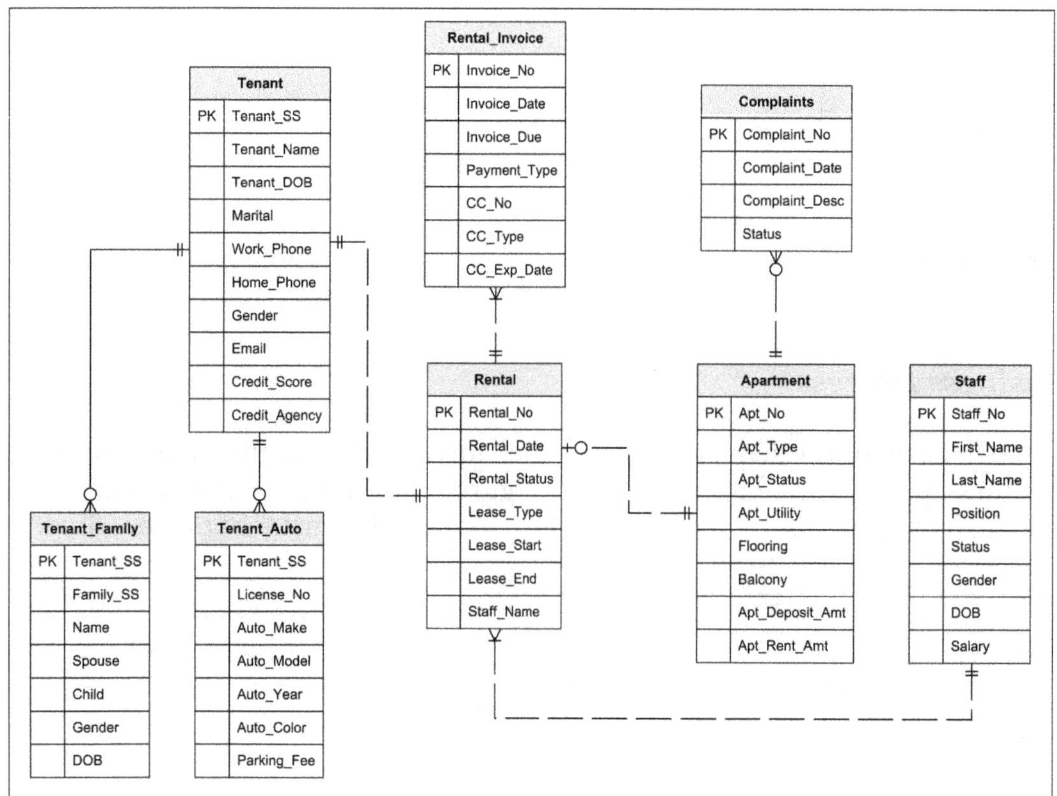

Figure 3-17: BR-14 associated ER model

BR-15:

Business rule statement "rental payments can be cash, check, or credit card" pertains to category 3 guideline that implies that the values taken by payment_type attribute in rental_invoice entity type should either be cash, check, or credit card. This rule can be included during the transformation of the entity type into relations as a value constraint.

Handle Complaints Business Process

This operational task deals with the sequence of activities involved in handling apartment complaints. The associated business process model is shown in Figure 3-18. It is again a swimlane model with three roles Tenant, Frontdesk, and Service involved in the handling of complaints.

Once again the business process model shows the logical specification. Some of the business rules associated with the business process are listed in Table 3-7 below the business process diagram.

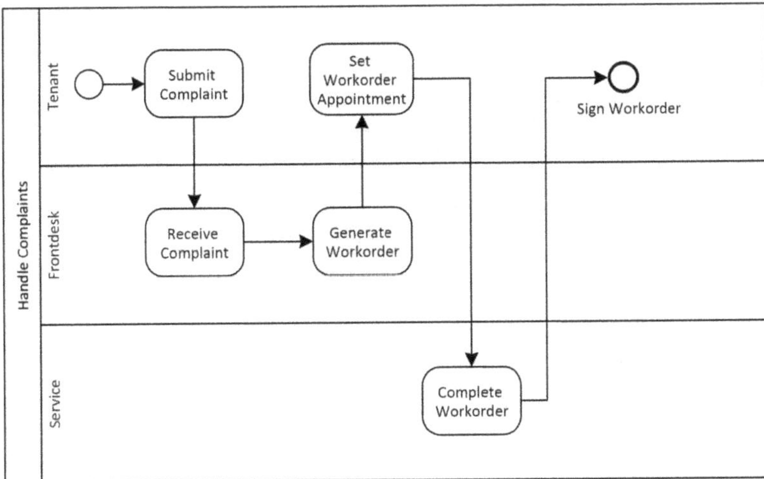

Figure 3-18: Handle Complaints Business Process Model

Business Rules ID	Business Rules Description
BR-16	Terms complaint, workorder, apartment relevant for business process.
BR-17	A complaint can be submitted by phone, in person, or Web site.
BR-18	A complaint must be associated with only one apartment.
BR-19	A complaint may be associated with rental if filed by a tenant.
BR-20	A pending complaint on a vacant apartment should remove rental reference.
BR-21	A workorder must be associated with only one complaint.
BR-22	A workorder must be generated within one business day.
BR-23	Tenant signature not necessary if tenant not in apartment after workorder completed.
BR-24	Only one contractor should be associated with a work order.

Table 3-7: Handle Complaints Business Process Business Rules

BR-16:

Business rule statement "terms complaint, workorder, apartment relevant for business process" pertains to category 1 guideline and implies that the business needs to record details on complaints, workorder, and apartment. Since complaint and apartment entity types have already been created in Create Rental business process data model, those entity type structures can be the starting point in the model. Workorder entity type can be created based on the details specified in workorder sheet with attributes like the date workorder received, work description, apartment number of the complaint, and so on. Based on observation, as a complaint will always be associated with an apartment, and an apartment could possibly be associated with multiple complaints, consequently the relationship between apartment and complaints entity type will be 1:N. This relationship is similar to the what exists in the data model for Create Rental business process. Also, based on observation and documentation the relationship between Workorder and

Complaints will be 1:N, since a Complaint may require one or more Workorders to complete, while a Workorder will always be associated with one Complaint. So the initial data model will be as shown in Figure 3-19.

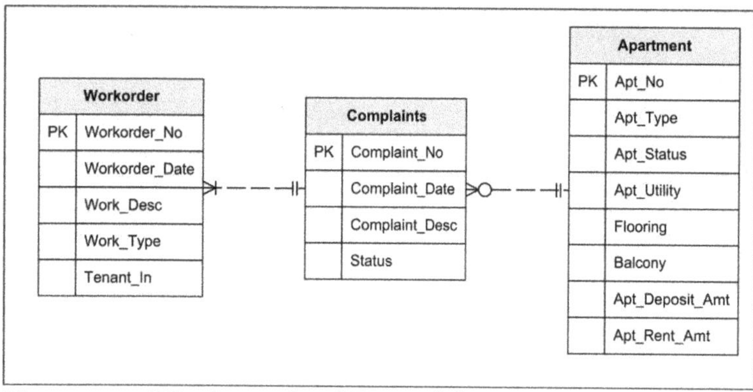

Figure 3-19: BR-16 associated ER model

BR-17:

Business rule statement "a complaint can be submitted by phone, in person, or Web site" pertains to category 4 guideline that is enforced through the business logic of Submit Complaint activity.

BR-18:

Business rule statement "a complaint must be associated with only one apartment" pertains to category 2 guideline. It specifies the minimum cardinality of complaints relationship with apartment. This reconfirms the database relationship as specified for BR-16 in Figure 3-19.

BR-19:

Business rule statement "a complaint may be associated with rental if filed by a tenant" pertains to category 1 and 3 guidelines. Reference to the term rental makes it a candidate for entity type as per category 1 guideline. The rental entity type created during the Create Rental business process can be utilized in the data model. Further, as per category 3, the business rule specifies a constraint on the complaint entity type in the form of a database relationship between complaint and rental. Based on observations and documentation, a complaint will be associated with only one rental (mandatory minimum and maximum cardinality) while a rental may be associated with no complaints (i.e. optional minimum cardinality) or many complaints (many maximum cardinality) during the tenure of the rental. Hence the relationship will be 1:N. Inclusion of these details now extends the previous version of the model as shown in Figure 3-20.

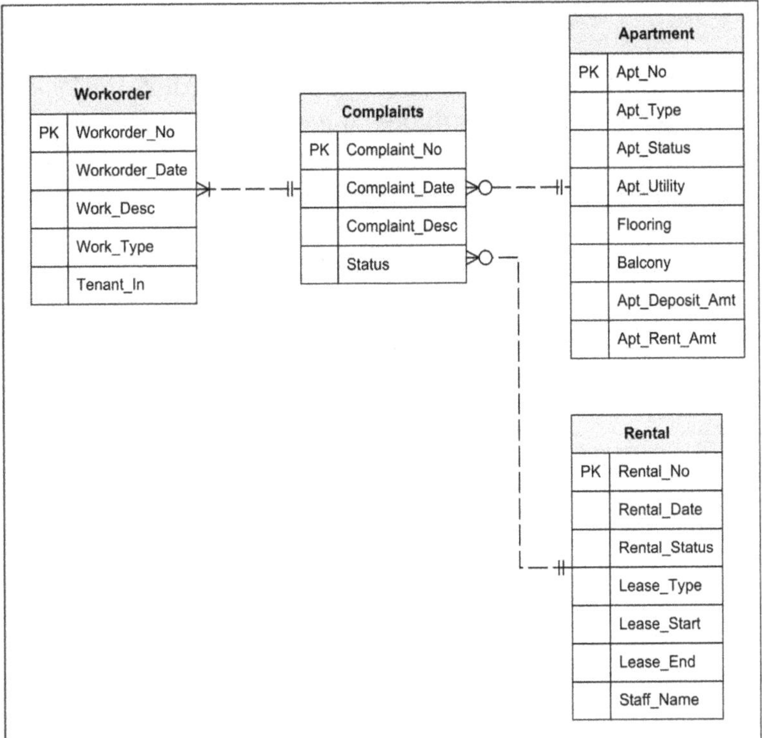

Figure 3-20: BR-19 associated ER model

BR-20:

Business rule statement "a pending complaint on a vacant apartment should remove rental reference" pertains to category 4 guideline that should be automatically enforced through the business logic attached to a change of rental status for an apartment.

BR-21:

Business rule statement "a workorder must be associated with only one complaint" pertains to category 2 guideline. It refers to the mandatory minimum cardinality from workorder entity type to complaints entity type. It also reconfirms the database relationship cardinalities between workorder and complaints as defined during BR-16 and shown in Figure 3-19 and Figure 3-20. It is enforced during the Generate Workorder activity.

BR-22:

Business rule statement "a workorder must be generated within one business day" pertains to category 4 guideline that should be enforced through the business logic of Receive Complaint activity.

BR-23:

Business rule statement "tenant signature not necessary if tenant not in apartment after workorder completed" pertains to category 3 guideline. It specifies a value constraint on the tenant_in attribute in Workorder entity type. This rule can be included during the transformation of the entity type into relations as a value constraint.

BR-24:

Business rule statement "Only one contractor should be associated with a workorder" pertains to category 1 and 2 guidelines. Reference to the term contractor makes it a candidate for entity type as per category 1 guideline. Relevant details on contractor entity type may be entered as attributes. Further, as per category 2 guideline, the business rule specifies a database relationship between Workorder and Contractor. Based on the business rule a Workorder will be associated with only one Contractor implies a mandatory minimum and maximum cardinality. On the other hand it is possible that a contractor may not have any Workorder or many Workorders. Hence the overall relationship will be 1:N. Inclusion of these details now extends the previous version of the model as shown in Figure 3-21.

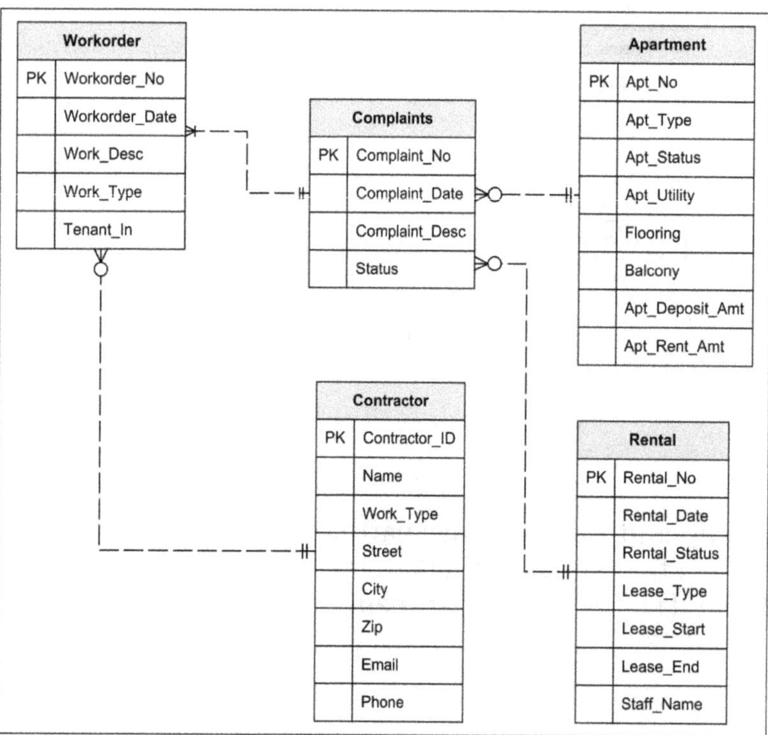

Figure 3-21: BR-24 associated ER model

Integrated Data Model

The individual data models of the three business processes of Superflex Apartment can be combined into a more unified and integrated data model. Figure 3-22 shows an integrated data model that now combines the Create Rental business process, Handle Rent business process, and Handle Complaints business process data models. Similarly data models of other business processes within the organization can be integrated to create a complete enterprise data model. Chapter 4 outlines the relational model concepts and the transformation of ER model into relational model. The relational model representation of the Superflex Apartment integrated model is outlined in Appendix A. The SQL script to install the database is listed in Appendix B.

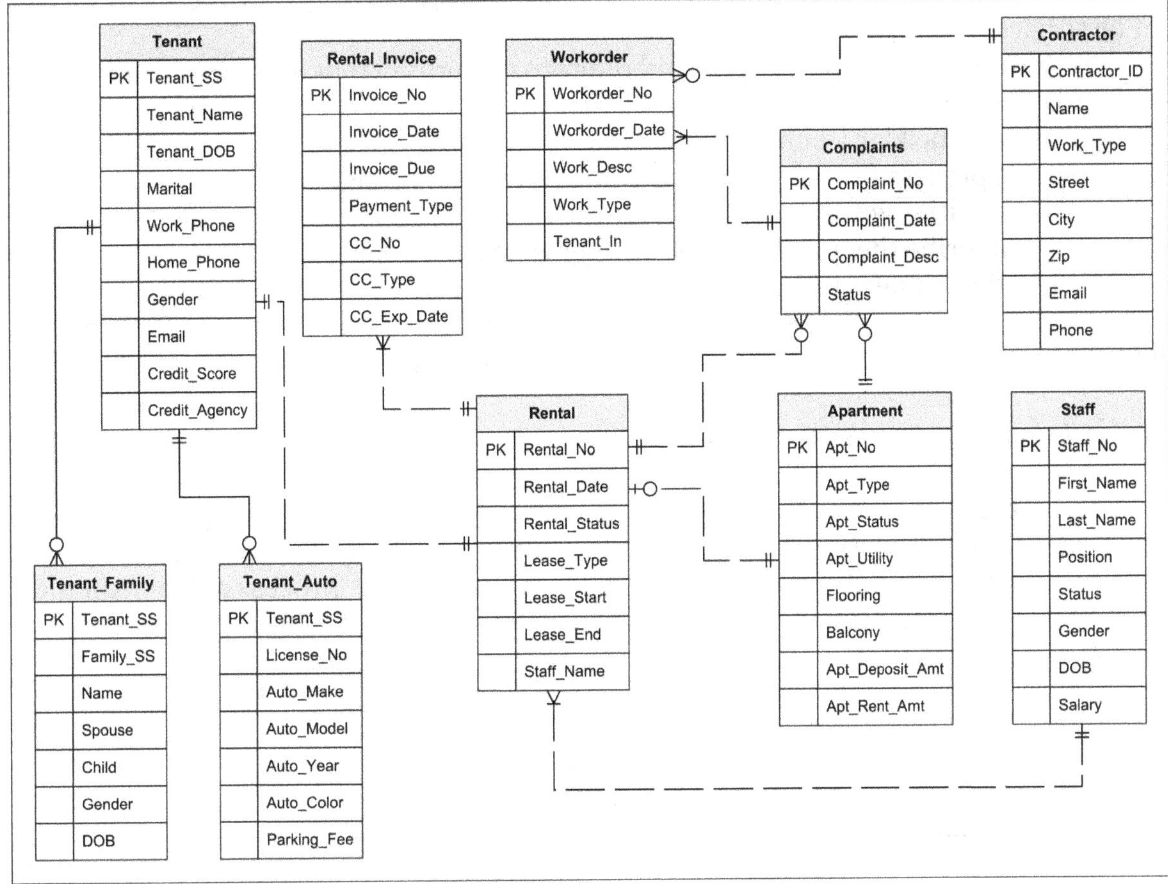

Figure 3-22: Superflex Apartment Data Model

Review Questions

1. Describe business process and its various types.
2. What are BPMN basic elements.
3. Describe the various types of business process activities.
4. Describe what is a business process gateway and its various forms.
5. Describe the purpose of swimlane business process element.
6. What are the four categories of business rules with respect to data modeling.
7. Describe the Constraints category of business rules.
8. Describe the Derivations category of business rules.

Review Exercises

1. A business process is a sequence of __________ related and structured activities to accomplish some task.
2. Business processes accomplish operational tasks limited to a ________ area like accounts payable or payroll.
3. Business processes accomplish operational tasks that ________ functional areas like sales order.
4. Business processes accomplish operational tasks that ______ across to another organization like supply chain just-in-time manufacturing.

5. A business process transforms a set of ______ into a set of _______ in the form of some product or service.
6. An ______ is represented as a small circle and refers to something that represents the initiation or conclusion of some work.
7. An ______ is either a task or a sub-process.
8. A ______ controls process flows by splitting it into alternate paths.
9. A _____ depicts activities within a pool.
10. Business rules describe the nature of operating policies of a business process in terms of the ______ that relate business terms to each other.
11. The _______ category emphasizes how a fact in one form that is transformed into some other knowledge or derived fact to support business process operations.

Problem Solving Exercises

3-1. Study the restaurant service operations business process model (Figure 3-23) and associated business rules (Table 3-8). Develop (i) an ER diagram based on the associated business rules and business term information, and (ii) indicate which business process activity should be manual, user, or service. Provide explanation for your choice. ER diagram should be based on crow-foot notation only.

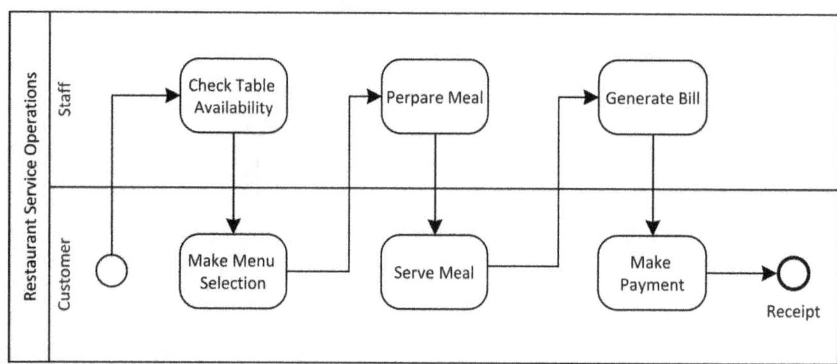

Figure 3-23: Restaurant Service Operation Business Process Model

Business Rules ID	Business Rules Description
BR-1	Terms Menu, SeatingTable, Booking, Server relevant for business process.
BR-2	A booking is taken care by one server. A server can attend to many bookings.
BR-3	It is possible for a server to have no bookings.
BR-4	Each booking is associated with at least one seatingtable.
BR-5	A seatingtable can service many bookings.
BR-6	Each booking is associated with one or more menu items.
BR-7	It is possible for a menu item to have not been ordered in any booking.

Table 3-8: Restaurant Service Operations Business Process Business Rules

Business term information that needs to be recorded:

- Menu term information will consist of the following: MenuID, its Name, Description, Price, Ingredient, and IngredientQuantity. There can be many ingredients with specific quantities for each menu item. The ID of Menu is MenuID.
- SeatingTable term information will consist of the following: TableID and details like number of seats and location. The ID of seating table is TableID.
- Server term information will consist of the following: ServerID, FirstName, LastName. The ID of server is ServerID.
- Booking term information will consist of the following: BookingID, ServingDate, PartySize, GuestName, NumberOfAdults, NumberOfChildren. The ID of server is BookingID.

3-2. Study the lead to forecast business process model (Figure 3-24) and associated business rules (Table 3-9). Develop (i) an ER diagram based on the associated business rules and business term information, and (ii) indicate which business process activity should be manual, user, or service. Provide explanation for your choice. ER diagram should be based on crow-foot notation only.

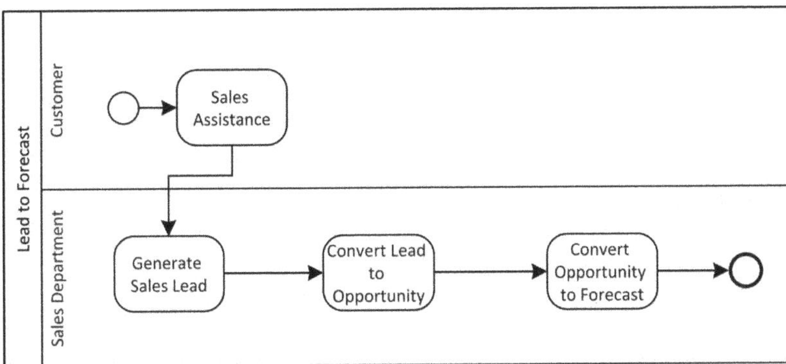

Figure 3-24: Lead to Forecast Business Process Model

Business Rules ID	Business Rules Description
BR-1	Terms SalesAgent, Customer, Product, SalesLead relevant for business process.
BR-2	SalesLead occurs when a customer requests the need for further assistance before placing an order.
BR-3	The salesagent records details about the customer and product.
BR-4	A customer can also be associated with multiple products.
BR-5	A product may not always have an interest from a customer.
BR-6	A salesaagent may initiate multiple salesleads.
BR-7	A customer can have multiple salesleads, while every saleslead must be associated with a customer.

Table 3-9: Lead to Forecast Business Process Business Rules

Business term information that needs to be recorded:

- SalesLead term information will consist of the following: SalesLeadID, LeadName, TimeFrame, LeadAmount, and MaturingPercent. The ID of SalesLead is SalesLeadID.
- Customer term information will consist of the following: CustomerID, Name, ContactType, ContactTitle, State, and Zip. The ID of Customer is CustomerID.

- Product term information will consist of the following: ProductID, Description, Price. The ID of Product is ProductID.
- SalesAgent term information will consist of the following: SalesAgentID, FirstName, LastName. The ID of SalesAgent is SalesAgentID.

3-3. Study the automobile rental web reservation business process model (Figure 3-25) and associated business rules (Table 3-10). Develop (i) an ER diagram based on the associated business rules and business term information, and (ii) indicate which business process activity should be manual, user, or service. Provide explanation for your choice. ER diagram should be based on crow-foot notation only.

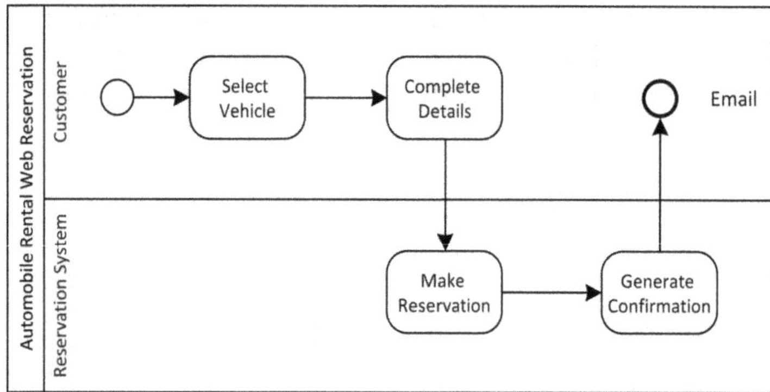

Figure 3-25: Automobile Rental Web Reservation Business Process Model

Business Rules ID	**Business Rules Description**
BR-1	Terms Customer Vehicle Rental relevant for business process.
BR-2	Only one vehicle per rental.
BR-3	Only one customer per rental.
BR-4	Repeat rental customers get 10% discount in Rental Amount.
BR-5	Rental vehicles must have less than 15000 miles.
BR-6	Rental vehicles with more than 10 minor dents are not allowed for future rentals.
BR-7	A vehicle can participate in many rentals.

Table 3-10: Automobile Rental Web Reservation Business Process Business Rules

Business term information that needs to be recorded:

- Customer term information will consist of the following: CustomerNo, CustomerName, Street, City, State, Zip, Phone, Email. The ID of Customer is CustomerNo.
- Vehicle term information will consist of the following: VIN (Vehicle Identification Number), ModelYear, AutoMake, AutoModel, OdometerReading, MinorDents, MajorDents. The ID of Vehicle is VIN.
- Rental term information will consist the following: RentalNo, RentalDate, PickUp_City, DropOff_City, PickUp_Time, DropOff_Time, Navigation, SkiRack, Infant_Seat, Collison_Insurance, RentalAmount, Tax, RentalTotal. The ID of Rental is RentalNo.

3-4. Extend problem 3-3 with the automobile rental business process model (Figure 3-26) and associated business rules (Table 3-11). In the business process model the Make Web Rental Reservation activity pertains to Figure 3-25 of problem 3-3. Develop (i) an ER diagram based on the associated business rules and business term information, and (ii) indicate which business process activity should be manual, user, or service. Provide explanation for your choice. ER diagram should be based on crow-foot notation only.

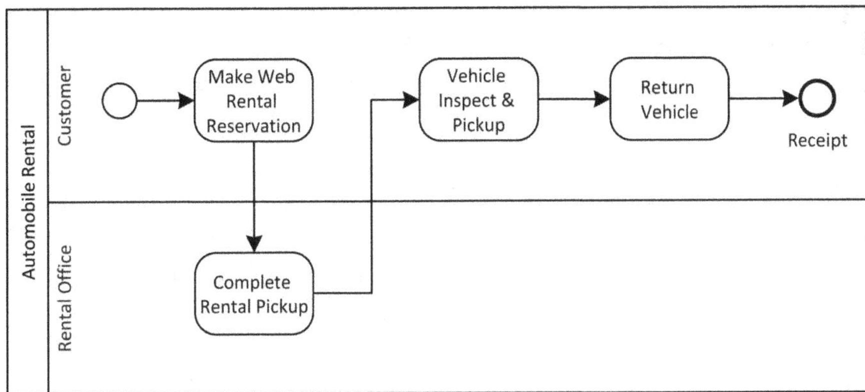

Figure 3-26: Automobile Rental Business Process Model

Business Rules ID	Business Rules Description
BR-1	Terms Registration, Vehicle, Rental, Location relevant for business process.
BR-2	A new customer first completes Web registration.
BR-3	A rental is always associated with a customer. The customer can visit the Web site again to make another reservation.
BR-4	The Web site generates a rental confirmation number with the Web rental rate.
BR-5	Every rental will have an assigned vehicle, but a vehicle may not be associated with a rental.
BR-6	A vehicle can be associated with many rentals over time.
BR-7	A rental is assigned to a location.
BR-8	A location may be taking care of multiple rentals.
BR-9	A vehicle may be stationed at multiple locations over time. A location can have multiple vehicles at its site.
BR-10	The vehicle rental rate is associated with the location where the vehicle is stationed.
BR-11	At the time of vehicle pickup, the StartOdometer reading is recorded as part of the rental. Also, at the conclusion of the rental, the EndOdometer reading is entered as part of the rental.

Table 3-11: Automobile Rental Business Process Business Rules

Business term information that needs to be recorded:

- Registration term information will consist of the following: RegistrationNo, FirstName, LastName, Address, Phone, and Email. The ID of Registration is RegistrationNo.
- Rental term information will consist of the following: ConfirmationNo, PickupDate, ReturnDate, WebRentalRate. The ID of Rental is ConfirmationNo.

- Vehicle term information will consist of the following: VIN, ModelYear, Odometer, Make, Type, and Model. The ID of Vehicle is VIN.
- Location term information will consist of the following: LocationID, State, City, LocationName. The ID of Location is LocationID.

3-5. Study the nursing home admission business process model (Figure 3-27) and associated business rules (Table 3-12). Develop (i) an ER diagram based on the associated business rules and business term information, and (ii) indicate which business process activity should be manual, user, or service. Provide explanation for your choice. ER diagram should be based on crow-foot notation only.

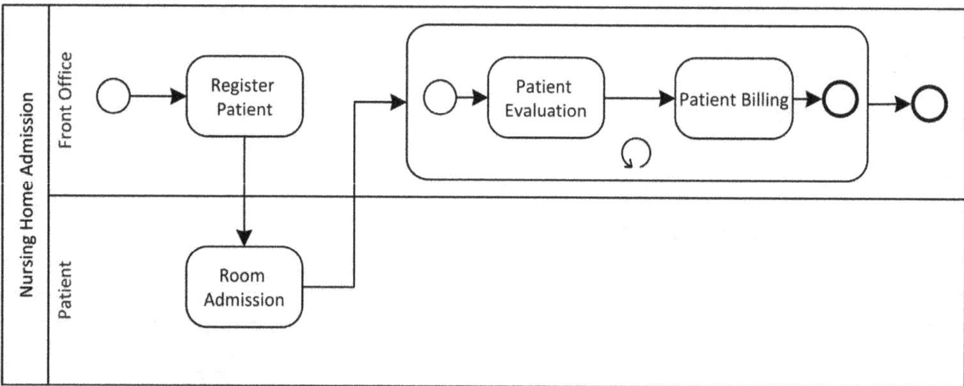

Figure 3-27: Nursing Home Admission Business Process Model

Business Rules ID	Business Rules Description
BR-1	Terms Family, Patient, Room, InsurancePolicy, InsuranceCo relevant for business process.
BR-2	Every patient is assigned a room. A patient can request a change to another room over time.
BR-3	A room will have only one patient at a time.
BR-4	Every patient must have some insurance policy.
BR-5	A patient can have multiple insurance policies.
BR-6	The nursing home may handle policies from different insurance companies (InsuranceCo term). Each patient insurance policy must belong to one of the associated insurance company.
BR-7	A patient can have multiple family members recorded. Also, a family can have multiple patients at the nursing home.

Table 3-12: Nursing Home Admission Business Process Business Rules

Business term information that needs to be recorded:

- Patient term information will consist of the following: PatientNo, FirstName, MiddleInitial, LastName, Phone, and Email. The ID of Patient is PatientNo.
- Room term information will consist of the following: RoomNo, TV, and Phone. The ID of Room is RoomNo.

- InsurancePolicy term information will consist of the following: PolicyNo, StartDate, EndDate, and PolicyDetails. The ID of InsurancePolicy is PolicyNo.
- InsuranceCo term information will consist of the following: CompanyID, Name, ContactPhone, ContactName, Address, and Email. The ID of InsuranceCo is CompanyID.
- Family term information will consist of the following: FamilyID, ContactName, PatientRelationship, Phone, Address, Email. The ID of Family is FamilyID.

3-6. Study the automobile insurance claim business process model (Figure 3-28) and associated business rules (Table 3-13). Develop (i) an ER diagram based on the associated business rules and business term information, and (ii) indicate which business process activity should be manual, user, or service. Provide explanation for your choice. ER diagram should be based on crow-foot notation only.

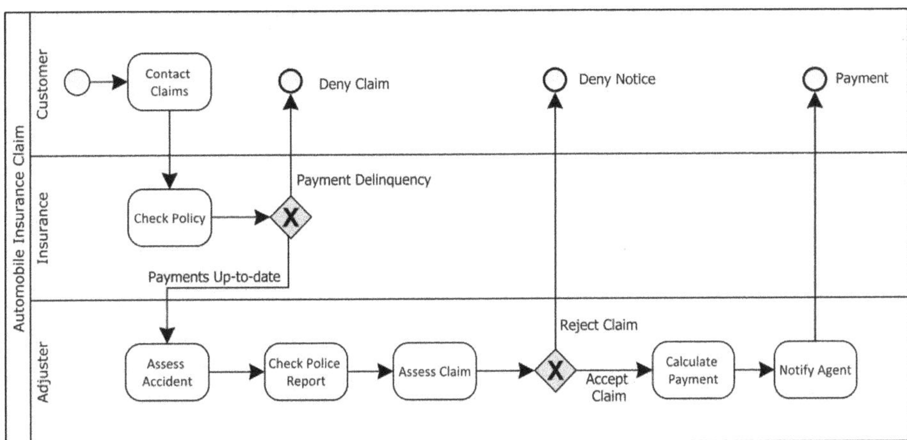

Figure 3-28: Automobile Insurance Claim Business Process Model

Business Rules ID	Business Rules Description
BR-1	Terms AutoPolicy, Claims, Agent, Adjustor relevant for business process.
BR-2	An auto policy may not have any claims in the beginning, but can have one or more claims over the life of the policy.
BR-3	An auto policy can include multiple vehicles.
BR-4	All auto policy payments are recorded.
BR-5	Only one agent must be associated with an auto policy.
BR-6	A claim must be handled by an adjustor. An adjustor may deal with many claims.
BR-7	A claim payment will incur a 10% rise in policy premium.
BR-8	Claims can be denied if policy payments are delinquent beyond 30 days.

Table 3-13: Automobile Insurance Claim Business Process Business Rules

Business term information that needs to be recorded:

- AutoPolicy term information will consist of the following: PolicyNo, YearPremium, EffectiveDate, ExpirationDate. The ID of AutoPolicy is PolicyNo information.

- AutoPolicyPayments details associated with each AutoPolicy will consist of the following information: PaymentNo, PaymentDate, DueDate, AmountDue, AmountPaid. The ID of AutoPolicyPayments is PaymentNo.
- Vehicle details associated with each AutoPolicy will consist of the following information: VIN (Vehicle Identification Number), ModelYear, AutoMake, AutoModel, BodilyInjuryAmt, AutoDamageAmt, MedicalPaymentsAmt, and UninsuredMotoristsAmt. The ID of each Vehicle is VIN.
- Claims term information will consist the following: ClaimNo, ClaimDate, AmountClaimed, AccidentStreet, AccidentState, AccidentZip, AmountPaid, ClaimStatus, PoliceReportNote, PoliceTicket, PoliceBlame, AdjusterBlame, BodilyInjuryStatus, AutoDamageStatus, SettlementDate, and RepairEstimate. The ID of Claims is ClaimNo information.
- Agent term information will consist the following: AgentNo, AgencyName, Street, City, State, Zip, Phone, and Email. The ID of Agent is AgentNo.
- Adjuster term information will consist the following: AdjusterNo, AdjusterName, Street, City, State, Zip, Phone, and Email. The ID of Adjuster is AdjusterNo.

Chapter 4. Introduction to Relational Model

Relational databases are the driving force behind the storage and manipulation of vast amounts of data that power any modern business organization. They are vital to the successful functioning of any modern organization. Businesses rely on relational databases to not only understand their operations, customer, and partners, but also support decision-making from a strategic standpoint. People come into contact with relational databases on a routine basis whenever they indulge in activities such as shopping online, supermarket checkout, online banking, airline reservation, or course registration.

A relational database is a repository of any data that an organization wishes to store for its operations and success. Such a repository can contain data on various aspects of organizational working like operations, customers, employees, business partners, organizational structure, and so on. Enterprise applications rely on relational databases to handle the data needed by the application. For instance, applications like enterprise resource planning (ERP), supply chain management (SCM), and customer relationship management (CRM) rely on relational databases to ensure efficient handling of vast amounts of organizational data. This chapter presents essential details on the relational model and its popular characterization as relational database.

Relational Model

Relational model organizes and structures data in the form of (i) two-dimensional tables called as relations, and (ii) database relationships among tables. A relational database is a logical collection of one or more tables with relationships among each other. Each such collection is referred as a *schema*. The rows of a table are referred as tuples or records, while the columns are referred as attributes or fields. Figure 4-1 is a sample collection of table names and relationships in an apartment complex database schema.

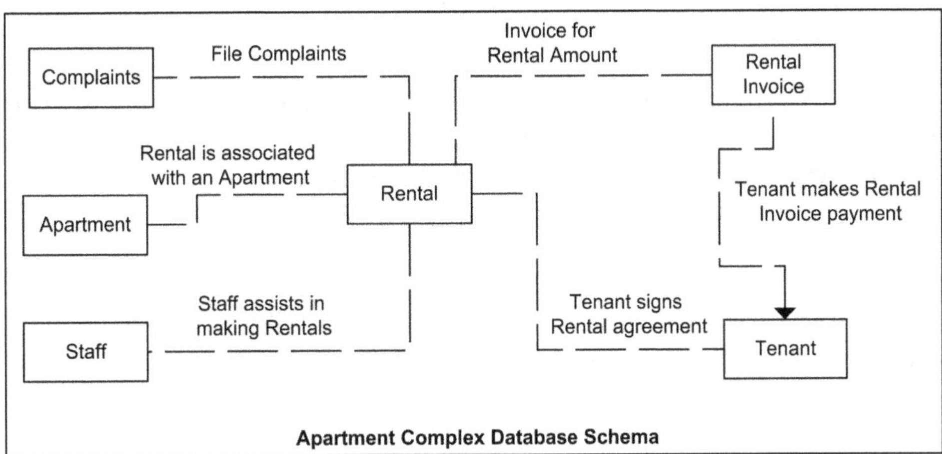

Figure 4-1: Tables and Relationships in Apartment Complex Database Schema

Each table refers to some *entity type* in an organization. Even though in general the terms entity type and entities are used interchangeably, there is a subtle difference between these terms. The term entity type refers to the definition of a table structure, while the values belonging to the entity type definition in the form of rows are referred as *entity instances* or *entities*. For example, as shown in Figure 4-2, the specification of the table Apartment along with its columns or attributes defines an entity type, while the values taken by the attributes in each row defines entity instances.

APARTMENT					
APT_NO	APT_TYPE	APT_STATUS	APT_UTILITY	APT_DEPOSIT_AMT	APT_RENT_AMT
100	0	V	Y	200	300
101	0	V	N	200	300
102	0	R	Y	200	300
...	...	...	...	...	...

← Entity Type Name

← Entity Instances

Figure 4-2: Apartment Table Example

Attributes of a table specify the characteristics of the entity type that an organization wishes to store. For example, the Apartment entity type contains data on different characteristics of an apartment important for an organization like apartment number (Apt_No), type of apartment (Apt_Type), status of the apartment (Apt_Status), apartment utilities (Apt_Utility), apartment deposit amount (Apt_Deposit_Amt), and apartment rent amount (Apt_Rent_Amt). Each row of the Apartment table is an instance of the values taken by the entity type apartment.

There are some basic rules that need to be followed while defining the table structure.

1. A table name is unique in the database schema.
2. Attribute names are unique within a table.
3. No two rows will be the same. In other words, duplicate rows are not allowed.
4. All attributes in a row are single valued only. In other words, an attribute cannot have more than one value in each row.
5. There is no ordering among rows or attributes.
6. Each table should have a *primary key*. Primary key is an attribute or a group of attributes in a table whose values are unique for each row of a table. In Figure 4-2, Apt_No attribute is the primary key of the Apartment table. Only one primary key specification should exist for each table.

Primary key specification is associated with a relational model integrity rule referred as *entity integrity*. Entity integrity implies that each table must have an attribute or combination of attributes with unique values in rows. Entity integrity ensures that entities in business are uniquely identified in a database.

Table definition in the database goes beyond the naming of the table and attributes. It also includes specification of the nature of data that can be stored for each attribute, and constraints on the nature of attribute values. Much of the table specification is accomplished through the SQL language.

Database Relationships

Tables in a relational model are often connected to each other through the concept of database relationships. Database relationships are a reflection of how data is utilized within the business environment. These relationships technically indicate a logical link between two tables at a time, and are also referred as binary relationships. For example, an apartment rental is always associated with some apartment; hence, the Rental table (entity type) representing the data of a rental will have a relationship with the Apartment table (entity type) representing the data of an apartment.

All database relationships in a relational model are defined (logically) through the concept of foreign key. Foreign key is an attribute in one table that appears as an attribute in another table and consequently provides a logical relationship between the two tables. The foreign key attribute contains values which are same as the primary key values of the other related table. Foreign key attribute is added to a table only if there is a relationship with another table. For example in Figure 4-3, Apt_No is the primary key of the table Apartment. Now if the Rental table has Apt_No as a foreign key attribute in its structure, it means that it can only have values that are same as Apt_No attribute values in the Apartment table. Foreign key attribute name need not be the same as the primary key attribute name of the related table. Often times, the table that is referenced by the foreign key (like Apartment table) is called the parent table, while the table with the foreign key (like the Rental table) is called the child table.

Foreign key specification is associated with a relational model integrity rule referred as *referential integrity*. Referential integrity implies that in database relationships, foreign key attribute values in one table must match the primary key attribute values of the related table. Referential integrity ensures that a database contains valid relationships.

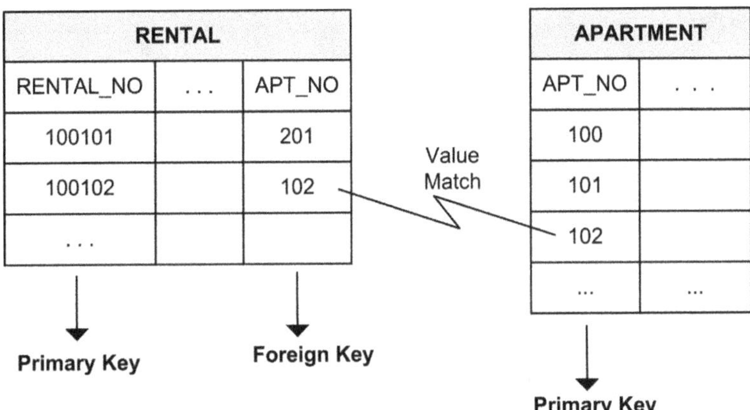

Figure 4-3: Database Relationship Example

Database relationships are based on how the rows of one table are associated with the rows of another table. These relationships can be expressed in three forms: one-to-one (1:1), one-to-many (1:N), and many-to-many (M:N).

One-to-One (1:1) Table Relationship

One-to-one (1:1) relationship exists if a row of one table is related to only one row of another table. To represent 1:1 relationship, foreign key attribute can be placed in either of the two tables (but not both). For example, suppose the Apartment table and Rental table of Figure 4-3 have 1:1 relationship. This implies that one row of Apartment table will have relationship (association) with only one row of Rental table, and vice-versa. To represent this relationship, the foreign key attribute will be added to either the Apartment table or the Rental table. In Figure 4-3 the foreign key (Apt_No) attribute appears in the Rental table.

One-to-Many (1:N) Table Relationship

One-to-many (1:N) relationship exists if a row of one table is related to many rows of another table. To represent 1:N relationship, the foreign key attribute should be placed in the table that represents the many part of the relationship, i.e. the table containing the many rows of the relationship. For example, suppose Staff table and Rental table have 1:N relationship as shown in Figure 4-4. This implies that one row of Staff table will have relationship (association) with many rows of Rental table. The Rental table now represents the many part of the relationship. So, the foreign key (Staff_No) is placed in the Rental table.

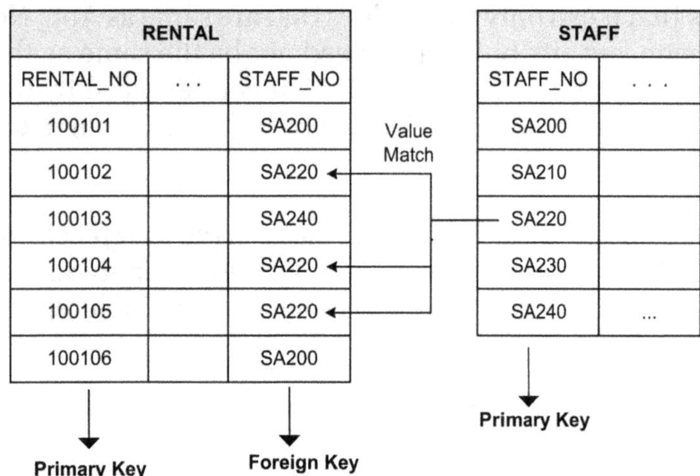

Figure 4-4: 1:N Relationship Example

Many-to-Many (M:N) Table Relationship

Many-to-many (M:N) relationship exists if a row of one table is related to many rows of another table and vice-versa. To represent M:N relationship, a new table is created. The attributes of the new table (referred as an intersection table) will include the primary key attributes of the tables that have M:N relationship. Further, the attributes of the new intersection table will together represent the primary key of the table, as well as become the foreign key attributes of their respective tables.

For example, suppose Product table and Product_Order table have M:N relationship as shown in Figure 4-5. This implies that one row of Product table is associated with may rows of Product_Order table, and each row of Product_Order table is also associated with many rows of Product table. In the figure, Product_Order table row having Order_Id value 1002 is associated with two products in the Product table having Product_Id values 10011 and 10015. Similarly, the Product_Order table row having Order_Id value 1004 is associated with three products in the Product table having Product_Id values 10011, 10013, and 10015. Conversely, Product table row having Product_Id value 10011 is associated with two rows in Product_Order table having Order_Id values 1002 and 1004, while the Product_Id value 10015 is associated with two Order_Id values 1002 and 1004.

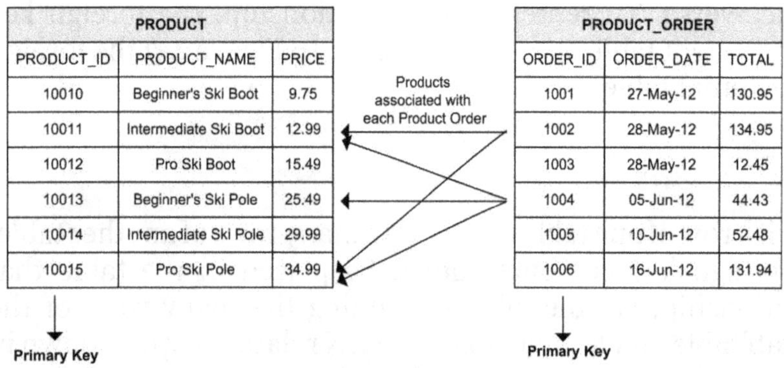

Figure 4-5: M:N Relationship Example

M:N relationship is represented through a new intersection table Order_Details as shown in Figure 4-6. The Order_Details table will at a minimum consist of the primary key attributes of Product and Product_Order tables, i.e. the Product_Id and Order_Id attributes. These Product_Id and Order_Id attributes in the intersection Order_Details table will together represent the primary key. Also, the Product_Id attribute in the intersection table Order_Details will be the foreign key attribute associating the Order_Details table with the Product table. Similarly, the Order_Id attribute in the intersection table Order_Details will be the foreign key attribute associating the Order_Details table with the Product_Order table.

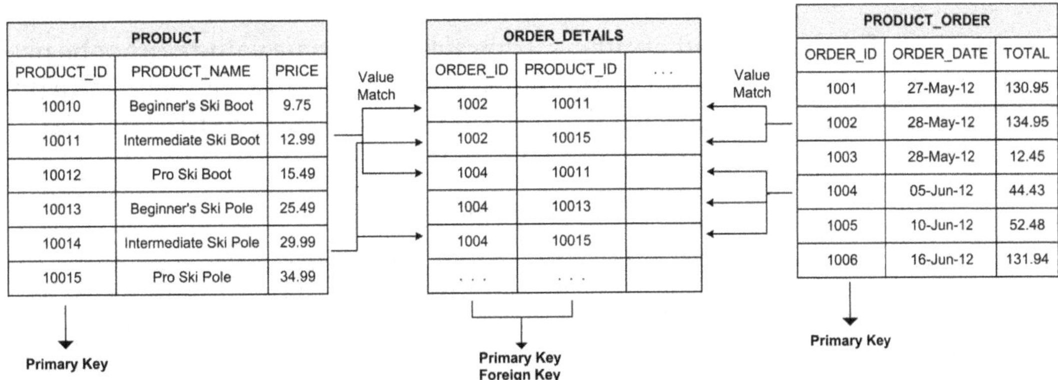

Figure 4-6: M:N Relationship Representation in Relational Model

Relational Database Language SQL

The database language to store and manipulate data in a relational model is called SQL (Structured Query Language). SQL is an ANSI standard language for relational database processing. SQL has two major components referred as Data Definition Language (DDL) and Data Manipulation Language (DML). DDL consists of statements to define the structure of tables and their relationships. It also consists of statements to control the administration of relational databases. DML consists of statements to manipulate data in existing tables. It consists of statements to insert a row in a table, delete rows from a table, update attribute values in a table or retrieve data from tables.

In this section the focus is on the Oracle SQL statements to define tables and relationships. Other aspects of the DDL component are covered in Chapter 5. All database object names like table names, attribute names, etc. in Oracle must follow the naming convention as shown in Table 4-1.

Naming Convention	Invalid Names Example
Spaces not allowed in between words.	Customer Order
Hyphens not allowed between words.	Customer-Order
Must begin with a letter	9Customer
Cannot exceed 30 characters	employee_social_security_numbers_column

Table 4-1: Oracle Naming Rules

Attribute Data Types

When a table is created, each attribute is assigned a data type, which specifies the kind of data that will be stored for that attribute. Data types also serve the purpose of error checking. For example, one cannot store a value "Jack" into an attribute assigned to hold a Date data type. Further, data types cause storage space to be more efficiently utilized by optimizing the way data is stored. The convention to define a data type is *attributename datatype-and-size.* For example, name varchar2(20). The following are some of the common Oracle data types.

Character Data Types

Character data types consists of alphabets and numbers. Character data type value cannot be used in calculations. The common character data types are: char and varchar2. Any character data type specification also includes the data size. Table 4-2 lists details of these Character data types.

Data Type	**Description**
CHAR	The char data type holds fixed-length character data up to a maximum size of 2000 characters. Char data type should be used for only fixed-length data having a restricted set of values. If no data size is defined, the default size for a char data type is one character. Using the char data type on attributes that might not fill the complete width forces the DBMS to add trailing blank spaces. For example, suppose a tenant_name attribute is declared as char(20) with a value "Mary Stackles." Now, in the database the actual storage will be "Mary Stackles" plus 7 blank spaces to the right of the last character.
VARCHAR2	The varchar2 data type stores variable length character data up to a maximum of 4,000 characters. If the inserted data values are smaller than the specified size, only the inserted values are stored, and the trailing blank spaces are not added to the end of the entry to make it fill the specified attribute size. For example, suppose a tenant_name attribute is declared as varchar2(20), with a value "Jack Ackerman." Now, in the database the actual storage will be "Jack Ackerman" only.

Table 4-2: Character Data Types

Numeric Data Types

The numeric data types store positive, negative, fixed, and floating-point numbers with precision up to 38 decimal places. Variations of the numeric data type are dec, decimal, double precision, float, integer, int, number, real, and smallint. Table 4-3 lists details of some of the common numeric data types.

Data Type	**Description**
INTEGER	An integer is a whole number with no digits to the right of the decimal point. suppose apt_no attribute is declared as integer.
NUMBER(p)	The number(p) data type is also utilized for integer data, where p is the precision for indicating the total number of digits. For example, suppose a tenant_ss attribute is declared as number(9).

NUMBER(p,s)	The number(p,s) data type is utilized to store numbers with fixed decimal digits. In the syntax p stands for precision and s stands for scale. For example, suppose a cost attribute is declared as number(5,2). This implies that all values will have two digits to the right of the decimal point, and there will be a total number of five digits. So valid cost attribute values are 25.95, 125.50, and so on.
NUMBER	The number data type is a floating-point specification. It is utilized for storing data with variable number of decimal places. The decimal point can appear anywhere, from before the first digit to after the last digit, or can be omitted. Floating point values are defined by not specifying either the precision or scale in the attribute value declaration. For example, suppose a student_gpa attribute is declared as number. The possible student_gpa values can be like 2.575, 3.5, 3.0, and so on.

Table 4-3: Number Data Types

Date Data Types

The Date data type stores dates from January 1, 4712 B.C. to December 31, 9999 A.D. The DATE data type stores the century, year, month, day, hour, minute, and second. The default date format is DD-MON-YY which stands for day of the month (DD), followed by month (MON), and the last two digits of the year (YY). The default time format is HH:MI:SS A.M., which indicates the hours (HH), minutes (MI), and seconds (SS) using the 12-hour clock. If no time is specified in a Date data type, the default time value is stored as 12:00:00 A.M. If no date is specified when a time is entered in a Date data type, the default date is the first day of the current month. DATE values are stored in a standard internal format in the database, so no length specification is required.

Large Object (LOB) Data Types

LOB data types can be used to store binary data, such as digitized sounds or images, or references to binary files from a word processor or spreadsheet. There are four LOB data types – BLOB, CLOB, BFILE, and NCLOB. Each of LOB data types is briefly described below in Table 4-4.

Large Object (LOB) Data Type	Description
BLOB	Binary LOB, stores up to 4 GB of binary data.
CLOB	Character LOB, stores up to 4 GB of character data.
BFILE	Binary File, storing a reference to a binary file located outside the database.
NCLOB	Character LOB that supports 2-byte character codes in the database.

Table 4-4: Various LOB Data Types

Create Table SQL

The SQL statement to create a new table is defined below. The CREATE TABLE keywords are followed by the name of the table. *All table names must be unique in the database.* The table attributes are listed through the "attribute data type & size" clause. The constraint declarations are optional.

```
CREATE TABLE tablename
(attribute1 data type & size [CONSTRAINT constraint declaration],
attribute2 data type & size [CONSTRAINT constraint declaration],
```

```
...
[CONSTRAINT constraint declaration . . .]);
```

Constraints are specifications which restrict the nature of attribute values. Constraints can be grouped into two categories: integrity constraints and value constraints. *All constraint names must be unique in the database.* SQL statements in Oracle are terminated by a semi-colon (;) sign.

Integrity Constraints

Integrity constraints are essential to preserve database integrity. They consists of *primary key constraint* and *foreign key constraint*. There can be only one primary key constraint in a table. A foreign key constraint in a table is optional as it depends on the database relationship. Both types of constraints can be placed *inline* as part of the definition of an individual attribute, or *out-of-line* clause as part of table definition so that it appears as a separate entry along with all the attributes of a table.

The general syntax for defining an inline primary key constraint occurs after an attribute data type declaration as "CONSTRAINT constraint-name PRIMARY KEY". For example, the following syntax creates the Product table. In the syntax, product_id, product_name, and price are attributes, while product_pk is the constraint name associated with the primary key attribute product_id of the table. The constraint name product_pk must be unique in the database.

```
create table product
(product_id integer constraint product_pk primary key,
product_name varchar2(30),
price number(5,2));
```

The syntax for the out-of-line primary key constraint declaration is "CONSTRAINT constraint-name PRIMARY KEY (attribute-name1 [,attribute-name2,...])". This syntax is generally used whenever the primary key consists of more than one attribute – called as composite primary key. For example, the following syntax creates a Tenant_Auto table, where the primary key consists of two attributes. Once again, the constraint name tenant_auto_pk must be unique in the database.

```
create table tenant_auto
(tenant_no integer,
license_no varchar2(6),
auto_make varchar2(15),
constraint tenant_auto_pk primary key (tenant_no,license_no));
```

The general syntax for defining an in-line foreign key constraint occurs after an attribute data type declaration as "CONSTRAINT constraint-name REFERENCES table-name". The foreign key attribute value has to match the primary key value of the referenced table. For example, the following syntax creates the Product_Order table with one foreign key attribute product_id. In the example, Product is the referenced table, and so the Product table primary key values will be checked with the values inserted for product_id attribute in the Product_Order table. The constraint names product_order_pk and product_order_fk must be unique in the database.

```
create table product_order
(order_id integer constraint product_order_pk primary key,
order_date date,
total number(5,2),
product_id integer constraint product_order_fk references product);
```

The syntax for the out-of-line foreign key constraint declaration is "CONSTRAINT constraint name FOREIGN KEY (attribute-name) REFERENCES table name [(primary-key-attribute)]". The primary-key-attribute entry is the name of the primary key of the referenced table. For example, the following syntax modifies the previous syntax to create Product_Order table with the foreign key clause at the end of the attribute declarations.

```
create table product_order
(order_id integer constraint product_order_pk primary key,
order_date date,
total number(5,2),
product_id integer,
constraint product_order_fk foreign key (product_id) references
product (product_id));
```

Value Constraints

Value constraints further conform the nature of data values that can be entered for an attribute. Value constraint types are *unique*, *not null*, *default*, and *check*. Multiple constraints for an attribute can be defined one after the other. All constraints except *not null* and *default* can be both in-line and out-of-line.

Unique Constraint

The unique constraint is identical to the primary key constraint except that null values are allowed. A table can have only one primary key constraint, but more than one unique constraint. Also, while a foreign key generally references a primary key, it can also reference an attribute with unique constraint. For instance, the following syntax creates the Sporting_Club table with unique constraint.

```
create table sporting_club
(club_id number(3) constraint sporting_club_pk primary key,
name varchar2(30) constraint sporting_club_name unique,
address varchar2(50));
```

It is also possible to have concatenated attributes defined with unique constraint. For instance, the following syntax creates a Tenant_Auto table wherein the concatenated attributes are defined as unique constraint.

```
create table tenant_auto
(tenant_ss number(9) constraint tenant_auto_fk references tenant,
license_no varchar2(6),
auto_make varchar2(15),
auto_model varchar2(15),
auto_year number(4),
auto_color varchar2(10),
constraint tenant_auto_pk primary key (tenant_ss,license_no),
constraint tenant_auto_lic_year (license_no,auto_year) unique);
```

Not Null Constraint

Not null constraint guarantees that an attribute has a value in a row. It must be declared inline with attribute definition. An attribute declared as primary key is also by default not null. For instance, the following syntax creates a Sporting_Club_NL table with not null constraint.

```
create table sporting_club_nl
(club_id number(3) constraint sporting_club_sp_pk primary key,
name varchar2(30) constraint sporting_club_sp_name not null,
address varchar2(50));
```

Default Constraint

The default constraint is utilized to assign a default value to an attribute. In this case, during a row insert operation it is not necessary to provide a value for the attribute. The default constraint does not require an explicit constraint name, and must be declared inline with attribute definition. For instance, the following syntax creates a Club_Activity_DF table with default constraint.

```
create table club_activity_df
(club_id number(3) constraint club_activity_df_pk primary key,
activity varchar2(50) default 'Hiking');
```

Check Constraint

A check constraint defines a discrete list of values that an attribute can contain. This list of values can be expressed within the constraint definition or expressed through a conditional expression.

A check constraint can also define a rule that is constructed from multiple attributes of a table. In this case the constraint must be declared as a separate constraint clause instead of being attached to a specific attribute. For instance, the following syntax shows a check constraint in the Rental table that ensures that the difference between lease_start attribute and lease_end attribute is six months or twelve months.

```
create table rental
(rental_no number(6) constraint rental_pk primary key,
rental_date date,
rental_status char(1),
lease_type varchar2(3),
lease_start date,
lease_end date,
apt_no number(3) constraint rental_apt_fk references apartment,
constraint rental_duration_ck check (((lease_end - lease_start) = 6) or ((lease_end - lease_start) = 12)));
```

Check constraint conditional expression attributes are limited to its table. If the conditional expression depends on values in other tables or needs to reference values before or after the changes on the attribute, the check constraint should not be used. Instead in such situations PL/SQL Triggers (outlined in later chapter) should be considered.

For instance, the following syntax shows a Rental table with a number of constraint specifications:

- attribute rental_date cannot have null values.
- attribute rental_status can have values that are either S or O or C or V.
- attribute lease_type will have a default value of One.
- attribute lease_type can also have values One or Six.

```
create table rental
(rental_no number(6) constraint rental_pk primary key,
rental_date date constraint rental_date_nn NOT NULL,
```

```
rental_status char(1)constraint rental_status_ck check ((rental_status = 'S') or (rental_status = 'O') or (rental_status = 'C')
or (rental_status = 'V')),
lease_type varchar2(3) default 'One' constraint lease_type_ck check ((lease_type = 'One') or (lease_type = 'Six')),
lease_start date,
lease_end date,
apt_no number(3) constraint rental_apt_fk references apartment);
```

The following syntax is an alternative to defining the same value constraints for the Rental table after the listing of attributes.

```
create table rental
(rental_no number(6) constraint rental_pk primary key,
rental_date date constraint rental_date_nn NOT NULL,
rental_status char(1),
cancel_date date,
lease_type varchar2(3) default 'One',
lease_start date,
lease_end date,
apt_no number(3) constraint rental_apt_fk references apartment,
constraint rental_status_ck check ((rental_status = 'S') or (rental_status = 'O') or (rental_status = 'C') or (rental_status = 'V')),
constraint lease_type_ck check ((lease_type = 'One') or (lease_type = 'Six'));
```

Referential Integrity Maintenance Options

Referential integrity is impacted when a row is deleted that contains a value referred to by a foreign key value in another table. For instance, in Figure 4-4, referential integrity will be impacted when rows in the Staff table (parent) are deleted. Since these rows have a relationship with the Rental table (child), the deletion of a row in Staff table will break the referential integrity by making the Rental table foreign key values orphans as they would be without a related primary key value.

There are three options to maintain referential integrity: *restrict*, *cascade*, and *set null*. The restrict option will not allow the deletion of a row in the parent table if its primary key value is referenced as a foreign key value in another table. This is the default option, and so is not explicitly allowed. The cascade option allows the deletion of rows in the parent table by also deleting all corresponding rows in the child table. The set null option also allows the deletion of rows in the parent table, but sets the corresponding rows in the child table to null. So with set null option the rows in the child table are not deleted. The set null option indicates an optional relationship. These options are added after the references clause of the create table statement as shown below.

```
create table rental_invoice
(invoice_no number(6) constraint rental_invoice_pk primary key,
invoice_date date,
invoice_due number(4),
cc_no number(16),
rental_no number(6) constraint rental_invoice_fk references rental
on delete cascade);

create table complaints
(complaint_no number(6) constraint complaints_pk primary key,
complaint_date date,
rental_complaint varchar2(100),
rental_no number(6) constraint complaints_fk1 references rental on delete set null);
```

Maintain Table Structure

Once the table has been created additional SQL statements are needed to maintain the table structure. Such maintenance involves modification of the table structure, removal of the table from the database, and the renaming of an existing table name. The modification of table structure is accomplished through the alter statement. The removal of a table from the database is done through the drop statement. The renaming of a table is performed through the rename statement.

ALTER Statement

The Alter statement performs many functions. It can be used to add an attribute to an existing table, modify the data type declaration of an existing attribute, add new constraints to a table, drop existing constraints from a table, and drop an attribute from a table. The syntax of Alter statement to add an attribute is:

```
ALTER TABLE tablename
ADD attribute-name   data-type-and-size  [ constraint specification ];
```

The following SQL statement adds an attribute "email" to the staff table.

```
ALTER TABLE staff
ADD email varchar2(25);
```

The syntax of Alter statement to modify an attribute's data type declaration is:

```
ALTER TABLE tablename
MODIFY attribute-name   new-data-type-and-size;
```

Modification of an attribute's data type declaration is allowed only if the existing data in the attribute being modified is compatible with the new specification. For example, one can change a varchar2 data type to a char data type, but not to a number data type. The following SQL statement modifies the data type of the attribute established (added in the previous example) in the staff table.

```
ALTER TABLE staff
MODIFY email varchar2(15);
```

The syntax of Alter statement to drop a constraint is:

```
ALTER TABLE tablename
DROP CONSTRAINT  constraint-name ;
```

The following SQL statement drops the foreign key constraint in the rental table.

```
ALTER TABLE rental
DROP CONSTRAINT rental_apt_fk2;
```

The syntax of Alter statement to add a constraint specification is:

```
ALTER TABLE tablename
ADD CONSTRAINT constraint-specification ;
```

The following SQL statement adds a foreign key constraint to the rental table.

```
ALTER TABLE rental
ADD CONSTRAINT rental_apt_fk FOREIGN KEY (apt_no) references apartment;
```

The syntax of Alter statement to drop an attribute from a table is:

```
ALTER TABLE tablename
DROP COLUMN attribute-name;
```

The following SQL statement drops the attribute established (added in the previous example) from the staff table.

```
ALTER TABLE staff
DROP COLUMN email;
```

DROP Statement

The Drop statement is used to remove a table from the database. This is a serious statement, because once the table is dropped, all the data that may have existed in the table is also deleted. The syntax of Drop statement is:

```
DROP TABLE tablename [CASCADE CONSTRAINTS];
```

This statement will not be successful if the table being dropped contains attributes referenced as foreign keys in other tables. The following SQL statement to drops the table supplier will generate error because the staff table is referenced through foreign keys in rental table.

```
DROP TABLE staff;
```

In this case, one can either drop all of the tables that contain the foreign key references first (like dropping purchase_order and products tables prior to dropping supplier table), or let the system drop the foreign key constraints in all of the associated tables with the Cascade Constraints option.

When the Drop Table statement is issued with the Cascade Constraints option, the system first drops all of the constraints associated with the table, and then drops the table. This allows the table to be dropped in any order, regardless of the foreign key constraints. The following SQL statement modifies the previous statement to drop the table supplier with the Cascade Constraints option. Now, the system will automatically drop the foreign key references to the staff table in rental table first before dropping the staff table from the database.

```
DROP TABLE staff cascade constraints;
```

RENAME Statement

The Rename statement allows the renaming of existing tables. The syntax is:

```
RENAME old-tablename TO new-tablename;
```

The following syntax renames sporting_clubs table to outdoor_clubs table.

```
RENAME staff TO employee;
```

Normalization

Normalization is a concept that enables attributes to collectively exist in a table such that the table structure does not become inconsistent during data manipulation. Normalization usually involves splitting tables into smaller tables thereby creating relationships between them. Normalization is based on two principles: modification anomalies and dependencies.

Modification Anomalies

Modification anomalies are unexpected inconsistencies that can occur during data manipulation operations. There are three types of modification anomalies: insert, update, and delete. To consider these anomalies consider the following single Rental table shown in Figure 4-7.

RENTAL Table

RENTAL_NO	RENTAL_DATE	LEASE_TYPE	LEASE_START	STAFF_FIRST_NAME	STAFF_LAST_NAME	APT_NO	APT_RENT_AMT
100101	12-Oct-11	One	1-Nov-11	Joe	White	201	500
100102	5-Dec-11	Six	1-Jan-12	Ann	Tremble	102	300
100103	15-Dec-11	Six	1-Jan-12	Ann	Tremble	203	500
100104	12-Mar-12	One	1-Apr-12	Susan	Brandon	101	300
100105	12-Apr-12	One	1-May-12	Joe	White	104	300
100106	15-Jul-12	One	1-Aug-12	Ann	Tremble	100	300

* RENTAL_NO is primary key

Figure 4-7: Rental Table with Modification Anomalies

Insert Anomaly:

An insert anomaly exists if some attribute value cannot be inserted in a table unless there is some additional data available. So, suppose a new staff member has joined the apartment complex. The new staff first name and last name cannot be inserted in the Rental table unless there is a new rental_no created. As rental_no is the primary key so without a rental_no value the new staff information cannot be inserted in a row.

Delete Anomaly:

A delete anomaly exists if deleting a row from a table results in unexpected loss of additional information. So, suppose the rental associated with rental_no 100104 is deleted. Now there will be loss of information on staff Susan Brandon as this was the only row containing this name.

Update Anomaly:

An update anomaly exists when it is necessary to modify multiple rows to revise a single fact. For example, suppose there is a new business rule that all apartments numbers from 100 to 105 will have their apartment rent changed to 350. This change will require modifying the apt_rent_amt value in four rows.

To deal with modification anomalies, application developers may circumvent them by developing additional programs to deal with inadvertent loss of data. A better approach is to modify the table design to remove these anomalies.

Functional Dependencies

Functional dependency is an important concept when analyzing a table for removing modification anomalies. A functional dependency is a relationship between attributes of a table. In general terms, attribute Y is functionally dependent on attribute X, if the value of X determines the value of Y. In other words, if we know the value of X, we can get the value of Y.

Functional dependencies are often found in real world situations. Suppose a smartphone manufacturer ties smartphone price and some features to the color of the smartphone. For instance, pink color smartphones may have a highest price, blue color smartphones will be priced less than pink smartphones, and black smartphones will have the lowest price. Now in the context of functional dependency the color of the smartphone is determining the smartphone price and other features. So if a smartphone table is created with attributes for color, price, processor, storage, and so on, then the color attribute value will determine other table attributes values.

Functional dependencies are written using the notation X -> Y, where X (attributes on the left side of the arrow) is referred as determinant. The functional dependency notation is read as: X attribute functionally determines Y attribute. Using the above example of smartphone table, Color -> Price, Processor, Storage. As primary key values are unique in each row of a table, often times primary key values can provide details on other attribute values in a row more accurately. So in the Rental table of Figure 4-7 consider two attributes Rental_No and Lease_Type. If we know the value of rental number (Rental_No attribute) we can find the duration (Lease_Type attribute) for that rental. This fact can be shown through the dependency Rental_No -> Lease_Type where Rental_No is the determinant.

Functional dependency determinant is not limited to single attribute. It can involve group of attributes. For example, study the following two functional dependencies.

Functional Dependency 1: Rental_No -> Rental_Date, Lease_Type, Lease_Start
Functional Dependency 2: Rental_No, Apt_No -> Apt_Rent_Amt

Functional dependency 1 implies that Rental_No attribute functionally determines the attributes (Rental_Date, Lease_Type, Lease_Start) on the right side of the arrow. Functional Dependency 2 implies that the determinant Rental_No and Apt_No attribute together functionally determine the Apt_Rent_Amt attribute value. Technically if X -> Y, Z, then it is possible to have equivalent functional dependencies like X -> Y and X -> Z. However, if there is a functional dependency X,Y -> Z, then it is not correct to split the determinant in equivalent functional dependencies like X -> Z and Y -> Z.

Normal Forms

Normal forms are rules that ensures a table has removed modification anomalies from its structure. Initially when the relational model was proposed E. F. Codd[1] there were three normal forms referred as first, second, and third normal forms (1NF, 2NF, 3NF). Later Boyce-Codd normal form (BCNF) was specified, and then the fourth and fifth normal forms (4NF, 5NF) were defined. Each successive normal form refines the previous normal form to remove additional anomalies. These normal forms are nested, i.e. a table in second normal form is also in the first normal form, and a table in fifth normal form is also in 1NF, 2NF, 3NF, BCNF, and 4NF. Generally, for most business database design purposes, normalization up to the third normal form is sufficient. The focus here will be on the first, second, third, and fourth normal forms.

---

[1] E.F. Codd, "A relational model of data for large shared data banks" Communications of The ACM, Vol. 13, No. 6, 1970, pp 377-387.

First Normal Form (1NF)

Any table that satisfies the basic rules of table structure (as outlined in the relational model section of this chapter) is in 1NF. These rules once again are: attribute names are unique within a table; no two rows will be the same or no duplicate rows; all attributes in a row are single valued; no ordering among rows or attributes; there is a primary key. The Rental table shown in Figure 4-7 is in 1NF.

Second Normal Form (2NF)

A table is in 2NF if all non-key attributes are dependent on all of the primary key. 2NF deals with partial dependency of non-key attributes on the primary key. 2NF primarily occurs in case the primary key consists of two or more attributes i.e. a table with composite primary key. This means that if a table has a single attribute as a primary key, it will by default be in 2NF, since every non-key attribute is dependent on the primary key so there is no scope for partial dependency. For example, consider the Rental_Staff table in Figure 4-8. The primary key of the table is a composite key consisting of Rental_No and Staff_No.

RENTAL_STAFF Table

RENTAL_NO	STAFF_NO	RENTAL_DATE	LEASE_TYPE	LEASE_START	STAFF_FIRST_NAME	STAFF_LAST_NAME
100101	SA200	12-Oct-11	One	1-Nov-11	Joe	White
100102	SA210	5-Dec-11	Six	1-Jan-12	Ann	Tremble
100103	SA210	15-Dec-11	Six	1-Jan-12	Ann	Tremble
100104	SA220	12-Mar-12	One	1-Apr-12	Susan	Brandon
100105	SA200	12-Apr-12	One	1-May-12	Joe	White
100106	SA210	15-Jul-12	One	1-Aug-12	Ann	Tremble

* RENTAL_NO, STAFF_NO is primary key

Figure 4-8: Rental_Staff Table with Second Normal Form Violation

The Rental_Staff table suffers from insert anomaly. Suppose a new staff member has joined the apartment complex, data on the new staff number like first name and last name cannot be inserted in the Rental_Staff table, unless there is a new rental_no created, as rental_no is part of the primary key, and primary key attributes cannot be having null values in a row.

The reason for insert anomaly is because there is a functional dependency Staff_No ->Staff_First_Name, Staff_Last_Name, which implies that the values of staff_first_name and staff_last_name are determined by the value of staff_no, and not rental_no. This functional dependency indicates that Staff_First_Name and Staff_Last_name attributes are not dependent on the entire composite primary key, but instead are dependent on part of the composite primary key implying partial dependency.

To correct the violation of the 2NF by the Rental_Staff table, the table is split into two tables Rental table and Staff table as shown in Figure 4-9. With the split details on a new staff can be inserted in the Staff table without a rental.

RENTAL Table

RENTAL_NO	RENTAL_DATE	LEASE_TYPE	LEASE_START
100101	12-Oct-11	One	1-Nov-11
100102	5-Dec-11	Six	1-Jan-12
100103	15-Dec-11	Six	1-Jan-12
100104	12-Mar-12	One	1-Apr-12
100105	12-Apr-12	One	1-May-12
100106	15-Jul-12	One	1-Aug-12

* RENTAL_NO is primary key

STAFF Table

STAFF_NO	STAFF_FIRST_NAME	STAFF_LAST_NAME
SA200	Joe	White
SA210	Ann	Tremble
SA210	Ann	Tremble
SA220	Susan	Brandon
SA200	Joe	White
SA210	Ann	Tremble

* STAFF_NO is primary key

Figure 4-9: Rental Table and Staff Table in Second Normal Form

Third Normal Form (3NF)

A table is in 3NF if it has no *transitive dependency*. A transitive dependency exists when there is a sequence of functional dependencies like X -> Y -> Z, wherein X is indirectly determining Z through the attribute Y. In essence the focus of 3NF is on dependencies among the non-key attributes. For example consider the Rental table in Figure 4-10. The primary key of the table is rental_no attribute. The Rental table is in 2NF. However, the Rental table will suffer from insert anomaly. Suppose the rent amount (Apt_Rent_Amt) of a new apartment number (Apt_No) has to be added to the Rental table. This insert of new rent amount cannot be done unless there is rental for the apartment in the form of a new rental_no value, since a row cannot be inserted with a blank primary key value.

RENTAL Table

RENTAL_NO	RENTAL_DATE	LEASE_TYPE	LEASE_START	APT_NO	APT_RENT_AMT
100101	12-Oct-11	One	1-Nov-11	201	500
100102	5-Dec-11	Six	1-Jan-12	102	300
100103	15-Dec-11	Six	1-Jan-12	203	500
100104	12-Mar-12	One	1-Apr-12	101	300
100105	12-Apr-12	One	1-May-12	104	300
100106	15-Jul-12	One	1-Aug-12	100	300

* RENTAL_NO is primary key

Figure 4-10: Rental Table with Third Normal Form Violation

The reason for insert anomaly is because there is a functional dependency Apt_No -> Apt_Rent_Amt, which is then part of a transitive dependency Rental_No -> Apt_No -> Apt_Rent_Amt. The transitive dependency implies that the values of Apt_Rent_Amt are indirectly determined by Rental_No.

To correct the violation of the 3NF in the Rental table, the table is split into two tables Rental table and Apartment table as shown in Figure 4-11. With the split details on a new apartment can be inserted in the Apartment table without a rental.

RENTAL Table

RENTAL_NO	RENTAL_DATE	LEASE_TYPE	LEASE_START
100101	12-Oct-11	One	1-Nov-11
100102	5-Dec-11	Six	1-Jan-12
100103	15-Dec-11	Six	1-Jan-12
100104	12-Mar-12	One	1-Apr-12
100105	12-Apr-12	One	1-May-12
100106	15-Jul-12	One	1-Aug-12

* RENTAL_NO is primary key

APARTMENT Table

APT_NO	APT_RENT_AMT
201	500
102	300
203	500
101	300
104	300
100	300

* APT_NO is primary key

Figure 4-11: Rental Table and Apartment Table in Third Normal Form

Fourth Normal Form (4NF)

Fourth normal form removes *multi-valued dependencies* (MVD). A multi-valued dependency exists when there are at least three or more attributes wherein one of the attribute determines multiple values of two or more attributes even though the attributes that are being associated with the single attributes are independent of each other. The notation for MVD is ->-> . For example, consider three attributes A, B, and C. A MVD exists if (i) A determines multiple values of B and C using the notation A ->-> B and A ->-> C, and (ii) B and C are independent of each other. Since A is independently determining the multiple values of B and C, placing the attributes together in a table will cause modification anomalies. The fourth normal form rule is that a table should not contain two or more independent multi-valued facts about an entity or no MVD. MVD is generally associated with primary key attributes of a table, wherein the primary key consists of two or more attributes.

MVDs are generalization of functional dependencies. A MVD where one value of A determines only one value of B and one value of C is a FD. So, a functional dependency can lead to a MVD.

Consider the Auto_Features table as shown in Figure 4-12. The three attributes have an MVD in the form of Auto_Make ->-> Auto_Model and Auto_Make ->-> Doors, where Auto_Model and Doors attribute values are independent of each other. The implication of the MVD is that it can result in modification anomaly. For instance, an insert anomaly can exist if a new Auto_Model attribute value has to be inserted for a new Auto_Make attribute value. This insert operation cannot be done unless there is a Door attribute value.

AUTO_FEATURES Table

AUTO_MAKE	AUTO_MODEL	DOORS
Subaru	Impreza	2
Subaru	Impreza	4
Subaru	Legacy	2
Subaru	Legacy	4
Honda	Accord	2
Honda	Accord	4

* All attributes together are primary key

Figure 4-12: Auto_Features Table with Fourth Normal Form Violation

The Auto_Features table violates the fourth normal form. To correct the violation of the 4NF in the Auto_Features table, the table is split into two tables Auto_Models table and Model_Doors table as shown in Figure 4-13. With the split details on a new AutoModel for a new AutoMake can be inserted in the Auto_Models table without a Door value.

AUTO_MODELS Table

AUTO_MAKE	AUTO_MODEL
Subaru	Impreza
Subaru	Legacy
Honda	Accord

* All attributes together are primary key

MODEL_DOORS Table

AUTO_MAKE	DOORS
Subaru	2
Subaru	4
Honda	2
Honda	4

* All attributes together are prim

Figure 4-13: Auto_Models Table and Model_Doors Table in Fourth Normal Form

General Guidelines to Facilitate Normalization

It is possible to ensure that tables in general are normalized before placing attributes in a table by (i) determining the functional dependency among the attributes, (ii) develop one table for each functional dependency wherein all the attributes in the functional dependency are also attributes of the table, and (iii) make the determinant the primary key of the ensuing table.

Entity relationship model by facilitating the development of tables (explained in the following section) assists in this process too, due to the concept of entity instances wherein the attribute in an instance is based on the entity identifier. As in the entity type structure the attributes of an entity type are dependent on entity identifier value for entity instances, there is a latent functional dependency from entity identifier to other attributes. Consequently the transformed tables from entity relationship model are more closer to normalized status. But, in spite of developing tables from entity relationship model, it is still possible that normal forms may be violated in the tables.

Role of Normalization During Database Design

Normalization can be applied in two ways to facilitate database design: (i) table refinement approach, or (ii) basic design approach. In the refinement approach, the ER Model is transformed into tables using the transformation rules, and then normalization concepts are applied. In this approach normalization is accomplished in an informal manner without the tedious process of recording functional dependencies. Normalization in this case ensures that keys and redundancies have not been overlooked.

The alternative design approach, normalization concepts are part of conceptual data model. So, instead of developing an ER model, functional dependencies are defined initially to develop relational model. An ER model is then generated (reverse engineered) from the relational database diagram. One of the drawbacks of this approach is that relationships can be overlooked.

This book emphasizes the table refinement approach as it simplifies development of the relational model with minimum normalization. Further, for novice data modelers, identifying relationships is much easier when entity type symbols are viewed compared to simply focusing on dependencies concepts. As ER model facilitates better communication and understanding of business process operations involving business rules, the table refinement approach is more appropriate.

Transform ER Model into Relational Model

Transformation of the ER model into a relational model is the process of moving the database development process from conceptual modeling to logical modeling. The transformation process also makes the data model more DBMS specific from an implementation standpoint. In general, the entity types become tables, while relationships among entity types are represented through the concept of foreign keys. The basic transformation guidelines for the various entity types and relationships with SQL statements are described now.

Entity Type Transformation

Each entity type becomes a table. The attributes of the entity type become the attributes of the corresponding table. The primary key of the entity type becomes the primary key of the table. Figure 4-14 shows the transformation of Staff entity type into Staff table. The figure shows the SQL statements for creating the Staff table. The primary key attribute Staff_No of Staff entity type is also the primary key of the corresponding table.

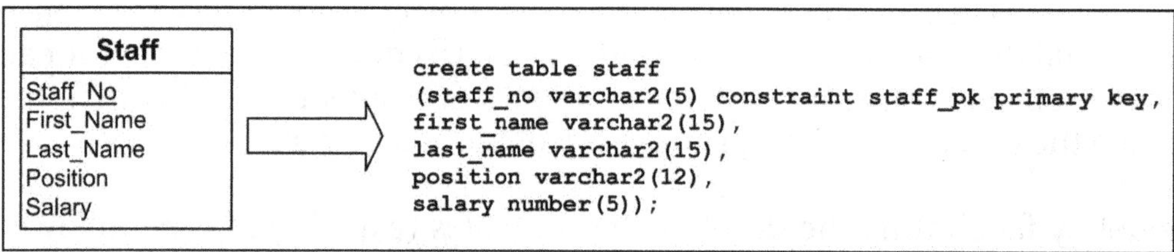

Figure 4-14: Representation of Entity Type as Database Table

Weak Entity Type Transformation

Each weak entity type becomes a table. The attributes of the weak entity type become the attributes of the corresponding table. The primary key of the weak entity type table can be created in two ways:

- If there is already a primary key of the weak entity type, then it is combined with the primary key of the entity type table which has an identifying relationship with the weak entity type.
- If there is no primary key of the weak entity type, then some or all of the attributes of the weak entity type are combined with the primary key of the entity type table which has an identifying relationship with the weak entity type.

Figure 4-15 shows the transformation of weak entity type Tenant_Auto along with Tenant entity type into their corresponding tables. Tenant_Auto is the weak entity type to Tenant entity type. The figure shows the SQL statements for creating the Tenant and Tenant_Auto table. The attributes of Tenant_Auto become the attributes of its corresponding table. Even though Tenant_Auto entity type already has a primary key, but since Tenant_Auto has an identifying relationship with Tenant, the primary key of Tenant_Auto table is formed by combining (or concatenating) the primary key of the Tenant entity type with the primary key of the Tenant_Auto entity type.

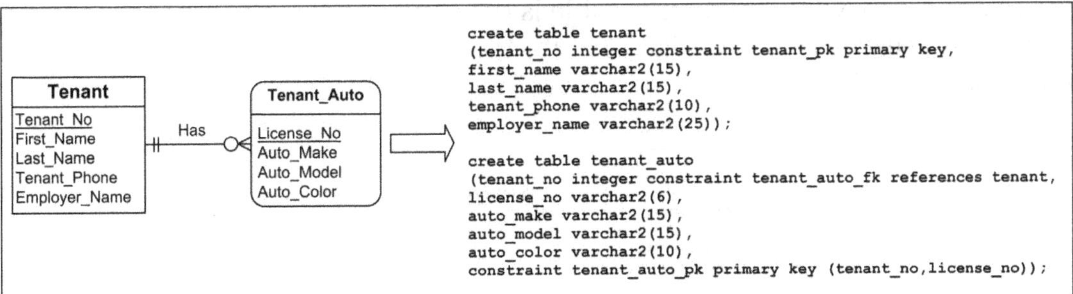

Figure 4-15: Representation of Weak Entity Type as Database Table

Essentially the primary key of the entity type table which has an identifying relationship with the weak entity type table is always combined with some attribute (or set of attributes) in the weak entity type table in a way that ensures uniqueness in weak entity table instances. Also, when the primary key of the entity type table which has an identifying relationship with the weak entity type table appears as part of the weak entity type table primary key, it is also specified as a foreign key in the weak entity type table. Instead of creating a concatenating primary key, sometimes for operational purposes a separate primary key called as a surrogate key is added to the weak entity type table.

One-to-One (1:1) Relationship Representation

If two entity types have 1:1 relationship, then their respective tables will also have 1:1 relationship. To specify 1:1 relationship between two tables, the foreign key attribute appears in one of the two tables (but not both). Figure 4-16 shows two entity types Rental and Apartment that have a 1:1 relationship. The figure shows the SQL statements for creating the Rental and Apartment table. To represent this 1:1 relationship, the foreign key (attribute Apartment_No) is placed in the Rental table.

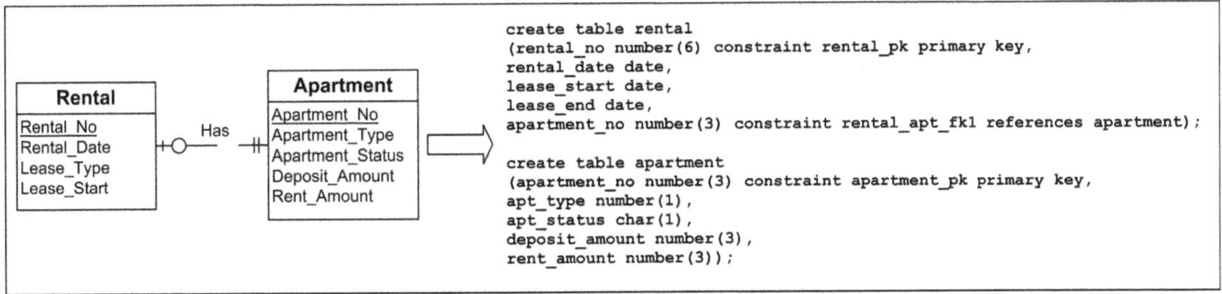

Figure 4-16: Representation of 1:1 Entity Relationship with Database Tables

One-to-Many (1:N) Relationship Representation

If two entity types have 1:N relationship, then their respective tables will also have 1:N relationship. To specify 1:N relationship between two tables, the foreign key attribute appears in the table that represents the many entity type in the ER model. Generally, the table that represents the one part of the relationship is also referred as the parent, while the table that represents the many part of the relationship is referred as the child. Also, if there is a 1:N relationship attribute, then this attribute is placed in the table that represents the many entity type or child table.

Figure 4-17 shows two entity types Staff and Rental with 1:N relationship. The figure shows the SQL statements for creating the Staff and Rental table. The Staff table is the parent as it represents the one part of the relationship, while the Rental table is the child as it represents the many part of the relationship. To represent this 1:N relationship, the foreign key (attribute Staff_No) is placed in the child (Rental) table.

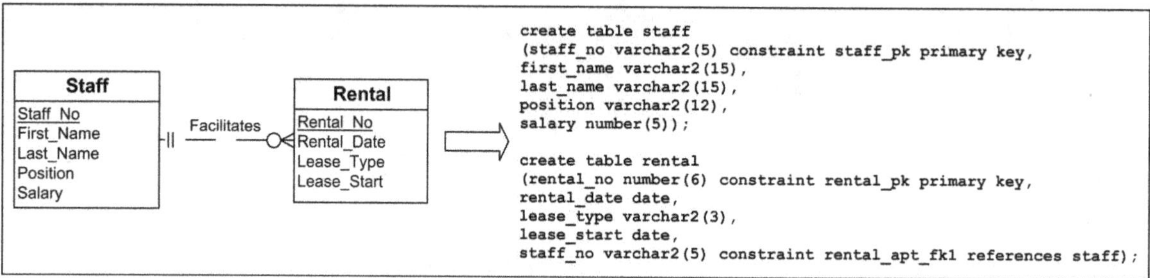

Figure 4-17: Representation of 1:N Entity Relationship with Database Tables

If the 1:N relationship is optional (or zero minimum cardinality) on both sides, then as an alternative a new separate table can be created which contains the primary key attributes of the two tables that have 1:N relationship. The primary key of this new table will be the attribute that represents the many entity type in the ER model. The attributes in this new table will also be specified as foreign keys to their respective relationship tables. Also, if there is a 1:N relationship attribute, then the attribute can be placed in this new separate table.

Figure 4-18 shows two entity types Staff and Rental that have 1:N relationship where the minimum cardinality is zero on both sides. The zero minimum cardinality implies that a Staff can exist without being associated with a Rental, and a Rental can exist without being associated with a Staff. For example, a Rental can be created directly through the Web site without any staff participation. Since the 1:N relationship is optional on both sides of the relationship, a new table is created which contains the primary key attributes of the Staff and Rental tables. The figure shows the SQL statements for creating the Staff, Rental, and Facilitates table, wherein the Facilitates table represents the optional 1:N relationship. The Facilitates table has the primary key of the Rental and Staff tables, wherein both the attributes are also the foreign keys to their respective tables. The primary key of the Facilitates table is Rental_No, as the Rental table is the child table.

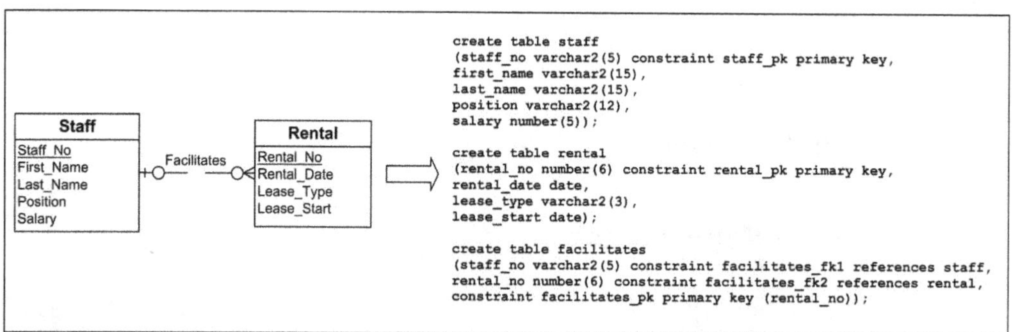

Figure 4-18: Representation of Optional 1:N Entity Relationship with Database Tables

Many-to-Many (M:N) Relationship Representation

A M:N relationship is represented by a new separate table referred as an intersection table. The attributes in the intersection table will be the primary key attributes of the tables that have the M:N relationship. Further, the attributes of the intersection table will also be the primary key of the table. Besides, the primary key attributes of the intersection table are also the foreign key attributes of their respective relationship tables. If there is a M:N relationship attribute, then this attribute can be placed in the new intersection table.

Figure 4-19 shows two entity types Rental and Complaints that have M:N relationship. To represent the M:N relationship, a new intersection table is created which contains the primary key attributes of the Rental and Complaints tables. The figure shows the SQL statements for creating the Staff, Rental, and Files table, wherein the Files table is the intersection table. The Files table has the primary key attributes of the Rental and Complaints tables, wherein both the attributes are also the foreign keys to their respective tables.

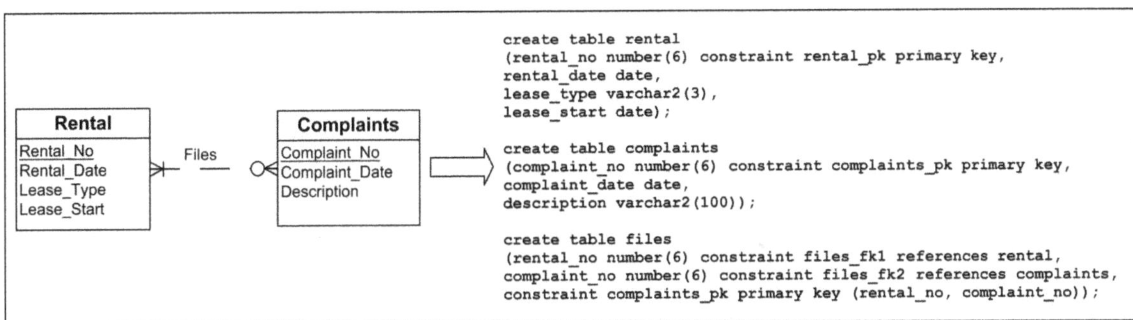

Figure 4-19: Representation of M:N Entity Relationship with Database Tables

Figure 4-20 shows that same two entity types Rental and Complaints with M:N relationship, but now there is a relationship attribute Status. To represent the M:N relationship with relationship attribute, the new intersection table is created which contains the primary key attributes of the Rental and Complaints tables, along with the Status attribute. The figure shows the SQL statements for creating the Staff, Rental, and Files table, wherein the Files table is the intersection table. The Files table has the primary key attributes of the Rental and Complaints tables, wherein both the attributes are also the foreign keys to their respective tables. The primary key of the Files table is combination of the attributes Rental_No and Complaint_No. Relationship attribute Status is the non-key attribute.

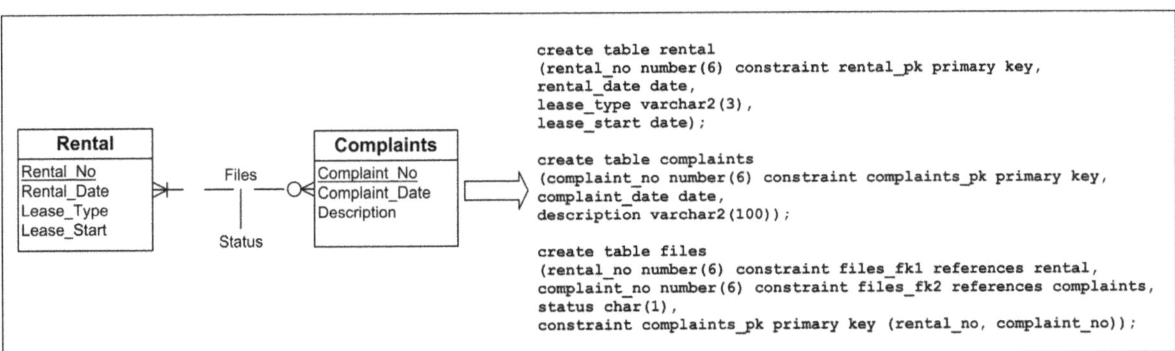

Figure 4-20: Representation of M:N Entity Relationship Attribute with Database Tables

M-Way Relationship Representation

M-Way relationships involving associate entity type is implemented similar to a M:N relationship with relationship attribute, where the intersection table represents the associate entity type. Since the associate entity type is a weak entity type, its transformation is similar to weak entity type and identifying relationship representation.

Figure 4-21 shows three entity types Rental, Complaints, and Files. Files entity type is an associate entity type. Files is also a weak entity type with identifying relationship with Rental and Complaints entity type. To represent this M-Way relationship with associate entity type, each entity type is transformed into separate tables, wherein their entity type attributes become table attributes. The figure shows the SQL statements for creating the Staff, Rental, and Files table. The Files table has the primary key attributes of the Rental and Complaints tables, wherein both the attributes are also the foreign keys to their respective tables. The primary key of the Files table is combination of the attributes Rental_No and Complaint_No. This transformation is similar to M:N relationship with relationship attribute.

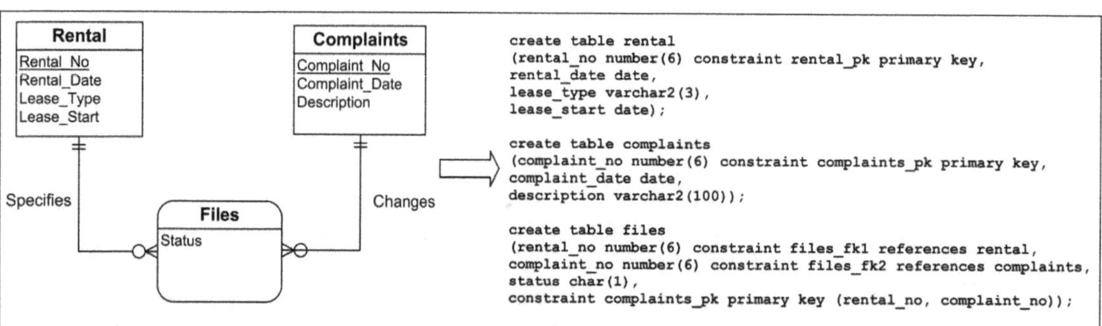

Figure 4-21: Representation of M-Way Relationship with Database Tables

Self-Referencing Relationship Representation

Self-referencing relationships follow the same guidelines as 1:1, 1:N, or M:N relationships. However, since these relationships refer to rows within a single entity type table, foreign key values refer to primary key values of the related rows in the same table.

In case of 1:1 self-referencing relationship, a foreign key attribute is added to the entity type table wherein only one of the relationship row contains the foreign key value. In case of 1:N self-referencing relationship, a foreign key attribute is added to the entity type table wherein the relationship row that represents the many part of the relationship contains the foreign key value. In case of M:N self-referencing relationship, a new intersection table is created that contains the primary key values of the relationship rows as attributes. All the attributes of the intersection table will be part of the primary key, and individually foreign keys.

Figure 4-22 shows Staff entity type that has a 1:N self-referencing relationship. The figure shows the SQL statement for creating the Staff table. Now in the Staff table some row will act as a parent row, while other rows related to it will act as child rows. To represent the 1:N relationship, the foreign key attribute Supervisor is added to the table. Supervisor will have values of the Staff_No attribute.

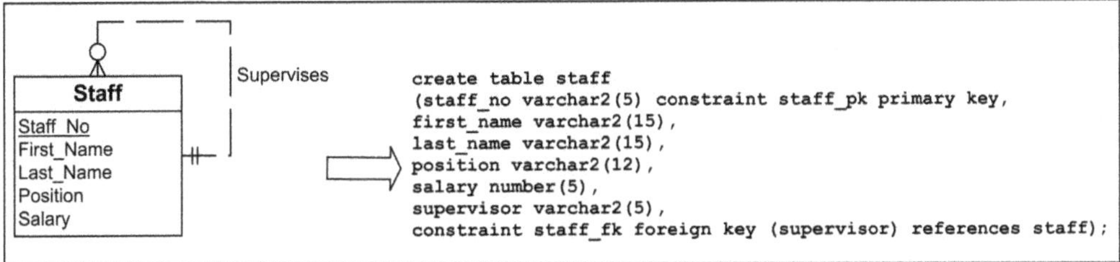

Figure 4-22: Representation of 1:N Self-Referencing Relationship with Database Tables

Generalization Hierarchy Representation

Each entity type in the generalization hierarchy becomes a table. The attributes of the entity types become the attributes of their respective tables. The primary key of the supertype entity type becomes the primary key of the supertype entity table. The primary key of the subtype entity type is the primary key of the supertype entity table, which should also be specified as a foreign key.

Figure 4-23 shows three entity types Person, Staff, and Tenant in a generalization hierarchy. Person is the supertype, while Staff and Tenant are subtypes. Each entity type is represented as a separate table. The figure shows the SQL statements for creating the Person, Staff, and Tenant tables. The primary key of supertype Person is also the primary key of its corresponding table. The subtype tables Staff and Tenant now also have the primary key of the supertype table Person as a primary key as well as foreign key.

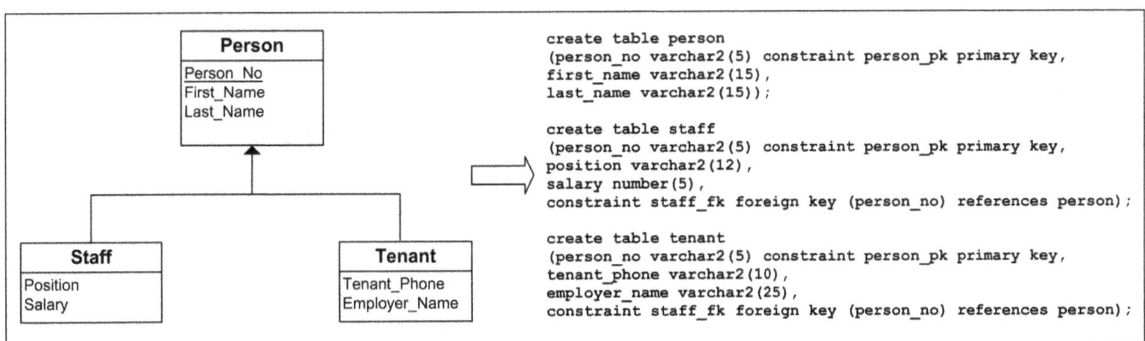

Figure 4-23: Representation of Generalization Hierarchy as Database Tables

Review Questions

1. What are the rules for defining the table structure in a relational database.
2. Explain the difference between the three database relationships.

3. Explain the difference between integrity constraints and value constraints.
4. Describe entity integrity and referential integrity.
5. Explain the options to maintain referential integrity.
6. Describe the transformation of the different database relationships in relational tables.
7. Describe the transformation of weak entity type into relational tables.
8. Explain the transformation of self-referencing relationship into relational tables.
9. Describe the principle of normalization.
10. Explain the various types of modification anomalies.
11. Describe functional dependencies.
12. Describe the principle of first normal form.

13. Describe the principle of second normal form.
14. Describe the principle of third normal form.
15. Describe the principle of fourth normal form.
16. Explain multi-valued dependency.

Review Exercises

1. The two components of SQL are ____________ and ______________.
2. The data type to store variable length character data is ____________.
3. Complete the syntax for creating a table supplier where supplier_no is the primary key.

```
create table supplier
(supplier_no number(3) ________________,
sname varchar2(15),
scity varchar2(10));
```

4. Complete the syntax for creating a table supplier_invoice where supplier_no is the foreign key to the table supplier.

```
create table supplier
(supplier_inv number(3),
invoice_date date,
invoice_total number(4,2),
supplier_no number(3) ________________);
```

5. The data type for numeric value 12.45 should be ____________.
6. The data type for numeric value 22335 should be ____________.
7. The ______________ value constraint keyword guarantees that an attribute always has a value.
8. The ______________ value constraint keyword specifies a discrete list of values an attribute can have.
9. To specify _________ relationship between two tables, the foreign key attribute appears in one of the two tables (but not both).
10. To specify _________ relationship between two tables, the foreign key attribute appears in the table that represents the many entity type in the ER model.
11. The attributes in the intersection table will be the ________ _________ attributes of the tables that have the M:N relationship.
12. To represent generalization hierarchy the primary key of the ________ entity table is also the primary key of the ________ entity table.
13. To represent generalization hierarchy the primary key of the ________ entity type is also a foreign key.
14. An _________ anomaly exists if some attribute values cannot be inserted unless there is some additional data available.
15. A _________ anomaly exists if deleting a row from a table results in unexpected loss of additional information.
16. An ________ anomaly exists when it is necessary to change multiple rows to modify a single fact.
17. An attribute Y is functionally dependent on attribute X, if the value of ______ determines the value of _______.
18. A table is in ________ if all non-key attributes are dependent on all of the primary key.
19. A table is in ________ if it has no transitive dependencies.

20. A table is in ________ if there are no multi-valued dependencies (MVD).
21. A transitive dependency exists when there is a sequence of functional dependencies where one attribute is indirectly determining another attribute.

Problem Solving Exercises

4-1. Consider the following table Activity_Clubs with primary key activity_id.

ACTIVITY_CLUBS

ACTIVITY_ID	NAME	CITY	STATE	PHONE
100	Hillside Mountain Club	Wichita	KS	3163997676
110	Branson Climbing Club	Branson	MO	4174485676
120	Cherokee Rafting Club	St. Charles	MO	3147780870

a. What is the entity type name for the table.
b. How many entity instances exist in the table.
c. What is the SQL statement to create the table Activity_Clubs.

4-2. Consider the following table Distributor with primary key distributor_id.

DISTRIBUTOR

DISTRIBUTOR_ID	NAME	CITY	STATE	PHONE
S500	Hillside Ski	Los Angeles	CA	7146654959
S510	Tiger Mountain	Los Angeles	CA	7143327878

a. What is the entity type name for the table.
b. How many entity instances exist in the table.
c. What is the SQL statement to create the table Distributor.

4-3. Consider the following table Items with primary key item_id and foreign key distributor_id. The foreign key in the Items table is associated with the Distributor table of problem 4-2.

ITEMS

ITEMS_ID	ITEM_NAME	PRICE	DISTRIBUTOR_ID
10010	Beginner's Ski Boot	9.75	S500
10011	Intermediate Ski Boot	12.99	S500
10012	Pro Ski Boot	15.49	S510
10013	Beginner's Ski Pole	25.49	S500
10014	Intermediate Ski Pole	29.99	S510

a. What is the entity type name for the table.
b. How many entity instances exist in the table.

c. What type of database relationship exists between Items table and Distributor table.
d. What is the SQL statement to create the table Items.

4-4. Consider the following table Membership with primary key membership_id and foreign key activity_id. The foreign key in the Membership table is associated with the Activity_Clubs table of problem 4-1.

MEMBERSHIP

MEMBERSHIP_ID	MEMBERSHIP_DATE	DURATION	ACTIVITY_ID
10010	12-JUN-08	4	100
10020	15-JUN-08	2	110
10030	21-JUN-08	5	120

a. What is the entity type name for the table.
b. How many entity instances exist in the table.
c. What type of database relationship exists between Membership table and Activity_Clubs table.
d. What is the SQL statement to create the table Membership.

4-5. Consider the following tables Emotions, Emotion_Details, and Emotion_Order. Primary keys are in bold, while foreign keys are in italics.

EMOTION

EMOTION_ID	NAME	PRICE
100	Floral Embrace	49.99
101	Red Bouquet	36.99
102	Musical Bouquet	49.99
103	Pink Perfection	44.99
104	Rose Elegance	34.99
105	First Bloom Bouquet	45.99

EMOTION_DETAILS

ORDER_ID	***EMOTION_ID***	QUANTITY
1001	100	1
1001	103	2
1002	103	1
1002	104	2
1003	103	1
1004	104	3
1004	105	1

EMOTION_ORDER

ORDER_ID	ORDER_DATE	TOTAL	SHIPPING
1001	27-MAY-08	86.97	6.00
1002	28-MAY-08	104.97	8.50
1003	28-MAY-08	34.95	6.00
1004	05-JUN-08	189.82	6.00

a. What is the entity type name for each table.
b. How many entity instances exist in each table.
c. What type of database relationship exists between Emotions table and Emotion_Order table.
d. What type of database relationship exists between Emotions table and Emotion_Details table.
e. What type of database relationship exists between Emotion_Details table and Emotion_Order table.
f. What is the SQL statement to create the tables Emotions, Emotion_Details, and Emotion_Order.

4-6. Transform the ER model shown in Figure 4-24 into a relational model with tables and relationships. Outline the SQL statements for specifying tables and relationships.

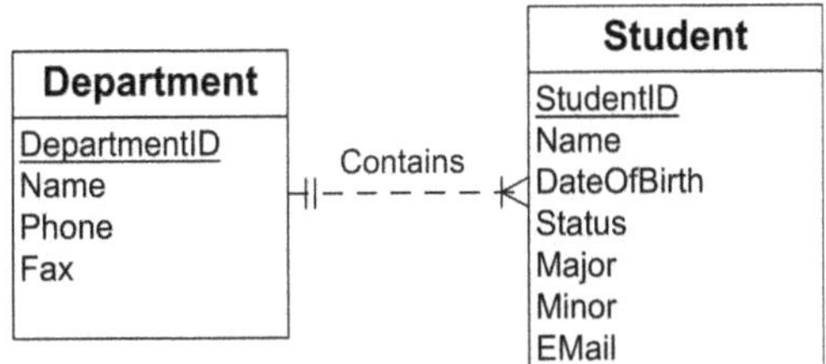

Figure 4-24

4-7. Transform the ER model shown in Figure 4-25 into a relational model with tables and relationships. Outline the SQL statements for specifying tables and relationships.

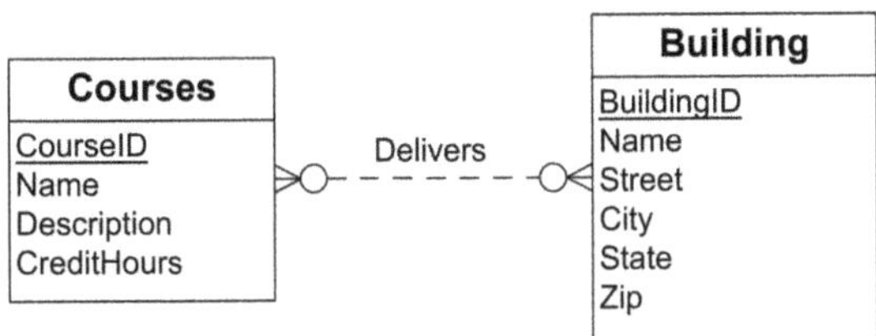

Figure 4-25

4-8. Transform the ER model shown in Figure 4-26 into a relational model with tables and relationships. Outline the SQL statements for specifying tables and relationships.

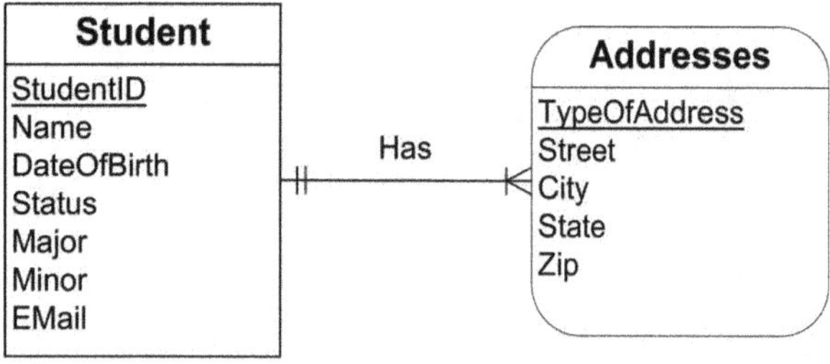

Figure 4-26

4-9. Transform the ER model in Figure 4-27 into a relational model with tables and relationships. Outline the SQL statements for specifying tables and relationships.

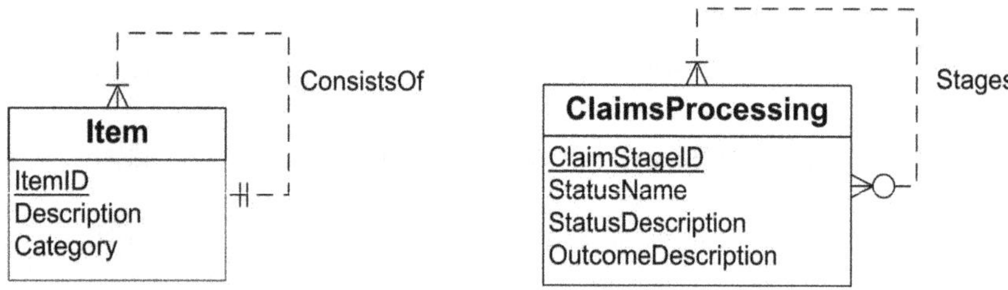

Figure 4-27

4-10. Transform the ER model of a University business process subset as shown in Figure 4-28 into a relational model with tables and relationships. Outline the SQL statements for specifying tables and relationships.

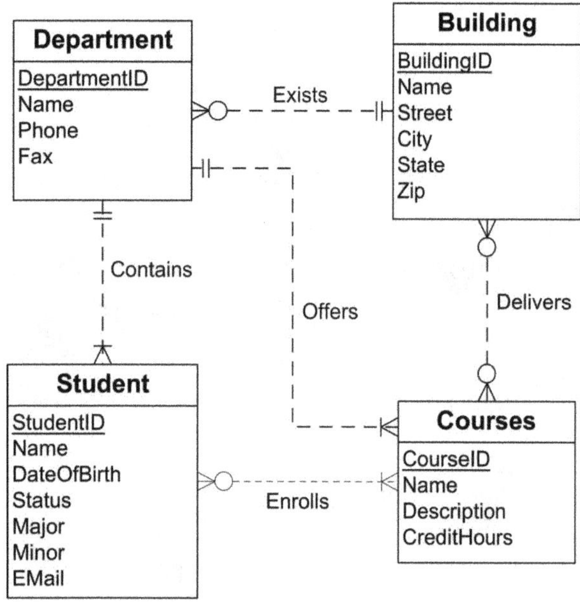

Figure 4-28

4-11. Transform the ER model of an Event reservations business process activity as shown in Figure 4-29 into a relational model with tables and relationships. Outline the SQL statements for specifying tables and relationships.

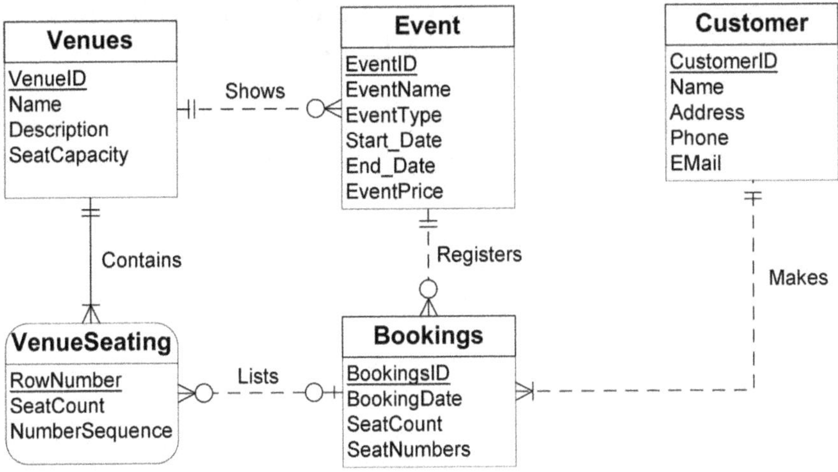

Figure 4-29

4-12. Transform the ER model of a Railway reservation business process activity as shown in Figure 4-30 into a relational model with tables and relationships. Outline the SQL statements for specifying tables and relationships.

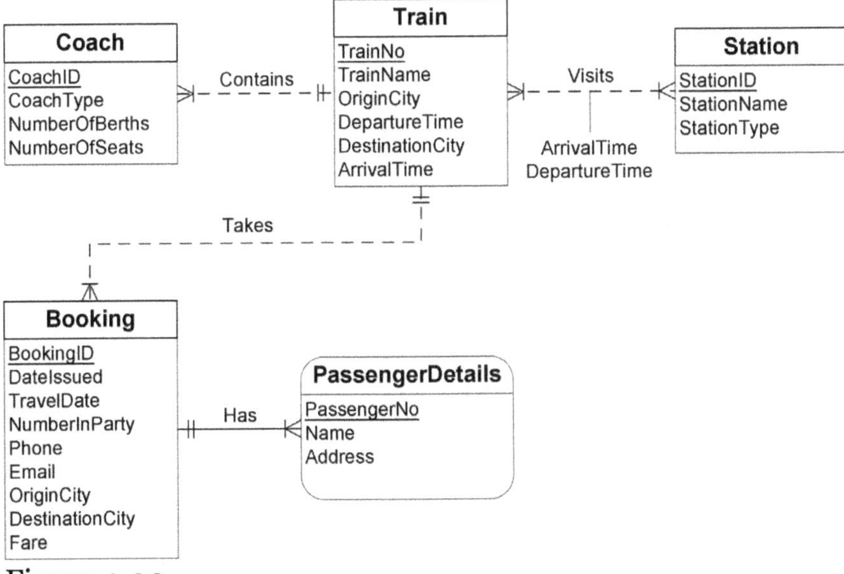

Figure 4-30

4-13. Transform the ER model of Chapter 3 problem 3-1 into a relational model with tables and relationships. Outline the SQL statements for tables and relationships.

4-14. Transform the ER model of Chapter 3 problem 3-2 into a relational model with tables and relationships. Outline the SQL statements for tables and relationships.

4-15. Transform the ER model of Chapter 3 problem 3-3 into a relational model with tables and relationships. Outline the SQL statements for tables and relationships.

4-16. Transform the ER model of Chapter 3 problem 3-4 into a relational model with tables and relationships. Outline the SQL statements for tables and relationships.

4-17. Transform the ER model of Chapter 3 problem 3-5 into a relational model with tables and relationships. Outline the SQL statements for tables and relationships.

4-18. Transform the ER model of Chapter 3 problem 3-6 into a relational model with tables and relationships. Outline the SQL statements for tables and relationships.

4-19. Study the following functional dependencies from a University business process.

StudentNumber -> FirstName, LastName, DegreeStatus, Gender, DOB, AdvisorName, GPA, Address, Email
DegreeStatus -> AdvisorName

a. Develop tables that are normalized from the given functional dependencies. Outline each table structure by providing a table name followed by the attributes list in parenthesis, wherein the primary key is underlined.
b. What normal form (if any) is violated due to the attributes listed in the functional dependencies.

4-20. Study the following functional dependencies from a University business process.

CourseNo, SectionNo -> CourseName, Description, BuildingNo, RoomNo, Capacity
CourseNo -> CourseName, Description
BuildingNo, RoomNo -> Capacity

a. Develop tables that are normalized from the given functional dependencies. Outline each table structure by providing a table name followed by the attributes list in parenthesis, wherein the primary key is underlined.
b. What normal form (if any) is violated due to the attributes listed in the functional dependencies.

4-21. Study the following functional dependencies from a Restaurant business process.

MenuName, IngredientName -> MenuDescription, Price, IngredientQuantity
MenuName -> MenuDescription, Price

a. Develop tables that are normalized from the given functional dependencies. Outline each table structure by providing a table name followed by the attributes list in parenthesis, wherein the primary key is underlined.
b. What normal form (if any) is violated due to the attributes listed in the functional dependencies.

4-22. Study the following functional dependencies from a Event Reservation business process:

EventName -> EventDescription, StartDate, EndDate, VenueName, SeatingCapacity, EventType
VenuName -> SeatingCapacity

a. Develop tables that are normalized from the given functional dependencies. Outline each table structure by providing a table name followed by the attributes list in parenthesis, wherein the primary key is underlined.

b. What normal form (if any) is violated due to the attributes listed in the functional dependencies.

4-23. Study the following Items table. Based on the provided data, list FDs that are *not true* among the attributes of the Items table where Item_Id is the determinant. Remember that it takes just two rows of different values to contradict a FD.

ITEMS

ITEMS_ID	ITEM_NAME	DISTRIBUTOR_NAME	CITY	STATE	PHONE
10010	Beginner's Ski Boot	Hillside Ski	Los Angeles	CA	7146654959
10011	Intermediate Ski Boot	Hillside Ski	Los Angeles	CA	7146654959
10012	Pro Ski Boot	Tiger Mountain	Los Angeles	CA	7143327878
10010	Beginner's Ski Boot	Hillside Ski	Los Angeles	CA	7146654959
10011	Intermediate Ski Boot	Tiger Mountain	Los Angeles	CA	7143327878

4-24. Study the Items table of problem 4-23. Based on the provided data, list FDs that are *true* among the attributes of the Items table where Item_Id is the determinant. Remember that it takes just two rows of different values to contradict a FD.

4-25. Study the Items table of problem 4-23. Based on the provided data, list FDs that are *not true* among the attributes of the Items table where Distributor_Name is the determinant. Remember that it takes just two rows of different values to contradict a FD.

4-26. Study the Items table of problem 4-23. Based on the provided data, list FDs that are *true* among the attributes of the Items table where Distributor_Name is the determinant. Remember that it takes just two rows of different values to contradict a FD.

4-27. Study the Items table of problem 4-23. Based on the provided data, list FDs that are *true* among the attributes of the Items table where Item_Name is the determinant.Remember that it takes just two rows of different values to contradict a FD.

Chapter 5. Structured Query Language (SQL)

This chapter extends the coverage of SQL language that was introduced in Chapter 4 with Data Manipulation Language (DML) statements[1]. DML statements are used for data retrieval and manipulation. Such statements allow for the insertion of rows in a table, modification of attribute values within a table, deletion of rows from a table, and retrieval of information from the tables. The chapter also covers some Oracle SQL functions and statements to facilitate enhanced database working.

The insertion of rows in a table is accomplished through the Insert statement; the modification of attribute values within a table is accomplished through the Update statement, and the deletion of rows from a table is accomplished through the Delete statement. The retrieval of information referred as a query is accomplished through the Select statement.

SQL Insert

Rows can be inserted into a table one row at a time. The Insert statement works in two ways: (i) to insert all attribute values into a row at once, or (ii) to insert only selected attribute values. The basic syntax of Insert statement is:

```
INSERT INTO tablename [(attribute1-name,  attribute2- name, . . .)]
VALUES (attribute1-value, attribute 2-value, . . .);
```

When all attribute values are being inserted, the optional listing of attribute names is not needed. Also, *when all table attribute values are being inserted in a row, the listing of attribute values should follow the existing sequence of attributes in the table (defined through the Create Table statement).* The following SQL statement inserts a row in order_details table that has three attributes (order_id, product_id, quantity).

```
insert into apartment
values (205,1,'R','Y','Carpet','N',300,400);
```

If an attribute does not have a value, a null keyword value should be used instead as a substitute for the blank value. The following SQL statement inserts a row in staff table that has values for only four of the eight attributes in the table (staff_no, first_name, last_name, position, status, gender, dob, salary).

```
insert into staff
values ('SA250', 'Susan', 'Kale', 'Supervisor', null, null, null, null);
```

If data for all attribute values will not be inserted, then those attributes for which data is available should be listed. In this case the sequence of attribute names in the syntax and their corresponding values should match. The following SQL statement inserts a row in sporting_clubs table that has values for only four of the eight attributes in the table (staff_no, first_name, last_name, position, status, gender, dob, salary).

```
insert into staff (staff_no, first_name, last_name, position)
values ('SA260', 'Susan', 'Kale', 'Supervisor');
```

---

[1] This chapter utilizes tables from Superflex Apartment database (refer Appendix A).

Insert Text with Quotation Mark

To insert text with quotation mark, one needs to enter the single quotation mark twice. The following SQL statement inserts a row in the contractor table, where the name attribute has a quotation string.

```
insert into contractor (contractor_id, name)
values ('C1016', 'Jimmy''s All Repairs');
```

Insert Values with Decimals

To insert values with decimals, the decimal point should be inserted with the value. The following SQL statement inserts a row in the tenant_auto table, where the parking_fee attribute has a decimal value.

```
insert into tenant_auto (tenant_ss,license_no,auto_color,parking_fee)
values (223056180,'REG532','Silver',45.50);
```

Insert Values in DATE Data Type

Date values are character strings. Oracle keeps date values in an internal format. The to_date function is used to transfer the date value (character string) into the internal format. The general syntax of the to_date function is TO_DATE('<date character string>', '<date format mask>'). Various date format masks exist in Oracle as shown in Table 5-1 below.

Format	**Description**	**Example**
MONTH	Name of month	June
MON	Three-letter abbreviation for month name.	JUN
MM	Two-digit numeric value of the month.	06
D	Numeric value for day of the week.	Wednesday = 4
DD	Numeric value for the day of the month (01-31).	25
DDD	Numeric value for the day of the year (01-366).	150
DAY	Name of the day of the week upto 9 characters.	Wednesday
DY	Three-letter abbreviation for day of the week.	WED
YYYY	Displays the four-digit year	2008
YYY or YY or Y	Displays the last three, two, or single digit of the year.	008, 08, 8
YEAR	Spells out the year.	TWO THOUSAND EIGHT

HH	Displays hours of the day using 12-hour clock.	06
HH24	Displays hour of the day using 24-hour clock.	17
MI	Displays minutes (0-59)	45
SS	Displays seconds (0-59)	35

Table 5-1: Date Format Masks

Format masks can be created by including front slashes, hyphens, and colons as separators between different date elements. For example, the format mask mm/dd/yy for October 15, 2012 would appear as 10/15/12. It is possible to include additional characters such as commas, periods, and blank spaces. For example, the format mask "day, month dd, yyyy" for January 15, 2012 would appear as "Sunday, January 15, 2012." Time mask can be like hh:mi:ss to stand for 04:35:50.

To insert date values, the to_date function can be defined as TO_DATE('5/15/2012', 'MM/DD/YYYY') for character string '05/15/2012.' Similarly '22-AUG-2012' would be represented as TO_DATE('22-AUG-2012', 'DD-MON-YYYY'). The following SQL statement inserts a row in the tenant_family table having a Date data type.

```
insert into tenant_family
values (123456789,444663434,'Kay Robin','Y','N','F',to_date('6/21/1965','mm/dd/yyyy'));
```

To insert time values in a Date attribute, use either the 24-hour clock or the 12-hour clock. The following examples show the use of 24-hour clock and 12-hour clock to insert a new row in rental table.

```
insert into rental (rental_no,rental_date)
values (100110,to_date('15:30','hh24:mi'));

insert into rental (rental_no,rental_date)
values (100111,to_date('2:30','hh:mi pm'));
```

SQL Update

The Update statement modifies attribute values in a table row. The syntax for Update statement is

```
UPDATE tablename
SET attribute1 = new-value1  [, attribute2 = new-value2, . . .]
[WHERE search condition ];
```

It is possible to update multiple attributes in a table using a single Update statement, but only one table can be updated at one time. Search conditions can be specified in the Where clause to make the update operation row specific. If the search condition is not specified, all rows of the table will have the new attribute value. The general syntax of the search condition is:

```
attribute-name  comparison-operator  expression/value
```

Every search condition is evaluated as either TRUE or FALSE. *Search condition values are case sensitive, and string expressions must be enclosed in single quotation.* The Table 5-2 below lists common comparison operators used in SQL.

Operator	**Description**	**Example**
=	Equal To	lease_type = 'One'
>	Greater Than	apt_deposit_amt > 300
<	Less Than	apt_deposit_amt < 300
>=	Greater Than or Equal To	invoice_no >= 1040
<=	Less Than or Equal To	invoice_no <= 1040
<>, !=, ^=	Not Equal To	lease_type <> 'Six'
LIKE	Pattern Matching Text Strings	tenant_name like 'M%' where % implies wildcard character indicating that part of the string can contain any characters. auto_make like '_o%' where _ implies a single character substitution.
BETWEEN	Range Comparison	apt_rent_amt between 300 and 600 (similar to apt_rent_amt >= 300 and apt_rent_amt <= 600)
IN	Determine if value part of a set.	cc_type in ('visa', 'discover')
NOT IN	Determine if value is not part of a set.	cc_type not in ('visa', 'discover')

Table 5-2: Comparison Operators

The following SQL statements illustrate the utilization of the Update statement.

1. Update a single attribute auto_make value in the tenant_auto table.

```
update tenant_auto
set auto_make = 'Toyota'
where license_no = 'SYK332';
```

2. Update two attributes auto_make and auto_color values in the tenant_auto table.

```
update tenant_auto
set auto_make = 'Volvo', auto_color = 'Green '
where license_no = 'ABC260';
```

Multiple search conditions can be combined using *AND* and *OR* operators. When the AND operator is used to combine two search conditions, both conditions must be true for the update statement to satisfy the search condition. When the OR operator is used to combine two search conditions, only one of the condition must be true for the update statement to satisfy the search condition. The following SQL statement will update the tenant_auto table using the AND operator.

```
update tenant_auto
set auto_model = 'S70', auto_color = 'Black '
where license_no = 'TTS430' and tenant_ss = '123456789 ';
```

SQL Delete

Delete statement deletes rows from an existing table. Deleting rows can be a dangerous operation, if the values are accidently deleted. The syntax of the Delete statement is:

```
DELETE FROM tablename
[WHERE search condition ];
```

Always include the Where clause in the Delete statement to ensure that the correct rows are deleted. If the Where clause is omitted, all table rows are deleted. For example, the following SQL statement will delete two rows from the complaints table where the rental_no is 100103.

```
delete from workorder
where complaint_no = '10013';
```

Saving Manipulation Changes

When data is inserted in a table row, the new row is not immediately visible to other users. The reason that happens is because Oracle does not save the new insertions in the database storage medium even though it generates the message that the row was successfully created. To save the new insertions permanently in the database, another statement called Commit has to be used. The following two SQL statements will permanently save the inserted row in the sporting_clubs table in the database.

```
insert into contractor (contractor_id, name)
values ('C1016', 'Branson Home Solutions');
commit;
```

The Commit statement also has to be used with other manipulation statements like Delete and Update. *In other words, no Insert, Delete, or Update operation in Oracle database is permanent unless the Commit statement is executed.* The Commit statement does not have to be executed after each manipulation statement. It can be done anytime in a session. However, it is a good idea to explicitly commit changes often so that the data will be available to other users, and the changes are saved in a timely manner.

Once data has been saved (Commit statement executed) it cannot be changed. To overcome situations when some manipulation statement results need to be cancelled, a statement called Rollback is used. Rollback undoes the changes since the last successful Commit statement execution. It is a way to remove the changes done previously in the session. For example, the following Insert statement will not be saved once the Rollback statement is executed.

```
insert into contractor (contractor_id, name)
values ('C1017', 'All Hours Plumbing');
rollback;
```

It is possible to rollback selectively using the Savepoint statement. Savepoint is a kind of marker that allows for partial rollback. The syntax of Savepoint is SAVEPOINT savepoint-name;.

The Savepoint name can be any Oracle object name. Multiple Savepoints can be created in a session, and then the Rollback statement can remove changes up to a particular Savepoint name. For example, consider the following list of Insert statements. The last Insert statement will not be saved once the Rollback statement is executed.

```
insert into contractor (contractor_id, name)
values ('C1018', 'Lexington Plumbing & Heating');

savepoint marker1;

insert into contractor (contractor_id, name)
values ('C1019', 'Solar Home Solutions');

savepoint marker2;

insert into contractor (contractor_id, name)
values ('C1020', 'Big Jon Repairs');

rollback to marker2;
```

SQL Query

SQL query is a powerful mechanism to retrieve information from a relational database. These queries range from listing of attributes from a single table to more complex criteria involving multiple tables. All retrieval of data from tables (also referred as a database query) is done through the Select statement[2]. Retrieval of data can be from a single table or it can involve multiple tables. Since the complete syntax of Select statement is quite complex, it will be explained gradually. The explanation will start with the minimal set, which will then be built upon with more complex extensions. Initially the focus is on querying from a single table. Later on, multi-table querying will be explained. The basic syntax of the Select query statement is as follows:

```
SELECT attributename1, attributename2, . . .
FROM tablename1;
```

There are two main keywords Select and From that are required in all query statements. The Select keyword clause contains a list of attributes whose values are desired in the output, while the From keyword clause lists the table name from which the attributes listed in the Select keyword clause will be generated. The result of any query is formatted as a tabular display with attribute names appearing as column names. For example, the following SQL query retrieves tenant_name and employer_name attribute values from the tenant table.

```
select tenant_name, employer_name
from tenant;
```

TENANT_NAME	EMPLOYER_NAME
Jack Robin	Kraft Inc.
Mary Stackles	Kraft Inc.
Ramu Reddy	MSU
Marion Black	MSU

---

[2] Query results always follow the SQL Query.

Venessa Williams Kraft Inc.

There are many optional keywords and entries possible in the Select keyword clause. These keywords and entries are as follows:

1. * symbol.
2. Distinct keyword.
3. Mathematical expressions.
4. Renaming of attribute names.
5. Concatenation of values and text.

* Symbol

The asterisk (*) symbol can be utilized if the query is supposed to list all attributes values from a table. In other words, instead of entering all the individual attribute names of a table in the Select keyword clause, the symbol * can be substituted instead. Further, if the symbol * is entered in the Select keyword clause, it should be the only entry. The following SQL query utilizes the * symbol.

1. Query: List all attributes of the tenant_auto table.

```
select * from tenant_family;
```

TENANT_SS	FAMILY_SS	NAME	SPOUSE	CHILD	GENDER	DOB
123456789	444663434	Kay Robin	Y	N	F	21-JUN-65
450452267	222664343	Sarla Reddy	Y	N	F	11-JUN-65
450452267	222663434	Anjali Reddy	N	Y	F	10-AUG-90
173662690	111444663	Terry Williams	Y	N	F	21-MAR-68
173662690	242446634	Tom Williams	N	Y	M	20-MAY-91

DISTINCT Keyword

The Distinct keyword ensures unique rows in the query output. The keyword removes duplicate rows from the query output. Two rows are considered duplicate if all attribute values match. The syntax of the Select keyword clause now is as follows:

```
SELECT [DISTINCT] attributename1, attributename2, . . .
FROM tablename1;
```

2. Query: List all apartment utilities (apt_utility attribute) and their rent amount (apt_rent_amt attribute) from the apartment table.

   To show the application of Distinct keyword two SQL queries are shown. The first query lists the output without the Distinct keyword. In the output of the first query as there are many duplicate rows, the second query utilizes the Distinct keyword to list the rows without the duplicate rows.

```
select apt_utility, apt_rent_amt from apartment;
```

APT_UTILITY	APT_RENT_AMT
Y	300

N	300
Y	300
N	400
Y	400
Y	500
Y	500
Y	700
Y	700

```
select distinct apt_utility, apt_rent_amt from apartment;
```

APT_UTILITY	APT_RENT_AMT
Y	700
Y	300
Y	400
Y	500
N	300
N	400

Mathematical Expressions

The utilization of mathematical expressions along with attribute names improves the versatility of the Select clause. The mathematical expression should contain attribute from the table listed in the From clause. Attribute values in the selected row are considered during the computing of the expression. The syntax of the Select keyword clause now is as follows:

```
SELECT [DISTINCT] attribute1, [expression], attribute2 . . .
FROM tablename1;
```

The following SQL query lists output involving a mathematical expression entry.

3. Query: Lists for each apartment number (apt_no attribute) the yearly rental amount.

   Query Logic: The yearly rental amount is a mathematical expression that multiplies the apartment rent amount (apt_rent_amt attribute) value by 12. Hence, apt_no attribute and the mathematical expression become the entries in the Select keyword clause.

```
select apt_no, apt_rent_amt*12 from apartment;
```

APT_NO	APT_RENT_AMT*12
100	3600
101	3600
102	3600
103	4800
104	4800

200	6000
201	6000
202	8400
203	8400

Renaming of Attributes Names

It is possible to rename attribute names in query output. Renaming of attributes is especially useful when mathematical expressions are listed in the Select keyword clause. Renaming is done through the alias feature in the Select clause in the following ways:

- the keyword AS followed by the new name, or
- having a space after the attribute name and following it with the new name, or
- enclosing the new name within double quotes.

The syntax of the Select keyword clause now is as follows:

```
SELECT [DISTINCT] attribute1 [AS   newname], [expression [ newname]], . . .
FROM tablename1;
```

The following two SQL queries illustrate the different styles of renaming feature.

4. Query: List for each apartment number (apt_no attribute) the yearly rental amount.

   Query Logic: The yearly rental amount is a mathematical expression that multiplies the apartment rent amount (apt_rent_amt attribute) value by 12. Hence, apt_no attribute and the mathematical expression become the entries in the Select keyword clause. In the query output, however, both the Select keyword clause attributes are renamed. The queries show two ways to rename Select clause attributes.

```
select apt_no apartment, apt_rent_amt*12 as yearly_rent
from apartment;
```

APARTMENT	YEARLY_RENT
100	3600
101	3600
102	3600
103	4800
104	4800
200	6000
201	6000
202	8400
203	8400

```
select apt_no "apartment", apt_rent_amt*12 as yearly_rent
from apartment;
```

apartment	YEARLY_RENT
100	3600
101	3600
102	3600
103	4800
104	4800
200	6000
201	6000
202	8400
203	8400

Concatenation of Values and Text

The concatenation symbols || in the Select clause allows the joining of text and attribute values to generate a more formal output. The following SQL query illustrates the utilization of the concatenation symbol including static text in query output.

5. Query: List the rental number (rental_no attribute) and the apartment number (apt_no attribute) values from the rental table in the form of a text statement with the utilization of the concatenation symbol.

```
select 'Rental Number '||rental_no||' belongs to apartment '||apt_no "Rental Statements"
from rental;
```

Rental Statements
Rental Number 100101 belongs to apartment 201
Rental Number 100102 belongs to apartment 102
Rental Number 100103 belongs to apartment 203
Rental Number 100104 belongs to apartment 101
Rental Number 100105 belongs to apartment 104
Rental Number 100106 belongs to apartment 100

Use of the concatenation symbol allows for any type of special formatting that may be required for output, like that for showing social security number as 123-456-7890 or phone number as (123) 456-7890.

WHERE Keyword

A common extension of the SQL query statement involves search conditions. Inclusion of search conditions in a database query is done through the Where keyword clause. The search conditions are similar to those shown in Table 5-2.

The attributes in the search condition should be from the table listed in the From keyword clause of the query. The general syntax of the SQL query statement with the Where keyword clause is as follows:

```
SELECT [DISTINCT] attribute1, attribute2, . . .
FROM tablename1
[WHERE search-condition];
```

The following SQL queries illustrate the utilization of the Where keyword clause with search conditions.

6. Query: List the apartment number (apt_no attribute) and apartment utility status (apt_utility attribute) values for all one-bedroom apartments in the apartment table.

   Query Logic: The output attributes in the Select clause will be apt_no and apt_utility attributes. For the search condition, the apartment table attribute that provides information on the type of apartment is apt_type attribute, wherein its value 1 indicates one-bedroom apartments. Hence, the search condition for the query will be apt_type = 1.

```
select apt_no, apt_utility
from apartment
where apt_type = 1;
```

APT_NO	APT_UTILITY
103	N
104	Y

7. Query: List the apartment number (apt_no attribute) and its rental status (apt_status attribute) values for all one-bedroom apartments in the apartment table that have utilities installed.

   Query Logic: The output attributes in the Select clause will be apt_no and apt_status attributes. For the search condition: (i) the apartment table attribute that provides information on the type of apartment is apt_type attibute, wherein its value 1 indicates one-bedroom apartments; (ii) the apartment table attribute that provides information on installation of utilities in apartments is apt_utility attibute, wherein its value Y indicates installation of utilities. Hence the search condition for the query will be apt_type = 1 and apt_utility = 'Y'.

```
select apt_no, apt_status
from apartment
where apt_type = 1
and apt_utility = 'Y';
```

APT_NO	APT_STATUS
104	R

Searching for NULL values

Sometimes the search condition of a query has to find rows where the value of an attribute is null. In this case the syntax of the search condition is WHERE attribute-name IS [NOT] NULL. The following SQL queris illustrate the use of null conditions.

8. Query: Lists complaint number (complaint_no attribute) and rental number (rental_no attribute) values in the complaints table where the status of a complaint is not determined.

   Query Logic: The output attributes in the Select clause will be complaint_no and rental_no attributes. For the search condition, the complaints table attribute that provides status of a complaint is the status attribute, wherein a blank (null) value indicates a non-determined status. Hence the search condition for the query will be status is null.

```
select complaint_no, rental_no
from complaints
where status is null;
```

COMPLAINT_NO	RENTAL_NO
10012	100105
10013	
10014	100103
10016	

9. Query: Lists complaint number (complaint_no attribute) and rental number (rental_no attribute) values in the complaints table where the complaint has a specified status.

   Query Logic: The output attributes in the Select clause will be complaint_no and rental_no attributes. For the search condition, the complaints table attribute that provides status of a complaint is the status attribute, wherein an existing value (not null) indicates a determined status. Hence the search condition for the query will be status is not null.

```
select complaint_no, rental_no
from complaints
where status is not null;
```

COMPLAINT_NO	RENTAL_NO
10010	100103
10011	100105
10015	100104

LIKE keyword

Like keyword is used for pattern matching. It finds matches to a pattern in character string. Such strings are enclosed in single quotations. Like keyword works with two wildcards characters to facilitate the search: the percent sign (%) and the underscore sign (_). The percent sign can serve as a substitute for multiple characters. For instance, the search condition apt_complaint like '%not working' searches in complaints table for all apt_complaint values that end with "not working" text. Similarly, the search condition rental_complaint like '%heater%' searches for all rental_complaint values in complaints table that have "heater" text in the attribute value. The underscore sign (_) can serve as a substitute for a single character. For instance, the search condition apt_no like '_03' searches for all apt_no values in complaints table where the first digit can be any value but the next two digits need to be 03. It is possible to combine both the wildcard characters in the same pattern search. For instance, the search condition auto_make like '_o%' searches for all auto_make values in tenant_auto table that can start with any character, have letter "o" as the second character, and then have any number of characters.

10. Query: List tenant names (tenant_name attribute) values which start with character 'M' and have the tenant date of birth values beyond 1979 from the tenant table.

    Query Logic: The output attribute in the Select clause will be tenant_name attribute. For the search condition: (i) the tenant table attribute that also provides information on the name of the tenant is tenant_name attibute, wherein pattern matching (Like keyword) has to be performed to get the tenant names that start with character M; (ii) the tenant table attribute that provides information on a tenant's date of birth is tenant_dob attribute, so the search has to find those date values that are greater than January 1, 1980. Hence the search condition for the query will be tenant_name like 'M%' and tenant_dob > '1-Jan-1980'. The format (dd-mon-yyyy) used for searching tenant_dob attribute date values is Oracle's default date format.

```
select tenant_name
from tenant
where tenant_name like 'M%'
and tenant_dob > '01-Jan-1980';
```

TENANT_NAME
Mary Stackles
Marion Black

ORDER BY Keyword

Next extension of the SQL query statement involves the sorting of query output. By default, the output of a query will be displayed in order of rows as they are selected. However, any re-ordering of the output can be accomplished through the Order By keywords in ascending or descending sequence. The Order By keyword clause requires a minimum of one attribute name from the attribute listed in the Select keyword clause. The Order By clause attribute name become the keys for sorting the output rows. The general syntax of the SQL query with the Order By keyword clause is as follows:

```
SELECT [DISTINCT] attribute1, attribute2, . . .
FROM tablename1
[WHERE search-condition ]
[ORDER BY attribute1 [DESC] [attribute2 [DESC]...]];
```

The Order By keyword clause should be the last keyword clause of the SQL query statement. If more than one attribute is listed in the Order By keyword clause, a multi-key sorting is performed. The default sorting order is ascending. The keyword for ascending is asc. To enable the descending sorting, the desc keyword must follow the attribute name. Rows are sorted in numeric order if the sort attribute (key) is having a number data type. The alphabetic order is adopted if the sort attribute (key) is having a char or varchar2 data type. The following SQL query illustrates the use of Order By keyword clause.

11. Query: List the automobile make (auto_make attribute) and the model year of the automobile (auto_year attribute) from the tenant_auto table for automobile models after 1995. The output must be listed in ascending sequence of the model year of the automobile.

    Query Logic: The output attributes in the Select clause will be auto_make and auto_year attributes. For the search condition, select rows where the tenant_auto table attribute auto_year has values greater than 1995. Hence the search condition for the query will be auto_year > 1995. Since the output has to be arranged in ascending sequence of the model year (auto_year) attribute, the Order By clause is utilized with auto_year as its only sort key.

```
select auto_make, auto_year
from tenant_auto
where auto_year > 1995
order by auto_year;
```

AUTO_MAKE	AUTO_YEAR
Ford	1999
Toyota	1999
Honda	1999
Toyota	2000
Volvo	2000
Honda	2001

Built-in Functions

There are five built-in functions that can be used in the SQL query statement. These functions and their descriptions are shown in Table 5-3.

Function	Description
COUNT(*) COUNT([DISTINCT] *attribute-name*)	Returns the number of rows. Returns the number of (distinct) values taken by the attribute.
SUM(*attribute-name*)	Returns the total of all values for the attribute.
AVG(*attribute-name*)	Returns the average of all values for the attribute.
MAX(*attribute-name*)	Returns the highest value of the attribute.
MIN(*attribute-name*)	Returns the lowest value of the attribute.

Table 5-3: SQL Built-in Functions

The data types of attributes involved with sum, avg, max, and min functions should be numeric. In general the built-in functions should be the only entries in the Select keyword clause. If attributes need to be placed along with the built-in functions in the Select keyword clause, the Group By keyword clause (explained later) should be utilized. The built-in function cannot be substituted for an expression or value in a search condition involving the Where keyword clause. These functions usage is now illustrated through the following SQL queries.

12. Query: How many apartments exist within the Superflex Apartment complex.

    Query Logic: The number of apartments that exist can be determined by counting the number of rows in the apartment table. The built-in function that counts the number of rows in a table is the count(*) function. Hence, the Select clause will have simply the count(*) entry.

```
select count(*)
from apartment;
```

COUNT(*)
9

13. Query: How many types of apartments exist within the Superflex Apartment complex.

Query Logic: Information on the types of apartments that exist is provided by the apt_type attribute in the apartment table. Now, a count of the various types of apartments can be determined by counting the number of rows that contain distinct apt_type attribute values. The built-in function that counts the distinct attribute values in a table is count(distinct attribute-name), which for the query will be count(distinct apt_type). Hence, the Select clause will have simply the count(distinct apt_type) entry.

```
select count(distinct apt_type)
from apartment;
```

```
COUNT(DISTINCTAPT_TYPE)
                      4
```

14. Query: What is the total amount due for rentals that have been billed to credit card visa.

Query Logic: Information on the amount due for rentals is provided by the invoice_due attribute in the rental_invoice table. The built-in function that would add the invoice_due attribute values will be the sum(attribute-name), which for the query will be sum(invoice_due). Hence, the Select clause will have simply the sum(invoice_due) entry. Now, the information on credit card visa will be provided by the attribute cc_type in the rental_invoice table. Hence, the query will also require a search condition like cc_type = 'visa'.

```
select sum(invoice_due)
from rental_invoice
where cc_type = 'visa';
```

```
SUM(INVOICE_DUE)
            6300
```

15. Query: What is the average amount due for rentals that have been billed to credit card mastercard.

Query Logic: Information on the amount due for rentals is provided by the invoice_due attribute in the rental_invoice table. The built-in function that would average the invoice_due attribute values will be the average(attribute-name), which for the query will be avg(invoice_due). Hence, the Select clause will have simply the avg(invoice_due) entry. Now, the information on credit card mastercard will be provided by the attribute cc_type in the rental_invoice table. Hence, the query will also require a search condition like cc_type = 'mastercard'.

```
select avg(invoice_due)
from rental_invoice
where cc_type = 'mastercard';
```

```
AVG(INVOICE_DUE)
    344.44444444444444444444444444444444444
```

16. Query: What is the highest rent charged for an apartment.

    Query Logic: Information on the rent charged for apartments is provided by the apt_rent_amt attribute in the apartment table. The built-in function that would return the highest value for apt_rent_amt attribute values will be the max(attribute-name), which for the query will be max(apt_rent_amt). Hence the Select clause will have simply the max(apt_rent_amt) entry.

```
select max(apt_rent_amt)
from apartment;
```

MAX(APT_RENT_AMT)
700

17. Query: What is the lowest rent charged for an apartment.

    Query Logic: Information on the rent charged for apartments is provided by the apt_rent_amt attribute in the apartment table. The built-in function that would return the lowest value for apt_rent_amt attribute values will be the min(attribute-name), which for the query will be min(apt_rent_amt). Hence the Select clause will have simply the min(apt_rent_amt) entry.

```
select min(apt_rent_amt)
from apartment;
```

MIN(APT_RENT_AMT)
300

Additional techniques to utilize built-in functions is provided in the Subquery sub-section within the Multi-Table Query section of this chapter.

GROUP BY Keyword

This extension of the SQL query statement involves the use of Group By keyword clause to perform grouping of selected rows based on similar attribute values. The general syntax of the SQL query statement along with the Group By keyword clause is as follows:

```
SELECT [DISTINCT] attribute1, [ attribute2 ], [ built-in function ], . . .
FROM tablename1
[WHERE search condition ]
[GROUP BY  attribute1, [ attribute2 ] . . .
[ORDER BY  attribute1  [DESC] [ attribute2  [DESC]...]];
```

The attributes in the Group By keyword clause should be from those that are listed in the Select keyword clause. If more than one attribute is listed in the Group By keyword clause, then there is an outer grouping of similar values, and for each such group value, an inner grouping of values for the other attribute occurs. There can be many attributes in the Group By keyword clause, but each such attribute must also be in the Select keyword clause list.

If the Group By clause is utilized in a query, it is now possible to have a built-in function in the Select keyword clause along with the other attribute entries. The built-in function in this case applies to the selected group. The following SQL queries illustrate the utilization of Group By keyword clause.

18. Query: List the different automobile types in the tenant_auto table, along with a count of each of these automobile types.

Query Logic: The automobile type information is provided by the auto_make attribute. The count of each automobiles types can be calculated by counting the number of times a specific automobile type appears in the tenant_auto table. This counting of rows can be accomplished by the built-in function count(*). Hence the Select clause will have auto_make, count(*) entries. Essentially the output requires a count of the number of times group of auto_make values appear in the tenant_auto table. As the output requires a built-in function value along with a table attribute, the Group By clause will have to be utilized. The Group By clause now will have the auto_make attribute.

```
select auto_make, count(*)
from tenant_auto
group by auto_make;
```

AUTO_MAKE	COUNT(*)
Ford	1
Toyota	2
Honda	2
Volvo	2

19. Query: List the different automobile types in the tenant_auto table.

Query Logic: The automobile type information is provided by the auto_make attribute. Hence the Select clause will have the attribute auto_make. As the output requires a listing of each auto_make group values, the Group By clause will be utilized. The Group By clause now will have the auto_make attribute.

```
select auto_make
from tenant_auto
group by auto_make;
```

AUTO_MAKE
Ford
Toyota
Honda
Volvo

20. Query: List the different automobile types and their corresponding models from the tenant_auto table, along with a count of each of these models.

Query Logic: The automobile type information is provided by the auto_make attribute, while the automobile model information is provided by the auto_model attribute. The count of each automobile model within an automobile type can be calculated by counting the number of times a specific automobile model appears within an automobile type in the tenant_auto table. This counting of rows can be accomplished by the built-in function count(*). Hence the Select clause will have auto_make, auto_model, and count(*) entries. Essentially the output requires a count of the number of times similar auto_model values appear within a group of auto_make value in the tenant_auto table. As the output requires a built-in function value along with a table attribute, the

Group By clause will have to be utilized. The Group By clause now will have the auto_make, auto_model attributes, thereby implying that for each auto_make group value, a second group of auto_model value is determined, and then a count of such auto_model values within the first group is calculated.

```
select auto_make, auto_model, count(*)
from tenant_auto
group by auto_make, auto_model;
```

AUTO_MAKE	AUTO_MODEL	COUNT(*)
Ford	Taurus	1
Honda	Civic	1
Toyota	Lexus	1
Toyota	Camry	1
Volvo	GL 980	1
Honda	Accord	1
Volvo	GL 740	1

HAVING Keyword

The Group By keyword clause can be extended with the Having keyword clause. The Having keyword clause is used to specify a search condition on the groups created through the Group By keyword clause. The Having keyword clause must occur only with the Group By keyword clause, and follow the Group By keyword clause syntax. The syntax of the Having keyword clause along with the Group By keyword clause is:

```
GROUP BY attribute1 [, attribute2 ...]
HAVING search-condition
```

The Having keyword clause search condition is different than the Where keyword clause search condition. The Where keyword clause search condition is utilized to do the initial selection of rows for the query output. The Having keyword clause search condition on the other hand is applied on the generated output rows, i.e. after the query output has been generated. Also, in general the built-in functions are not part of the Where keyword clause search condition. But, such functions can be utilized as part of the search condition with the Having keyword clause. The following SQL query illustrates the utilization of Having keyword clause.

21. Query: List the different automobile types in the tenant_auto table, along with a count of at least two or more of these automobile types.

    Query Logic: The automobile type information is provided by the auto_make attribute. The count of each automobiles types can be calculated by counting the number of times a specific automobile type appears in the tenant_auto table. This counting of rows is accomplished by the built-in function count(*). Hence the Select clause will have auto_make, count(*) entries. As the output requires a built-in function value along with a table attribute, the Group By clause will is utilized that will have the auto_make attribute. Now since the final output only requires those rows which have the count(*) value greater than one, the Having clause can be utilized with the search condition count(*) > 1.

```
select auto_make, count(*)
from tenant_auto
group by auto_make
having count(*) > 1;
```

AUTO_MAKE	COUNT(*)
Toyota	2
Honda	2
Volvo	2

DECODE Function

The decode function in the Select keyword clause is similar to the case or if..then..else structures found in programming languages. The function compares an attribute or search value to values in the list. If a match is found, then the specified output value is returned. If no match is found, then the default value is returned. If no default value is defined, a null value is returned as the result.

The syntax for the decode function is DECODE(MatchValue, List1, Result1, List2, Result2, ..., Default). MatchValue is the search list or attribute name. List1 represents the first value to be matched in the search list. Result1 represents the output value to be returned if List1 entry and MatchValue match. List2 and Result2 pair follow the logic similar to List1 and Result1, and so on. The Default is the output value if no match is found. The following SQL query illustrates the utilization of decode function.

22. Query: List the apartment number and its status in the form of text "Rented" "Vacant" or "Not Available."

    Query Logic: Apartment number information is provided by the apt_no attribute in the apartment table. The apartment status information is provided by the apt_status attribute in the apartment table. The apt_status values are V for vacant or R for rented. So the decode function can be utilized to display the text "Vacant" or "Rented" instead of V or R values with the default display of "Not Available". The Select keyword clause will have apt_no attribute and the decode function.

```
select apt_no,
decode(apt_status,'R','Rented','V','Vacant','Not Available') "Status"
from apartment;
```

APT_NO	Status
100	Rented
101	Rented
102	Rented
103	Vacant
104	Rented
200	Vacant
201	Rented
202	Vacant
203	Rented

CASE Function

The case function in the Select keyword clause provides functionality similar to the decode function. The syntax for the case function is:

```
CASE attribute  WHEN List1 THEN Result1
      [WHEN List2 THEN Result2
       WHEN ... ]
      ELSE Default
END
```

The case attribute values are considered for search. List1 represents the first value for matching. Result1 represents the output to be returned if List1 entry matches the attribute value. The other list and result entries have similar logic. The Default is the value to return if no match is found. The following SQL query illustrates the utilization of the case function. The query is similar to the example that illustrates utilization of decode function.

23. Query: List the apartment number and its status in the form of text "Rented" "Vacant" or "Not Available."

```
select apt_no, (case apt_status when 'R' then 'Rented'
when 'V' then 'Vacant'
else 'Data Error!' end) "Status"
from apartment;
```

APT_NO	Status
100	Rented
101	Rented
102	Rented
103	Vacant
104	Rented
200	Vacant
201	Rented
202	Vacant
203	Rented

Multi-Table Query

Queries involving more than one table require proper linking of tables. Linking of tables is accomplished through two approaches – join or subquery. Joins can be of two types – inner join and outer join. It is possible to have both approaches in the same SQL query statement.

Subquery

A subquery is created when there is another query inside a SQL query statement. These subqueries can exist in the Where clause, the Select clause, and the From clause. The inside query is called the subquery, while the main query is called the outer query.

Subquery in Where Clause

The purpose of subquery in Where clause is to fulfill a search condition in the outer query. The utilization of subqueries limits the processing of the outer query by using the subquery to create intermediate results. Subqueries can return one of more values and can also be nested with additional subqueries themselves. The general syntax of the subquery approach is:

```
SELECT attribute1, attribute2, . . .
FROM tablename
WHERE search-attribute  {[=] | [IN]}  (SELECT attribute
                                       FROM tablename
                                       [WHERE  search conditions])
. . .;
```

The first Select keyword query is called the outer query. The second Select keyword query within the parenthesis is called the subquery. The search attribute in the Where keyword clause of the outer query is linked with the attribute values returned by the subquery Select keyword clause. There are two operators (= or IN) linking the outer query search attribute with the subquery. If the subquery will return a single value then the = operator can be used. But, if subquery returns multiple values, then the IN operator should be used.

The subquery should not have more than one attribute in the Select keyword clause. The subquery can also contain a subquery (called as nested subquery) by becoming the outer query for another subquery associated with its search condition. It is possible for the outer query to have more than one subquery associated with different search attributes in its search condition.

The use of subquery is possible when the condition attribute of a SQL query is in one table, while the output attributes are in a separate table. The linking of the outer query table with the inner query table occurs over attributes that share a common domain. This common domain concept generally applies to the primary key and foreign key combinations. In other words, the Where keyword clause search attribute of the outer query and the Select keyword clause attribute of the subquery should correspond to the primary key and foreign key combinations. Many times the output attribute table and the condition attribute table have no direct primary or foreign key link. In this case other tables that can facilitate the link are utilized. The following SQL queries illustrate the utilization of the subquery approach.

24. Query: List the tenant_name and tenant_dob attribute values for those tenants that drive Volvo automobiles.

Query Logic: The attributes for output (tenant_name and tenant_dob) are in the tenant table. Hence these attributes appear in the outer query Select keyword clause. However, the information on what automobile a tenant drives is in the auto_make attribute in the tenant_auto table. Thus tenant_auto attribute should be part of the outer query search condition. However, since the auto_make attribute is in a separate table tenant_auto, the tenant_auto table becomes part of the outer query search condition through a subquery. The primary key of tenant appears as foreign key in tenant_auto table. Consequently the search condition in the outer query tenant table will find those tenant_ss attribute values in the inner query table tenant_auto that have auto_make attribute value 'Volvo.'

```
select tenant_name, tenant_dob
from tenant
where tenant_ss in (select tenant_ss
from tenant_auto
where auto_make = 'Volvo');
```

TENANT_NAME	TENANT_DOB
Jack Robin	21-JUN-60
Venessa Williams	12-MAR-70

25. Query: List the tenant_name and tenant_dob attribute values for those tenants who live in apartment number 203.

Query Logic: The attributes for output (tenant_name and tenant_dob) are in the tenant table. Hence these attributes appear in the outer query Select keyword clause. However, information on the apartment in which a tenant lives is part of the tenant's rental details. The rental table has information on apartment number (apt_no) associated with a rental_no. Thus the apt_no attribute of the rental table should be part of the outer query search condition. However, since the apt_no attribute is in a separate table rental, the rental table becomes part of the outer query search condition through a subquery. The primary key of rental appears as foreign key in tenant table. Consequently the search condition in the outer query tenant table will find that rental_no attribute value in the inner query table rental that has apt_no attribute value 203.

```
select tenant_name, tenant_dob
from tenant
where rental_no = (select rental_no
from rental
where apt_no = 203);
```

TENANT_NAME	TENANT_DOB
Ramu Reddy	11-APR-62

26. Query: List the tenant_name and tenant_dob attribute values for those tenants who live in apartments that have apartment utilities installed.

Query Logic: The attributes for output (tenant_name and tenant_dob) are in the tenant table. Hence these attributes appear in the outer query Select keyword clause. However, the information on whether an apartment has utilities installed is provided by the apt_utility attribute having a value "Y" in the apartment table. Thus the apt_utility attribute of the apartment table should be part of the outer query search condition. However, since the apt_utility attribute is in a separate table, it becomes part of the outer query search condition through a subquery. But, the apartment table and the rental table have no direct database relationship or link with each other. So, a third table rental is selected. The primary key of rental appears as foreign key in tenant table, and the primary key of apartment appears as foreign key in rental. Consequently the search condition in the outer query tenant table will first find that the rental_no attribute value in the inner query table rental, which in turn will have its own subquery that finds apt_no values that have apt_utility value "Y."

```
select tenant_name, tenant_dob
from tenant
where rental_no in (select rental_no from rental
where apt_no in (select apt_no from apartment
where apt_utility = 'Y'));
```

TENANT_NAME	TENANT_DOB
Jack Robin	21-JUN-60
Mary Stackles	02-AUG-80

Ramu Reddy	11-APR-62
Venessa Williams	12-MAR-70

Subquery with Built-in Functions

Since a built-in function cannot be used as Where keyword clause search value, it is possible to use a subquery instead as a substitute for the search value expression. The following SQL queries illustrates this technique.

27. Query: List the first and last name of staff whose salaries are greater than the average staff salaries.

    Query Logic: Information on the staff first and last name is provided by the first_name and last_name attributes in the staff table. Hence, the Select keyword clause will have the first_name, last_name entries. Now, the information on staff salaries is provided by the salary attribute in the staff table. To determine which staff has their salary more than the average salary of all staff would require a search condition like salary > avg(salary). But, since a built-in function cannot be used as a search condition value, a subquery instead will be substituted to provide this value. Hence, the query will have a search condition like salary > (select avg(salary) from staff).

```
select first_name, last_name
from staff
where salary > (select avg(salary) from staff);
```

FIRST_NAME	LAST_NAME
Terry	Ford
Susan	Brandon

Subquery in Select Clause

A subquery in the Select keyword clause should generate a scalar value that is then passed to the main outer query. In other words, the subquery in Select keyword clause is not allowed to pass more than one row and more than one column value. The following SQL query illustrates this technique.

28. Query: Lists the first and last name of staff and the difference between the staff salary and the average staff salary for those staffs' whose salaries are greater than the average staff salaries.

    Query Logic: Information on the staff first and last name is provided by the first_name and last_name attributes in the staff table. So, the Select keyword clause will have the first_name, last_name entries. Now for the display of difference between the staff salary and the average staff salary in the Select keyword clause, a mathematical expression is developed wherein the average staff salaries are calculated through a subquery. Since by default the mathematical expression becomes the column heading, a renaming of the expression is done.

    Now, the information on staff salaries is provided by the salary attribute in the staff table. To determine which staff has their salary more than the average salary of all staff would require a search condition like salary > avg(salary). But, since a built-in function cannot be used as a search condition value, a subquery instead will be substituted to provide this value. Hence, the query will have a search condition like salary > (select avg(salary) from staff).

```
select staff_no, first_name, last_name,
salary-(select avg(salary) from staff) as SalaryDiff
from staff
where salary > (select avg(salary) from staff);
```

STAFF_NO	FIRST_NAME	LAST_NAME	SALARYDIFF
SA220	Terry	Ford	17600
SA230	Susan	Brandon	10600

Subquery in From Clause (Inline View)

A subquery in the From keyword clause is also referred as an Inline View. In this case the subquery output serves as a temporary table for outer query. The subquery data can thereafter be referenced by the Select and Where keyword clauses of the query. It is temporary because the data from the subquery is not stored in the database. The following SQL query illustrates this concept.

29. Query: List the apartment numbers (apt_no) and apartment rent amount (apt_rent_amt) from apartment table in descending order of apt_no.

```
select apt_no, rent
from (select apt_no, apt_rent_amt rent
from apartment
order by apt_rent_amt desc)
where apt_no like '2%';
```

APT_NO	RENT
202	700
203	700
200	500
201	500

Join (Inner Join)

Join (inner join) in database query is an alternative approach to perform a multi-table query. There are two approaches to perform inner join. In the traditional approach there are two essential entries: the first entry requires the query to list all the tables involved in the From keyword clause; and the second entry involves the use of the Where keyword clause to define the search condition that links the query tables through a special type of search condition called as join condition. The linking of tables occurs over attributes that share a common domain. This common domain concept generally applies to the primary key and foreign key combinations. In other words, the search attribute of one table and the value attribute of the second table should correspond to the primary key and foreign key combinations. The general syntax of the traditional join approach is:

```
SELECT attribute1, attribute2, . . .
FROM tablename1, tablename2, . . .
WHERE tablename1.attribute = tablename2.attribute
and  search conditions . . .;
```

The attributes in the Select keyword clause can be from any of the tables listed in the From keyword clause. The join condition attributes need not be listed in the Select keyword clause. The linking of tables occurs two tables at a time. If more than two tables are involved in the query, then there will be tables that will serve as intermediary between the other tables. For example, say the From keyword clause has tableA, tableB, and tableC. In such case tableA may link with tableB, and tableB many link with tableC to form a chain of interconnected tables for the query. If the output attribute tables and the condition attribute tables have no direct primary key or foreign key link, other tables can facilitate the link. The join condition can be stated in any order in the Where keyword clause along with other search conditions.

Inner joins are also referred as equality join or equijoin as the join is based on values in one table being equal to values in another table. If the attribute names in the tables involved in the query are not unique it is necessary to have the tablename prefix before the attribute names to provide a more specific reference. If the join condition is excluded by mistake, the query will still give results, but the outcome will be voluminous based on the relational algebra concept of cartesian product. In cartesian product every row in one table is joined with every row of the other table. The following SQL queries illustrate the inner join traditional approach.

30. Query: List the tenant_name, tenant_dob, and license_no attribute values for those tenants that drive Volvo automobiles.

    Query Logic: The attributes (tenant_name, tenant_dob, and license_no) in the Select keyword clause come from two tables. The tenant_name and tenant_dob attributes are in the tenant table, while license_no attribute is in the tenant_auto table. So now both of these tables should be in the From keyword clause. Information on tenants that drive Volvo automobiles is provided by the auto_make attribute in the tenant_auto table (which is also listed in the From keyword clause). So, the search condition will be auto_make = 'Volvo'. Since there are two tables in the From keyword clause, the database relationship between tenant and tenant_auto tables will provide the join condition in the Where keyword clause. The join condition will link the primary key (tenant_ss) of tenant table with the foreign key (tenant_ss) in tenant_auto table as tenant.tenant_ss = tenant_auto.tenant_ss.

```
select tenant_name, tenant_dob, license_no
from tenant, tenant_auto
where tenant.tenant_ss = tenant_auto.tenant_ss
and auto_make = 'Volvo';
```

TENANT_NAME	TENANT_DOB	LICENSE_NO
Jack Robin	21-JUN-60	TTS430
Venessa Williams	12-MAR-70	LLT668

31. Query: List the tenant_name, lease_end, and apt_no attribute values for those tenants who live in Studio types apartments.

    Query Logic: The attributes (tenant_name, lease_end, and apt_no) in the Select keyword clause come from two tables. The tenant_name attribute is in the tenant table, while the lease_end and apt_no attributes are in the rental table. So now both of these tables should be in the From keyword clause. Information on tenants who live in Studio types apartments is provided by the apt_type attribute value of 0 in the apartment table. Hence, the apartment table is also added to the From keyword clause, and the search condition in the Where keyword clause becomes apt_type = 0.

Since there are overall three tables in the From keyword clause, a join condition that links two tables at a time needs to be determined based on their database relationships with each other. As apartment table is related to rental table, the join condition that links primary key (apt_no) of apartment table with the foreign key (apt_no) in the rental table will be rental.apt_no = apartment.apt_no. Similarly as the tenant table is related to the rental table, the join condition that links the primary key (rental_no) of rental table with the foreign key (rental_no) in the tenant table will be tenant.rental_no = rental.rental_no. These two join condition make all the three query tables inter-related with each other.

The attributes apt_no and rental_no appear in two tables, hence these attribute names need to be qualified with their respective table names. This qualification is necessary in order to prevent the DBMS from generating error.

```
select tenant_name, lease_end, apartment.apt_no
from tenant, rental, apartment
where tenant.rental_no = rental.rental_no
and rental.apt_no = apartment.apt_no
and apt_type = 0;
```

TENANT_NAME	LEASE_END	APT_NO
Marion Black	31-MAR-18	101
Mary Stackles	30-NOV-16	102

Inner Join Keyword

The second approach to inner join utilizes either of the two specialized keywords: inner join or natural join. In the case of Inner Join keyword, the From keyword clause in the query will have the Inner Join keyword between the tables that need to be joined followed by the join condition that links the two tables through their primary key and foreign key combinations. The SQL query syntax involving the Inner Join keyword is:

```
SELECT attribute1, attribute2, . . .
FROM tablename1 INNER JOIN  tablename2
ON join-condition1
[INNER JOIN tablename3 ON join-condition2 . . .]
WHERE search-conditions  . . .;
```

In the above syntax, the join-condition1 is similar to the join condition linking tablename1 and tablename2 in the WHERE keyword clause of the traditional syntax, i.e. tablename1.attribute = tablename2.attribute. The join-condition2 for tablename3 should now link tablename3 through its associated ON keyword entry with tablename1 or tablename2. The previous two SQL queries based on the traditional inner join approach rewritten with the Inner Join keyword are as follows:

32. Query: List the tenant_name, tenant_dob, and license_no attribute values for those tenants that drive Volvo automobiles. (this query is same as query 7 of Multi-Table Query section)

```
select tenant_name, tenant_dob, license_no
from tenant inner join tenant_auto
on tenant.tenant_ss = tenant_auto.tenant_ss
where auto_make = 'Volvo';
```

TENANT_NAME	TENANT_DOB	LICENSE_NO
Jack Robin	21-JUN-60	TTS430
Venessa Williams	12-MAR-70	LLT668

33. Query: List the tenant_name, lease_end, and apt_no attribute values for those tenants who live in Studio types apartments. (this query is same as query 8 of Multi-Table Query section)

```
select tenant_name, lease_end, apartment.apt_no
from tenant inner join rental
on tenant.rental_no = rental.rental_no
inner join apartment on rental.apt_no = apartment.apt_no
where apt_type = 0;
```

TENANT_NAME	LEASE_END	APT_NO
Marion Black	31-MAR-18	101
Mary Stackles	30-NOV-16	102

Natural Join Keyword

In the case of Natural Join keyword, the From keyword clause in the query will have the Natural Join keyword between the tables that need to be joined. The SQL query syntax involving the Natural Join keyword is:

```
SELECT attribute1, attribute2, . . .
FROM tablename1 NATURAL JOIN  tablename2 [NATURAL JOIN tablename3 . . .]
WHERE search conditions . . .;
```

In this syntax, the DBMS automatically accomplishes the linking of tables around the Natural Join keyword using the primary key and foreign key combinations as specified through their database relationship. The previous two SQL queries based on the traditional inner join approach rewritten with the Natural Join keyword are as follows:

34. Query: List the tenant_name, tenant_dob, and license_no attribute values for those tenants that drive Volvo automobiles. (this query is same as query 7 of Multi-Table Query section)

```
select tenant_name, tenant_dob, license_no
from tenant natural join tenant_auto
where auto_make = 'Volvo';
```

TENANT_NAME	TENANT_DOB	LICENSE_NO
Jack Robin	21-JUN-60	TTS430
Venessa Williams	12-MAR-70	LLT668

35. Query: List the tenant_name, lease_end, and apt_no attribute values for those tenants who live in Studio types apartments. (this query is same as query 8 of Multi-Table Query section)

```
select tenant_name, lease_end, apt_no
from tenant natural join rental natural join apartment
where apt_type = 0;
```

TENANT_NAME	LEASE_END	APT_NO
Marion Black	31-MAR-18	101
Mary Stackles	30-NOV-16	102

Outer Join

Outer join extends the inner join approach by also returning rows that do not have a match as specified in the join condition. There are three forms of outer join – left outer join, right outer join, and full outer join. Left outer join and right outer join list the unmatched rows of only one table, while the full outer join lists unmatched rows of both tables. In outer join, one table is declared as an outer table, while the other table is declared as an inner table. The outer table is the one from which the unmatched rows will be listed. Oracle's traditional approach for outer join required the use of the plus (+) symbol. Alternatively, specific outer join keywords like left join, right join, and full join can also be utilized.

The Oracle's traditional plus symbol (+) serves as an outer join marker to frame the outer join condition. The syntax for this approach involves placing the plus (+) symbol with the join condition in the Where keyword clause as outer-tablename.attribute=inner-tablename.attributename (+). In this syntax, a null value is inserted for the attributes in the inner-tablename that do not have matching rows in the outer-tablename. The plus (+) symbol can be placed on either side of the equality (=) operator, wherein the tablename.attribute having the sign becomes the inner-tablename. The use of + outer join marker yields only the left outer join or the right outer join. The following SQL queries illustrate the outer join with the + outer join marker.

36. Query: List the rental_no, apt_no, and apt_type attribute values for all apartments with utilities installed that have not been rented yet.

    Query Logic: The attributes (rental_no, apt_no, and apt_type) in the Select keyword clause come from two tables. The rental_no attribute is in the rental table, the apt_no attribute is in both rental and apartment table, and apt_type attribute is in the apartment table. So now both of these tables should be in the From keyword clause. Information on whether an apartment has utilities installed is provided by the apt_utility attribute having a value "Y" in the apartment table. Thus the apt_utility attribute of the apartment table will be the search condition in the Where keyword clause as apt_utility = 'Y'. Since there are two tables in the From keyword clause, the database relationship between apartment and rental tables will provide the join condition in the Where keyword clause. The join condition will link the primary key (apt_no) of apartment table with the foreign key (apt_no) in rental table as apartment.apt_no = rental.apt_no.

    To get apartments that have not been rented yet implies getting apt_no attribute values in apartment table that have no matching apt_no attribute values in the rental table. This requires an outer join where the outer-table is apartment and the inner-table is rental. The join condition is now extended with the + outer join marker beside the inner-table as apartment.apt_no = rental.apt_no (+).

```
select rental_no, apartment.apt_no, apt_type
from apartment, rental
where apartment.apt_no = rental.apt_no (+)
and apt_utility = 'Y';
```

```
RENTAL_NO   APT_NO   APT_TYPE
```

100106	100	0
100102	102	0
100105	104	1
	200	2
100101	201	2
	202	3
100103	203	3

Left Join Keyword

Left outer join includes all rows that match the join condition along with those rows in the first (left) table of the syntax that are unmatched with rows from the second (right) table of the syntax. The left join keyword in the From keyword clause indicates left outer join. The SQL query statement syntax is:

```
SELECT attribute1, attribute2, . . .
FROM tablename1 LEFT JOIN  tablename2
ON join-condition1 [...]
WHERE search-conditions  . . .;
```

In the above syntax, unmatched rows of tablename2 are filled with null values. The following query illustrates left join.

37. Query: List rental_no and complaint_no attribute values for those rentals that have registered a complaint along with those rentals that do not have any complaint.

Query Logic: The attributes (rental_no and complaint_no) in the Select keyword clause come from two tables. The rental_no attribute is in the rental table and complaint table, while the complaint_no attribute is in the complaints table. So now both of these tables should be in the From keyword clause. Since there are two tables in the From keyword clause, the database relationship between complaints and rental tables will provide the join condition in the Where keyword clause. The join condition will link the primary key (rental_no) of rental table with the foreign key (rental_no) in complaints table as rental.rental_no=complaints.rental_no.

To get rentals that do not have any complaints registered implies getting rental_no attribute values in rental table that have no matching rental_no attribute values in the complaints table. This requires an outer join where the outer-table is rental and the inner-table is complaints. To utilize the left join keyword, the outer-table will be on the left of the keyword as rental left join complaints.

```
select rental.rental_no,complaint_no
from rental left join complaints
on rental.rental_no=complaints.rental_no;
```

RENTAL_NO	COMPLAINT_NO
100103	10010
100105	10011
100105	10012
100103	10014
100104	10015

```
100102
100106
100101
```

Right Join Keyword

Right outer join includes all rows that match the join condition along with those rows in the second (right) table of the syntax that are unmatched with rows from the first (left) table of the syntax. The right join keyword the From keyword clause indicates right outer join. The SQL query statement syntax is:

```
SELECT attribute1, attribute2, . . .
FROM tablename1 RIGHT JOIN  tablename2
ON join-condition1 [...]
WHERE search-conditions  . . .;
```

In the above syntax, unmatched rows of tablename1 are filled with null values. The following query illustrates right join.

38. Query: List rental_no and complaint_no attribute values for those complaints that are associated with rentals along with those complaints that are not associated with any rental.

Query Logic: The attributes (rental_no and complaint_no) in the Select keyword clause come from two tables. The rental_no attribute is in the rental table and complaint table, while the complaint_no attribute is in the complaints table. So now both of these tables should be in the From keyword clause. Since there are two tables in the From keyword clause, the database relationship between complaints and rental tables will provide the join condition in the Where keyword clause. The join condition will link the primary key (rental_no) of rental table with the foreign key (rental_no) in complaints table as rental.rental_no=complaints.rental_no.

To get complaints that do not have any rentals registered implies getting complaint_no attribute values in complaints table that have either a null rental_no attribute value or have no matching rental_no attribute values in the rental table. This requires an outer join where the outer-table is complaints and the inner-table is rental. To utilize the right join keyword, the outer-table will be on the right of the keyword as rental right join complaints.

```
select rental.rental_no,complaint_no
from rental right join complaints
on rental.rental_no=complaints.rental_no;
```

RENTAL_NO	COMPLAINT_NO
100103	10010
100105	10011
100105	10012
	10013
100103	10014
100104	10015
	10016

Full Join Keyword

Full outer join includes all rows that match the join condition along with those rows that are unmatched in both tables. The full join keyword in the From keyword clause indicates full outer join. The SQL query statement syntax is:

```
SELECT attribute1, attribute2, . . .
FROM tablename1 FULL JOIN tablename2
ON join-condition1 [...]
WHERE search-conditions . . .;
```

In the above syntax, the unmatched rows in both tables are filled with null values. The following query illustrates full join.

39. Query: List rental_no and complaint_no attribute values for those complaints that are associated with rentals along with those complaints that are not associated with any rental, and vice-versa.

Query Logic: This query combines the previous left join query (i.e. query 14 of Multi-Table Query section) and right join query (i.e. query 15 of Multi-Table Query section) . In essence, the full outer join generates unmatched rows from both tables, besides the matching rows.

```
select rental.rental_no,complaint_no
from rental full join complaints
on rental.rental_no=complaints.rental_no;
```

RENTAL_NO	COMPLAINT_NO
100103	10010
100105	10011
100105	10012
	10013
100103	10014
100104	10015
	10016
100102	
100106	
100101	

Self Join

Sometimes a query may require the same table to be queried more than once. This type of query is called a self-join. To perform self-join a table alias may need to be created. A table alias is an alternate name given to a table in the From keyword clause. The syntax of table alias is: tablename aliasname. When a table alias is defined, then the alias name should be used in the query instead of the table name. Table alias can be used also in a regular query. An illustration of self join is outlined in Exists Subquery section query 17.

Inequality Join

Inequality join occurs when the join condition is not based on the equality of values. In this case the join operator can be any other operator instead of the = operator.

Exists Subquery

Exists and not exists are logical operators associated with a subquery in the Where keyword clause that return a true or false status value depending on the presence or absence of rows in the subquery. In this case the subquery is related to the outer query through its search condition. If the subquery returns one or more rows, then the exist condition evaluates as true, and the related row in the outer query is retrieved. If the subquery returns no rows, then the exist condition evaluates as false, and the related row in the outer query is not retrieved.

Even though a subquery is utilized in the SQL query, the operation of the subquery is different. The subquery is not fulfilling a search condition of the outer query in the traditional sense. The DBMS selects a row of the outer query and then executes the subquery to see if there is any row returned by it. If there is a row returned, the exist condition is considered true, and the row of the outer query is placed for output. So, essentially the subquery is executed for each row of the outer query. The following query illustrates the utilization of exists condition.

40. Query: List the rental_no attribute values for those rentals that have been paid with different credit cards.

    Query Logic: As the rental_no attribute value pertaining to rental payments is needed in the output, the rental_no attribute in the Select keyword clause will come from the rental_invoice table. Information on the type of credit card used for rental payments is provided by the cc_type attribute in the rental_invoice table. To know which rental_no has been paid with different credit cards, the rental_invoice table has to have two table instances. Now the query will check for the cc_type value for each rental_no value in one table instance, and compare it with the cc_type value for similar rental_no value in the second table instance. The table instances now will be like a self-join requiring table aliases.

    This comparison will be done through a subquery with the exists search condition of the outer query. In essence for each match of rental_no value in the subquery where the cc_type values are different, the exists condition of the outer query is deemed true, and consequently the outer query rental_no value is selected for output.

```
select distinct rental_no
from rental_invoice a
where exists
(select * from rental_invoice b
where a.rental_no = b.rental_no
and a.cc_type <> b.cc_type);
```

RENTAL_NO
100101
100105

41. Query: List the rental_no attribute values for those rentals that have been paid with the same credit card.

Query Logic: This query is a variation of the previous query (i.e. query 17 of Multi-Table Query section). Now, the comparison will be done through a subquery with the not exists search condition of the outer query. In essence for each match of rental_no value in the subquery where the cc_type values are different, the exists condition of the outer query is deemed false, and consequently the outer query rental_no value is selected for output.

```
select distinct rental_no
from rental_invoice a
where not exists
(select * from rental_invoice b
where a.rental_no = b.rental_no
and a.cc_type <> b.cc_type);
```

RENTAL_NO
100104
100103
100102

ANY and ALL Keywords

Keywords any and all may be used with a set of values in the Where keyword clause. If the values in the condition are preceded by keyword ALL, the condition will only be true if satisfied by all values. The ALL comparison condition in a way is used to compare a value to a list or subquery. It must be preceded by =, !=, >, <, <=, >= condition operators and followed by a list or subquery. The values in the list in a way are connected through logical AND operator.

If the values in the condition are preceded by keyword ANY, the condition will only be true if satisfied by any (one or more) values. The ANY comparison condition can also be used to compare a value to a list or subquery. It must be preceded by =, !=, >, <, <=, >= condition operators and followed by a list or subquery. The values in the list in a way are connected through the logical OR operator.

If the values are generated through a subquery, and the subquery is empty, then the ALL condition operator returns true while the ANY condition operator returns false. It is possible to use the keyword SOME instead of keyword ANY. The following query illustrates the use of these keywords.

42. Query: List all credit card types that have been used for amounts greater than 300, 400, 500.

    Query Logic: Information on credit card types is provided by cc_type attribute in rental_invoice table. Since there might be repetitious credit card types in the output, the Select keyword clause will have the distinct keyword for displaying unique cc_type values. Information on invoice amounts is provided by invoice_due attribute in rental_invoice table. To find which cc_type values have been used for invoice_due amounts greater than 300, 400, and 500, the search condition can use the All operator or alternately use the AND logical operator to combine the individual conditions to check for each value.

```
select distinct cc_type
from rental_invoice
where invoice_due > all (300,400,500);
```

CC_TYPE
visa

discover

43. Query: List all credit card types that have been used for any amount greater than 300, 400, 500.

Query Logic: Information on credit card types is provided by cc_type attribute in rental_invoice table. Since there might be repetitious credit card types in the output, the Select keyword clause will have the distinct keyword for displaying unique cc_type values. Information on invoice amounts is provided by invoice_due attribute in rental_invoice table. To find which cc_type values have been used for any invoice_due amounts greater than 300, 400, and 500, the search condition can use the Any operator or alternately use the OR logical operator to combine the individual conditions to check for each value.

```
select distinct cc_type
from rental_invoice
where invoice_due > any (300, 400,500);
```

CC_TYPE
visa
mastercard
discover

44. Query: List the cc_no, cc_type and total of invoice due payments for those credit cards that has been used the most (in terms of dollar payments).

Query Logic: The Select clause will have attributes cc_no, cc_type, and sum(invoice_due) built-in function. Since the built-in function is used with other attributes the Group By keyword clause will be used in the query. To ascertain credit cards that have been used the most, the Having search condition will be developed that will check which of the sum(invoice_due) value is greater than all values in a list that is generated by a subquery that retrieves the sum(invoice_due) value for various cc_no and cc_type values.

```
select cc_no, cc_type, sum(invoice_due)
from rental_invoice
group by cc_no, cc_type
having sum(invoice_due) >= all
(select sum(invoice_due)
from rental_invoice
group by cc_no,cc_type);
```

CC_NO	CC_TYPE	SUM(INVOICE_DUE)
1234567890123456	visa	3500

Set Operators

Sometimes there might be a need to combine query results of two separate queries. Common set operators like UNION, UNION ALL, INTERSECT, and MINUS can be utilized to combine the results of two separate queries into a single result. Table 5-4 explains their purpose.

Set Operator	Description
UNION	Output consists of all rows from both queries, but no duplicate rows.
UNION ALL	Output consists of all rows from both queries, but displays all duplicate rows.
INTERSECT	Output consists of only rows common to both queries.
MINUS	Output consists of rows returned by first query minus the common rows returned by the second query.

Table 5-4: SQL Set Operators

The general syntax of the set operators is query1 set-operator query2. The rules for using the set operators are:

- Both queries must have the same number of attributes in the Select keyword clause.
- The data type of corresponding attributes in the Select keyword clause of both the queries have to match.

45. Query: Generate a list of all tenant and their family members social security numbers, name, and date of births in the apartment complex.

Query Logic: The information on a tenant's social security numbers, name, and date of births is provided by the attributes tenant_ss, tenant_name, and tenant_dob respectively from the tenant table. Consequently, tenant_ss, tenant_name, and tenant_dob become the Select keyword clause entries of a query on tenant table. Similarly information on a tenant's family social security numbers, name, and date of births is provided by the attributes family_ss, name, and dob respectively from the tenant_family table. Consequently, family_ss, name, and dob become the Select keyword clause entries of a query on tenant_family table.

Now, to get the output in three columns of social security number, name, and date of birth, the two queries can be combined through the union operator. By default, the first query Select keyword clause attribute names become the output column headings.

```
select tenant_ss, tenant_name, tenant_dob
from tenant
union
select family_ss, name, dob
from tenant_family;
```

TENANT_SS	TENANT_NAME	TENANT_DOB
111444663	Terry Williams	21-MAR-68
123456789	Jack Robin	21-JUN-60
173662690	Venessa Williams	12-MAR-70
222663434	Anjali Reddy	10-AUG-90
222664343	Sarla Reddy	11-JUN-65
223056180	Marion Black	25-MAY-81
242446634	Tom Williams	20-MAY-91
444663434	Kay Robin	21-JUN-65

450452267	Ramu Reddy	11-APR-62
723556089	Mary Stackles	02-AUG-80

Rownum

Rownum is an Oracle attribute for listing row numbers. Rownum attribute can appear in the Select keyword clause along with other attributes names, or be part of a condition in the Where keyword clause. There are rules on the use of rownum attribute.

1. The Where keyword clause with rownum attribute must contain an inequality. Further the inequality must be only < or <= condition operator. It will not work with >, >=, =,<> condition operators.
2. The rownum attribute in the Select keyword clause must not appear with *.

The following SQL queries illustrate the application of rownum attribute.

46. Query: List the row numbers and staff names (first_name, last_name attributes) from the customer table.

```
select rownum,first_name,last_name
from staff;
```

ROWNUM	FIRST_NAME	LAST_NAME
1	Joe	White
2	Ann	Tremble
3	Terry	Ford
4	Susan	Brandon
5	Julia	Roberts

47. Query:List the staff names (first_name, last_name attributes) beyond the third row from the staff table.

Note: This query will return nothing because the rownum attribute in Where clause has > condition operator.

```
select first_name,last_name from staff where rownum > 3;
```

no rows selected

48. Query: List the first five staff names (first_name, last_name attributes) from the staff table.

```
select first_name,last_name from staff where rownum < 6;
```

FIRST_NAME	LAST_NAME
Joe	White
Ann	Tremble
Terry	Ford
Susan	Brandon
Julia	Roberts

49. Query: List the first two staff names (first_name, last_name attributes) from the staff table.

```
select first_name,last_name from staff where rownum <3;
```

FIRST_NAME	LAST_NAME
Joe	White
Ann	Tremble

Database Views

Database Views are sort of pseudo tables that do not actually store data. A View stores a query, and is then used to access data in the underlying tables (referred as base tables). Figure 5-1 shows the basic processing of a View.

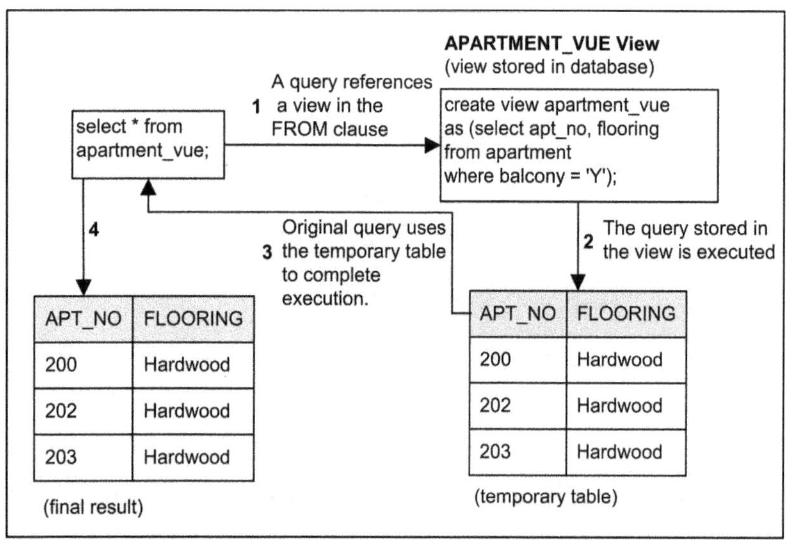

Figure 5-1: Processing of Database View

When a query references a View, the query contained in the View is processed and the results are treated as a virtual or temporary table. Views can assist users who do not have the training to create complex SQL queries, as well as restrict users to sensitive data. The general syntax is:

```
CREATE VIEW view-name [(column1, column2, ...)]
AS database-query;
```

The view-name should be unique within the database. The optional column names (column1, column2, ...) are utilized if the columns of the View will have different names from the corresponding Select keyword clause entries in the database query. Views have restrictions with regard to certain data manipulation operations like insert, update or delete. The following SQL statement illustrates the creation of a View followed by its query.

50. View: Create a View rental_details based on a SQL query that retrieves Rental_no, apt_no, apt_type, and apt_rent_amt attribute values from the rental and apartment tables.

```
create view rental_details as
(select rental_no, rental.apt_no, apt_type, apt_rent_amt
from rental, apartment
where rental.apt_no = apartment.apt_no);
```

Once the View has been created it can be queried just like any other table. The following query retrieves data from the rental_details View.

```
select * from rental_details;
```

RENTAL_NO	APT_NO	APT_TYPE	APT_RENT_AMT
100106	100	0	300
100104	101	0	300
100102	102	0	300
100105	104	1	400
100101	201	2	500
100103	203	3	700

Views can be dropped from the database by using the syntax DROP VIEW view name;. The previously created View rental_details can be dropped from the database as follows:

```
drop view rental_details;
```

A View is generally read-only. However to perform insert, update, delete operations on Views such that the corresponding base tables are affected, it is necessary that the View (i) includes primary key (or foreign key) of base tables, (ii) contains all the required attributes of the base tables, and (iii) does not include Group By keyword clause or Distinct keyword.

Materialized View

A Materialized View stores the data defined by the View query, so that the data can be retrieved without executing the View query again. In other words, a materialized View allows replication of data. There are many reasons for storing duplicate data as Materialized View:

- Complex queries on large databases may require a significant amount of processing, which can then affect the transactional processing of the system. Replicating data for reporting and analysis allows better transactional processing.
- Remote users can improve query performance by replicating data to a local database.
- Data analysis needs may require data to be frozen for specific time for comparison purposes.

Of course there are also some drawbacks to Materialized Views, like additional storage space is required to store View data, and modifications to Materialized Views require synchronization with base tables. The syntax for Materialized View is:

```
CREATE MATERIALIZED VIEW view-name [(column1, column2, ...)]
[REFRESH COMPLETE]
[START WITH start-date NEXT refresh-date]
AS database-query;
```

where refresh complete option stores a new copy of the View query results; and start with option clause specifies the timing for view refresh.

The following SQL statement illustrates the creation of a Materialized View followed by its query.

51. Create a Materialized View rental_details_vue based on a SQL query that retrieves rental_no, apt_no, apt_type and apt_rent_amt attribute values from the rental and apartment tables.

```
create materialized view rental_details_vue
refresh complete
start with sysdate next sysdate+7
as (select rental_no, rental.apt_no, apt_type, apt_rent_amt
from rental, apartment
where rental.apt_no = apartment.apt_no);
```

Similar to database Views, Materialized Views can be dropped from the database by using the syntax DROP MATERIALIZED VIEW view name;. The previously created Materialized View rental_details_vue can be dropped from the database as follows:

```
drop materialized view rental_details_vue;
```

Sequences

Sequences are database objects that automatically generate sequential list of numbers (integers). They are useful for creating unique primary key attribute values or unique surrogate keys. Attributes using values from sequences must have a number data type. The general syntax to create a sequence is as follows (curly brackets indicate one of the two options can be used but not both):

```
CREATE SEQUENCE sequence-name
[INCREMENT BY number ]
[START WITH  start-value ]
[{MAXVALUE  final-value | NOMAXVALUE}]
[{MINVALUE  minimum-value  | NOMINVALUE}]
[{CYCLE | NOCYCLE}]
[{CACHE number-of-sequence-values-to-cache | NOCACHE}]
[{ORDER | NOORDER}];
```

Every sequence must have a unique name and must follow the Oracle naming convention. The Create Sequence keyword clause is the only required clause in creating a sequence; the rest of the clauses are optional. Creating a sequence is a DDL statement. Table 5-5 describes the optional clauses.

Keyword	Description	Default Value
INCREMENT BY	Value by which sequence incremented.	INCREMENT BY 1
START WITH	The sequence start value.	START WITH 1
MAXVALUE	The maximum value to which sequence can increment.	NOMAXVALUE, which allows sequence to be incremented to 1* 1027
MINVALUE	The minimum value for a decrementing sequence.	NOMINVALUE
CYCLE	Indicates that when the sequence reaches its MAXVALUE, it cycles back and starts again from the MINVALUE.	NOCYCLE, which indicates that sequence should stop at the MAXVALUE

CACHE	Whenever a sequence value is requested, the server automatically generates several sequence values and saves them in the server memory area called a cache to improve system performance.	20 sequence numbers are cached.
NOCACHE	Directs the server not to cache any sequence values.	
ORDER	Ensures that the sequence numbers are granted in exact order in which requested.	NOORDER, which indicates no order in number generation.

Table 5-5: Sequence Syntax Keywords

The following SQL statement creates a sequence apartment_sequence that starts with value 100, and increments each value by 10.

```
create sequence apartment_sequence
start with 300
increment by 10;
```

Sequences can be used with the Insert statement to insert attribute values in a row through the convention of placing a ".nextval" suffix after the sequence name. In other words, whenever a sequence has to be utilized to automatically insert values for an attribute in the Insert statement, the entry sequence-name.nextval should be used, where sequence-name is the name of the sequence. The following SQL statement inserts a row in the apartment table wherein the apt_no attribute value is generated by apartment_sequence sequence.

```
insert into apartment
values (apartment_sequence.nextval,3,'R','Y','Hardwood','Y',500,700);
```

It is possible to determine the current sequence value by running a SQL query with currval keyword on the dual system table. More details on dual system table is explained in the Data Dictionary section of this chapter. The syntax of the SQL query for determining the current sequence value is:

```
SELECT sequence-name.CURRVAL FROM DUAL;
```

The following SQL query provides the current value of the previously created sequence apartment_sequence.

```
select apartment_sequence.currval
from dual;
```

```
CURRVAL
      310
```

It is also possible to determine the next sequence value by running a SQL query with nextval keyword on the dual system table. The syntax of the SQL query for determining the next sequence value is:

```
SELECT sequence-name.NEXTVAL FROM DUAL;
```

The following SQL query provides the next sequence value of the previously created sequence club_id_sequence.

```
select apartment_sequence.nextval
from dual;
```

```
NEXTVAL
      320
```

Once the next sequence value has been generated, the previous sequence value cannot be accessed using the sequence statement. This restriction prevents a user from accidently using the same sequence value as the primary key for two different rows. The currval keyword can only be used in the same database user session and immediately after using the nextval keyword statement. For instance, to confirm the currval database session restrictions, try exiting the SQL editor, start it again, and then try to use the currval statement as shown below. The database will return an error.

```
select apartment_sequence.currval from dual;

Error starting at line : 1 in command -
select apartment_sequence.currval from dual
Error report -
ORA-08002: sequence APARTMENT_SEQUENCE.CURRVAL is not yet defined in this session
```

In the next chapter 6 on PL/SQL language a shorter mechanism for finding the sequence current value (currval) and next value (nextval) is provided through Example 4 in the Assignment Statement section. Sequences are dropped from the database through the following SQL statement.

```
DROP SEQUENCE sequence-name;
```

Oracle SQL Functions

There are many SQL functions provided by Oracle to facilitate database retrieval. These functions are in addition to the standard SQL built-in functions.

Date Functions

The sysdate function retrieves the current system date and time from the database server. There are many variations of the sysdate function. To just retrieve the current date or time, a SQL query with sysdate as the only entry in the Select keyword clause on dual table can be developed as shown below.

```
select sysdate from dual;
```

```
SYSDATE
22-DEC-18
```

If you retrieve the sysdate value along with other attributes you can omit the dual table from the From keyword clause, as the following query illustrates.

52. Query: List the contractor_id attribute, name attribute, and sysdate information from the contractor table.

```
select contractor_id, name, sysdate
from contractor;
```

```
CONTRACTOR_ID  NAME                     SYSDATE
C1011          Tony Home Repairs        22-DEC-18
C1012          Mr Fix It                22-DEC-18
C1013          Sunny Home Solutions     22-DEC-18
C1014          Affordable Repairs       22-DEC-18
```

Table 5-6 describes some of the date functions.

Function	Description
ADD_MONTHS(*input date, number of months to add*)	Returns a date that is a specific number of months after the input date.
LAST_DAY(*input date*)	Returns a date that is the last day of the month for the entered input date.
MONTHS_BETWEEN(*input date1, input date2*)	Returns the number of months between two dates (including fractions).

Table 5-6: Oracle Date Functions

Oracle SQL date functions can be utilized in two ways: (i) they can be associated with attributes in the Select keyword clause, or (ii) they can be part of a search condition in the Where keyword clause involving attributes with date data types. The following SQL queries illustrate the use of SQL date functions.

53. Query: List for each rental_no attribute, new lease renewal dates (lease_end attribute) that extend the existing lease renewal dates by two months. The new lease renewal date output column should be named new_renewals.

```
select rental_no, add_months(lease_end,2) as new_renewals
from rental;
```

```
RENTAL_NO  NEW_RENEWALS
   100101  31-JUL-17
   100102  31-JAN-17
   100103  30-JUN-17
   100104  31-MAY-18
   100105  30-JUN-18
   100106  30-SEP-18
```

54. Query: List the last day of the current month.

```
select last_day(sysdate)
from dual;
```

```
LAST_DAY(SYSDATE)
31-DEC-18
```

55. Query: List the last date of the month before which the complaint number 10011 complaint has to be completed (complaint_date attribute).

```
select last_day(complaint_date)
from complaints
where complaint_no = 10011;
```

LAST_DAY(COMPLAINT_DATE)
31-AUG-18

56. Query: List the number of months between the date the lease ends (lease_end attribute) and an input date for rental number 100102.

Note: There are two queries showing the positive and negative results. If the first date is greater than the second date, the result is positive otherwise it is negative.

```
select months_between(lease_end,to_date('9/30/16','mm/dd/yy'))
from rental
where rental_no = 100102;
```

MONTHS_BETWEEN(LEASE_END,TO_DATE('9/30/16','MM/DD/YY'))
2

```
select months_between(to_date('9/30/16','mm/dd/yy'),lease_end)
from rental
where rental_no = 100102;
```

MONTHS_BETWEEN(TO_DATE('9/30/16','MM/DD/YY'),LEASE_END)
-2

57. Query: List the rental number (rental_no attribute) and apartment number (apt_no attribute) of those rentals that are due 60 days after the entered date of 9/30/17.

```
select rental_no, apt_no
from rental
where lease_end >= to_date('9/30/17','mm/dd/yy')+60;
```

RENTAL_NO	APT_NO
100104	101
100105	104
100106	100

58. Query: List the rental number (rental_no attribute) and apartment number (apt_no attribute) of those rentals that are due 60 days before the entered date of 9/30/11.

```
select rental_no, apt_no
from rental
where lease_end <= to_date('9/30/11','mm/dd/yy')-60;
```

```
RENTAL_NO  APT_NO
   100101     201
   100102     102
   100103     203
```

59. Query: List the complaints (complaint_no attributes) that had their workorder generated in less than 2 days.

```
select complaints.complaint_no
from complaints, workorder
where complaints.complaint_no = workorder.complaint_no
and (workorder_date - complaint_date) < 2
```

```
COMPLAINT_NO
       10010
       10011
       10014
       10016
```

Number Functions

There are many Oracle SQL functions to manipulate numeric data retrieved through a SQL query. To use these numeric functions, enter the function in the Select keyword clause. Table 5-7 describes some of these functions.

Function	Description	Example
ABS(*number*)	Returns the absolute value of a number.	ABS(25) = 25
CEIL(*number*)	Returns the value of a number rounded to the next highest integer.	CEIL(65.99) = 66
FLOOR(*number*)	Returns the value of a number rounded down to the integer value.	FLOOR(65.99) = 65
MOD(*number, divisor*)	Returns the remainder of a number and its divisor.	MOD(17,10) = 7
POWER(*number, power*)	Represents the value representing a number raised to the specified power.	POWER(3,2) = 9
ROUND(*number, precision*)	Returns a number rounded to a specified precision.	ROUND(35.99,0) = 36
SIGN(*number*)	Returns a value 1 if the number is positive, value -1 if the number is negative, value 0 if the number is zero.	SIGN(25) = 1
TRUNC(*number, precision*)	Returns a number truncated to the specified precision. Default precision is 0.	TRUNC(34.95,1) = 34.9

Table 5-7: Oracle Number Functions

The following SQL query illustrates the way numeric functions can be utilized.

60. Query: List the absolute value of the number of months between the date the lease ends (lease_end attribute) and an input date for rental number 100102.

Note: Without the abs function the result would have been negative.

```
select abs(months_between(lease_end,to_date('3/15/17','mm/dd/yy')))
from rental
where rental_no = 100102;
```

```
ABS(MONTHS_BETWEEN(LEASE_END,TO_DATE('3/15/17','MM/DD/YY')))
                    3.51612903225806451612903225806451612903
```

Character Functions

There are a number of character functions provided by Oracle SQL. These functions provide ways to manipulate text data retrieved by a SQL query. To use character functions, enter the function in the Select keyword clause. Table 5-8 describes some of these functions. These functions also make it possible to embed format masks with data values such as social security numbers or telephone numbers using the concatenation || symbol.

Function	**Description**	**Example**	**Example Result**
CONCAT(*string1, string2*)	Combines two strings.	concat('Ford','Taurus')	FordTaurus
INITCAP(*string*)	Returns the string with initial letter only in upper case.	initcap('DR')	Dr
LENGTH(*string*)	Returns the length of the input string.	length('Jack')	4
LPAD(*string, number of characters to add, padding characters*)	Returns the value of the string with sufficient padding of the entered character on the left side.	lpad('Jack',8,'*')	****Jack
RPAD(*string, number of characters to add, padding characters*)	Returns the value of the string with sufficient padding of the entered character on the right side.	rpad('Jack',8,'*')	Jack****
REPLACE(*string, search string, replacement string*)	Returns the string with every occurrence of the search string replaced with the replacement string.	replace('Toyota','o','d')	Tdydta
SUBSTR(*string, start position, length*)	Returns a subset of the input string, starting at the start position and of the specified length.	substr('Velvet',1,3)	Vel
UPPER(*string*)	Returns the input string in upper case.	upper('Fall')	FALL
LOWER(*string*)	Returns the input string in lower case.	lower('Fall')	fall

Table 5-8: Oracle Character Functions

The following SQL queries illustrates the way character functions can be utilized.

61. Query: List automobile make (auto_make attribute) and year (auto_year attribute) of all automobiles in the tenant_auto table. The output should combine the two attribute values.

```
select concat(auto_make,auto_year)
from tenant_auto;
```

```
CONCAT(AUTO_MAKE,AUTO_YEAR)
Ford1999
Volvo1990
Toyota2000
Honda2001
Toyota1999
Honda1999
Volvo2000
```

62. Query: List the tenant_name, rental_no, and work_phone attribute values from tenant table. The output should display the work_phone attribute value in format like 999-999-9999.

```
select tenant_name, rental_no,
'('||substr(work_phone,1,3)||')'||substr(work_phone,4,3)||'-'||
substr(work_phone,7,10) "Work Phone"
from tenant;
```

TENANT_NAME	RENTAL_NO	Work Phone
Jack Robin	100101	(417)345-2323
Mary Stackles	100102	(417)545-3320
Ramu Reddy	100103	(417)836-2323
Marion Black	100104	(417)425-7766
Venessa Williams	100105	(417)555-7878

Format Masks

Whenever data is retrieved from numeric or date data type attributes, the output values appear in the default date and number formats. It is possible to utilize format masks to display data in a different format. Such output display is accomplished through the to_char function. The to_char function has the following syntax: TO_CHAR(attribute-name, 'format mask'). The date format masks are similar to those listed in Table 5-1. The numeric format masks are shown in Table 5-9.

Format Mask	**Description**	**Example**
99999	Number of 9s determine display width.	34345
099999	Displays leading zeros.	034345
$99999	Prefix a dollar before the value.	$34345

99999MI	Displays "-" before negative values.	-34345
99999PR	Displays negative values in angle brackets.	<34345>
99,999	Displays a comma in the indicated position.	34,345
99999.99	Displays a decimal point in the indicated position.	34345.00

Table 5-9: Numeric Format Masks

The following SQL queries illustrate the utilization of format masks. The to_char function column in output is renamed, otherwise the column heading will be the function name.

63. Query: List the rental_no attribute and the date the lease started (lease_start attribute) from the rental table. The lease_start attribute value should be in mm/dd/yyyy format.

```
select rental_no, to_char(lease_start,'mm/dd/yyyy') as lease_start_date
from rental;
```

RENTAL_NO	LEASE_START_DATE
100101	06/01/2016
100102	06/01/2016
100103	11/01/2016
100104	04/01/2017
100105	05/01/2017
100106	08/01/2017

64. Query: List the apt_no attribute and apartment's deposit amount (apt_deposit_amt attribute) for those apartments that have no utility (apt_utility attribute). The apt_deposit_amt attribute output value should be formatted with the $ prefix.

```
select apt_no, to_char(apt_deposit_amt,'$999.99') deposit
from apartment
where apt_utility = 'N';
```

APT_NO	DEPOSIT
101	$200.00
103	$300.00

65. Query: List the rental_no attribute and the rental_date attribute time values from the rental table. The rental_date attribute value in output should be formatted in "hh:mi" am/pm format.

```
select rental_no,to_char(rental_date,'hh:mi pm') rental_date
from rental;
```

RENTAL_NO	RENTAL_DATE
100101	12:00 am
100102	12:00 am
100103	12:00 am
100104	12:00 am

100105 12:00 am

100106 12:00 am

Review Questions

1. How are foreign keys handled during the dropping of a table from the database.
2. What actions can be performed using the Alter statement?
3. Explain how manipulation changes are saved permanently in the database.
4. Explain the purpose of Rollback and Savepoint statements.
5. What are script files? Describe the nature of their content.
6. List the basic keywords necessary to develop a SQL query.
7. What are the different ways to give custom names to output columns?
8. What is the purpose of Where keyword clause?
9. How is the query output sorted? Explain.
10. Explain the various built-in functions provided by SQL.
11. Provide the rationale for the Having keyword in SQL query.
12. How many attributes can be listed in the Select keyword clause of a subquery?
13. Explain the difference between inner joins and outer joins.
14. Describe the purpose and structure of database views.
15. Describe an inline view.
16. Outline the purpose and working of sequences.
17. Which Oracle Date function gives the number of months between two dates? Explain.
18. Outline the purpose of Oracle Number functions. Give at least two examples.
19. Explain the working of concat function.
20. Explain the usefulness of to_char function.
21. What are the three Oracle data dictionary views? Explain their purpose.

Review Exercises

1. The syntax to add an attribute email to sporting_clubs table is:
   ______________ add email ___________ ;
2. The syntax to drop constraint customer_fk from table customer is:
   ______________ drop constraint customer_fk;
3. The syntax to modify the data type of attribute price to number(7,2) in table product is:
   alter table product ____________________;
4. Complete the following syntax to drop a table having foreign keys links automatically removed.
   drop table sporting_clubs _________________;
5. To save the new insertions permanently in the database a ____________ statement should be executed.
6. A text file that contains a sequence of SQL statement is called _____________ file.
7. The basic syntax of the SQL query statement requires two keywords ____________ and __________.
8. Entry in the Select keyword clause that shows all attributes from a table is ____________.
9. Entry in the Select keyword clause that ensures unique rows in query result is ____________.
10. The keywords of in SQL query that sorts the query output are _____________.
11. The built-in function that counts the number of rows in a table is ______________.
12. There are __________ built-in functions that can be used in a query statement.
13. The keywords in SQL query that performs grouping of selected rows based on similar attribute values are _____________.

14. The keyword in SQL query that outlines a search condition on the groups created is ____________.
15. Queries involving more than one table require proper ____________ of tables.
16. The ____________ is used to fulfill a search condition in the outer query.
17. The condition to join tables in a SQL query is specified by the ____________ ____________ in the Where keyword clause.
18. The ____________ function in the Select keyword clause takes a specific value and compares it to values in the list.
19. ____________ outer join includes all rows that match the join condition along with those rows in the first (left) table that are unmatched with rows from the second (right) table.
20. ____________ outer join includes all rows that match the join condition along with those rows in the second (right) table that are unmatched with rows from the first (left) table.
21. ____________ outer join includes all rows that match the join condition along with those rows that are unmatched in both tables.
22. The keywords to create a view are ____________ ____________.
23. Views can be dropped from the database using the ____________ ____________ keywords.
24. ____________ view is a temporary table generated through a subquery in the From keyword clause.
25. ____________ are database objects that automatically generate sequential list of numbers.
26. The function that retrieves the current system date and time from the database is called ____________.
27. The function to apply format masks for display of database data is ____________.
28. The command to show the attribute list for a table is ____________.
29. The Oracle attribute for listing row numbers in a table is ____________.
30. ____________ is created to improve query performance.
31. A ____________ is an alternate name for an object that references the owner name as well as the object name.
32. The two types of synonyms are ____________ and ____________.
33. Complete the syntax to retrieve list of tables existing in an Oracle user account.
    select table_name from ____________;
34. Complete the syntax to retrieve list of sequences existing in an Oracle user account.
    select sequence_name from ____________;

Problem Solving Exercises

5-1. Create a table kr_customer with the following attributes as shown below. Name attribute is the primary key of the table. Choose appropriate data types for attributes.

Name	City	Status
Jackie Foods	Memphis	P
Tom Construction	Kansas City	R
Indie Professional	Memphis	P

5-2. Create a table kr_salesperson with the following attributes as shown below. Name attribute is the primary key of the table. Choose appropriate data types for attributes.

Name	Age	Salary
Tom Selleck	40	50150

Jeremy Mack	35	100300
Anita Raina	38	65500
Kerry Kao	28	35600
Joe Walton	45	110500

5-3. Create a table kr_order with the following attributes as shown below. Order_Number attribute is the primary key of the table. Customer_Name is a foreign key linked to KR_Customer table. Salesperson_Name is a foreign key linked to KR_Salesperson table. Choose appropriate data types for attributes.

Order_Number	Customer_Name	Salesperson_Name	Amount
100	Jackie Foods	Anita Raina	700
200	Indie Professional	Tom Selleck	1200
300	Tom Construction	Joe Walton	1500
400	Jackie Foods	Tom Selleck	850
500	Indie Professional	Jeremy Mack	455
600	Jackie Foods	Joe Walton	1500
700	Tom Construction	Anita Raina	860

5-4. Create a script file that inserts rows in the above tables.

5-5. Superflex Apartment database: Create a script file that inserts the following rows in sporting_clubs table. The attribute names are the column heading.

Club_ID	Name
150	Central Climbing Club
160	Steinbeck Sports Club

5-6. Outdoor Clubs database: Modify the price of Product_ID 10011 to 15.75 in the product table.

5-7. Outdoor Clubs database: Modify the price of Product_ID 10020 to 6.99 in the product table.

5-8. Extend problem 5-4 script file with the following rows in kr_order table. The attribute names are the column heading.

Order_Number	Customer_Name	Amount
800	Jackie Foods	550
900	Indie Professional	780

5-9. Extend problem 5-8 by deleting Order_Number 500 from kr_order table.

5-10. Change the data type of Customer_Name attribute in kr_order table.

5-11. Change the data type of Salesperson_Name attribute in kr_order table.

5-12. Outdoor Clubs database: Add an attribute "Fee" with numeric data type in the sporting_clubs table. Issue SQL Update statements for individual rows that insert appropriate values for the Fee attribute.

5-13. Outdoor Clubs database: Add an attribute "Club_Created" with date data type in the sporting_clubs table. Issue SQL Update statements for individual rows that insert appropriate values for the Club_Created attribute.

5-14. Outdoor Clubs database: Delete rows from the purchase_order table for supplier_id belonging to supplier "Hillside Ski."

5-15. Outdoor Clubs database: Delete rows from sporting_clubs table for all sporting clubs in state "NY." Due to the 1:N (parent-child) database relationship between sporting_clubs table and club_membership and club_activity tables, sequence the delete operation such that rows in child tables are deleted first for sporting_clubs in state "NY."

5-16. Outdoor Clubs database: List the product_id, product_name, and price attribute values from the product table.

5-17. Outdoor Clubs database: List the product_id, product_name, and price attribute values from the product table where price is greater than 10.

5-18. Outdoor Clubs database: How many customers are listed in the customer table.

5-19. Outdoor Clubs database: List the first_name, last_name attribute values for all customers who have placed a product order. (Use subquery).

5-20. Outdoor Clubs database: List the first_name, last_name attribute for all customers who have placed a product order. (Use join).

5-21. Outdoor Clubs database: List the sporting club name, duration, first_name, last_name attribute values for customers who have club membership.

5-22. Outdoor Clubs database: How many product orders are there for each payment_type attribute value.

5-23. Outdoor Clubs database: What is average quantity for each product order.

5-24. Outdoor Clubs database: List all product name which end with word "Pole."

5-25. Outdoor Clubs database: List the customer name (first_name, last_name attributes) along with their club membership (membership_id attribute). If a customer does not have club membership, the output should show null.

5-26. Outdoor Clubs database: List all products (product_name attribute) along with the number of times each product has been re-ordered.

5-27. Outdoor Clubs database: List the supplier_id and supplier name attribute values, and the number of products each supplier has provided.

5-28. Outdoor Clubs database: List the supplier_id, supplier name attribute values, and the number of products each supplier has provided. However, only those suppliers who have supplied more than two products should be listed.

5-29. Outdoor Clubs database: List all products product_id and product_name attribute values and their remaining stock (calculated through the expression quantity_in_stock - reorder_point).

5-30. Outdoor Clubs database: List all products product_id and product_name attribute values and their remaining stock (calculated through the expression quantity_in_stock - reorder_point). List only those rows where the remaining stock is more than the average reorder_qty attribute value.

5-31. Outdoor Clubs database: Create a database view product_view containing product table product_name and price attributes, supplier table name and city attributes.

5-32. Query the previously created database view product_view (problem 5-31)to list all products name (product_name attribute), and supplier name (name attribute) located in Los Angeles.

5-33. Outdoor Clubs database: Create a database view customer_view containing customer table's first_name and last_name attributes, product order table's order_id attribute, product table's product_name attribute, and order_details table's quantity attribute.

5-34. Query the previously created database view customer_view (problem 5-33) to list those customers names (first_name and last_name attributes) who have ordered more than two products.

5-35. Query the previously created database view customer_view (problem 5-33) to list average quantity per product name (product_name attribute).

5-36. Superflex Apartment database: List the name of each child that is in a rental unit.

5-37. Superflex Apartment database: List the rental invoice invoice_no attribute value for each invoice from November 2010.
5-38. Superflex Apartment database: List the apt_no attribute value for each apartment that is currently vacant.
5-39. Superflex Apartment database: For each apartment, list the apartment number and rental amount. Order this in descending order based on rental amount.
5-40. Superflex Apartment database: For each tenant's automobile auto_make attribute, list the number (count) for each make.
5-41. Superflex Apartment database: List the length of the lease for each rental.
5-42. Superflex Apartment database: For each apartment's apt_no attribute, list the name of each tenant.
5-43. Superflex Apartment database: List the number of payments made on each credit card for apartment rentals, including the credit card type.
5-44. Superflex Apartment database: List the number of automobiles listed for each rental (rental_no attribute) and apartment (apt_no attribute).
5-45. Superflex Apartment database: List the amount of rent collected per month if all apartments are rented and the tenants pay their rent.
5-46. Superflex Apartment database: List the amount of rent collected based on the apartment that are rented and the tenants pay their rent.
5-47. Superflex Apartment database: List the apartment (apt_no attribute) which is the most expensive.
5-48. Superflex Apartment database: List the number of complaints filed by various rentals (rental_no attribute).
5-49. Superflex Apartment database: List the rentals (rental_no attribute) that has the most complaints.
5-50. Superflex Apartment database: List the tenant name (tenant_name attribute) of the oldest tenant.
5-51. Superflex Apartment database: List the number of tenants in each apartment. Make sure you also count the tenant and include any empty apartments.
5-52. Superflex Apartment database: List the name of any member of the tenant family that is older than the tenant itself.
5-53. Outdoor Clubs database: Delete rows from the purchase_order table for supplier_id belonging to supplier "Hillside Ski." (use SQL subquery for search condition)
5-54. Outdoor Clubs database: Delete rows from club_activity and sporting_clubs table for all sporting clubs in state "NY." (use SQL subquery for search condition)
5-55. Outdoor Clubs database: Update the reorder_qty attribute value to 10 in the product table for supplier "Tiger Mountain." (use SQL subquery for search condition)

5-56. Create a script file that
(i) creates a sequence kr_order_sequence, starting at 1000. The sequence increments by 100.
(ii) Use this sequence to insert the following rows in kr_order table created in problem 5-3.

Order_Number	Customer_Name	Salesperson_Name	Amount
1000	Jackie Foods	Anita Raina	700
1100	Indie Professional	Tom Selleck	1200
1200	Tom Construction	Joe Walton	1500
1300	Jackie Foods	Tom Selleck	850

5-57. Outdoor Clubs database: List the membership_id and customer_id attributes, along with the dates on which the club memberships expire.
5-58. Outdoor Clubs database: List order_id attribute, order_date attribute, and shipping time (the number of days it takes to ship order).
5-59. Outdoor Clubs database: List order_id attribute, order_date attribute, and shipping time (the number of days it takes to ship order) for those orders where the shipping time is greater than the average of such time.
5-60. Outdoor Clubs database: List the first_name attribute and last_name attribute of customers who had their products shipped in less than 5 days.
5-61. Outdoor Clubs database: List the first four product_name attribute values in the product table.
5-62. Outdoor Clubs database: List the first two order_id attribute values where the payment type is credit card.
5-63. List the attributes and their data types for product_order and customer tables.
5-64. Show all the constraints in the database.
5-65. Show all the constraints in the order_details table.
5-66. Show all the tables in the database.

Chapter 6. Introduction to PL/SQL Language

SQL has no structured logic capabilities. To facilitate application development as well as database operations pertaining to business rules beyond the conceptual data model, Oracle developed a programming language native to its database called PL/SQL. PL/SQL is also referred to as a database language as it is embedded within the Oracle database. This chapter introduces PL/SQL language structure along with its database and application building capabilities. There are many examples in the chapter that are numbered for quick reference.

As PL/SQL is embedded within the Oracle database, PL/SQL is utilized to develop business rules and their associated logic on the database server in the form of stored program units. Oracle uses SQL within the framework of its PL/SQL language for the transfer and retrieval of data from the database. PL/SQL provides the ability to combine SQL queries for more complex database retrieval and manipulation, thereby making it also a powerful transaction processing language. As the database is shared among business applications, these stored program units are also shared among business applications. The utilization of stored program units for application development enhances database processing for applications.

There are many benefits to adopting PL/SQL for database interaction in comparison to inline SQL wherein applications directly interact with the SQL engine.

- Faster processing of database requests.
- Better structuring of business applications by concentrating database access in one layer.
- Reduce overhead of communicating potentially large amounts of interim data back and forth between application program and database. This results in lower network traffic.
- A natural language to develop business logic in the database.
- Better enforcement of data integrity and business rules.
- Database level security for PL/SQL stored program units.
- Improved database server security by preventing SQL injection (a technique to maliciously exploit applications that use client-supplied data in SQL statements) attacks.

The interaction of SQL with PL/SQL is seamless. PL/SQL allows data manipulation and query statements of SQL to be included directly within its program unit structure. The inclusion of SQL within the PL/SQL program unit is based on the application logic of the program unit. Understanding how to embed SQL within the application logic is similar to the logic scenarios of other programming languages.

PL/SQL Program Unit Interaction with the Database Server

Even though the PL/SQL program units are stored in the Oracle DBMS, they are relatively separate modules within the server. The interaction of PL/SQL program units with the database server is channeled through the PL/SQL Engine. The interaction occurs through the SQL statements as shown in Figure 6-1.

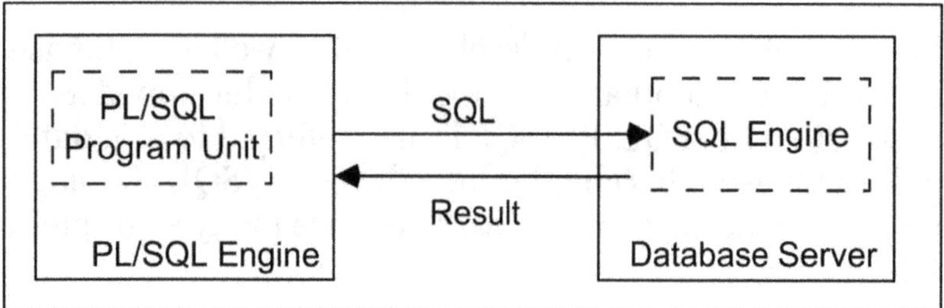

Figure 6-1: PL/SQL Engine Interaction with Database Server

The PL/SQL program units primarily deal with database data. One of the key elements during this interaction pertains to the handling of SQL operations. When any SQL statement is submitted to the SQL engine, it processes and returns the results back to the PL/SQL program unit. SQL engine does not intermittently release results so as to allow the program unit to continue processing on the side. This implies that for SQL statements like Insert, Update, and Delete where the results are either success or failure due to some error, the PL/SQL program unit gets the resulting status immediately. However, in the case of a SQL query, the entire query output is returned to the program unit. Consequently, it is the job of the PL/SQL program unit to store the query results for processing.

PL/SQL Program Unit Structure

A PL/SQL program unit consists of a standard structure referred as a PL/SQL block. It consists of three sections – declarative, executable, and exception handling. The PL/SQL block structure with sections and related keywords is shown in Figure 6-2. Each declaration ends with a semi-colon (;). Each SQL or PL/SQL statement also ends with a semi-colon (;).

```
[DECLARE
. . . variables, user-defined exceptions . . .]

BEGIN
. . . SQL and PL/SQL statements . . .

[EXCEPTION
. . . error-handling statements  (SQL and PL/SQL statements) . . .]

END;
```

Figure 6-2: PL/SQL Block

Table 6-1 below provides a brief description of the sections along with each sections inclusion status within a PL/SQL block.

Block Section	**Section Description**
Declarative *(Optional)*	Specified with the keyword DECLARE. This section defines all the variables and user-defined exceptions that will be referenced within the Executable section. The variables in this section may store database values like rental_no attribute value, a table row, or some temporary value.

Executable *(Mandatory)*	Specified within the BEGIN and END keywords. This section is the heart of the PL/SQL block. It contains all the processing logic involving SQL and PL/SQL statements.
Exception Handling *(Optional)*	Specified with the EXCEPTION keyword. This section includes actions (or error handlers) when errors arise within the Executable section.

Table 6-1: PL/SQL Block Description

The PL/SQL program units are categorized into named or anonymous(unnamed) units. The standard PL/SQL block of Figure 6-2 is also referred as an anonymous PL/SQL program unit. If a named PL/SQL program unit is developed, the top line of the PL/SQL block will include a header line. The header line will define the name, the type of program unit, any parameters (values) it is supposed to receive or return, and other characteristics. These PL/SQL program units can be developed based on the needs of the development environment. Table 6-2 provides a brief description of these program units.

PL/SQL Program Unit	**Description**
Anonymous Block	Unnamed PL/SQL block that can be embedded within an application or run through a SQL editor.
Stored Procedure or Function	Named PL/SQL block in the database that can accept input and can be invoked repeatedly.
Application Procedure or Function	Named PL/SQL block in an application that can accept input and can be invoked repeatedly.
Package	Named PL/SQL module that groups related procedures, functions, and identifiers together.
Database Trigger	A PL/SQL block that is associated with a database table or database system and is executed in response to a database event.
Application Trigger	A PL/SQL block that is executed in response to an application event.

Table 6-2: PL/SQL Program Unit Descriptions

PL/SQL programs can be developed in any PL/SQL development environment like Oracle SQL Developer (www.oracle.com). Each PL/SQL statement ends with a semi-colon. PL/SQL keywords are not case sensitive. A PL/SQL development environment recognizes an anonymous block when the PL/SQL program begins with keyword "declare" or "begin."

PL/SQL Variables and Data Types

PL/SQL is a strongly typed language, which means that all variables must be declared prior to their use in the executable section of the program unit. For instance, if a SQL query is included in a program unit, variables are needed to hold the data retrieved from the database. On the other hand, if the program unit performs a calculation, a variable is needed to hold the resulting value.

Each variable in the PL/SQL program unit has a data type. The type of data that needs to be stored determines the type of variable needed. The data type also dictates the storage format, restrictions on how the variable can be used, and the valid values which may be placed for that variable. Since SQL is embedded within the PL/SQL language, the SQL names and data types can be used within PL/SQL. All PL/SQL variable names must follow the Oracle naming standard as outlined in Chapter 4.

PL/SQL offers a comprehensive set of predefined scalar and composite data types. A scalar data type is a singular data type as it is not made up of other variable components. A composite data type has internal structure or components. The major data types are explained in this chapter.

Scalar Data Type

The scalar data type holds a single value, and falls into one of four categories: number, character, integer, boolean, and date. It is similar to data types available for table attributes like *char, varchar2, number, and date* (explained in Chapter 4). All variable declarations have the following syntax "variable-name data-type-and-size". Some examples of variable declarations are:

```
current_name varchar2(30);
state char(2);
count1 number(3);
```

Additionally, the PL/SQL language includes data types like *boolean, binary_integer, simple_integer, and pls_integer*. Boolean is a "logical" data type. It can be assigned the value of true, false or null. The binary_integer data type allows you to store signed integers. The range of magnitude of binary_integer is $-2^{31} + 1$ through $2^{31} - 1$.

Variables declared as pls_integer also store signed integers. The magnitude range for this data type is -2147483647 through 2147483647. Oracle recommends pls_integer for all integer calculations which do not fall outside of its range. Pls_integer values require less storage than number values, and operations on pls_integer use machine arithmetic, making them more efficient.

Variable Initialization

Sometimes a starting or initial value is needed for a variable. This is accomplished in PL/SQL through initialization during variable declaration. Initialization means that the variable will already contain a value when the executable section of the program unit (begin/end section) starts processing the program logic. Some examples of variable declarations with initialization are:

```
current_name varchar2(30) default 'Jack Trench';
state char(2) default 'MO';
count1 number(3) default 123;
status boolean default FALSE;
```

Assignment operator symbol ":=" (explained later) can also be used in place of keyword default to accomplish the same result. In practice, the assignment operator symbol is more widely used.

Not Null and Constant

The not null option will require that the variable always contain a value. This value can change during the program unit execution, but the variable must always contain a value. For instance, the following declaration initializes variable "current_name" with not null option, thereby implying that this variable must always store some value.

```
current_name varchar2(30) not null default 'Jack Trench';
```

The constant option can be added to the variable declaration to require the variable to always contain a specific value within the program unit. In other words, the constant option can keep the value of the variable from being changed within the program unit. For example, the following declaration initializes variable state with a fixed value "MO" throughout the program unit.

```
state constant char(2) default 'MO';
```

Reference Data Type

There are two special data types in PL/SQL that can be referred as reference data types that allow a PL/SQL variable (i) to have direct reference and use of a table attribute data type, or (ii) provide a way to reference a table row or a row of output from a SQL query. Reference data types reduce errors when the database values have to be stored in variables. It ensures that the developer does not have to check the data type of a database table attribute as it matches correctly with the declared variable. Further, if changes are made to the database structure, such as making an attribute size longer, the developer does not have to be concerned about modifying the variable declaration separately.

Direct Reference to a Table Attribute Data Type

The syntax of reference data type that references the data type of a table attribute in database is:

```
variablename   tablename.attributename%TYPE;
```

For instance, the following declaration for a variable named "current_apt_no" stores data similar to apt_no attribute in apartment table:

```
current_apt_no apartment.apt_no%type;
```

Reference a Table Row or a SQL Query Output Row

The syntax of reference data type that refers to an entire row of a table or SQL query output is:

```
variablename   table or query-name%ROWTYPE;
```

The query-name involves the use of a concept called cursor (explained later). For instance, the declaration for a variable named rental_row that will store one row of rental table will be written as:

```
rental_row rental%rowtype;
```

Since rental_row variable stores a row of the rental table, each attribute of the row will be accessed using the syntax "variable-name.attribute-name". So, to access the lease_type attribute value, the syntax reference will be rental_row.lease_type. Rowtype declarations are also used to define table-based records (explained later).

Composite Data Types

Variables can be defined that store multiple scalar values through more complex data types called as collections and records. Collections consist of associative arrays, nested tables, varrays, and PL/SQL record.

ASSOCIATIVE ARRAYS

An associative array data type (also known as index-by tables) is similar to a one-dimensional array that is expressed as a set of key-value pairs. It is like a simple version of a database table in server memory which is useful when used with small number of rows, such as simple lookup tables. It consists of two elements – a primary key that indexes the table, and the actual value having its own data type. The key can either be an integer or a string. To declare an associative array, the data type is declared first followed by the variable for that type, as shown in the following syntax:

```
TYPE typename IS TABLE OF scalar data type [NOT NULL]
  INDEX BY [BINARY_INTEGER | PLS_INTEGER | VARCHAR2(size-limit)];
variablename typename;
```

For instance, variables auto_make_table and auto_model_table are two variables having associative array data type auto_type.

```
TYPE auto_type IS TABLE OF varchar2(10)
  INDEX BY BINARY_INTEGER;
auto_make_table auto_type;
auto_model_table auto_type;
```

To fill the associative array, both "key" and "value" should be assigned directly with the assignment operator (:=) using the syntax "plsql-arrayname(key) := value". The first key value does not have to be 1, and the associated values do not have to be inserted sequentially. The only restriction on the key value is that it must be unique within the array table structure. Table 6-3 shows the array values.

Key	Value
1	Ford
2	Volvo
3	Toyota
4	Honda

Table 6-3: Table Data Type Values

The following anonymous block program unit fills the associative array auto_make_table as shown in Table 6-3.

```
declare
TYPE auto_type IS TABLE OF varchar2(10)
  INDEX BY BINARY_INTEGER;
auto_make_table auto_type;
begin
auto_make_table(1) := 'Ford';
auto_make_table(2) := 'Volvo';
auto_make_table(3) := 'Toyota';
auto_make_table(4) := 'Honda';
end;
```

To reference an item in the associative array the syntax is plsql-arrayname(key). For instance, auto_make_table(2) will reference the second value "Volvo." As the associative array table values are stored in the memory of the database server, it can grow as large as needed, depending on available server memory.

Associative array tables can also be used to store multiple values called as table of records. Such tables are useful for storing lookup information from database tables that are used many times within a program unit. By storing the information in an associative array table, the program unit does not have to repeatedly query the database, which improves processing performance. The table declaration uses the rowtype reference data type as shown below.

```
TYPE complaint_type IS TABLE OF complaints%rowtype
  INDEX BY BINARY_INTEGER;
complaint_table complaint_type;
```

In the above declaration the complaint_type data type holds a row of complaints table. A table of records is filled programmatically similar to a table of single value, but now it will expand horizontally with all attributes of the table.

There are many special keywords attached to an associative array that helps in its manipulation. These features are outlined in the Table 6-4.

Keyword	Description	Examples	Results
COUNT	Returns the number of rows in the table	auto_make_table.count	4
DELETE (row key) DELETE(first key to be deleted, last key to be deleted)	Deletes a specific table row or a range of rows.	auto_make_table.delete auto_make_table.delete(2) auto_make_table.delete(1, 2)	Deletes all rows. Deletes row with index value 2. Deletes rows with index values 1 through 2.
EXISTS(row key)	Returns TRUE or FALSE if the specified row exists.	IF auto_make_table.exists(2)	Returns TRUE if the item associated with key value 2 exists.
FIRST	Returns the key value of the first item in the table.	auto_make_table.first	1
LAST	Returns the key value of the last item in the table.	auto_make_table.last	4
NEXT(row key)	Returns the value of the key of next row after the specified row.	auto_make_table.next(2)	If current row key = 2, returns 3
PRIOR(row key)	Returns the value of the key of row before the specified row.	auto_make_table.prior(3)	If current row key = 3, returns 2

Table 6-4: PL/SQL Associative Array (Table) Processing Keywords

NESTED TABLES

Nested tables represent sets of values. They are also one-dimensional arrays with no upper bound. One can model multi-dimensional arrays by creating nested tables whose elements are also nested tables. They use sequential numbers as subscripts.

Nested tables can also be stored in database tables and manipulated through SQL. Within the database, nested tables are column types that hold sets of values. Oracle stores the rows of a nested table in no particular order. When a nested table is retrieved from the database into a PL/SQL variable, the rows are given consecutive subscripts starting at 1. That gives array-like access to individual rows.

Nested tables differ from arrays in two important ways: (i)the size of a nested table can increase dynamically, and (ii) they might not have consecutive subscripts. One can delete elements from a nested table using the built-in procedure *delete*. The built-in function *next* lets you iterate over all the subscripts of a nested table, even if the sequence has gaps. The syntax to define a PL/SQL type for nested tables is:

```
TYPE typename IS TABLE OF scalar data type [NOT NULL];
variablename  typename;
```

The following anonymous block program unit defines and fills a nested table auto_make_table.

```
declare
type nested_type is table of varchar2(30);
auto_make_table nested_type;
begin
auto_make_table := nested_type('Ford','Volvo','Toyota','Honda');
end;
```

VARRAYS

Varrays (short for variable-size arrays) hold a fixed number of elements (although you can change the number of elements at runtime). They use sequential numbers as subscripts. One can define equivalent SQL types, allowing varrays to be stored in database tables. They can be stored and retrieved through SQL, but with less flexibility than nested tables.

A varray has a maximum size, which is specified in its type definition. Its index has a fixed lower bound of 1 and an extensible upper bound. A varray can contain a varying number of elements, from zero (when empty) to the maximum specified in its type definition. The syntax to define a PL/SQL type for varrays is:

```
TYPE typename IS {VARRAY | VARYING ARRAY} (size_limit)
  OF scalar data type [NOT NULL];
variablename  typename;
```

where size_limit is a positive integer literal representing the maximum number of elements in the array. The following anonymous block program unit defines and fills a varray auto_make_table.

```
declare
type varray_type is varray(5) of varchar2(10);
auto_make_table varray_type;
```

```
begin
auto_make_table := varray_type('Ford','Volvo','Toyota','Honda');
end;
```

To store nested tables and varrays inside database tables, it is necessary to declare SQL types using the *create type* statement. The SQL types can be used as columns or as attributes of SQL object types.

PL/SQL RECORD

A PL/SQL record is a composite data structure, similar to a record structure in a high-level programming language. PL/SQL records can be table based, cursor based, or programmer defined. These composite data structures utilize the cursor concept (explained later) for storing values. A PL/SQL record can be visualized as a row of data. It can contain all the contents of a row.

Table-based Record

A table-based record represents the structure of a table row. This is useful in situations when the application is reading (or writing) rows from (to) database tables. The individual attributes are accessed using the dot notation. The syntax for a table-based record is:

```
variable-name     table-name%ROWTYPE;
```

For instance, the following program unit below declares a variable tenant_rec that stores one row of tenant table. The SQL query in the begin/end block of the program will transfer all attribute values for the specific row to variable tenant_rec. To access individual row values the syntax will be variable-name.attribute-name. So, to access the marital attribute value the syntax will be tenant_rec.marital.

```
declare
tenant_rec tenant%rowtype;
begin
select *
into tenant_rec
from tenant
where tenant_ss = 123456789;
end;
```

Programmer-defined Record

A programmer-defined record is similar to records in high-level programming language. To declare a record variable, a type declaration must be made first followed by the variable name. The syntax is:

```
TYPE record-variable-type-name IS RECORD
  (field-1        datatype,
  field-2         datatype,
  .
  .
  .
  field-i datatype);
record-variable        record-variable-type-name;
```

For instance, the program unit below declares a variable tenant_rec that stores a record of the type my_tenant_type. The record will hold three variable values. The SQL query in the executable section of the program unit will transfer the three attribute values for the specific row to variable tenant_rec. To access individual values the syntax will be variable-name.record-type-variable. So, to access the employer_name attribute value the syntax will be tenant_rec.employer_name.

```
declare
type my_tenant_type is record
  (ss tenant.tenant_ss%type,
  name tenant.tenant_name%type,
  employer varchar2(20));
tenant_rec my_tenant_type;
begin
select tenant_ss, tenant_name, employer_name
into tenant_rec
from tenant
where tenant_ss = 123456789;
end;
```

Cursor-based Record

Cursor-based records are described through the explicit cursors concept later in the chapter.

SQL Statements Within Program Unit

Due to the seamless integration of SQL with PL/SQL, SQL statements can be entered directly within the executable section of a PL/SQL block. The approach to embed SQL statements within a PL/SQL block is illustrated now.

DATA MANIPULATION

Data manipulation statements are often required in applications. The following examples illustrate utilization of different DML statements to accomplish database operations within a PL/SQL block. Even though each example has only one DML statement, it is possible to combine multiple DML statements in one PL/SQL block depending on the application or business logic.

1. A PL/SQL anonymous block program unit that inserts a new row in rental table.

```
begin
insert into rental (rental_no, rental_date, staff_no, apt_no)
values(rental_sequence.nextval,sysdate,'SA200',103);
commit;
end;
```

2. A PL/SQL anonymous block program unit that modifies the staff_no value for rental_no 100103 in rental table.

```
begin
update rental
set staff_no = 'SA200'
where rental_no = 100103;
commit;
end;
```

3. A PL/SQL anonymous block program unit that deletes complaint_no 10010 from the complaints table.

```
begin
delete from complaints
where complaint_no = 10010;
commit;
end;
```

SQL QUERY

SQL query statements can be embedded in the executable section of a PL/SQL block to retrieve data from the database. When a SQL query is included in a PL/SQL block, the Select keyword clause is followed by a Into clause. The Into clause lists the variables that are to hold the values that are returned by the database server. *A SQL query embedded within the executable section of the PL/SQL block must return only one row.* SQL Cursors section later in the chapter has more details on how SQL queries are handled in a PL/SQL block.

4. A PL/SQL anonymous block program unit that retrieves one row of staff_no and apt_no attribute values for rental_no 100103 from the rental table.

```
declare
staff_no_text rental.staff_no%type;
apt_no_text rental.apt_no%type;
begin
select staff_no, apt_no
into staff_no_text, apt_no_text
from rental
where rental_no = 100103;
end;
```

Interactive PL/SQL Anonymous Block Program Unit

It is possible to create interactive anonymous block program units. To generate such interactivity substitution variables are utilized. Substitution variables can replace values in any SQL query in a PL/SQL anonymous block program unit. These substitution variables at runtime prompt the user for values. There are two substitution variable types:

1. Single ampersand (&) defined as "&variable-name".
2. Double ampersand (&&) defined as "&&variable-name".

Single ampersand (&) in a PL/SQL program unit indicates a variable that holds a value during program unit runtime. Double ampersand (&&) in a PL/SQL program unit is a variable that retains its value for the session until the variable is reset or deleted.

The following PL/SQL anonymous block program unit prompts the user for rental_no and rental_complaint attribute values input, and then inserts a row in complaints table. In the program unit, &complaint_desc and &rental_no_in are the variables that make the program unit interactive. Note: char or varchar2 data type variables should be entered with single quotes.

```
declare
complaint_desc complaints.rental_complaint%type;
rental_no_in complaints.rental_no%type;
begin
insert into complaints (complaint_no,complaint_date,rental_complaint, rental_no)
values(complaints_sequence.nextval,sysdate,&complaint_desc,&rental_no_in);
commit;
end;
```

PL/SQL Statements

Business and application logic structures can be implemented through relevant PL/SQL statements. Such statements consists of assignment statements, selection statements, and iteration statements. Besides the logic structure statements there are also comment statements, display statements, and special statements. PL/SQL statements can span many lines.

Comment Statement

Comment statements are not executed, but utilized for documentation purposes. Comments can be inserted anywhere in the program. There are two types of comment statements: single line or multi-line. Single line comment statements have two hyphens (- -) at the beginning of the line. Multi-line comment statements start with the symbols /* and end with symbols */. For instance, the following code shows the two types of comment statements.

```
-- This is a single line comment statement.
/* This is a multiple line comment statement. It can be created
  anywhere in the program */
```

Display Statement

Display statements in PL/SQL show variable data or text string in a PL/SQL development environment. The general display statement is DBMS_OUTPUT.PUT_LINE. DBMS_OUTPUT is a standard Oracle built-in package (program unit) that users can access. This package has a put_line program unit that displays the content in one line. There are many other program units in the package which provide different options for displaying variable data or text string. The syntax of the statement is:

```
DBMS_OUTPUT.PUT_LINE({variable | text string } [|| { variable | text string } ...]);
```

The text string values must be enclosed in single quotation marks. The concatenation symbol is used to separate entries in the statement. The following PL/SQL anonymous block program unit displays variable data and text string.

```
declare
last_name varchar2(5) default 'Kay';
begin
dbms_output.put_line('Last Name is ' ||last_name);
end;
```

Assignment Statement

The assignment statement assigns a value to a variable. In PL/SQL, the assignment operator symbol is :=. The name of the variable is on the left side of the assignment operator, while the value is placed on the right side of the operator. The value can be a literal (actual value), or another variable, or an arithmetic expression. The assignment operator can also be used to initialize variables in the declaration section of the program. The following examples show different ways of using the assignment statement in program units.

1. Create a PL/SQL anonymous block that assigns a value to a variable last_name.

```
declare
```

```
last_name varchar2(5);
begin
last_name := 'Kay';
end;
```

2. Create a PL/SQL anonymous block that assigns a value to a variable temp_name and then assigns variable temp_name to another variable first_name.

```
declare
first_name varchar2(5);
temp_name char(5);
begin
temp_name := 'Jack';
first_name := temp_name;
end;
```

3. Create a PL/SQL anonymous block that initializes variables in the declaration section.

```
declare
state char(2) := 'MO';
count1 number(2) := 10;
begin
-- plsql statements
end;
```

4. Create a PL/SQL anonymous block that assigns the currval and nextval values of the database sequence apartment_sequence1 to variables temp_curr and temp_next.

```
declare
temp integer;
temp1_next integer;
temp2_next integer;
begin
temp1_next := apartment_sequence1.nextval;
temp2_next := apartment_sequence2.nextval;
dbms_output.put_line(temp1_next ||' '||temp2_next);
end;
```

Sequence Logic

Sequence logic refers to an ordered execution of SQL or PL/SQL statements. The following PL/SQL anonymous block program unit illustrates the sequence logic concept.

5. A PL/SQL anonymous block that inserts a new staff with interactive input of staff first name and last name. It then updates the existing staff_no with the new staff_no for rental 100106. Example logic flowchart is shown in Figure 6-3.

```
declare
temp integer;
temp1_curr integer;
begin
insert into staff (staff_no, first_name, last_name)
values('SA'||staff_sequence.nextval,&first_name,&last_name);
temp1_curr := staff_sequence.currval;
update rental
set staff_no = 'SA'||temp1_curr
where rental_no = 100106;
```

```
dbms_output.put_line('Update completed');
end;
```

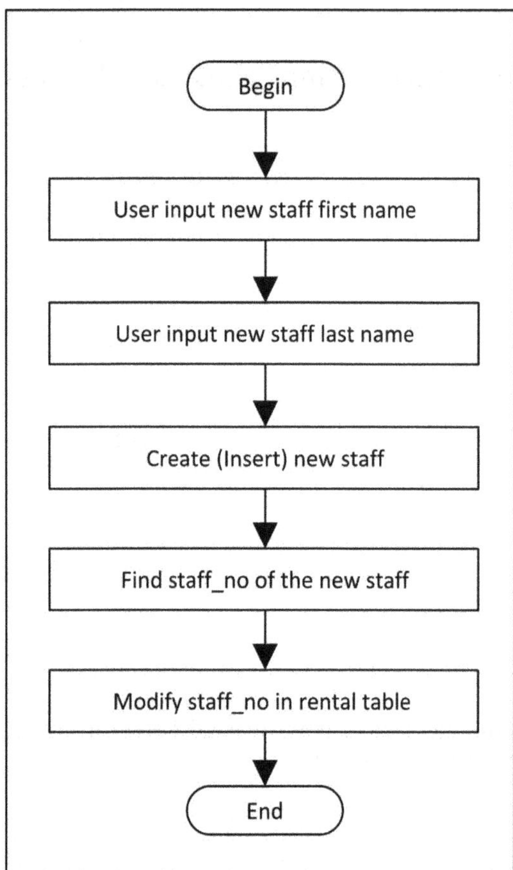

Figure6-3: Logic flowchart of Example 5

Selection Logic

Selection logic refers to the execution of SQL or PL/SQL statements depending on some condition. In other words, the logic sequences the processing statements based on the result of some condition that is evaluated as true or false. PL/SQL language provides a *if/then* statement that implements the selection logic. The syntax of PL/SQL selection logic statement is:

```
IF condition THEN
   ... PL/SQL statements (if condition is true) ...
[ELSE
   ... PL/SQL statements (if condition is false) ...]
END IF;
```

Every *if* keyword must have a corresponding *end if* keyword. The condition can either use a condition structure involving a comparison operator or a boolean variable. The condition structure has the syntax "variablename comparison-operator value". Table 5-5 provides a list of comparison operators with examples.

Operator	Description	Usage Example
=	Equal	total = 8

<>	Not Equal	total <> 8
!=	Not Equal	total != 8
>	Greater Than	total > 8
<	Less Than	total < 8
>=	Greater Than or Equal To	total >= 8
<=	Less Than or Equal To	total <= 8

Table 6-5: PL/SQL Comparison Operators

The condition structure can consist of one or more conditions joined using the logical operator keywords *AND* or *OR*. Two conditions joined with the AND operator are true if both the conditions evaluate as true, while the conditions joined with the OR operator are true if either of the condition evaluates as true. Also, the if/then/else statements can be *nested*. Nested statements involve using another if/then/else combination within an existing if/then/else statement. The following PL/SQL anonymous block program units illustrate the selection logic concept.

6. Create a PL/SQL anonymous block that assigns a text value to variable x_found if auto_maker and auto_style interactive variables have correct values using the "or" operator. Reference data types are used to complete declarations of variables auto_maker and auto_style. The program unit displays the x_found variable text value.

```
declare
x_found varchar2(20);
auto_maker tenant_auto.auto_make%type;
auto_style tenant_auto.auto_model%type;
begin
if (&auto_maker = 'Toyota' or &auto_style = 'Camry') then
  x_found := 'Correct Match';
else
  x_found := 'Match not correct';
end if;
dbms_output.put_line(x_found);
end;
```

7. Create a PL/SQL anonymous block that assigns a text value to variable x_found if auto_maker and auto_style interactive variables have correct values using the "and" operator. Reference data types are used to complete declarations of variables auto_maker and auto_style. The program unit displays the x_found variable text value.

```
declare
x_found varchar2(20);
auto_maker tenant_auto.auto_make%type;
auto_style tenant_auto.auto_model%type;
begin
if (&auto_maker = 'Ford' and &auto_style = 'Taurus') then
  x_found := 'Correct Match';
else
  x_found := 'Match not correct';
end if;
dbms_output.put_line(x_found);
end;
```

8. Extend the sequence logic example 5, by creating a new PL/SQL anonymous block that that inserts a new staff with interactive input of staff first name, last name, and staff status. If the staff status is R then update the existing staff_no with the new staff_no for rental 100106 and display message "Update completed" otherwise display the message "Update not completed." Example logic flowchart shown in Figure 6-4.

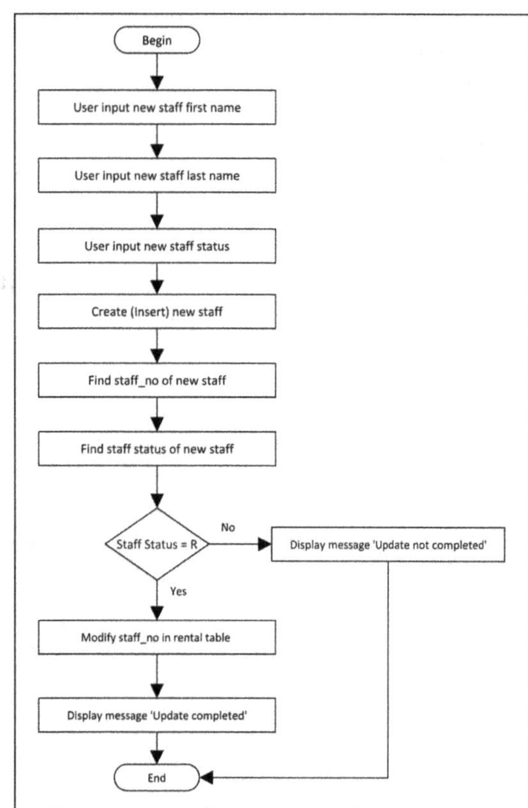

Figure 6-4: Logic flowchart of Example 8

```
declare
temp integer;
temp1_curr integer;
status_curr staff.status%type;
begin
insert into staff (staff_no, first_name, last_name, status)
values('SA'||staff_sequence.nextval,&first_name,&last_name,&staff_status);
temp1_curr := staff_sequence.currval;
select status into status_curr from staff where staff_no = 'SA'||temp1_curr;
if status_curr = 'R' then
  update rental
  set staff_no = 'SA'||temp1_curr
  where rental_no = 100106;
  dbms_output.put_line('Update completed');
else
  dbms_output.put_line('Update not completed');
end if;
end;
```

A variation of the if/then/else statement is the *if/elsif* statement. The if/elsif statement allows the testing of many different conditions and is similar to case statement used in other programming languages. The syntax of the statement is:

```
IF condition1 THEN
   ... PL/SQL statements (if condition1 is true) ...
[ELSIF condition2 THEN
   ... PL/SQL statements (if condition2 is true) ...]
[ELSIF condition3 THEN
   ... PL/SQL statements (if condition3 is true) ...]
...
ELSE
   ... PL/SQL statements (if none of the conditions are true) ...
END IF;
```

9. Extend the selection logic example 8, by creating a new PL/SQL anonymous block that that inserts a new staff with interactive input of staff first name, last name, position, and staff status. If the staff status is R and the position is either Manager or Supervisor then update the existing staff_no with the new staff_no for rental 100106 and display message "Update completed." Also if the staff status is T and the position is either Manager then update the existing staff_no with the new staff_no for rental 100106 and display message "Update completed." Otherwise display the message "Update not completed."

```
declare
temp integer;
temp1_curr integer;
status_curr staff.status%type;
position_curr staff.position%type;
begin
insert into staff (staff_no, first_name, last_name, position, status)
values('SA'||staff_sequence.nextval,&first_name,&last_name,&position,&staff_status);
temp1_curr := staff_sequence.currval;
select position,status into position_curr, status_curr
from staff
where staff_no = 'SA'||temp1_curr;
if status_curr = 'R' and position_curr = 'Supervisor' then
  update rental
  set staff_no = 'SA'||temp1_curr
  where rental_no = 100106;
  dbms_output.put_line('Update completed');
elsif status_curr = 'R' and position_curr = 'Manager' then
  update rental
  set staff_no = 'SA'||temp1_curr
  where rental_no = 100106;
  dbms_output.put_line('Update completed');
elsif status_curr = 'T' and position_curr = 'Manager' then
  update rental
  set staff_no = 'SA'||temp1_curr
  where rental_no = 100106;
  dbms_output.put_line('Update completed');
else
  dbms_output.put_line('Update not completed');
end if;
end;
```

CASE Statement

The PL/SQL case keyword statement is another type of statement for selection logic. The syntax is as follows:

```
CASE selector
   WHEN expression-1 THEN statement-1;
   WHEN expression-2 THEN statement-2;
   . . .
   WHEN expression-n THEN statement-n;
   [ELSE statement-i;]
END CASE;
```

A *selector* is a value or a variable. Based on the selector, the program unit determines which *When* keyword clause should be executed. Each *When* keyword clause has an expression that is evaluated against the selector, and if the comparison is true, the statement following the then keyword is executed. The selector is evaluated only once. The When keyword clauses are evaluated sequentially. Whenever the first When keyword clause expression matches with the selector, the other When keyword clauses following it are ignored. If no When keyword clause expression matches the value of the selector, the Else keyword clause is executed.

SEARCHED CASE Statement

A variation of the previous PL/SQL case statement is a searched case statement. The *searched case* statement has search conditions that yield boolean values of *true, false or null.* When a particular search-condition evaluates as true, the statement following the then keyword is executed. If no search-condition yields true, the Else keyword clause is executed. The syntax is as follows:

```
CASE
   WHEN search-condition-1 THEN statement-1;
   WHEN search-condition-2 THEN statement-2;
   . . .
   WHEN search-condition-n THEN statement-n;
   [ELSE statement-i;]
END CASE;
```

Iteration Logic

Iteration logic occurs when SQL or PL/SQL statements are executed repeatedly a fixed number of times or until a condition is satisfied. These statements can represent simple sequence logic to more complex logic involving combination of sequence, selection, and even iteration logic. PL/SQL language provides different types of keywords to implement the iteration logic. These syntax are discussed below.

- Statement with keywords *loop/end loop* to repeat SQL or PL/SQL statements until the condition in the *if/then* clause is true. The keyword *exit* transfers control to the statement immediately after the keyword *end loop*. The if/then clause with exit keyword can be anywhere between the loop and end loop keywords. The optional *continue* keyword clause tests for the condition associated with the *when* keyword, which if satisfied, immediately completes the current iteration of the loop and passes control to the next iteration of the loop. The syntax is:

```
LOOP
  ... PL/SQL statements ...
  [CONTINUE [WHEN condition]]
  IF condition THEN
    EXIT;
```

```
  END IF;
  ... PL/SQL statements ...
END LOOP;
```

- Statement with keywords *loop/end loop* to repeat SQL or PL/SQL statements until the condition in the *exit when* clause is true. The exit when clause can be anywhere between the loop and end loop keywords. The optional *continue* keyword clause tests for the condition associated with the *when* keyword, which if satisfied, immediately completes the current iteration of the loop and passes control to the next iteration of the loop. The syntax is:

```
LOOP
  ... PL/SQL statements ...
  [CONTINUE [WHEN condition]]
  EXIT WHEN condition;
  ... PL/SQL statements ...
END LOOP;
```

- Statement with keywords *while/end loop* to repeat SQL or PL/SQL statements until the condition associated with the *while* clause is true. Before each iteration of the loop, the condition is evaluated. If the condition is true, the sequence of statements are executed, and then control resumes to the top of the loop. If condition is false or null, the loop is skipped and control passes to the next statement after the end loop keyword. The syntax is:

```
WHILE condition
LOOP
  ... PL/SQL statements ...
END LOOP;
```

- Statement with keywords *for/end loop* to repeat SQL or PL/SQL statements for a fixed number of times. The statement requires a variable (*count-variable*) to count the number of iterations. The *start-value* is the starting value for the defined variable, and the *end-value* is the final value for the variable. Each time the statements within the loop and end loop keywords are executed, the variable is automatically incremented by 1.

```
FOR count-variable IN start-value .. end-value
LOOP
  ... PL/SQL program statements ...
END LOOP;
```

The following PL/SQL anonymous block program units illustrate the iteration logic concept.

10. A PL/SQL anonymous block that insert rows in a new table abc with one attribute sno. The SQL statement to create the table abc is followed by the PL/SQL anonymous block program unit. The program unit logic is shown in Figure 6-5.

```
create table abc (sno number(2));

declare
tcount number(2) :=10;
begin
loop
insert into abc values (tcount);
```

```
tcount := tcount + 1;
exit when tcount > 15;
dbms_output.put_line('Value inserted '||tcount);
end loop;
end;
```

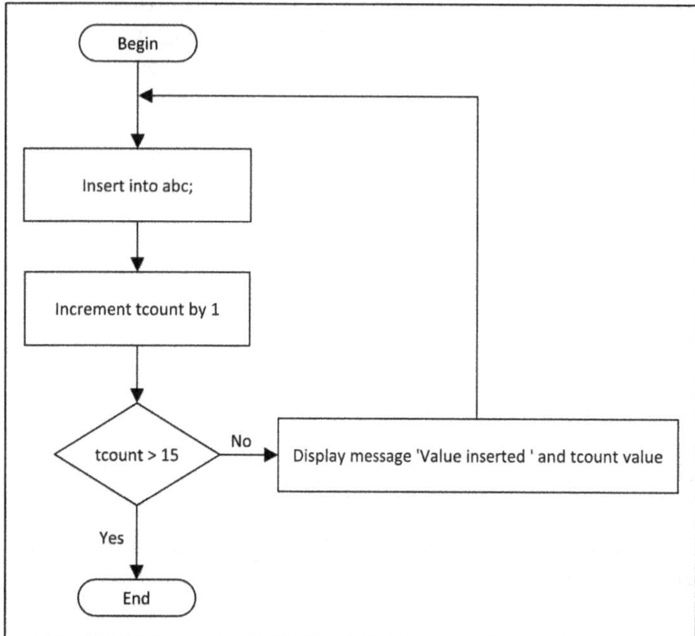

Figure 6-5: Logic flowchart of Example 10

11. A PL/SQL anonymous block that insert rows in a new table counter_table with one attribute counter2. The program unit inserts 8 rows in the table using the if/then exit keyword clause. The SQL statement to create the table counter_table is followed by the PL/SQL anonymous block program unit source.

```
create table counter_table
(counter2 number(2));

declare
count_loop number(2) := 1;
begin
loop
insert into counter_table
  values (count_loop);
dbms_output.put_line('Row Number '||count_loop);
if count_loop = 8 then
  exit;
end if;
count_loop := count_loop + 1;
end loop;
end;
```

12. A PL/SQL anonymous block that insert rows in a new table counter_table with one attribute counter2. The program unit inserts 7 rows in the table with continue keyword using the exit keyword clause. There are two dbms_output statements. The first dbms_output statement will be displayed all the time. Due to the continue keyword condition, the second dbms_output message

will be displayed after the second iteration. The SQL statement to create the table counter_table is followed by the PL/SQL anonymous block program unit source.

```
create table counter_table
(counter2 number(2));

declare
count_loop number(2) := 1;
begin
loop
insert into counter_table
  values (count_loop);
dbms_output.put_line('Row Number '||count_loop);
count_loop := count_loop + 1;
continue when count_loop < 3;
if count_loop = 8 then
  exit;
end if;
dbms_output.put_line('After Continue '||'Row Number '||count_loop);
end loop;
end;
```

13. A PL/SQL anonymous block that insert rows in a new table counter_table with one attribute counter2. The program unit inserts 8 rows in the table using the exit when keyword clause. The SQL statement to create the table counter_table is followed by the PL/SQL anonymous block program unit source.

```
create table counter_table
(counter2 number(2));

declare
count_loop number(2) := 10;
begin
loop
exit when count_loop = 18;
insert into counter_table
  values (count_loop);
dbms_output.put_line('Row Number '||count_loop);
count_loop := count_loop + 1;
end loop;
end;
```

14. A PL/SQL anonymous block that inserts rows in a new table counter_table with one attribute counter2. The program unit insert 8 rows in the table using the while/loop iteration statement. The SQL statement to create the table counter_table is followed by the PL/SQL anonymous block program unit source.

```
create table counter_table
(counter2 number(2));

declare
count_loop number(2) := 20;
begin
while count_loop < 28
loop
insert into counter_table
  values (count_loop);
dbms_output.put_line('Row Number '||count_loop);
```

```
count_loop := count_loop + 1;
end loop;
end;
```

15. A PL/SQL anonymous block that insert rows in a new table counter_table with one attribute counter2. The program unit insert 11 rows in the table using the for/loop iteration statement. The SQL statement to create the table counter_table is followed by the PL/SQL anonymous block program unit source.

```
create table counter_table
(counter2 number(2));

begin
for count_loop in 50 .. 60
loop
insert into counter_table
  values (count_loop);
end loop;
end;
```

LABEL Statement

An executable statement in PL/SQL program unit can be labeled. To label a particular section of PL/SQL block simply add "<<your-label-name-here>>" in front of that section. The label name cannot be more than 30 characters and has to start with a letter. No need to end the label with a semi-colon (;). Labels can be the target of a GOTO statement, EXIT statement, references to variables with the same name, nested loops identification, and so on. The following example illustrates the use of label statement.

16. A PL/SQL anonymous block shows how a nested loop with labels improves the readability of the program unit.

```
declare
 s1 integer := 0;
 i1 integer := 0;
 j1 integer;
begin
 <<outer_loop>>
 loop
  i1 := i1 + 1;
  j1 := 0;
  <<inner_loop>>
  loop
   j1 := j1 + 1;
   s1 := s1 + i1 * j1; -- Sum several products
   exit inner_loop when (j1 > 5);
   exit outer_loop when ((i1 * j1) > 15);
  end loop inner_loop;
 end loop outer_loop;
 dbms_output.put_line('The sum of products equals: ' || to_char(s1));
end;
```

PL/SQL Cursors

A cursor is a variable or reference name given to a SQL query that retrieves database data. The cursor concept is the primary approach to retrieve database data in a PL/SQL program unit. There are two types of cursors – implicit cursor and explicit cursor. Implicit cursor is declared automatically whenever a SQL statement is issued within the begin and end keywords (executable section) of a PL/SQL program unit. Consequently all DML (insert, update, delete SQL statements) and SQL query statements in executable section of a PL/SQL program unit are implicit cursors. Explicit cursors on the other hand is a SQL query that is defined in the Declare section of the program unit. The explicit cursor can handle any number of output rows returned by the database server.

Implicit Cursor

An implicit cursor is created automatically whenever a DML or a SQL query is executed within the executable section of a PL/SQL program unit. For purposes of implicit cursor, the standard SQL query syntax is modified to include an Into keyword clause. The Into keyword clause specifies the local variables that are to hold the attribute values that are returned by the database server. *An implicit cursor SQL query must generate only one row of output*. The number of variables in the Into clause should be the same as the number of attributes in the Select keyword clause. The transfer of attribute values listed in the Select keyword clause to the variables in the Into keyword clause will follow the sequence of their corresponding list. The implicit cursor SQL query syntax is defined below followed by examples of program units.

```
SELECT attribute1, attribute2, ...
INTO variable1, variable2, ...
FROM tablename ...
...;
```

17. Create a PL/SQL anonymous block that retrieves and displays the values of auto_make and auto_model attribute values for license_no 'SYK332' from the tenant_auto table.

    Since the SQL query will retrieve only one row of output, the implicit cursor can be utilized. The declaration section has variables make_in and model_in. Once the implicit cursor SQL query is executed by the SQL engine the auto_make value is stored in the variable make_in, while the auto_model value is stored in the variable model_in.

```
declare
make_in tenant_auto.auto_make%type;
model_in tenant_auto.auto_model%type;
begin
select auto_make, auto_model
into make_in, model_in
from tenant_auto
where license_no = 'SYK332';
dbms_output.put_line('Auto make is '||make_in||
' and model is '||model_in);
end;
```

There are implicit cursor attributes that provide useful information on the execution of SQL query or data manipulation statements. These implicit cursor attributes are: %found, %isopen, %notfound, and %rowcount. Any reference to these attributes in the PL/SQL program unit requires the SQL prefix in reference to the SQL cursor. Also, the implicit cursor attributes are not substitutes for DBMS errors. Table 6-6 describes these keyword attributes. Keep in mind, PL/SQL returns an error when no data is selected.

Keyword Attribute	Description
sql%notfound	Evaluates as "true" if an Insert, Update, or Delete statement affected no rows, or a Select Into statement returned no rows. Otherwise, it yields "false." This keyword attribute is the logical opposite of %found.
sql%found	Evaluates as "true" if an Insert, Update, or Delete statement affected one or more rows, or a Select Into statement returned one or more rows. Otherwise, it yields "false."
sql%rowcount	Returns the number of rows affected by an Insert, Update, or Delete statement, or returned by a Select Into statement.
sql%isopen	Always yields "false" because Oracle closes the SQL cursor automatically after executing its associated SQL statement.

Table 6-6: Implicit Cursor Keyword Attributes

18. Create a PL/SQL anonymous block that updates the rental table with an input apt_no attribute value for an input rental_no attribute value. Only those rentals that have lease_type attribute value of 'Six' should be updated. If the update is successful, a message 'Update Successful' is displayed, otherwise a message 'Update Failed' is displayed.

Since the SQL Update statement is utilized, the implicit cursor sql%found attribute can be checked as a condition (selection logic) for displaying the appropriate message. If the sql%found attribute returns true, then the update was successful, otherwise the update failed. The program unit logic is shown in Figure 6-6.

```
declare
begin
update rental
set apt_no = &in_apt_no
where rental_no = &rental_no
and lease_type = 'Six';
if sql%found then
dbms_output.put_line('Update Successful');
else
dbms_output.put_line('Update Failed');
end if;
end;
```

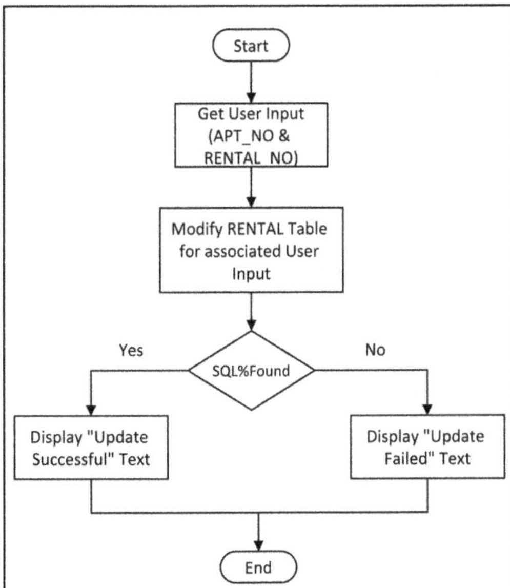

Figure 6-6: Logic flowchart of Example 18

19. Create a PL/SQL anonymous block that checks whether the employer for a tenant for an input rental_no attribute value is 'MSU.' If the tenant works for MSU display the message "Tenant Academic" otherwise display the message "Tenant Professional."

The program unit needs data from three attributes: tenant_name, employer_name, and rental_no. All of these attributes are in the tenant table. The SQL query will retrieve tenant_name attibute value from the tenant table for employer_name having "MSU" value for an input rental_no value. Since the SQL query will retrieve only one row of output, an implicit cursor can be utilized. The implicit cursor attribute sql%found can be checked as a condition (selection logic) for displaying the appropriate message.

```
declare
tctr integer;
begin
select count(*)
into tctr
from tenant
where rental_no = &rental_no
and employer_name = 'MSU';
if sql%found and tctr = 0 then
dbms_output.put_line('Tenant Professional');
end if;
if sql%found and tctr = 1 then
dbms_output.put_line('Tenant Academic');
end if;
end;
```

Explicit Cursor

Explicit cursors are variable names given to a SQL query in the declare section of the program unit. Once the explicit cursor has been defined, it is processed within the *begin* and *end* keywords (executable section) of the program unit. *Explicit cursors should always be used if the SQL query returns more than one row of output*. The syntax of the explicit cursor definition is:

```
CURSOR cursor-name  IS
SELECT attribute1, ...
FROM tablename...
[WHERE  search condition  ...] ...;

variable1  cursor-name%rowtype;
```

The cursor-name is a PL/SQL variable name followed by the regular SQL query statement. Along with the cursor declaration, a local variable (variable1) needs to be declared having the rowtype reference data type. The local variable is necessary to facilitate cursor processing. Once the cursor has been defined, the processing of the cursor (shown through the flowchart in Figure 6-7) is as follows:

1. Open the cursor:
   a. Opening the cursor essentially (i) executes the SQL query statement attached to the cursor-name variable, and (ii) stores the query output rows returned from the database server under the cursor-name variable.
2. Fetch the stored cursor row into the local variable having the rowtype reference data type:
   a. Fetching the cursor row essentially transfers the current (or first) row of the cursor to the rowtype local variable.
   b. Once the row contents have been transferred to the rowtype local variable, the individual attribute values of the cursor row can be now accessed using the syntax *rowtype-local-variable.attribute*.
   c. This fetching of cursor rows is done sequentially till the end of rows in cursor is reached.
   d. An exit condition to test the end of cursor rows is included in the processing.
3. Close the cursor:
   a. Closing the cursor releases the SQL query results. To get the query results again, the cursor will have to be reopened again.

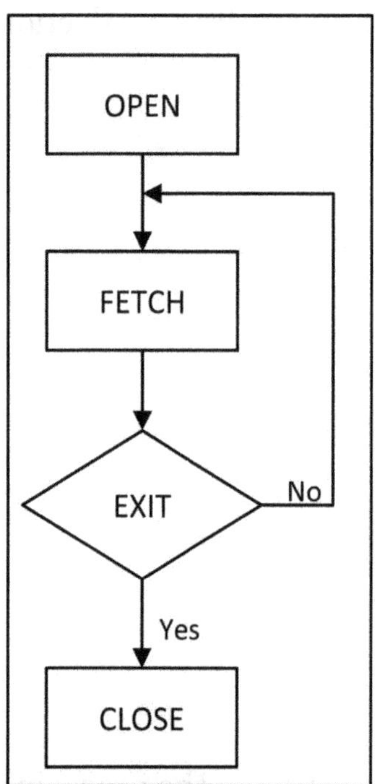

Figure 6-7: Explicit Cursor Processing Logic

Similar to implicit cursor attributes, there are explicit cursor attributes that provide useful information to further facilitate its processing. These explicit cursor attributes are: *%found, %isopen, %notfound, and %rowcount.* Any reference to these attributes in the PL/SQL program unit requires the cursor name prefix in reference to the defined cursor. Table 6-7 describes these keyword attributes.

Keyword Attributes	**Description**
cursor-name%notfound	Evaluates as "true" if a cursor has no further rows to fetch, and "false" when there are rows remaining.
cursor-name%found	Evaluates as "true" if a cursor has rows remaining to fetch, and "false" when there are no rows remaining.
cursor-name%rowcount	Returns the number of rows that a cursor has fetched so far.
cursor-name%isopen	Returns "true" if the cursor is open, and "false" if cursor is closed.

Table 6-7: Explicit Cursor Keyword Attributes

There are two ways to perform explicit cursor processing. The first approach (syntax shown below) opens the cursor through the Open keyword clause. It then utilizes the Fetch keyword clause to transfer each row from cursor-name to the rowtype variable, and then checks for the end of rows in cursor-name through the Exit When keyword clause. The cursor-name%notfound is the explicit cursor keyword attribute that determines the defined cursor's end of rows. The cursor is closed through the Close keyword clause.

```
BEGIN
OPEN  cursor-name;
LOOP
FETCH  cursor-name  INTO rowtype-variable;
EXIT WHEN  cursor-name%NOTFOUND;
... pl/sql statements ...
END LOOP;
CLOSE  cursor-name;
END;
```

20. List the auto_make, auto_model attribute values of all cars listed in the tenant_auto table that belong to model year 2000 and beyond. The program unit logic is shown in Figure 6-8.

```
declare
cursor auto_cursor is
select auto_make, auto_model
from tenant_auto
where auto_year > 1999;
auto_row auto_cursor%rowtype;
begin
open auto_cursor;
loop
fetch auto_cursor into auto_row;
exit when auto_cursor%notfound;
dbms_output.put_line('Make is ' ||auto_row.auto_make|| ' and model is ' ||auto_row.auto_model);
end loop;
close auto_cursor;
end;
```

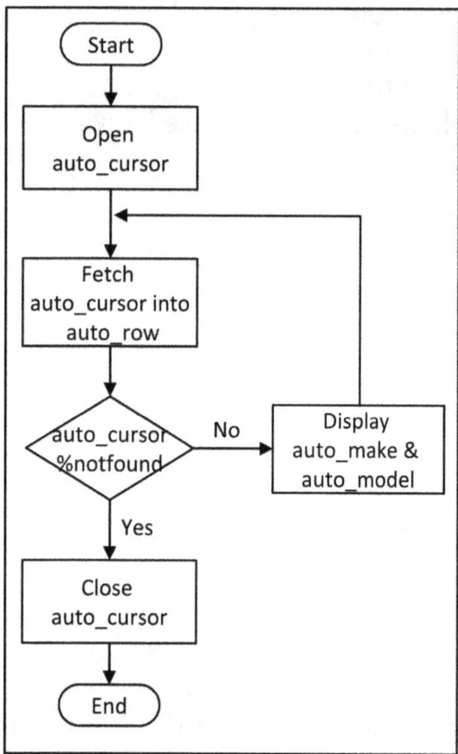

Figure 6-8: Logic flowchart of Example 20

The second approach toward explicit cursor processing uses a variation of the PL/SQL iteration logic *for/end loop* statement. In this approach (syntax shown below), the opening of the cursor is done automatically when the for loop starts; the fetching of cursor rows from cursor-name to rowtype-variable is done automatically; the exit condition to check the end of rows in cursor-name is also automatic; and, once the loop ends, the cursor is automatically closed. Each iteration of the loop is associated with the fetching of the next cursor rows from cursor-name to rowtype-variable.

```
BEGIN
FOR rowtype-variable  IN  cursor-name
LOOP
... pl/sql statements ...
END LOOP;
END;
```

Essentially, with the second approach, there is no need to explicitly open the cursor, fetch the cursor rows, check for the end condition, and close the cursor. The PL/SQL engine implicitly performs these operations now.

21. List the auto_make, auto_model attribute values of all cars listed in the tenant_auto table that belong to model year 2000 and beyond. Utilize the second approach for explicit cursor processing.

```
declare
cursor auto_cursor is
select auto_make, auto_model
from tenant_auto
where auto_year > 1999;
auto_row auto_cursor%rowtype;
begin
for auto_row in auto_cursor
```

```
loop
dbms_output.put_line('Make is '||auto_row.auto_make||
            ' and model is '||auto_row.auto_model);
end loop;
end;
```

Cursor Processing Guidelines

PL/SQL language provides for complex data retrieval and processing. Often times this may involve multiple cursors, where the results of one cursor query may be the condition for another cursor query. Figure 6-9 provides a schematic view of nested cursor data retrieval. The basic approach to perform SQL query processing using cursors within a program unit should be as follows:

- Determine what data needs to be retrieved. This includes the attribute names and their respective tables.
- Determine how many SQL queries (cursors) will be required to facilitate complete retrieval.
- Determine the nature of each query type, ie. whether it is an implicit cursor query or an explicit cursor query.
- In case of multi-query retrieval, sequencing of SQL queries is important – referred as cursor nesting. Such nesting is accomplished by placing the attribute value of one cursor query as the search value of the second cursor query's search condition, and so on.

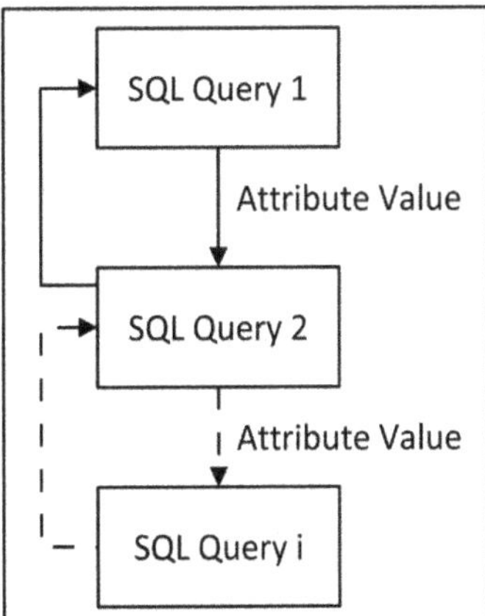

Figure 6-9: Nested Cursor Logic

22. List apartments which have utility, and for such apartments display the credit card payment count summary. The program unit should list as output attribute Rental_no, apt_no, apt_utility, and cc_type values along with a count of the number of times the specific credit card has been used for payment. Figure 6-10 shows the flowchart logic of the nested cursor processing example.

The program unit has two explicit cursors – utility_cursor and count_cursor. These two explicit cursors are nested through the rental_no attribute value of utility_cursor. The explicit cursor queries are as follows:

utility_cursor: Retrieve rental_no, apt_no, and apt_utility attribute values from apartment and rental tables.

count_cursor: Retrieve cc_type attribute, count(*) from rental_invoice where the rental_no is the same as rental_no of utility_cursor.

```
declare
cursor utility_cursor is
select rental_no,apartment.apt_no apartment_no,apt_utility
from apartment,rental
where rental.apt_no = apartment.apt_no;
utility_row utility_cursor%rowtype;

cursor count_cursor is
select cc_type, count(*) as Card_Used
from rental_invoice
where rental_no = utility_row.rental_no
group by cc_type;

count_row count_cursor%rowtype;
cc_type_in char(10);

begin
open utility_cursor;
loop
  fetch utility_cursor into utility_row;
  exit when utility_cursor%notfound;
  dbms_output.put_line('Rental '||utility_row.rental_no||
        ' for Apartment '||utility_row.apartment_no||
        ' with Utility '||utility_row.apt_utility);
  dbms_output.put_line(' CC Number '||'Times Card Used');
  dbms_output.put_line(' --------- '||'---------------');
  open count_cursor;
  loop
    fetch count_cursor into count_row;
    exit when count_cursor%notfound;
    cc_type_in := count_row.cc_type;
    dbms_output.put_line(cc_type_in||'      '|| count_row.card_used);
  end loop;
  close count_cursor;
end loop;
close utility_cursor;
end;
```

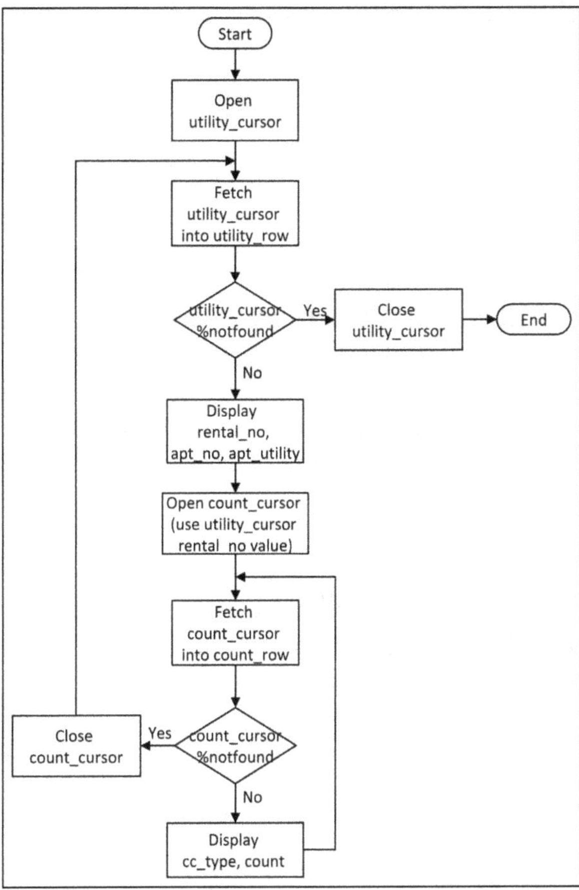

Figure 6-10: Logic flowchart of Example 22

Database Access Using Cursors

Aside from explicit cursor processing there are other forms of cursor processing available in PL/SQL. These can be in the form of parameterized cursors, cursor variables, or cursors for updates.

Parameterized Cursors

Explicit cursors can be defined in PL/SQL that take input parameters. This feature makes the cursor more flexible. The syntax for declaring a PL/SQL explicit cursor with parameters is:

```
CURSOR cursor name (parameter1 IN datatype, [parameter2 IN datatype, ...])
[RETURN return_spec] IS
select statement;
```

For instance, the following cursor declaration has an input parameter that is utilized in the cursor query. The cursor query fetches tenant_name and employer_name attribute values from the tenant and tenant_auto tables where the auto_color attribute value matches the input parameter value.

```
cursor tenant_cursor (color_in tenant_auto.auto_color%type) is
  select tenant_name, employer_name
  from tenant, tenant_auto
  where tenant.tenant_ss = tenant_auto.tenant_ss
  and auto_color = color_in;
```

If a cursor loop is used to process tenant_cursor, it will be done as follows:

```
for tenant_row in tenant_cursor('Red')
loop
...
end loop;
```

Cursor Variables

Cursor variables are special type of explicit cursors. For these variables there is no need to have a SQL query associated with them at the time of declaration. Consequently different SQL queries can be associated with cursor variables at different times in the program unit. Furthermore, cursor variables can be passed as parameters to other program units. This results in the cursor being opened in one program unit, possibly a few rows being fetched in that program unit, and the rest of the processing happening in another program unit.

Creating a cursor variable involves a data type called as *ref cursor* data type, and a variable declaration using this data type. The processing is handled like an explicit cursor using the open, fetch, and close statements. However, the open statement for the cursor variable provides the query to be processed. The syntax to define the cursor variable is:

```
TYPE cursor-variable-type-name IS REF CURSOR
  [RETURN return-type];
cursor-variable          cursor-variable-type-name;
```

The Return keyword clause is used to constrain the type of SQL query that will be associated with the cursor at a later time. If the Return keyword clause is missing, any SQL query can be associated with the cursor. Cursor variables that are declared with the Return keyword clause are sometimes referred to as *constrained cursor variables.*

The syntax to OPEN cursor variables with a SQL query is:

```
OPEN cursor-variable FOR sql-statement;
```

If the cursor variable is a constrained variable, the return type of the variable must be consistent with the select list used in the SQL query of the open statement. Otherwise, a *rowtype_mismatch* exception will be generated by the system. The SQL query statement must be explicitly stated; it should not be a value of a string variable. Once opened, a cursor variable works in the same manner as explicit cursors.

23. Create an interactive PL/SQL anonymous block program unit that opens and displays selected attributes from apartment, rental or tenant_family tables based on the input table name value.

```
declare
type cur_type is ref cursor;
c1 cur_type;
apartment_rec apartment%rowtype;
rental_rec rental%rowtype;
family_rec tenant_family%rowtype;
tname varchar2(10);

begin
tname := &enter_name;
```

```
if tname = 'APARTMENT' then
open c1 for select * from apartment;
elsif tname = 'RENTAL' then
open c1 for select * from rental;
elsif tname = 'FAMILY' then
open c1 for select * from tenant_family;
else
dbms_output.put_line('Make proper selections.');
end if;

if tname = 'APARTMENT' then
loop
fetch c1 into apartment_rec;
exit when c1%notfound;
dbms_output.put_line(apartment_rec.apt_no||' '|| apartment_rec.apt_utility);
end loop;
end if;

if tname = 'RENTAL' then
loop
fetch c1 into rental_rec;
exit when c1%notfound;
dbms_output.put_line(rental_rec.rental_no||' '||rental_rec.lease_end);
end loop;
end if;

if tname = 'FAMILY' then
loop
fetch c1 into family_rec;
exit when c1%notfound;
dbms_output.put_line(family_rec.name||' '||family_rec.dob);
end loop;
end if;
end;
```

Cursor for Update

In many instances it may be necessary to retrieve rows from the database and perform processing on each row, including data manipulation like update or delete operations. Cursor for Update is an extension of explicit cursor, that allows for the Oracle server to (i) keep track of which physical database row (rowid attribute) corresponds to the row in the cursor, and then (ii) lock the rows retrieved with the cursor query for incoming updates via the cursor. The cursor for update syntax is as follows:

```
CURSOR cursor-name IS
select-statement FOR UPDATE [NOWAIT];
```

The *nowait* option controls what will occur if the rows being retrieved by the cursor are already locked by another transaction. If this option is excluded, the statement will wait indefinitely for the needed rows to unlock and become available. The nowait option can raise server error if the desired rows are currently locked.

In addition, at the time of SQL update or delete operations, the *where current of* cursor clause may be added to instruct the server to update/delete the physical row of the table that corresponds to the row of the cursor that is currently being processed. The extended syntax for SQL update operations is as follows:

```
UPDATE table-name
SET new-values
WHERE CURRENT OF cursor-name;
```

The extended syntax for SQL delete operations is as follows:

```
DELETE FROM table-name
WHERE CURRENT OF cursor-name;
```

24. List the position and salary attributes from the staff table, and based on the position attribute value perform different salary increments. The "Assistant" is given a 20% salary increment, the "Manager" is given a 40% salary increment, while the "Supervisor" is given a 50% salary increment.

```
declare
cursor staff_cursor is
select position, salary
from staff
for update nowait;
staff_row staff_cursor%rowtype;
increment staff.salary%type;
begin
for staff_row in staff_cursor
loop
if staff_row.position = 'Assistant' then
increment := staff_row.salary * 1.20;
end if;
if staff_row.position = 'Manager' then
increment := staff_row.salary * 1.40;
end if;
if staff_row.position = 'Supervisor' then
increment := staff_row.salary * 1.50;
end if;
update staff
set salary = increment
where current of staff_cursor;
end loop;
commit;
end;
```

Review Questions

1. What are the different parts of a PL/SQL block?
2. Define the two reference data types.
3. How many types of PL/SQL program units can be created?
4. What PL/SQL statement implements decision logic?
5. What PL/SQL statement implements iteration logic?
6. Describe an implicit cursor.
7. Explain an explicit cursor.
8. What are nested cursors?
9. What statement is used to display PL/SQL program unit output?
10. What are paremeterized cursors?
11. Describe use of cursor variables?
12. Explain rationale of cursor for update?

Review Exercises

1. PL/SQL is a database programming language that extends the ____________ language with structured logic capabilities.
2. The keyword for the declaration section of a typical PL/SQL program is ______________.
3. The keyword for the executable section of a typical PL/SQL program is ______________.
4. The keyword for the exception section of a typical PL/SQL program is ______________.
5. An ____________ ______________ is a PL/SQL program that has no name, but can be run through SQL Plus.
6. A ______________ is a named PL/SQL program that can accept input and can be invoked repeatedly.
7. A ______________ is a named PL/SQL program that will always return some value.
8. A ______________ is a named PL/SQL program that is associated with a database table, and is executed in response to a database event.
9. The following declaration refers the data type of invoice_name variable to ____________ attribute.
   invoice_name customer.last_name%type;
10. A PL/SQL ______________ data type is similar to a one-dimensional array.
11. The following PL/SQL statement assigns ______________ to ______________.
    last_name := temp_name;
12. Complete the following syntax:
    if total >= 10 then
    t_desc := 'condition met';
    else t_desc := 'condition not met';
    __________;
13. Complete the following syntax:
    loop
    insert into counter_table values (count_loop);
    ___________;
14. An ____________ cursor is a SQL query statement defined within the BEGIN/END block of the program.
15. An ____________ cursor can handle only one row of result returned by the database server.
16. An ____________ cursor is a SQL query statement defined in the declare section of the program.
17. An ____________ cursor can handle any number of rows returned by the database server.
18. Complete the following syntax:
    loop
    fetch customer_cursor into customer_row;
    exit when _______________________;
    end loop;
19. The name of the cursor being processed below is ____________.
    for invoice_row in customer_order
    loop
    dbms_output.put_line('Inside Cursor');
    end loop;
20. The following statements pertain to the processing of an ____________ cursor.
    for invoice_row in customer_order
    loop
    dbms_output.put_line('Inside Cursor');
    end loop;

Problem Solving Exercises

6-1. Outdoor Clubs database: Create a PL/SQL anonymous block program unit that displays for each sporting club, membership details in the form of membership_id, membership_date, first_name, last_name, and duration attribute values. For those sporting clubs that do not yet have any membership, "No Membership Yet" message should be displayed. Save the PL/SQL anonymous block program unit as a script file.

6-2. Outdoor Clubs database: Create a PL/SQL anonymous block program unit that displays product_name attribute values from the product table, and a status text based on the price attribute value. Save the PL/SQL anonymous block program unit as a script file. The rules for categorizing the price status text display are:

Price Range	Price Status
< $5.00	Low
Between 5 and 20	Medium
> 20	High

A partial display of program unit output is shown below:

```
Product Name                 Price Status
------------------------    ------------
Beginner's Ski Boot           Medium
Intermediate Ski Boot         Medium
Pro Ski Boot                  Medium
Beginner's Ski Pole           High
```

6-3. Outdoor Clubs database: Create a PL/SQL anonymous block program unit that counts how many products listed in the product table fall within the price range categories shown below. Save the PL/SQL anonymous block program unit as a script file. The rule for categorizing price ranges are:

Price Range	Price Status
< $5.00	Low
Between 5 and 20	Medium
> 20	High

The program unit output is as follows:

```
Product Count Price Status
------------- ------------
2             Low
5             Medium
5             High
```

6-4. Outdoor Clubs database: Create a PL/SQL anonymous block program unit that displays the product_name and price attribute values for those products that have been ordered in quantities of more than 3. Save the PL/SQL anonymous block program unit as a script file.

6-5. Outdoor Clubs database: Create a PL/SQL anonymous block program unit that lists the product_name attribute value and a *demand status* text display. The *demand status* text display is determined by counting the number of times a product has been ordered so far. The *demand status* text display will be either "Low Demand" or "High Demand". Low Demand is displayed if the product has been ordered less than 2 times. High Demand is displayed if the product has been ordered more than 2 times. Save the PL/SQL anonymous block program unit as a script file.

6-6. Outdoor Clubs database: Create a PL/SQL anonymous block program unit that displays the activity attribute values listed in the club_activity table along with a count of the clubs in the sporting_clubs table that provide the activity. Save the PL/SQL anonymous block program unit as a script file.

6-7. Outdoor Clubs database: Create a PL/SQL anonymous block program unit that displays the activity attribute value listed in the club_activity table along with the name of the clubs in the sporting_clubs table that provide the activity. Save the PL/SQL anonymous block program unit as a script file. A partial display of program unit output is shown below:

```
Hiking
---------
Hillside Mountain Club
Branson Climbing Club

Canoeing
---------
Cherokee Rafting Club
White Plains Club
```

6-8. Outdoor Clubs database: Create a PL/SQL anonymous block program unit that displays the first_name and last_name attribute value from the customer table along with a list of club activities for those customers who have club membership. Save the PL/SQL anonymous block program unit as a script file.

6-9. Outdoor Clubs database: Create a PL/SQL anonymous block program unit that displays the customer first_name and last_name attribute values and a customer status text display. The customer status text display is determined by counting the number of times a customer has placed an order so far. The customer status text display will be either "Average Customer" or "Good Customer". Average Customer is displayed if the customer has ordered less than 2 times. Good Customer is displayed if the customer has ordered 2 or more times. Save the PL/SQL anonymous block program unit as a script file.

6-10. Outdoor Clubs database: Extend problem 6-1 to take care of a business rule to support a promotion where sporting clubs based in Missouri (state MO) want to reduce their club membership amount by $50 to generate club memberships. Save the PL/SQL anonymous block program unit as a script file.

6-11. Outdoor Clubs database: Extend problem 6-1 to take care of a business rule to encourage memberships in sporting clubs based in Missouri (state MO) by adding a bonus month to their existing and new club memberships.

6-12. Outdoor Clubs database: Extend problem 6-3 to take care of a business rule to increase the price of our lower priced products due to high operational cost. So those products that have Low price status, add $1 to their product price.

6-13. Outdoor Clubs database: Extend problem 6-4 by implementing a business rule of having sufficient inventory for high demand products (i.e. products that have been ordered in quantities of more than 3). For such products increment the reorder_qty of these products by 3. Save the PL/SQL anonymous block program unit as a script file.

6-14. Outdoor Clubs database: Extend problem 6-5 by implementing a business rule of not carrying products that have low demand. Consequently, the program unit will reduce the price of products that have low demand by $1. Save the PL/SQL anonymous block program unit as a script file.

6-15: Outdoor Clubs database: Extend problem 6-5 by implementing a business rule to stop carrying products that have low demand. So, once the report is displayed delete products that have low demand. Make sure all related tables also have those products references deleted.

Chapter 7. PL/SQL Stored Programs

PL/SQL stored program units in the database are identified by their name and type. The anonymous PL/SQL block program unit structure of chapter 6 is extended by giving it a name and specifying its type. This chapter introduces the PL/SQL stored procedure, function, packages, and triggers, along with an explanation of the exception section of the PL/SQL block and dynamic SQL[1]. There are many examples in the chapter that are numbered for quick reference.

PL/SQL Procedure

A PL/SQL stored procedure is a named PL/SQL block structure that is stored on the database server. It can receive multiple input parameters (values), can return multiple output values, or can return no output values. A procedure is defined through the header statement attached to a PL/SQL block. The general syntax of a stored procedure is:

```
CREATE [OR REPLACE] PROCEDURE procedure-name
    [( parameter1 mode datatype, parameter2 mode datatype, ...)] {IS|AS}
... declaration statements ...
BEGIN
... pl/sql program statements ...
END;
```

The procedure-name must conform to the Oracle naming standard. The parameter list is optional. *Parameters* can be variables or constants. The *parameter mode* defines how the parameter values can be accessed in the program unit. Parameter modes can be "in," "out," or "in out." Table 7-1 describes these different modes.

Parameter Mode	Description
IN	Parameter is passed to the procedure as a read-only (input) value that cannot be changed in the program unit.
OUT	Parameter is passed to the procedure as a write-only (output) variable. It can appear on the left side of an assignment statement in the program unit.
IN OUT	Combination of IN and OUT modes. The parameter value is passed with some input value which can then be changed in the program unit as an assignment variable.

Table 7-1: Procedure Parameter Modes

A parameter can be declared with no mode specification, in which case the default is "in" mode. The parameter data type does not require a data type size precision. The following program units illustrate the procedure concept.

1. Create a procedure auto_list that lists the auto_make and auto_model attribute values of all automobiles listed in the tenant_auto table that belong to model year (auto_year attribute) 2000 and beyond. (Note: The procedure has no parameter).

---

[1] This lesson utilizes tables from Superflex Apartment database (refer Appendix A).

```
create or replace procedure auto_list is
cursor auto_cursor is
  select auto_make, auto_model
  from tenant_auto
  where auto_year > 1999;
auto_row auto_cursor%rowtype;
begin
open auto_cursor;
loop
 fetch auto_cursor into auto_row;
 exit when auto_cursor%notfound;
 dbms_output.put_line('Make is '||auto_row.auto_make||
           ' and model is '||auto_row.auto_model);
end loop;
close auto_cursor;
end;
```

2. Create a procedure auto_list2 that lists the auto_make and auto_model attribute values of all automobiles listed in the tenant_auto table that belong to some input model year (auto_year attribute) and beyond. (Note: The procedure has an input parameter that is used in the search condition of the explicit cursor query).

```
create or replace procedure auto_list2 (year_in in number) is
cursor auto_cursor is
  select auto_make, auto_model
  from tenant_auto
  where auto_year > year_in;
auto_row auto_cursor%rowtype;
begin
open auto_cursor;
loop
 fetch auto_cursor into auto_row;
 exit when auto_cursor%notfound;
 dbms_output.put_line('Make is '||auto_row.auto_make||
           ' and model is '||auto_row.auto_model);
end loop;
close auto_cursor;
end;
```

3. Create a procedure auto_list3 that lists the auto_make and auto_model attribute values of all automobiles listed in the tenant_auto table that belong to some input model year (auto_year attribute) and beyond. The procedure also returns the values of auto_make and auto_model attributes. (Note: The procedure has an input parameter that is used in the search condition of the explicit cursor query, and two output parameters that will contain the values of the auto_make and auto_model attributes).

```
create or replace procedure auto_list3
          (year_in IN number, make_out OUT varchar2,
              model_out OUT varchar2) IS
cursor auto_cursor is
  select auto_make, auto_model
  from tenant_auto
  where auto_year > year_in;
auto_row auto_cursor%rowtype;
begin
for auto_row in auto_cursor
loop
 make_out := auto_row.auto_make;
 model_out := auto_row.auto_model;
 dbms_output.put_line('Make is '||make_out||
           ' and model is '||model_out);
end loop;
```

```
end;
```

4. Create a procedure complaint_status with two input parameters representing complaint_no and status attributes of complaints table. The procedure updates the status attribute value for the input complaint_no when the input status value is different from the stored value.

```
create or replace procedure complaint_status (complaint_in IN number,
                                              status_in IN varchar2) AS
status_out complaints.status%type;
begin
select status
into status_out
from complaints
where complaint_no = complaint_in;
if status_out = status_in then
dbms_output.put_line('Update not required.');
else
update complaints
set status = status_in
where complaint_no = complaint_in;
dbms_output.put_line('Update completed.');
end if;
commit;
end;
```

Call Procedure from another PL/SQL Program Unit

Procedures communicate with other program units. This communication occurs when a procedure is called from another PL/SQL program unit or application. The call to a procedure from another PL/SQL program unit involves the name of the procedure and its parameters. The syntax is:

```
procedure name [(parameter1, parameter2, ...)];
```

It is important that the same number of parameters are included when calling a procedure as in the definition of the procedure. Also, the sequence of the parameter data types during the calling of the procedure should match the sequence of the parameter data types listed in the procedure definition. Figure 7-1 illustrates the concept of PL/SQL procedures interacting with each other.

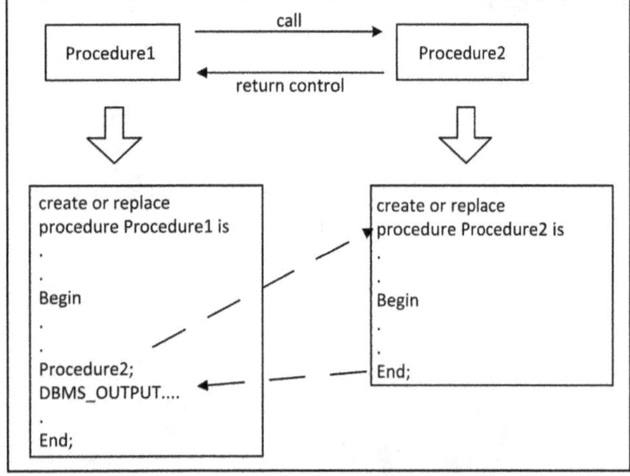

Figure 7-1: Interaction among PL/SQL Procedures

5. Create a procedure calling_procedure that calls the procedures auto_list, auto_list2, and auto_list3 outlined in previous examples. Define local variables to display the output mode parameter of auto_list3.

```
create or replace procedure calling_procedure IS
auto_out1 tenant_auto.auto_make%type;
auto_out2 tenant_auto.auto_model%type;
begin
dbms_output.put_line('Start auto_list procedure');
auto_list;
dbms_output.put_line('Start auto_list2 procedure');
auto_list2(1999);
dbms_output.put_line('Start auto_list3 procedure');
auto_list3(1999, auto_out1, auto_out2);
dbms_output.put_line('Value of auto_out1 is '||auto_out1);
dbms_output.put_line('Value of auto_out2 is '||auto_out2);
end;
```

PL/SQL Function

A PL/SQL stored function is a named PL/SQL block on the server like a procedure, except that it *returns a single value* that is assigned to a variable in the calling program unit. It can receive multiple input parameters (values). A function is defined through the header statement attached to a PL/SQL block. The general syntax of a function is:

```
CREATE [OR REPLACE] FUNCTION function-name
            (parameter1 mode datatype, parameter2 mode datatype, ...)]
            RETURN datatype IS
... declaration statements ...
BEGIN
... pl/sql program statements ...
RETURN return-value;
END;
```

The function-name must conform to the Oracle naming standard. The parameter list is optional. The *parameters*, their *modes*, and their working is similar to procedures (refer Table 7-1). Along with the parameter list, the header statement has a *return* keyword followed by the data type of the value that will be returned by the function. There must be at least one "return" keyword clause in the body of the function. The following program unit illustrates the creation of function.

6. Create a function tenant_function with one input parameter. The input parameter is the tenant_ss attribute value in tenant table. The function returns the tenant_name value for the input tenant_ss attribute value.

```
create or replace function tenant_function (ss_in in number)
  return varchar2 IS
name_in tenant.tenant_name%type;
begin
select tenant_name
into name_in
from tenant
where tenant_ss = ss_in;
return name_in;
end;
```

A function is called by another program unit (procedure or function) either (i) through the assignment statement or (ii) as a substitute for a value that has to be placed in the calling program unit. The syntax of calling a function through the assignment statement is "variable := function-name [(parameter1, ...)]." The syntax of calling a function as a substitute for value is "function-name [(parameter1, ...)]." The number and sequence of the parameter data types during the calling of the function should match the sequence of the parameter data types listed in function definition. The following example illustrates the calling of a function by a procedure.

7. Create a procedure auto_tenant_list that lists the Auto_make, auto_model, and tenant_name attribute values for all automobiles that belong to model year (auto_year attribute) 2000 and beyond. The procedure calls the function tenant_function outlined in example 6 to get the tenant name.

```
create or replace procedure auto_tenant_list IS
cursor auto_cursor is
  select auto_make, auto_model, tenant_ss
  from tenant_auto
  where auto_year > 1999;
auto_row auto_cursor%rowtype;
tenant_in tenant.tenant_name%type;
begin
open auto_cursor;
loop
 fetch auto_cursor into auto_row;
 exit when auto_cursor%notfound;
 tenant_in := tenant_function(auto_row.tenant_ss);
 dbms_output.put_line('Make '||auto_row.auto_make|| ' and model ' ||
         auto_row.auto_model || ' is for '|| tenant_in);
end loop;
close auto_cursor;
end;
```

Boolean Function

Boolean functions are special type of functions that do not return a value. Instead, they return status condition as "true" or "false." The boolean function requires the function header to contain the return data type as boolean. Also, in the body of the function the return statement should be followed by either "true" or "false" keyword. The boolean function syntax is:

```
CREATE [OR REPLACE] FUNCTION function-name [(parameter1 mode datatype,
                             parameter2 mode datatype,...)]
                             RETURN BOOLEAN IS
... declaration statements ...
BEGIN
... pl/sql program statements ...
RETURN {TRUE | FALSE};
END;
```

8. Create a boolean function tenant_boolean_func with one input parameter. The input parameter is the tenant_ss attribute value in the tenant table. The function returns status "true" or "false" depending on whether there is a tenant name in the tenant table.

```
create or replace function tenant_boolean_func (ss_in IN number)
        return boolean is
```

```
cursor tenant_cursor is
select tenant_name
from tenant
where tenant_ss = ss_in;
tenant_row tenant_cursor%rowtype;
begin
open tenant_cursor;
fetch tenant_cursor into tenant_row;
if tenant_cursor%found then
return true;
else return false;
end if;
close tenant_cursor;
end;
```

Boolean functions are called from other program units through (i) the condition of an if/then statement, or (ii) declaring a variable of data type boolean, and then assigning the boolean function to the boolean variable and thereafter checking if the boolean variable value is true or false . For instance, if the following PL/SQL selection statement is entered in the calling program unit, the condition will be true if the boolean function returns a "true" status value.

```
IF tenant_boolean_func THEN
... pl/sql statements...;
END IF;
```

On the other hand, if the following PL/SQL selection statement is entered in the calling program unit, the condition will be true if the boolean function returns a "false" status value.

```
IF NOT(tenant_boolean_func) THEN
... pl/sql statements...;
END IF;
```

9. Create a procedure check_tenant with one input parameter that calls the boolean function tenant_boolean_func outlined in example 8 to display a message on whether the tenant exists or not.

Version 1:
```
create or replace procedure check_tenant (ss_in number) is
begin
if tenant_boolean_func(ss_in) then
dbms_output.put_line('Tenant Exists');
else
dbms_output.put_line('Tenant Does Not Exist');
end if;
end;
```

Version 2:
```
create or replace procedure check_tenant (tenant_ss_in number) is
tname boolean;
begin
tname := tenant_boolean_func(tenant_ss_in);
if tname = true then
 dbms_output.put_line('Tenant Exists');
else
 dbms_output.put_line('Tenant Does Not Exists');
end if;
end;
```

Inline Function

It is possible to use functions directly in SQL query statements. Such functions are referred as *inline functions*. In order to develop inline functions some basic rules have to be followed:

- The function must use only "in" parameter mode.
- The data types of the function input parameter values, and the function return values must correspond to the Oracle database data type – eg. varchar2, char, number, date, and so on.
- Function must be stored in the database as a database object.

10. Create a function age with one input parameter that calculates the age of a person. The input parameter will have a date data type.

```
create or replace function age (input_date in date) return number IS
computed_age number;
begin
computed_age := trunc((sysdate - input_date)/365);
return computed_age;
end;
```

The function age calculates a person's age by subtracting the date of birth from the current system date, and then dividing the result by 365. Since the calculation can contain decimals, the trunc SQL function is used. The use of the function in a SQL query statement is as follows:

```
select tenant_name, age(tenant_dob)
from tenant;
```

PL/SQL Package

A PL/SQL package is a collection of logically related procedures and functions. It is like a code library that performs related tasks. A PL/SQL package consists of two separate source components – the *package specification*, and *package body*. The package name in the package specification source must be the same as the package name in the package body source.

Package Specification

The package specification is the public interface of the package. It is also called the package header, and contains definitions of variables, procedures, functions, exceptions, cursors, types that are included in the package body. The elements of a package specification (variables, cursors, procedures, functions) can be defined in any order. The syntax of package specification is:

```
CREATE [OR REPLACE] PACKAGE package-name IS
[... variable declarations ...]
[... procedure definitions ...]
[... function definitions ...]
END;
```

The variables in the package specification can be referenced by any program within the package. Variables can also include cursor variables. Variables in a package specification are defined similar to their declaration in a PL/SQL block. For example, count1 number(2). Cursors in a package specification are defined similar to any explicit cursor declaration in a PL/SQL block. For example,

```
cursor package_cursor is
select auto_make, auto_model, auto_year, auto_color
from tenant_auto;
```

Procedure definition in a package involves the listing of the procedure header or definition statement line. For example,

```
PROCEDURE auto_list2 (year_in IN number);
PROCEDURE auto_tenant_list;
```

Function definition in a package involves the listing of the function header or definition statement line. For example,

```
FUNCTION tenant_function (ss_in IN number) RETURN varchar2;
```

The definitions of procedures and functions in a package specification are called *forward declarations*, because the program unit definitions are only declared here. The actual program unit source is described in the package body. Following is a package specification for a package titled sample_package.

```
create or replace package sample_package IS
count1 number(2);
cursor package_cursor is
  select auto_make, auto_model, auto_year, auto_color
  from tenant_auto;
procedure auto_list2 (year_in in number);
procedure auto_tenant_list;
function tenant_function (ss_in in number) return varchar2;
end;
```

Package Body

The package body contains the source of the program units declared in the package specification. The package body must be created using the package name of an existing package specification. The same name ties the specification and the body units together. In addition, all procedure and function definition statements must match exactly with their corresponding declarations in the package specification. Also, *package specification should be created before the package body*, otherwise an error will occur. The package body is optional, because sometimes a package contains only variable declarations and no other program units. The syntax of package body is:

```
CREATE [OR REPLACE] PACKAGE BODY  package-name  IS
[... variable declarations ...]
[... cursor definitions ...]
[... named program unit blocks ...]
END;
```

In the syntax, the package-name is name of the package defined in the package specification source component. Variables and cursors declared in the beginning of package body are private to the package body program units. Each named program unit like procedure or function can have its own variable or cursor declarations. However such declarations are local to only that program unit. The following is a description of the package body of a package titled sample_package. The package specification of sample_package has already been defined in package specification subsection.

```
create or replace package body sample_package is
```

```
procedure auto_list2 (year_in in number) is
cursor auto_cursor is
  select auto_make, auto_model from tenant_auto
  where auto_year > year_in;
auto_row auto_cursor%rowtype;
begin
for auto_row in auto_cursor
loop
dbms_output.put_line('Make is '||auto_row.auto_make||
   ' and model is '||auto_row.auto_model);
end loop;
end;

procedure auto_tenant_list is
cursor auto_cursor is
  select auto_make, auto_model, tenant_ss from tenant_auto
  where auto_year > 1999;
auto_row auto_cursor%rowtype;
tenant_in tenant.tenant_name%type;
begin
for auto_row in auto_cursor
loop
tenant_in := tenant_function(auto_row.tenant_ss);
dbms_output.put_line('Make '||auto_row.auto_make|| ' and model ' ||
     auto_row.auto_model || 'is for '|| tenant_in);
end loop;
end;

function tenant_function (ss_in in number) return varchar2 is
name_in tenant.tenant_name%type;
begin
select tenant_name into name_in
from tenant
where tenant_ss = ss_in;
return name_in;
end;
end;
```

Programs within a package are accessed through the convention *package-name.package-specification-program*. For example Figure 7-2 shows a variable tenant_name in a program unit that is assigned the return value of the function tenant_function within the package sample_package.

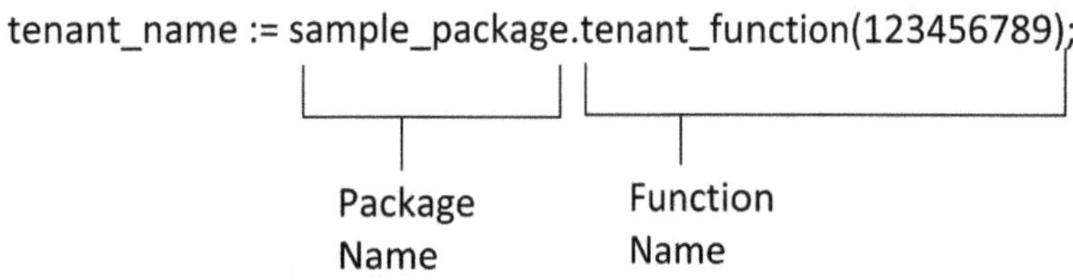

Figure 7-2: Access Package Programs

Package program units can have *public* or *private* scope. Any definition declared in the package specification component is considered public, which means that it can be referenced from outside of the package by other program units. On the other hand, definitions are considered private if they can be called only from other program units within the same package.

Exceptions

Exceptions are optional runtime error handling statements defined after the exception keyword in the executable section of a PL/SQL program unit. When an error occurs during the execution of a PL/SQL program unit, an exception is raised. Immediately, the logic control of the program unit is transferred to the exception section of the program unit.

Exceptions are classified in two broad categories – system exceptions and user-defined exceptions. Figure 7-3 illustrates the two categories.

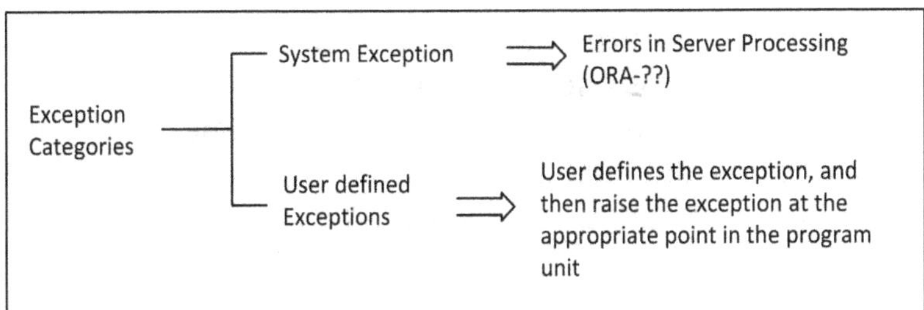

Figure 7-3: Exception Category

System exceptions are raised implicitly (automatically), and they correspond to errors during database processing. Errors generated by the Oracle database server during processing have an ORA prefix. System exceptions are of two types – predefined exception and undefined exception. User defined exceptions also work in the same manner, except that the user has to define the exception first, and then utilize a raise statement to generate an exception at the appropriate point in the program unit.

The syntax for handling exceptions within a PL/SQL block is shown in Figure 7-4. In the figure exception-name1, exception-name2, and so on entries refer to the exception names. Oracle database errors that have not been given exception names can be handled using the When Others clause in the exception section.

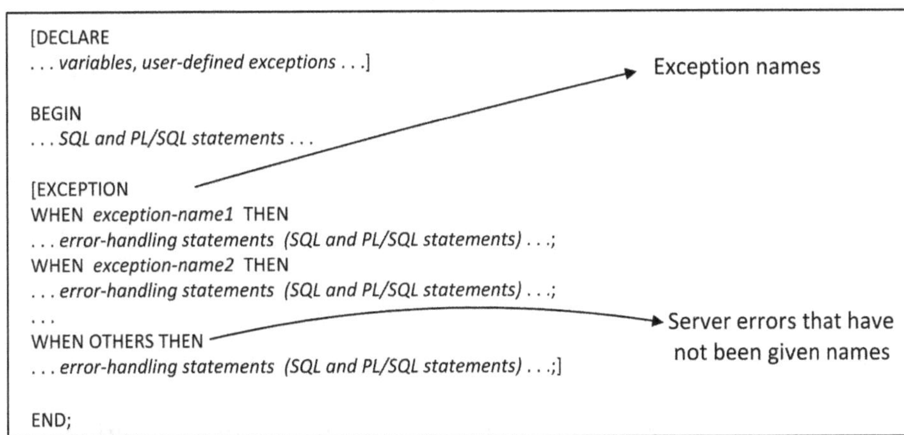

Figure 7-4: Handling Exceptions

Predefined Exceptions

Predefined exceptions are names (called as exception name) given to common server errors that already have been recognized by Oracle. To following Table 7-2 provides a sample list of some of the common server errors and their respective exception names.

Server Error Number	Exception Name	Description
ORA-00001	DUP_VAL_ON_INDEX	Unique constraint on primary key violated.
ORA-01403	NO_DATA_FOUND	Query returns no records.
ORA-01422	TOO_MANY_ROWS	Query returns more rows than expected.
ORA-06502	VALUE_ERROR	Error in truncation, arithmetic, or conversion operation.

Table 7-2: Sample Predefined Exceptions

To facilitate display of server errors that are not listed in the When clause, two predefined functions sqlcode and sqlerrm can be utilized. Function sqlcode returns the error number, while the function sqlerrm returns the message description associated with the error. If a SQL statement executes successfully, sqlcode is equal to "0" and sqlerrm contains the string "ORA-0000: normal, successful completion." The following program units illustrate the utilization of predefined exceptions to handle runtime errors in a PL/SQL program unit.

11. Create a procedure exception_test1 that inserts a row in the staff table.

```
create or replace procedure exception_test1 IS
begin
insert into staff (staff_no, first_name, last_name)
values ('SA230', 'Kane', 'Chin');
commit;
dbms_output.put_line('Row Inserted');
end;
```

Since the staff_no (primary key) value in the Insert statement is already existing in the staff table, an Oracle runtime error ORA-00001: unique constraint violated occurs.

The procedure exception_test1 is now modified with the exception section as shown below. The exception name dup_val_on_index corresponds to the ORA-00001 server error.

```
create or replace procedure exception_test1 IS
begin
insert into staff (staff_no, first_name, last_name)
values ('SA230', 'Kane', 'Chin');
commit;
dbms_output.put_line('Row Inserted');
exception
  when dup_val_on_index then
  dbms_output.put_line('Duplicate Primary Key Value.');
  dbms_output.put_line('Correct Insert Statement.');
end;
```

The execution of the modified exception_test1 procedure with the use of exception section now displays the following dbms_output message:

```
Duplicate Primary Key Value.
Correct Insert Statement.
```

12. Create a procedure exception_test2 that queries the staff table with wrong staff_no attribute value.

The procedure utilizes the sqlerrm function. To utilize the sqlerrm function, a variable having varchar2 data type with maximum length of 512 is declared. This length is necessary, as the maximum length of an Oracle error message is 512.

```
create or replace procedure exception_test2 IS
  staff_in staff.staff_no%type;
  first_in staff.first_name%type;
  last_in staff.last_name%type;
  error_message varchar2(512);
begin
select staff_no, first_name, last_name
into staff_in, first_in, last_in
from staff
where staff_no = 'SA340';
dbms_output.put_line('Row Found');
exception
  when too_many_rows then
  dbms_output.put_line('Too Many Rows.');
  dbms_output.put_line('Correct Query Statement.');
  when others then
  error_message := sqlerrm;
  dbms_output.put_line('Program encountered the following error:');
  dbms_output.put_line(error_message);
end;
```

The procedure runtime now displays the following message:

```
Program encountered the following error:
ORA-01403: no data found
```

Undefined Exceptions

Undefined exceptions are those server errors that do not have a predefined exception name. To utilize undefined exceptions, exception details must be first defined in the declaration section of the program unit. During this definition process the exception name is associated with a specific server error number. Then the exception can be called in the exception section of the program unit the same way as a predefined exception. The syntax to declare an undefined exception in a PL/SQL block is:

```
DECLARE
. . . variables, . . .
exception-name  EXCEPTION;
PRAGMA EXCEPTION_INIT( exception-name, Oracle-error-number );
```

Pragma is a keyword that is used to provide an instruction to the compiler. The exception-name is an Oracle variable. The Oracle-error-number is the Oracle server error number that must have the prefix hyphen (-) before the error number. The leading zeros of the error number can be ignored.

13. Create a procedure exception_test3 that inserts a row in the complaints table.

```
create or replace procedure exception_test3 IS
error_message varchar2(512);
begin
insert into complaints (complaint_no,complaint_date, rental_no)
values (complaints_sequence.nextval,sysdate,100108);
commit;
```

```
dbms_output.put_line('Row Inserted');
exception
  when dup_val_on_index then
  dbms_output.put_line('Duplicate Primary Key Value.');
  dbms_output.put_line('Correct Insert Statement.');
  when others then
  error_message := sqlerrm;
  dbms_output.put_line('Program encountered the following error:');
  dbms_output.put_line(error_message);
end;
```

The procedure is tested with a wrong foreign key value for the rental_no attribute to ensure that it generates a run time error message ORA-02291: integrity constraint violated - parent key not found.

Since the runtime server error is not a predefined exception server error, the undefined exception approach can be utilized. The procedure exception_test3 is now modified to include the undefined exception to trap the Oracle error number ORA-02291.

```
create or replace procedure exception_test3 IS
e_foreign_key_error EXCEPTION;
PRAGMA EXCEPTION_INIT(e_foreign_key_error, -2291);
error_message varchar2(512);
begin
insert into complaints (complaint_no,complaint_date,rental_no)
values(complaints_sequence.nextval,sysdate,100108);
commit;
dbms_output.put_line('Row Inserted');
exception
when e_foreign_key_error then
dbms_output.put_line('Wrong Foreign Key Value.');
dbms_output.put_line('Correct Insert Statement.');
when dup_val_on_index then
dbms_output.put_line('Duplicate Primary Key Value.');
dbms_output.put_line('Correct Insert Statement.');
when others then
error_message := sqlerrm;
dbms_output.put_line('Program encountered the following error:');
dbms_output.put_line(error_message);
end;
```

The procedure runtime now displays the following message:

```
Wrong Foreign Key Value.
Correct Insert Statement.
```

User-Defined Exceptions

User-defined exceptions are those exceptions that are not caused due to server errors, but rather due to non-enforcement of business rules or integrity of the database. User-defined exceptions have to be defined in the declaration section of the program unit through the syntax *exception-name exception*, where the exception-name is an Oracle variable. The user-defined exception is raised through the statement *raise exception-name* in the executable section of the program unit.

Once user-defined exceptions have been declared, they are generally invoked through the PL/SQL selection statements. The syntax of a PL/SQL block with user-defined exception is shown below.

```
DECLARE
. . . variables . . .
exception-name1 EXCEPTION;
BEGIN
. . . SQL and PL/SQL statements . . .
IF condition THEN
  RAISE exception-name1;
END IF;
. . .
[EXCEPTION
WHEN exception-name1 THEN
. . . error-handling statements (SQL and PL/SQL statements) . . .;
WHEN exception-name2 THEN
. . . error-handling statements (SQL and PL/SQL statements) . . .;
. . .
WHEN OTHERS THEN
. . . error-handling statements (SQL and PL/SQL statements) . . .;]
END;
```

14. Create a procedure exception_test4 that updates the employer_name attribute with null value in the tenant table.

The procedure validates a business rule that a tenant must be employed (i.e. must have an employer_name attribute value). So, if a SQL update statement assigns a null value to the employer_name attribute, it will violate the business rule, resulting in the raising of the associated exception (e_employer).

```
create or replace procedure exception_test4
        (tenant_in number, employer varchar2 default null) IS
e_employer_error exception;
employer_out varchar2(5);
error_message varchar2(512);
begin
update tenant
set employer_name = employer
where tenant_ss = tenant_in;
select employer_name into employer_out
from tenant where tenant_ss = tenant_in;
if employer_out is null then
  raise e_employer_error;
else commit;
end if;
exception
  when e_employer_error then
  dbms_output.put_line('A tenant must have an employer.');
  dbms_output.put_line('The Update is void.');
  when others then
  error_message := sqlerrm;
  dbms_output.put_line('Program encountered the following error:');
  dbms_output.put_line(error_message);
end;
```

The procedure runtime below will display the message below the anonymous block:

```
begin
```

```
exception_test4(723556089);
end;

A tenant must have an employer.
The Update is void.
```

Exception Usage

Unlike many programming languages where a run-time error such as stack overflow or division by zero stops normal processing and returns control to the operating system, exception handling mechanism in PL/SQL "bulletproofs" the PL/SQL program units in a way that it can continue operating in the presence of errors. This is achieved by placing PL/SQL anonymous block program units inside stored program units as shown in Figure 7-5.

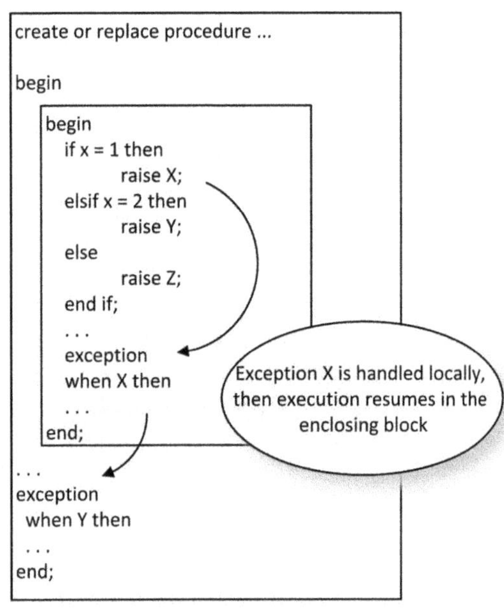

Figure 7-5: Exception Usage

When an exception is raised, PL/SQL looks for the exception handler inside the enclosed anonymous block unit first, closes the current block, and the program continues in the outer block unit from the next statement. If there is no exception handler in the enclosed anonymous block, PL/SQL exits the enclosed block and looks for it in the outer block, i.e. the exception reproduces itself in successive enclosing blocks until a handler is found or there are no more blocks to search. In the latter case, PL/SQL returns an unhandled exception error to the host environment.

Using exceptions in program units for error handling have several benefits.

- Without exception handling, every time a SQL statement is executed, one may have to check for execution errors:

```
BEGIN
SELECT ...
-- check for 'no data found' error
SELECT ...
-- check for 'no data found' error
SELECT ...
```

-- check for 'no data found' error

In this case, as error processing is not clearly separated from normal processing, it can complicate the logic flow.

- Exceptions improve readability by isolating error-handling routines.
- Exceptions improve reliability. One need not check for an error at every point it might occur. Just add an exception handler in the PL/SQL block. If the exception is ever raised in that block (or any sub-block), it will be handled.

15. Create a procedure exception_test5 that inserts a row in the staff table.

The procedure contains an anonymous block program unit. The anonymous block program unit inserts a row in the staff table. During procedure execution, the anonymous block program unit generates a runtime error. The exception handler of the anonymous block program unit is executed, and the control is transferred to the statement in the procedure after the anonymous block program unit. The procedure query is thereafter executed and the associated message displayed.

```
create or replace procedure exception_test5 is
staff_in staff.staff_no%type;
first_in staff.first_name%type;
last_in staff.last_name%type;
error_message varchar2(512);
begin
  begin
  insert into staff (staff_no, first_name, last_name)
  values ('SA230', 'Kane', 'Chin');
  commit;
  dbms_output.put_line('Row Inserted');
  exception
    when dup_val_on_index then
    dbms_output.put_line('Duplicate Primary Key Value.');
    dbms_output.put_line('Correct Insert Statement.');
  end;

select staff_no, first_name, last_name
into staff_in, first_in, last_in
from staff
where staff_no = 'SA240';
dbms_output.put_line('Row Found');
exception
when others then
dbms_output.put_line('Program encountered the following error:');
dbms_output.put_line(sqlerrm);
end;
```

The procedure runtime will display the following message:

```
Duplicate Primary Key Value.
Correct Insert Statement.
Row Found
```

Raise Application Error

Raise_application_error is a procedure in the built-in package dbms_standard. This procedure allows developers to create meaningful error messages for a specific application. Oracle reserves error codes in the range of -20000 to -20999 for these user-defined errors. The syntax is:

RAISE_APPLICATION_ERROR(error-number, error-message, [keep-errors]);

Parameter error-number is the number of the error that a developer associates with a specific error message. This can be any number between -20999 and -20000. The error-message parameter is the text of the error, and it can contain up to 512 characters. The optional parameter keep-errors is a boolean parameter. If keep-errors is set to "true," the new error will be added to the list of errors that has been raised already. If keep-errors is set to "false," the new error replaces the list of errors that has been raised already. The default value for the parameter keep-errors is "false."

Figure 7-6 illustrates the use of the syntax. The raise_application_error procedure works with user-defined exceptions. It associates the number of the error with the text of the error. Therefore, as an exception, it does not have a specific name associated with it. Raise_application_error procedure is useful for the following reasons:

- Ability to provide customized error messages.
- Ability to transfer error messages just like server errors to third party programs accessing the database (if dbms_output is limited to PL/SQL editors).
- Ability to invoke error handling from anywhere in the program.
- Rollback a transaction from a database trigger (explained in the next lesson).

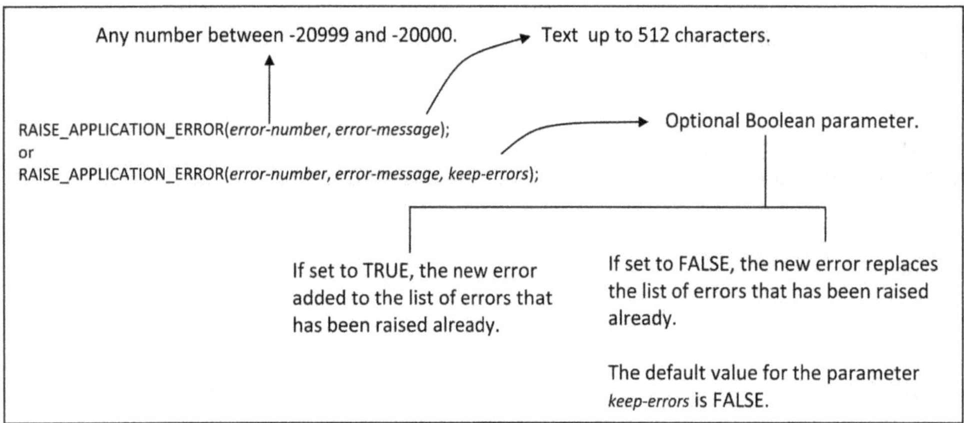

Figure 7-6: Raise_Application_Error specifications

The following program units illustrate the utilization of raise_application_error procedure.

16. Create a procedure cc_count that displays a count of the number of times a credit card has been used for rental payment.

    In the procedure, the raise_application_error text is displayed if the procedure is executed with an input parameter value that is not "visa," "mastercard" or "discover."

```
create or replace procedure cc_count (cc_type_in in varchar2) IS
count_in number(3);
```

```
begin
if (cc_type_in in ('visa','mastercard','discover')) then
select count(*)
into count_in
from rental_invoice
where cc_type = cc_type_in;
dbms_output.put_line(cc_type_in||' has be used '||count_in||' times.');
else
raise_application_error(-20000,'Wrong input value');
end if;
end;
```

17. Create a procedure employers that displays a specific tenant's employer_name attribute value.

    In the procedure, the raise_application_error message is displayed if the procedure is executed with an input parameter that is not a valid tenant_name attribute value. The procedure illustrates the placing of raise_application_error procedure within a predefined exception.

```
create or replace procedure employers (tenant_name_in in varchar2) IS
emp1 varchar2(20);
begin
select employer_name into emp1
from tenant
where tenant_name=tenant_name_in;
dbms_output.put_line(emp1);
exception
when no_data_found then
raise_application_error(-20001,'Wrong input value');
end;
```

18. Create a procedure kraft_employers that displays a specific tenant's employer_name attribute value.

    The procedure displays the raise_application_error message if the input parameter tenant_name attribute value has an employer_name value of "MSU." The procedure illustrates the placing of raise_application_error procedure with user-defined exception in the exception section of the program unit.

```
create or replace procedure kraft_employers (tenant_name_in in varchar2) IS
emp1 varchar2(20);
error2 exception;
begin
select employer_name into emp1
from tenant
where tenant_name=tenant_name_in;
dbms_output.put_line(emp1);
if emp1 = 'MSU' then
raise error2;
end if;
exception
when no_data_found then
raise_application_error(-20001,'Wrong input value');
when error2 then
raise_application_error(-20001,'Wrong Employer');
end;
```

Database Trigger

A trigger is a named PL/SQL program unit that is stored in the database and executed in response to a specific database event. The specific event is associated with either a table, a view, a schema, or the database, and is one of the following:

- A database manipulation (DML) statement on table (delete, insert, or update).
- A database definition (DDL) statement (create, alter, or drop).
- A database operation (servererror, logon, logoff, startup, or shutdown).

Triggers are used for different purposes like:

- Enforcing referential integrity.
- Enforcing complex business rules that cannot be defined by using integrity constraints.
- Maintaining complex security rules.
- Automatically generating values for derived columns.
- Collecting statistical information on table access.
- Preventing invalid transactions.
- Providing value auditing.

Triggers are quite different from the procedures, functions, or packages that are explicitly called by name for execution. Unlike the other PL/SQL program units which are independent of database tables, triggers are always associated with and attached to database tables. Besides, database triggers cannot accept input parameters. The size of the trigger cannot be more than 32K.

Triggers are executed (referred as *fired*) only when the triggering event occurs. When a trigger fires, all operations performed become part of the transaction. For example, if a trigger program unit has been defined to fire before a SQL Insert statement on the rental table, this trigger fires every time an insert operation is performed on the table. A trigger can fire at exactly one of the following timing points:

- Before the triggering statement executes.
- After the triggering statement executes.
- Before each row that the triggering statement affects.
- After each row that the triggering statement affects.

Table Trigger

Trigger on database table are program units attached to the table. Its definition includes specification of the trigger event associated with the database table, trigger timing, and trigger levels. Figure 7-7 provides a schematic view of the elements in a trigger definition.

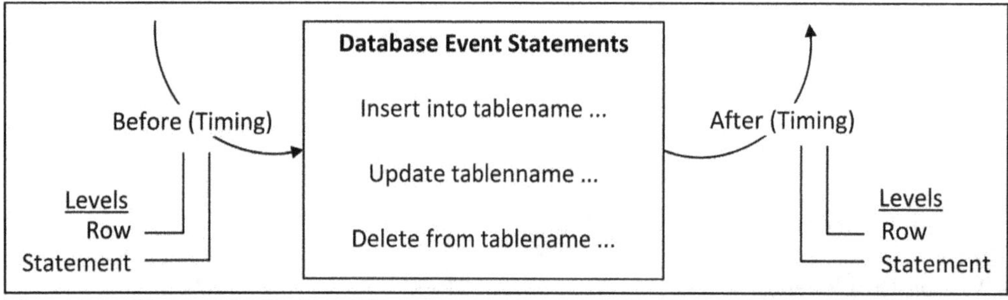

Figure 7-7: Trigger Definition Elements

A DML trigger is associated with the DML event that is applied to a table. Consequently, the trigger is fired (or executed) when the DML statement on the table is executed. One can specify multiple DML statements together in the syntax, or just one.

Trigger timing refers to the time when the execution of the trigger will occur. There are two sets of timings associated through the *before* and *after* keywords. The "before" timing in the trigger definition implies that the trigger will be fired prior to the completion of the trigger database event (insert, update, or delete operation). The "after" timing in the trigger definition implies that the trigger will be fired after the actual trigger database event (insert, update, or delete operation) is completed.

There are two levels of triggers associated with the scope of a trigger. These levels are generally referred as *row* and *statement* levels. "Row" level trigger fires for each row affected by the associated trigger database event. The "statement" trigger fires only once per associated database event. The default is "statement" level.

For example, if the trigger is defined as a "row" level trigger, then during the database event associated with say a SQL Update statement, one can have the trigger fire once for each row that is being updated. So if the update affects 20 rows, the trigger will fire 20 times. On the other hand, if the trigger is defined as a "statement" level trigger, then it would fire just once for the SQL Update statement. In other words, even if the update operation is updating 20 rows, the trigger will fire just once. Figure 7-8 provides a schematic view of the difference between a "statement" and "row" level triggers.

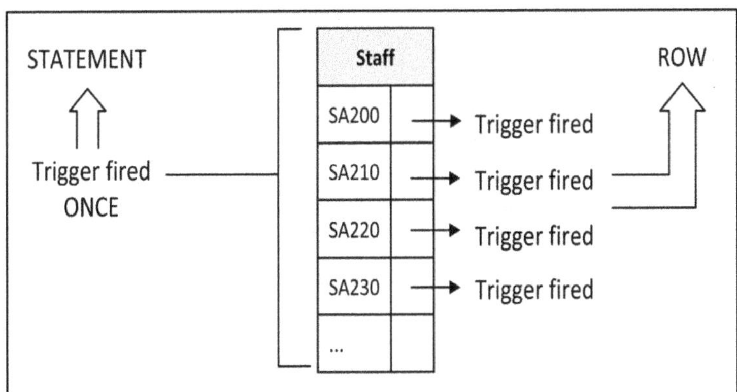

Figure 7-8: Scope of Statement level and Row level Trigger

Table 7-3 summarizes the elements in trigger definition.

Element	Values	Description
Event	INSERT, UPDATE, DELETE	Statement that causes trigger to fire
Timing	BEFORE, AFTER	Timing of whether trigger fires before or after the event
Level	ROW, STATEMENT	Whether trigger fires once for each triggering event statement, or once for each affected row by the triggering event statement

Table 7-3: Trigger Definition Details

The general syntax for creating a trigger is:

```
CREATE [OR REPLACE] TRIGGER trigger-name
[BEFORE | AFTER | INSTEAD OF]
[INSERT | DELETE | UPDATE [OF attribute1 [,attribute2[, ...] ] ] ]
ON [tablename | viewname]
[COMPOUND TRIGGER]
[FOLLOWS trigger-name2]
[ENABLE | DISABLE]
[ REFERENCING {OLD [AS] old-name [NEW [AS] new-name]
        | NEW [AS] new-name [OLD [AS] old-name] } ]
[FOR EACH ROW]
[WHEN (condition)]
DECLARE
...
BEGIN
... pl/sql statements ...
END;
```

- The BEFORE keyword implies that the trigger fires before executing the triggering event statement, while the AFTER keyword implies that the trigger fires after executing the triggering event statement. The INSTEAD OF keyword implies that the trigger is on database views (discussed later).
- The DELETE keyword indicates that the triggering event is a SQL Delete statement; the INSERT keyword indicates that the triggering event is a SQL Insert statement; the UPDATE [OF attribute1, ...] keyword indicates that the triggering event is a SQL Update statement that may also be associated optionally with the columns or attributes listed.
- The tablename entry is the name of the table on which the trigger is defined. The viewname is the name of the database view on which the trigger is defined. For triggers on database views, the trigger type must be defined as "instead of."
- The COMPOUND TRIGGER option allows the trigger to fire at more than one timing point. Compound triggers make it easier to program an approach where you want the actions you implement for the various timing points to share common data. A compound trigger has a declaration section and a section for each of its timing points.
- The FOLLOWS trigger-name2 clause specifies the relative firing order of triggers of the same type. In essence this clause indicates that the trigger being created should fire after some other trigger-name2 specified trigger. The trigger-name2 specified trigger must already exist, must be defined on the same table as the current trigger being created, and must have been successfully compiled. They need not be enabled. The FOLLOWS clause in a way guarantees execution order for triggers defined with the same timing point.
- The ENABLE or DISABLE option explicitly enables or disables a trigger at creation time, with the enabled state as the default. An enabled trigger executes its trigger body if a triggering statement is entered and the trigger restriction (if any) evaluates to "true." A disabled trigger does not execute its trigger body, even if a triggering statement is entered and the trigger restriction (if any) evaluates to "true." Of course one can also issue a SQL Alter statement (outlined later in the section) to ENABLE the trigger.
- The REFERENCING keyword indicates correlation names that can be used to refer to the old and new values of the row attributes that are being affected by the trigger.
- FOR EACH ROW clause designates the trigger to be a ROW level trigger. Such a trigger is fired once for each row that is affected by the triggering event. If this clause is omitted, the trigger is a STATEMENT level trigger. A statement trigger is fired only once, when the triggering event is met.
- The WHEN condition clause specifies the trigger condition that must be satisfied for the trigger to be fired.

- There are certain restrictions that apply to statements within the execution block of the trigger. Some of these restrictions are:
  - A trigger may not issue transactional control statements like commit, savepoint, or rollback. When a trigger fires, all operations performed become part of the transaction.
  - Any function or procedure called by a trigger may not issue a transactional control statement.

In general, to reference an attribute value before the triggering event, the prefix "old" can be used like :OLD.attribute_name. For instance, if an update or delete trigger has a reference like :old.invoice_due on the rental_invoice table, it would indicate the value of invoice_due attribute prior to the change (update or delete operation). However, in the case of an insert trigger on the rental_invoice table the value of :old.invoice_due would be null, as there is no existing row prior to the SQL operation.

Similarly to reference an attribute value after the triggering event is complete the prefix "new" can be used like :NEW.attribute_name. For instance, if an update or insert trigger has a reference like :new.invoice_due on the rental_invoice table, it would indicate the value of invoice_due attribute after the change (update or insert operation). However, in the case of a delete trigger on the rental_invoice table the value of :new.invoice_due is null, as the reference row does not exist in the table after the SQL operation.

The "new" or "old" references are only allowed for "row" level triggers. They are not allowed for "Statement" level triggers. Also, the condition in the When keyword clause does not require the colon (:) prefix for new or old attribute reference. The following program units illustrate the operation of triggers.

19. Create a row level trigger staff_insert_before that fires before an insert operation on the staff table. The trigger also displays the insert attribute values.

```
create or replace trigger staff_insert_before
before insert
on staff
For each row
Begin
dbms_output.put_line('before insert of ' ||:new.first_name||' '||:new.last_name);
end;
```

The trigger can be tested with the following SQL Insert statement:

```
insert into staff (staff_no, first_name, last_name)
values ('SA400','John','Doe');
```

20. Create a statement level trigger staff_update_before that fires before an update operation on the staff table. The trigger also displays a text message.

```
create or replace trigger staff_update_before
before update
on staff
begin
dbms_output.put_line('before updating some staff ');
end;
```

The trigger can be tested with the following SQL Update statement.

```
update staff set dob = sysdate;
```

The output will show that 7 rows were updated, but still being a statement level trigger the text message will be displayed once.

21. Create a row level trigger staff_update_before that fires before an update operation on the STAFF table. The trigger also displays a text message along with the existing value of last_name attribute and the new dob attribute value.

```
create or replace trigger staff_update_before
before update
on staff
for each row
begin
dbms_output.put_line('before updating some staff '|| :old.last_name||:new.dob);
end;
```

The trigger can be tested with the following SQL Update statement.

```
update staff set dob = sysdate;
```

The output will show the dbms_output statement message and values for each row. Notice that the trigger is fired for each row that is updated.

Trigger Exceptions

Triggers become part of the transaction of a statement. So, when the transaction would raise any exceptions the whole statement is rolled back. However, in the absence of the rollback statement to block a trigger from completion, the raise application error exceptions are utilized. For instance, the following row level update trigger staff_dob on the staff table prevents any update of dob attribute value in the staff table.

```
create or replace trigger staff_dob
Before update of dob on staff
For each row
Begin
Raise_application_error(-20000,'cannot change date of birth');
End;
```

Special IF statements

A trigger can determine if it is executing because of an insert, update, or delete event with calls to special functions: *inserting*, *updating*, and *deleting*. These functions are declared in package dbms_standard. As the dbms_standard is a default package in Oracle server for each user, it is not necessary to specify the package name with the program units of that package. The package definition is as follows:

```
create [or replace] package dbms_standard is
  function inserting return boolean;
  function deleting return boolean;
  function updating return boolean;
  function updating  (column-name varchar2)  return boolean;
  . . .
end dbms_standard;
```

Inside the PL/SQL block of a trigger one can use the if/then statement to determine which statement caused the firing of the trigger. This is especially useful if the trigger is associated with multiple database events like insert, update, or delete operations in its definition. For instance, the following trigger staff_trigger_status checks these special functions.

```
create or replace trigger staff_trigger_status
before insert or update or delete on staff
for each row
Begin
if inserting then
dbms_output.put_line('inserting person: ' || :new.last_name);
elsif updating then
dbms_output.put_line('updating person: ' ||
:old.last_name || ' to ' || :new.last_name);
elsif deleting then
dbms_output.put_line('deleting person: ' || :old.last_name);
end if;
end;
```

Mutating Tables

Mutating tables is a common error (ORA-4091) if triggers are not managed properly. It is caused by "row" level triggers, because the "statement" level trigger is fired in its entirety either before or after the triggering DML statement. The mutating table error occurs when an update or delete trigger encounters a SQL Select or Update statement in the body of the trigger that references the same trigger table. However, *table mutation error does not occur for an insert trigger*. The mutating table concept is explained through the following program units.

22. Create an update trigger staff_read_mutate on the staff table that also attempts to query the staff table.

```
create or replace trigger staff_read_mutate
after update of dob on staff
for each row
declare
last_name_in staff.last_name%type;
begin
select last_name
into last_name_in
from staff
where staff_no = 'SA200';
dbms_output.put_line(last_name_in);
end;
```

Now test the trigger with the following SQL Update statement:

```
update staff
set dob = to_date('1/12/85','mm/dd/yy')
where staff_no = 'SA200';
```

Oracle SQL Developer will display the "ORA-04091: table STAFF is mutating, trigger/function may not see it" mutating table error.

23. Create an update trigger staff_update_mutate on the staff table that also attempts to update the staff table.

```
create or replace trigger staff_update_mutate
after update of dob on staff
for each row
begin
update staff
set salary = 25000
where staff_no = 'SA200';
dbms_output.put_line('Update performed');
end;
```

The trigger generates mutating table error when executing the following SQL Update statement:

```
update staff
set dob = to_date('1/12/85','mm/dd/yy')
where staff_no = 'SA200';
```

24. Create an insert trigger staff_insert_mutate on the staff table that also attempts to query and update the staff table.

```
create or replace trigger staff_insert_mutate
before insert on staff
for each row
declare
last_name_in staff.last_name%type;
begin
update staff
set dob = to_date('1/12/85','mm/dd/yy')
where staff_no = 'SA200';
select last_name
into last_name_in
from staff
where staff_no = 'SA200';
dbms_output.put_line(last_name_in);
end;
```

Now the trigger runs with no errors and generates the dbms_output message when executing the following SQL Insert statement.

```
insert into staff (staff_no, first_name, last_name)
values ('SA330', 'Kane', 'Chin');
```

WORKAROUND FOR TABLE MUTATION

Since it is possible to reference any attribute value within a row of the trigger table using the "old" or "new" prefix, one can still access attributes required by the SQL Select statement in the body of the trigger. The "old" prefix allows access to row values "before" the trigger is fired, while the "new" prefix allows access to row values "after" the trigger is fired. For instance, Example 22 trigger staff_read_mutate on the staff table is now modified to access row values from the staff table. The trigger will display the dbms_output message during an update operation.

```
create or replace trigger staff_read_mutate
after update of dob on staff
for each row
declare
last_name_in staff.last_name%type;
begin
--select last_name
```

```
--into last_name_in
--from staff
--where staff_no = 'SA200';
dbms_output.put_line(:old.last_name);
end;
```

Similarly any modification of an attribute value within a row can be done through an assignment statement instead of a SQL Update statement. For instance, Example 23 trigger staff_update_mutate on the staff table is now modified to enable change of salary value in the staff table. The trigger will display the dbms_output message during an update operation.

```
create or replace trigger staff_update_mutate
before update of dob on staff
for each row
begin
--update staff
--set salary = 25000
--where staff_no = 'SA200';
:new.salary := 25000;
dbms_output.put_line('Update performed');
dbms_output.put_line('Old Salary '||:old.salary);
dbms_output.put_line('New Salary '||:new.salary);
end;
```

MUTATING TABLES WITH DATABASE RELATIONSHIP

Another situation when table mutating error occurs is if the trigger has statements to change the primary key, foreign key or unique key columns of the table the trigger is triggering off. In this case the table mutate error is encountered when querying a table other than the table on which the trigger is based. This happens when a foreign key reference is present with an "on delete cascade" option.

A row level trigger on the parent table will mutate if the child table is being referred to in the trigger for a delete transaction. This will only happen if the foreign key in the child table is created with the on delete cascade option. No mutation occurs if the parent table is being referred in a trigger in the child table.

Implementing Business Rules through Triggers

Business rules reflect guidelines that affect data during business operations. Triggers are useful in implementing such business rules. Consider the following examples of triggers implementing business rules.

25. Create an update trigger trigger_apartment_bu on the apartment table that implements a business rule: no apartment should be rented if there are complaints pending on the apartment.

    The trigger is fired every time a change is made from 'V' to 'R' in the value of the apt_status attribute. It checks to see if there are any complaints for the apartment. If any complaint is pending, then the update is cancelled and the raise_application_error message is displayed.

```
create or replace trigger apartment_bu
before update on apartment
for each row
when (old.apt_status='V')
declare
cursor complaint_cursor is
select complaint_no,status
```

```
from complaints
where apt_no=:old.apt_no;
complaint_row complaint_cursor%rowtype;
error1 exception;
begin
for complaint_row in complaint_cursor
loop
if complaint_row.status is null then
raise error1;
end if;
end loop;
exception
when no_data_found then
dbms_output.put_line('Update Ok');
when error1 then
raise_application_error(-20100,'Update Cancelled');
end;
```

The trigger generates raise_application_error when executing the following SQL Update statement:

```
update apartment
set apt_status = 'R'
where apt_no = 103;
```

26. Create an insert trigger tenant_auto_bi on the tenant_auto table that implements a business rule: if the rental_status attribute value for the tenant is "S" then the tenant should not be allowed to have any vehicle registered for parking.

```
create or replace trigger tenant_auto_bi
before insert on tenant_auto
for each row
declare
status_t char(2);
error1 exception;
begin
select rental.rental_status into status_t
from rental,tenant
where rental.rental_no=tenant.rental_no
and tenant.tenant_ss=:new.tenant_ss;
if status_t = 'S' then
raise error1;
end if;
exception
when error1 then
raise_application_error(-20100,'Insert Cancelled');
end;
```

As rental_no 100106 has the rental_status attribute value "S" the trigger generates raise_application_error when executing the second of the following two SQL Insert statements:

```
insert into tenant (tenant_ss, tenant_name, rental_no)
values (667756789,'Tracy Austin',100106);
insert into tenant_auto (tenant_ss,license_no,auto_make,auto_model)
values (667756789,'DJK933','Lexus','RX350');
```

System Trigger

System triggers refer to triggers that are fired by DDL statements or database system events rather than DML statements. DDL events include statements like create, alter, drop, grant, and so on. The database system events include logon, logoff, startup, shutdown, and servererror. The syntax of system trigger is the same as DML statements triggers with the On keyword clause now indicating the trigger to be database or schema level trigger.

```
CREATE [OR REPLACE] TRIGGER trigger-name
[BEFORE | AFTER]
[List of DDL or Database System Events]
[ON DATABASE | SCHEMA]
...
BEGIN
... pl/sql statements ...
END;
```

The "on database" option implies that the trigger fires when anyone logs into the database, regardless of the schema. This option can be used to maintain a typical audit of who and when the database has been accessed. This option further implies that the trigger is specific to the schema in which it is created.

27. Create a trigger chk_rental_alter that blocks any attempt to execute a SQL Alter statement in the schema in which the trigger is defined. The trigger will instead display an dbms_output message along with the raise_application_error message.

```
create or replace trigger chk_rental_alter
before alter
on schema
declare
error1 exception;
begin
dbms_output.put_line('System Trigger successful');
raise error1;
exception
when error1 then
raise_application_error(-20100,'Alter Cancelled');
end;
```

The trigger can be tested with the following SQL Alter statements.

```
alter table rental
modify least_type char(3);
alter table apartment
modify flooring char(10);
```

INSTEAD OF Trigger

Database views have limitations with respect to SQL Insert, Update, or Delete statements. These limitations occur especially when the views are created through the joining of multiple tables. To overcome this limitation, *instead of* triggers can be defined, which fire when a user issues a DML statement associated with a view. The mechanism of instead of triggers is that when the user tries to insert, update, or delete a row in a view, the trigger performs the associated insert, update, or delete operation on the table underlying the view.

Instead of triggers are attached to specific database views. There is no "before" or "after" specifications, instead only row level operations. The trigger body specifies one or more SQL commands that modify the tables underlying the view. The table attributes to be modified must be contained in the view and are referenced using the "old" qualifier. The following trigger program units illustrate the application of such triggers.

28. Create a view rental_view on a SQL query that lists rental_no, tenant_name, invoice_no and invoice_due attributes from rental, tenant, and rental_invoice tables. Then, create the instead-of trigger rental_delete on rental_view view, which deletes a row from the rental_invoice table.

```
create view rental_view as
select rental.rental_no, tenant_name, invoice_no, invoice_due
from rental, tenant, rental_invoice
where rental.rental_no = rental_invoice.rental_no
and rental.rental_no = tenant.rental_no;

create or replace trigger rental_delete
instead of delete on rental_view
For each row
Begin
delete from rental_invoice
where invoice_no = :old.invoice_no;
end;
```

Test the rental_delete trigger through the following SQL Delete statement which deletes a row from the rental_invoice table.

```
delete from rental_view
where invoice_no = 1006;
```

Trigger Guidelines

- Do not define triggers that duplicate database features. For instance, do not define triggers to reject bad data if the same checking is done through constraints.

- Limit the size of triggers. If the trigger logic requires much more than 60 lines of PL/SQL code, it may be better to put most of the code in a stored program unit and then invoke it from the trigger. The size of the trigger cannot exceed 32K.

- Do not create recursive triggers. For instance, if there is an "after update" trigger on a table, and the trigger itself issues a SQL statement on the same table, the trigger may fire recursively until it runs out of memory.

- Although triggers are useful for customizing a database, excessive use of triggers can result in complex interdependencies. For instance, when a trigger fires, a SQL statement within the trigger can fire other triggers, resulting in cascading triggers. The Oracle server only allows up to 32 triggers to cascade at simultaneously.

Dynamic SQL

SQL statements in a PL/SQL program unit can be categorized as static or dynamic. Static SQL statements are those where the database objects are validated when the program is compiled. Dynamic SQL statements are SQL queries that are entered as text strings, and then compiled and validated at runtime.

The advantage of dynamic SQL is the possibility of structuring SQL query statements dynamically based on user inputs, including DDL statements like create, alter, and drop. This is useful when one wants to create program units that contain SQL queries that use search condition that are based on dynamic conditions, such as attribute name or table name. Also, it provides the ability to create or alter database table structures such as creating a temporary table to generate a report, and then drop the table.

Two methods are available for implementing dynamic SQL with PL/SQL - DBMS_SQL and Native Dynamic SQL. The DBMS_SQL is a PL/SQL built-in package that offers a programmatic API. Native Dynamic SQL allows the placement of dynamic SQL statements directly into the PL/SQL code, and can then be utilized in server-side programs. In this lesson the native dynamic SQL approach is outlined.

Native Dynamic SQL

Native dynamic SQL (sometimes also referred as embedded dynamic SQL) is performed through the *execute immediate* statement. Supported statements include DML, DDL, SQL, and PL/SQL anonymous blocks. An extension of *execute immediate* statement for queries only, involves the use of ref cursors so that a statement may be passed at runtime instead of being given declaratively. The syntax of the native dynamic SQL statement is as follows:

```
EXECUTE IMMEDIATE dynamic-sql-string
  [INTO {define-variable1 [, define-variable2] ... | plsql-record}]
  [USING [IN | OUT | IN OUT] bind-variable1 [,
      [IN | OUT | IN OUT] bind-variable2] ...]
  [{RETURNING | RETURN} INTO bind-variable3 [, bind-variable4] ...];
```

where dynamic-sql-string may be any of non-query DML, single row query, anonymous PL/SQL block, call statement, transaction control statement, DDL or session control command. Define-variables are matched positionally to items in the select list. Where a PL/SQL record is given to retrieve the results of the query, the elements of the record must match the items in the select list as would be the case with a static SQL statement.

In the syntax, bind-variables can be bound to place holders in a dynamic SQL string. Place holders are indicated by a colon prefix and are matched positionally to variables in the USING clause. Where duplicate place holders are present in a statement, the handling will vary depending on the type of statement involved. If the statement is DML, and the same place holder is referenced more than once, then the corresponding bind-variable must appear the same number of times in the USING clause. If the statement is a PL/SQL block, then the corresponding bind-variable is given only once, its position matching that of the first occurrence of the place holder. However, table or column names cannot be passed as bind variables.

Bind-variables can be *in*, *out* or *in out* depending on their usage. In a standard DML statement all binds will have the default IN mode. However if the statement has a returning clause or is a PL/SQL block or stored program unit call, then the result of the execution may be that bind variables are assigned values. In this case, just as with parameters to a stored procedure or function, it is necessary to indicate the fact by specifying the mode as "out" or "in out" as appropriate.

An execute immediate statement:

- prepares the given string.
- binds any arguments passed in the "using" clause.
- executes the statement.

- when defined as a query, fetches the single row into the define variables or PL/SQL record given in the "into" clause.
- deallocates and clears up as necessary.

If more than one row matches the search criteria a "too_many_rows" exception will be raised. Similarly if no rows are returned the result is a "no_data_found" exception. In these cases the ref cursor method should be used instead. The syntax involving ref cursors in dynamic SQL is:

```
OPEN cursor-variable FOR dynamic-query-string
  [USING bind-variable1 [, bind-variable2] ...];
```

where cursor-variable is a weakly typed cursor variable. A weakly typed cursor variable is one that is declared without a return type and so may be used with any query. A strongly typed cursor variable has a return record type and may only be used with queries that return records of that type.

Just as with execute immediate, the "using" clause maps bind variables positionally to place holders (prefixed by colons) in the query statement. However because the statement must be a query the mode of all bind variables is always "in" and so is not specified. Data type restrictions are the same as for execute immediate. Fetching Data using the ref cursor is similar to cursor processing. It may include fetch and close statements along with cursor% attributes (notfound, found, rowcount, isopen). The following program units illustrate the application of Dynamic SQL.

29. Create a PL/SQL anonymous block that creates a table test1. (Note: The program unit utilizes Dynamic SQL to run a DDL Create Table statement.)

```
declare
str varchar2(200);
begin
str := 'create table test1 (tst varchar2(120))';
execute immediate str;
end;
```

30. Create a PL/SQL anonymous block that inserts a row into the table created by example 29 with bind variables for row attribute values. (Note: The program unit utilizes Dynamic SQL to run a SQL Insert statement.)

```
declare
str varchar2(200);
val1 varchar2(6) := 'hello';
begin
str := 'insert into test1 values (:1)';
execute immediate str using val1;
end;
```

31. Create a PL/SQL anonymous block that inserts a row into the table created by example 29 with attribute values placed directly.

```
declare
str varchar2(200);
--val1 varchar2(6) := 'hello';
begin
str := 'insert into test1 values (''hello2'')';
execute immediate str;
end;
```

32. Create a PL/SQL anonymous block that inserts a row into the table created by example 29 where the table name is a variable that may not known until runtime.

```
declare
str varchar2(200);
val1 varchar2(6) := 'test1';
begin
str := 'insert into '||val1||' values (''hello3'')';
execute immediate str;
end;
```

33. Create a PL/SQL anonymous block that retrieves data with a SQL query where the table name is a bind variable.

```
declare
stud varchar2(40);
val1 varchar2(10) := 'customer';
str varchar2(200);
begin
str := 'select last_name from '||val1||' where customer_id = 102';
execute immediate str into stud;
dbms_output.put_line('Last Name is '||stud);
end;
```

34. Create a PL/SQL anonymous block that retrieves data with a SQL query and an unknown table name involving multiple rows. (Note: The anonymous PL/SQL block can also be created as a procedure with an input parameter 'val1.')

```
declare
type my_curs_type is ref cursor;
curs my_curs_type;
t_rec tenant%rowtype;
str varchar2(512);
val1 varchar2(10) := 'tenant';
begin
str := 'select * from '||val1||'';
open curs for str;
loop
fetch curs into t_rec;
exit when curs%notfound;
dbms_output.put_line(t_rec.tenant_name||' '||t_rec.tenant_dob);
end loop;
close curs;
end;
```

The dbms_output message will be as follows:

```
Jack Robin 21-JUN-60
Mary Stackles 02-AUG-80
Ramu Reddy 11-APR-62
Marion Black 25-MAY-81
Venessa Williams 12-MAR-70
```

35. Create a procedure search_db that retrieves data with unknown table name, attribute name, and condition value involving multiple rows. The procedure has input parameters for the unknown entries of the query. (Note: The condition value has to be passed as a bind variable.)

```
create or replace procedure search_db (table1 varchar2,attr1  varchar2,cond1 varchar2) is
type my_curs_type is ref cursor;
curs my_curs_type;
t_rec tenant%rowtype;
str varchar2(512);
begin
str := 'select * from '||table1||' where '||attr1||' = :j';
open curs for str using cond1;
loop
fetch curs into t_rec;
exit when curs%notfound;
dbms_output.put_line(t_rec.tenant_name);
end loop;
close curs;
end;
```

Test the procedure with the following statement:

```
execute search_db('tenant','employer_name','MSU');
```

The dbms_output message will be as follows:

```
Ramu Reddy
Marion Black
```

Review Questions

1. Define the structure of a PL/SQL procedure.
2. What are the different types of parameter modes in a PL/SQL procedure?
3. Explain the main difference between a PL/SQL procedure and PL/SQL function.
4. What is the difference between a boolean function and an inline function?
5. How can a PL/SQL function be utilized within a SELECT clause of a SQL query.
6. What are exceptions. List their various types?
7. How are undefined exceptions defined?
8. How can one create an undefined exception.
9. What is the relevance of user-defined exception?
10. What is the purpose of raise_application_error?
11. What are the two elements of a package?
12. How is a package referenced by another program?
13. What is the basic purpose of a trigger?
14. Describe the various levels of trigger.
15. Describe the nature of table mutation.
16. In what way can triggers support referential integrity?
17. Describe the difference between the system triggers and DML based triggers.
18. How can triggers be utilized with database views?
19. What is the difference between static SQL and dynamic SQL?
20. Describe the concept of native dynamic SQL.

Review Exercises

1. ___________ _______________ is an integrated, interactive environment to create, execute, and debug PL/SQL programs.

2. A PL/SQL ________________ can receive multiple input parameters or can return multiple output values.
3. The parameter mode _______ indicates that the parameter is passed as a read-only (input) value that cannot be changed in the program.
4. The parameter mode _______ indicates that the parameter is passed as a write-only (output) value that can be assigned a value in the program.
5. The following statement is a call to the _______ program.
   ```
   auto_list(1999, 'Jack Model');
   ```

6. The following statement is a call to the _______ program having _______ parameters.
   ```
   auto_list(1999, 'Jack Model');
   ```
7. A PL/SQL ________________ can receive multiple input parameters, but must return a single value.
8. The PL/SQL ____________ statement that returns a value from a function.
9. Complete the following syntax of a definition line:
   create function abc (id_in number) ________ varchar2

10. The variable id_in is an __________ parameter in following syntax of a definition line.
    ```
    create function abc (id_in number) ______ varchar2;
    ```

11. Complete the following syntax of a definition line:
    ```
    create function xyz (id_in varchar2) ______ boolean
    ```

12. A ____________ function is a special type of PL/SQL function that does not return a value.
13. A function used in a SQL statement is referred as an ___________ function.
14. Exceptions in a PL/SQL program map an Oracle __________ error to error-handling statements.
15. Exception name is a name given to an Oracle ____________ error.
16. The entry no_data_found in the following statement is an ____________.
    ```
    exception
    when no_data_found then
    dbms_output.put_line('error has occured');
    ```

17. The Oracle server error mapped to an exception name is ____________.
    ```
    e_xyz exception;
    pragma exception_init(e_abc,-2291);
    ```

18. The entry e_invoice_error in the following statement is an ____________.
    ```
    if invoice_no is null then
    raise e_invoice_error;
    end if;
    ```
19. Raise_application_error is a ______________ exception.
20. A PL/SQL ______________ is a collection of logically related procedures and functions.
21. A PL/SQL package consists of two components ________________ and ______________.
22. Variables in a _________________ can be referenced by any program within the package.

23. The following statement refers to the ____________ package.
    test_all.auto_list(1999);

24. The entry auto_list(1999) in the following statement refers to a PL/SQL ____________.
    test_all.auto_list(1999);

25. A PL/SQL ______________ is a collection of compiled programs.
26. PL/SQL programs that execute in response to database events like insert, update, and delete are called database ____________.

27. A database ____________ can fire before or after a triggering event.
28. Database ____________ are necessary to enforce referential integrity with respect to cardinality specifications.
29. ____________ triggers fire when a user issues a DML statement associated with a view.
30. ____________ SQL statements are entered as text strings, which are then compiled and validated at runtime.
31. Native dynamic SQL is performed through the ____________ ____________ statement.

Problem Solving Exercises

7-1. Outdoor Clubs database: Create a procedure "ex7_membership" that displays membership_id, first_name, last_name, and city attribute values for all customers who have club membership. Save the procedure source as a script file.

7-2. Outdoor Clubs database: Create a procedure "ex7_order_details" that displays from the product_order table, order_id, order_date, and total attribute values for an input customer_id value. Include an exception that maps the Oracle server error for an invalid customer_id input, and displays a message "Customer ID not correct. Try again!." Save the procedure source as a script file.

7-3. Outdoor Clubs database: Create a procedure "ex7_membership_duration" that receives an input Date value and displays from the club_membership table, the membership_id, customer first_name, and customer last_name attribute values along with a *time status* calculated value for the time remaining with respect to the input date, membership_date and duration values. If the input date is beyond the membership time duration, a message should display "Membership has expired." Input the date in format dd-MON-yy. Use the Save the procedure source as a script file.

7-4. Outdoor Clubs database: Create a procedure "ex7_membership_status" that displays membership_id, duration, first_name, last_name, city attribute values for customers who have club membership, along with the name attribute value of the sporting_club. The value of the sporting_club name should be returned by a function "ex7_clubname." Save the procedure and function source as separate script files.

7-5. Outdoor Clubs database: Add an attribute "qty_ordered" to the product table with data type integer. Now, create a procedure "ex7_add_quantities" that adds the quantities that have been ordered for each product so far, and updates those values for the qty_ordered attribute in the product table. For those products that do not yet have an order, the value inserted for the attribute should be zero. At the end of processing display the product_id, qty_ordered values. Save the procedure source as a script file.

7-6. Outdoor Clubs database: Create a procedure "ex7_new_order" with input parameters of customer_id, product_id, quantity, payment_type attribute values to inserts a new order in the product_order table. Use sysdate for order_date attribute value. The ship_date is 5 days after the order_date. Before inserting the new order, the procedure checks a boolean function "ex7_check_quantity" on whether the quantity ordered is available in stock. If the quantity ordered is more than stock available, the procedure displays a message "Order cannot be accepted." Use the sequence product_order_sequence of the Outdoor Clubs & Product database script to insert the new order_id value. Include exceptions that map Oracle server errors for invalid inputs of customer_id, product_id, and payment_type. The exception displays different message for each input error. For invalid customer_id the message is "Customer ID not correct. Try again!." For invalid product_id the message is "Product ID not correct. Try again!." For invalid payment_type the message is

"Payment Type not correct. Try again!." Save the procedure and function source as separate script files.

7-7. Outdoor Clubs database: Create a script file that adds an attribute "fee" with data type integer to the sporting_clubs table. The fee attribute holds the amount of fee charged per month by a sporting club. Use the following table to update the sporting_clubs table with the fee data.

CLUB_ID	FEE
100	$ 50
110	$ 75
120	$ 85
130	$ 60

Now, create a procedure "ex7_new_membership" that inserts a new row of club membership. The procedures has input parameters of duration, payment_type, club_id, customer_id attribute values. Use the current date as membership_date attribute value. The new club membership amount attribute value is determined by a call to a function "ex7_membership_amount." The function uses the fee value in the sporting_clubs table to calculate the amount value. The formula for amount value is "duration * fee." The procedure displays membership_id, membership_date, and amount attribute values.

Include exceptions that map Oracle server errors for invalid inputs of customer_id, club_id, and payment_type. The exception displays different message for each input error. For invalid customer_id the message is "Customer ID not correct. Try again!." For invalid club_id the message is "Club ID not correct. Try again!." For invalid payment_type the message is "Payment Type not correct. Try again!." Save the procedure and function source as separate script files.

7-8. Outdoor Clubs database: Create a procedure "ex7_supplier_update" that contains two input parameters. The first input parameter is a supplier_id attribute value that is used to delete the supplier from the supplier table. The second input parameter is also another supplier_id attribute value that is used to update the deleted supplier entry (of the first input parameter) in the product and purchase_order table with a new supplier value. Create a boolean function "ex7_supplier_exist" to determine if the two input parameter supplier_id attribute values exists before proceeding with the data manipulations. If the suppliers do not exist, then display a message "Invalid Suppliers. Run program unit again!." If the supplier does exist, then after completing the manipulations display the product_id attribute values that have the new updated supplier entry. Save the procedure and function source as separate script files.

7-9. Outdoor Clubs database: Create a procedure "ex7_activity_count" with one input parameter. The input parameter is the activity attribute value. The procedure displays the input activity value along with a count of the clubs in the sporting_clubs table that provide the activity. Create a function "ex7_activity_check" that checks whether the input activity exists in the database. If the input activity is not listed in the club_activity table, the procedure displays a message "Activity not in Database" based on the function "ex7_activity_check." Save the procedure and function source as separate script files.

7-10. Outdoor Clubs database: Create a procedure "ex7_cust_activity" with two input parameters. The input parameters are the attributes first_name and last_name in the customer table. The procedure displays the list of activity values for the sporting club for which the customer has club membership. If the customer name do not have club membership the procedure displays a message "Customer is still not a club member" utilizing the function "ex7_check_member." Create a function "ex7_check_member" that checks whether the customer has club membership.

Include an exception that maps the Oracle server error for invalid input, and displays a message "Customer names not correct. Try again!." Save the procedure and function source as separate script files.

7-11. Outdoor Clubs database: Create a procedure "ex7_purchase_details" that displays po_no, quantity, and product_name attribute values for each purchase_order along with the supplier city attribute value. The supplier city attribute value should be returned by a function "ex7_supplier_city." Save the procedure and function source as separate script files.

7-12. Outdoor Clubs database: Create a procedure "ex7_membership_duration2" that displays membership_id, duration, first_name, last_name, city attribute values for customers who have club membership, along with the name attribute value of the sporting_club. The value of the sporting_club name should be returned by a function "ex7_club name." For those customers that do not yet have any membership, display first_name, last_name, city attribute values along with a message "No Membership Yet." The procedure checks a boolean function "ex7_check_membership2" on whether the customer has membership. Save the procedure and function source as separate script files.

7-13. Outdoor Clubs database: Create a package "ex7_product_category" consisting of two procedures similar to problem 6-2 and 6-3 of Chapter 6. The first procedure of the package (similar to problem 6-2) should be named "ex7_product_price." The second procedure of the package (similar to problem 6-3) should be named "ex7_product_count." Save the package source as a script file.

7-14. Outdoor Clubs database: Create a package "ex7_order_member" that has two procedures. The first procedure should be named "ex7_club_member." This procedure creates a new club membership. It contains input parameters for attributes duration, payment_type, club_id, and customer_id. Club membership is $50 per month. The procedure displays membership_id, membership_date, and amount attribute values. Use the current date for membership_date attribute.

The second procedure named "ex7_new_order" creates a new product order with a maximum of 3 products in an order. The input parameters for the new product order are (i) the three products and their respective ordered quantities are referred as product_id1 and quantity1, product_id2 and quantity2, and product_id3 and quantity3, and (ii) attributes customer_id and payment_type. If there are less than 3 products, then null should be used for input. The procedure displays order_id, order_date, ship_date, total attribute values. The ship_date attribute value is 5 days after the order_date attribute value. Use the current date for order_date attribute. The procedure inserts a row in product_order table, rows in order_details table, and updates the quantity_in_stock attribute value in the product table. Save the package source as a script file.

7-15. Outdoor Clubs database: Create a package "ex7_membership" that has one procedure and two functions. The procedure is named "ex7_new_member." It creates a new club membership. The procedure has input parameters for attributes duration, payment_type, name of sporting club, first_name of customer, and last_name of customer. Club membership is $50 per month. The procedure will display membership_id, membership_date, customer_id and amount attribute values. Use the current date for membership_date attribute.

The first function "ex7_check_club" checks to see if the sporting club exists. If the club does not exist, the membership is denied with a message "This club is not attached to the database." The second function "ex7_check_customer" checks to see if the customer exists. If the customer does not exist, a new customer is created to complete the club membership. Save the package source as a script file.

7-16. Outdoor Clubs database: Create a package "ex7_status_check" that has one procedure and one function. The procedure is named "product_status" with one input parameter for attribute product_id. The procedure displays product_name, associated supplier name, and a message. The message will either display a total of the quantity ordered for the product, or a text "Not Ordered so far." The value of quantity ordered is determined by a function "product_qty." Create the function product_qty that determines the total quantity ordered for the input product_id attribute value. Save the package source as a script file.

7-17. Outdoor Clubs database: Create a trigger "product_reorder_au" that is associated with an update operation on the product table. The trigger checks to see whether during the update of the quantity_in_stock attribute, if its value gets lower than the reorder_point attribute value for a product. When this situation occurs, the trigger automatically inserts a new purchase order in the purchase_order table. The new purchase order will use the existing supplier_no attribute value for the product in the product table, and the quantity attribute value will be same as the reorder_qty value for the product in the product table. Save the trigger source as a script file.

7-18. Outdoor Clubs database: Create a trigger "product_order_ai" that is associated with an insert operation on the product_order table. The trigger automatically adds a shipping and handling charge of $ 6 to whatever is the tabulated value of the total attribute. The tabulated value is the sum of (price * quantity) for all products in the product order. Save the trigger source as a script file.

7-19. Outdoor Clubs database: Create a trigger "sporting_clubs_ai" that maintains the relationship between sporting_clubs and club_activity tables with respect to insert operations in both tables. The default club_activity is 'Walking.' Save the trigger source as a script file.

7-20. Outdoor Clubs database: Create two triggers "product_supp_ai" and "product_supp_ai2" that maintain the relationship between supplier and product tables with respect to insert operations in both tables. Save the trigger source as a script file.

7-21. Outdoor Clubs database: Create a database view "purchase_supp_view" containing po_no, quantity, supplier name, and product_name attributes. Now create a instead-of trigger on purchase_supp_view with respect to delete operation on purchase_order table. Save the view definition and the trigger source as a script file.

7-22. Outdoor Clubs database: Create a database view "product_supp_view" containing product_name, price, supplier name, and supplier city attributes. Now create a instead-of trigger on product_supp_view with respect to insert operation on supplier table. Save the view definition and the trigger source as a script file.

7-23. Outdoor Clubs database: Create a view "customer_ord_view" containing first_name, last_name, order_id, product_name, quantity attributes. Now create a instead-of trigger on customer_ord_view with respect to insert operations on customer table. Save the view definition and the trigger source as a script file.

7-24. Outdoor Clubs database: Create a procedure "search_info1" that uses a dynamic SQL to find the values pertaining to tables customer or product. The procedure has one input parameter to enter a table name (customer or product). The procedure displays first_name, last_name, and city attribute values if the input parameter is customer table, or product_name and price if the input parameter is product table. Save the procedure source as a script file.

7-25. Outdoor Clubs database: Create a procedure "search_info2" that uses a dynamic SQL to find the values pertaining to tables customer or product. The procedure has two input parameters. The first input parameter can be used to enter a table name (customer or product). The second input parameter can be used to enter an attribute name. The possible attribute names are first_name, last_name, and city if the first input parameter table name is customer; or product_name and price attribute names if the first input parameter is product. The procedure should display all the rows for the input attribute name. Save the procedure source as a script file.

7-26. Outdoor Clubs database: Create a procedure "search_info3" that uses a dynamic SQL to find the values pertaining to customer or product tables. The procedure has three input parameters. The first input parameter can be used to enter a table name (customer or product). The second and third input parameters are supposed to complete a search condition in the SQL query. The second input parameter can be used for an attribute name for the search condition. The third input parameter can be some condition value associated with the attribute name of the second parameter. The conditional operator for the search condition in the query will be = sign. The procedure displays first_name, last_name, and city attribute values if the first input parameter is customer table, or product_name and price if the first input parameter is product table. Save the procedure source as a script file.

7-27. Outdoor Clubs database: Create a procedure "insert_info1" that uses a dynamic SQL to insert a row in a table. The procedure has five input parameters. The first input parameter refers to some table in the database, the second parameter is some attribute of the table, the third parameter is the value of the second parameter attribute, the fourth parameter is also some attribute of the table, and the fifth parameter is the value of the fourth parameter attribute. For example, insert a row with first_name, last_name attribute values in customer table. Save the procedure source as a script file.

7-28. Outdoor Clubs database: Create a trigger "product_price_updt" that is associated with an update operation on the product table. The trigger enforces a business rule that there should not be any price increase beyond 10% of the existing price on any product. Save the trigger source as a script file.

7-29. Outdoor Clubs database: Create a trigger "club_mem_state" that is associated with an insert operation on the club_membership table. The trigger enforces a business rule that a customer can only be associated with a sporting club which is in the same state in which the customer resides. Hence, during the insert of a new club membership, the trigger checks to see whether the customer's state attribute value matches the sporting club's state attribute value. If the customer's state attribute value does not match the sporting club's state attribute value, the trigger automatically assigns any sporting club which is in the same state as the customer's state. Save the trigger source as a script file.

7-30. Outdoor Clubs database: Create a trigger "club_mem_amt" that is associated with an insert operation on the club_membership table. The trigger enforces a business rule that a customer will be charged a fee of $50 per month if the sporting club is in the same state in which the customer resides (i.e. an in-state fee), otherwise the fee will be $75 per month (i.e. out-of-state fee). Hence, during the insert of a new club membership, the trigger automatically computes the amount value (i.e. fee * duration) based on the customer state value and sporting club state value. Save the trigger source as a script file.

7-31. Outdoor Clubs database: Create an update trigger "purchase_quantity_updt that implements a business rule on the purchase_order table that blocks any quantity reduction from the supplier beyond 5 units within a purchase order. Save the trigger source as a script file.

Chapter 8. PL/SQL Web

PL/SQL is not only a database language but also an application language well suited for Web applications. In this chapter, the Web component of PL/SQL is explored along with the basics of the Internet, Web architecture for applications, and HTML statements to create a Web page.

Web Essentials

Internet is a worldwide collection of computer networks that are connected to each other for sharing and exchanging of information. The *World Wide Web* (or simply the *Web*) is part of the Internet that provides information to computers connected to the Internet. The Web organizes its resources in a common way so that the information can be easily stored, transferred, and displayed among the various types of computers connected to it. Businesses use the Web regularly for everything from advertising to retailing.

The exchange of information on the Web is done through an electronic document called a *Web page*. Each page contains information ranging from simple text to complex multimedia. A variation of the Internet is called *Intranet*. An intranet is an internal network like an Internet, but available within the organization. An Intranet allows employees to share information, e-mail, and perform other activities.

Web pages on the Internet are classified as *static* or *dynamic*. A static Web page displays the same content during a session. A dynamic Web page content changes frequently during a session. Dynamic Web pages generally use the database at the back-end to display varying information on the Web page.

Web Architecture

Web architecture is the setup of hardware and software to facilitate Internet working. There are two types of Web architectures: two-tier architecture and three-tier architecture. The two-tier architecture is sufficient for displaying static Web pages. To display dynamic Web pages, the three-tier architecture is required.

The two-tier architecture consists of multiple computers (referred as clients) connected to a server computer as shown in Figure 8-1. The client computers have a software referred to as a *Web Browser*, while the server computer contains a *Web Server* software. The basic role of a Web browser is to take requests for Web pages from users, and then display those pages within the browser window. This is also referred as *rendering* of a Web page. To get the Web page, the browser needs an address (called as URL) of where the Web page is stored. Once that address is provided, the browser locates the Web page on the Internet, retrieves it, and displays it in the browser's window.

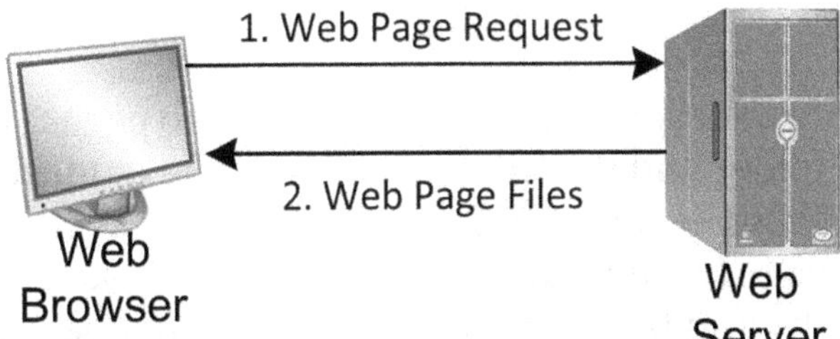

Figure 8-1: Web Browser and Server Interaction

The URL stands for Uniform Resource Locator. Each Web page has a unique URL, and to view a Web page its URL must be known. For instance, the URL http://www.myoracle.com/index.html retrieves information from the www.myoracle.com Web site.

The browser divides the URL into three parts. The first part of the URL is the HTTP protocol keyword represented as http://. This indicates that the Web page should be retrieved using the HTTP protocol. An extension of HTTP protocol is HTTPS. HTTPS protocol is used for additional security in the form of a Secure Socket Layer (SSL) on top of the HTTP protocol.

The second part of the URL is the *domain*. In this example it is "www.myoracle.com" which identifies a (server) machine on the Internet. A domain ends with characters that give a general indication of the site's purpose, such as .com, .org, .net, .gov, .edu, and so on. There are also many country suffixes such as .uk for United Kingdom, .de for Germany, and so on.

The middle portion of the domain provides specific information on the site being accessed. In the above example it is "myoracle" which stands for MyOracle corporation. For name recognition, most organizations use their own name or a familiar abbreviation for it. The leftmost part of the domain use "www" as a convention to identify the address as a website.

Each machine connected to the Internet, is assigned an address referred as an *IP address* or *Internet Protocol address*. IP address are four numbers separated by decimal points. It is possible to use this numeric IP address in URL for machine identification. But it is better to use aliases like "www.myoracle.com" instead of some numeric IP address as it is easier to remember. Also, another advantage of using alias is that the system administrators can associate an alias with another IP address if required without affecting the access to the site on the Internet.

When an alias is used instead of the numeric IP address in a URL, the browser has to translate the alias into a numeric IP address before it can request a Web page. To resolve the alias numeric IP address, the browser contacts a specific type of server known as a Domain Name System server, or DNS server.

Once the browser reads the URL and identifies the IP address of the machine to contact, as well as the specific path and resource requested, it initiates the request. It connects to the IP address using a specific point of connection on the target server called a *port*. Port is an entry point (identified as a number) that is configured on the server machine to handle incoming requests. Generally, systems administrators configure their machines to use port 80 as the default for HTTP Web documents. For this reason, the port number is usually not included in the URL, but the port can be included (after the domain) if needed by ending the domain name by a colon followed by the port number. The above URL example can also be written as http://www.oracle.com:80/index.html.

Through the connection that it has established, the browser sends a request for the Web page. The Web server processes the request by looking for the folder and the file requested. If the request is for a static Web page, it is transmitted back to the browser immediately. Requests for dynamic Web pages may take longer as the Web page may have to be generated. The URL in this case may invoke the scripts that produces the page dynamically, and then transmit the completed page to the browser. If the server cannot find the resource being requested, it returns an error message to the browser. The Web server also manages the Web site setup, besides transferring Web contents to a Web browser.

Although the user apparently requests a single Web page, that Web page may in turn initiate additional requests for files to complete the Web page. When rendering a Web page, the browser may find that the page contains several other files (like image files, audio files, etc.) that need to be also retrieved. Once the browser has received all the additional files, it assembles the Web page for display in the browser window. Examples of Web browsers are Chrome, Edge, Internet Explorer, Firefox, Opera, Safari, and so on.

To incorporate dynamic (or database) content in Web pages the two-tier architecture is extended to a three-tier architecture as shown in Figure 8-2. Three-tier architecture is split into three parts: the client, the Web/Application server, and the database server (DBMS).

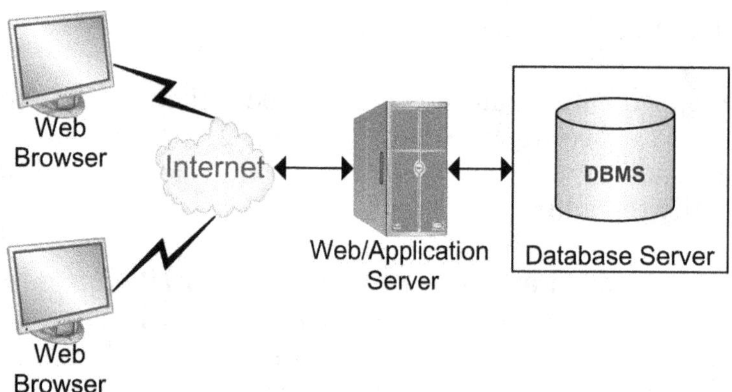

Figure 8-2: Web Framework

The database level is the DBMS software (Database Management System Software) that provides the database information for the Web page. The Web/application server is referred as the *middle-tier*. The middle-tier Web server listens for requests for Web pages from the clients Web browser. When the client machines' Web browser requests Web pages from the middle-tier, the Web server routes the request to the application server for processing. The application server facilitates the retrieval of information from the database server. Once the request is processed, the Web server sends the Web page to the browser that requested it. Web servers and application servers maybe on separate machines or same machine.

Web Application

A Web application is an application deployed on the Web. It can be a Web page or a series of Web pages. Web applications generally utilize dynamic Web pages to enhance application interactivity. The purpose of a Web application is to allow organizations and users to accomplish various tasks like obtaining information, shopping, customer relationship, and so on. Web applications have evolved from traditional round-trip updates of Web pages to a more desktop application style of Web page processing. Deploying an application on the Web provides an organization a way (i) to extend its reach beyond the borders of the organization, and (ii) perform various organizational activities in an optimal way.

A Web page is written in a language called HTML (Hypertext Markup Language). HTML is not a programming language, but a language that consists of markers (or tags) that specify how content would appear in a Web browser. Creating a Web page with HTML can be quite tedious. To simplify Web page development, many Web authoring software like Dreamweaver have emerged. These software require little understanding of HTML to develop Web pages.

Each Web page by default is stored as a file with file type *.html* or *.htm*. Web pages may also have special file types like .asp (for Active Server Pages), .jsp (for Java Server Pages), and so on. Web pages are grouped together to form a Web site. A Web site links individual Web pages in a hierarchical structure as shown in Figure 8-3. Every Web site has some goal or purpose, and the Web pages within the site are developed for achieving this objective. For example, a retail company Web site will have Web pages to enable selling of products. Web pages in this case will include display of products, ordering of products, customer support operations, and so on.

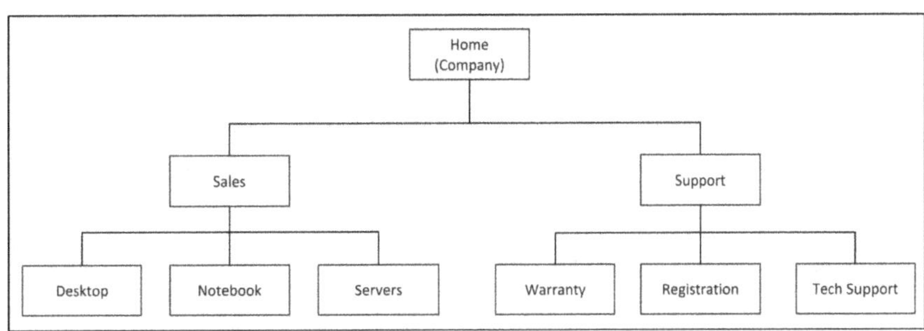

Figure 8-3: Web site hierarchy

The top most Web page of the hierarchy is typically called the *home* page. Home page contains the links to other Web pages of the Web site. It is possible to have links to all Web pages from the home page or have links to selective Web pages lower in the hierarchy. The home page filename is generally named on the Web server as *default* or *index*.

Designing the layout of a Web page is a very specialized domain. It can affect how users interact with the screen, respond to color schemes and artwork, and how to effectively present information. A typical Web page layout can consist of word processor type margin areas on all four sides of a page. In the middle of the Web page is the area to display the page content. The top margin area typically has a *banner* containing the page title. Below the banner there may be a *navigation bar* with links to other pages of the site. Navigation bars may also appear in other margin areas too. Margin areas also have *mail links*, links to external Web sites, or some text. To ensure consistency in layout across the Web site or a Web application, entries in the margin areas may remain the same among the Web pages of the site.

HTML is sufficient for developing static Web pages. However, if the Web page contains database data, HTML by itself is not sufficient. Consequently, database driven dynamic Web pages require regular programming language syntax to be mixed with HTML markers. For example, Visual Basic is a programming language that can be mixed with HTML to create Active Server Pages (ASP). Web page design for dynamic Web pages is a fusion of two areas: Web page layout design and Web page logic design.

The programming language within a Web page is referred as a *scripting* language. There are many scripting languages. Some scripting languages work within the browser (referred as client-side languages), while other scripting languages work at the server level (referred as server-side languages). For example, Javascript is a programming language that executes within a browser on the client machine. VBScript on the other hand is a programming language that executes within the server. Server-side scripts are useful if the application will be accessed by many users through different kinds of browsers.

To provide desktop like capabilities in Web applications, server-side scripts are complemented with (i) client-side scripts like Javascript, and (ii) XML type data formats. The Javascript language facilitates desktop like handling of Web applications within the Web browser window, while the JSON, XML languages provide the data format to ease the transfer of data from the database server to the Web browser. The AJAX (asynchronous Javascript and XML) concept encapsulates the mechanism for providing desktop capabilities to Web applications.

Oracle developed a server-side scripting approach to facilitate database driven dynamic Web pages through their PL/SQL Web Toolkit. A variation of PL/SQL Web Toolkit is called as PL/SQL Server Pages (PSP). The PL/SQL Web Toolkit uses the database language PL/SQL as a scripting language along with HTML to generate database driven dynamic Web pages. Since PL/SQL is optimized for database operations, the resulting Web pages are more efficient in database interactivity. PL/SQL Web Toolkit generated Web pages are stored within the Oracle server (DBMS). To enhance the capability of the PL/SQL toolkit Web page, it is possible to embed it with other Javascript or JSON or XML AJAX characteristics.

Hypertext Markup Language (HTML)

HTML is the language of the World Wide Web. This chapter provides a brief overview of HTML. HTML is not a programming language, but rather a markup language. A Web page in HTML is a plain text (ASCII) file containing letters, numbers, and other printable characters along with embedded special markup codes. These markup codes are often called as *tags*. HTML tags are used to mark-up HTML elements. Any text editor or word processor can be used to create the HTML layout of a Web page.

HTML uses two key symbols for tag specification. These symbols constitute what is often called an angle bracket – less than symbol (<) and greater than symbol (>). All HTML code is enclosed between these two symbols. For example, <head> indicates a Web page header tag.

All HTML tags appear in pairs. In between the tag pairs the content is placed. The beginning tag is like <some-tag>, while the closing tag is like </some-tag>. For example <title>PL/SQL Web Page</title> defines the display window title "PL/SQL Web Page" in the browser. <title> marks the beginning of the windows title text, while the </title> is the end of the title text. HTML tags are not case-sensitive.

Tags can have attributes. Attributes can provide additional information about the HTML elements on your page. The attributes are placed before the closing bracket of the starting tag. The value of the attribute must be enclosed within double quotation marks. For example, there is a tag <body> that defines the body element of a HTML page. With an added bgcolor attribute like <body bgcolor="red">, the background color of the Web page in browser becomes red. Another example, consider the <img> tag that shows an image/video on a Web page. The <img> tag can be configured with a number of attributes including the src attribute, which specifies the filename of the image file or video clip. The SRC attribute within the <img> tag appears as <img src="mypicture.gif">. Some of the basic HTML tags are as follows.

Main Elements

Document Type

The document type tag <!DOCTYPE> is the very first statement in a Web page. It makes sure the Web site renders correctly in various browsers. The tag tells the browser which HTML or XHTML specification the document uses. XHTML is the next generation of HTML. It emphasizes writing tags in lower case as well as requiring closing of tag elements.

A HTML document is validated against a Document Type Definition (DTD). Before an HTML file can be properly validated, a correct DTD must be added as the first line of the file. The HTML 4.01 Transitional DTD includes everything in the strict DTD plus deprecated elements and attributes. For example, <!DOCTYPE HTML PUBLIC "-//W3C//DTD HTML 4.01 Transitional//EN" "http://www.w3.org/TR/html4/loose.dtd">

<html> Element

Every Web page must begin and end with the <html> element. These are the first and last tags of the document. For example the following is a Web page with only one line "My First Web Page."

<head> and <body> Elements

The HTML statements in a Web page appear in two sections – the head and body. The head part of the page uses <head> ... </head> tag pairs. The <head> tag contains information that is placed at the start of a Web page. It contains general information, also called meta-information, about a document. The tags inside the head element should not be displayed by a browser. Only few tags are legal inside the head section. These are: <base>, <link>, <meta>, <title>, <style>, and <script> as shown in Table 8-1.

HTML Tag	Description
<title> ... </title>	Defines the Web page title that appears in the browser's title bar.
<base> . . . </ base>	Defines a base URL for all the links on a page.
<style> ... </style>	Defines a style sheet.
<link> ... </link>	Defines an external link between the existing Web page and an external source.
<script> ... </script>	References embedded scripts.
<meta> ... </meta>	Defines Web page document properties.

Table 8-1: Common tags in Head section of a Web page

Following the <head> tag is the <body> tag that defines the HTML elements that represent the content of the Web page. The attributes of the <body> tag determines the appearance of the Web page. Some of the common attributes of the <body> tags are in Table 8-2.

Attribute	Determines
background	The background image.
bgcolor	The background color.
text	Text color.
link	The color of an unvisited link.
Table 8-2: Common attributes of Body tag	

A simple Web page is shown below, along with its appearance in a Web browser in Figure 6-5:

```
<html>
<head>
<title>PL/SQL Web Page</title>
</head>
<body>
My First Web Page.
</body>
</html>
```

Additional Elements

Headings: Headings are defined with the <h1> to <h6> tags. <h1> defines the largest heading. <h6> defines the smallest heading. HTML automatically adds an extra blank line before and after a heading.

Paragraphs: Paragraphs are defined with the <p> tag. HTML automatically adds an extra blank line before and after a paragraph.

Line Breaks: The <br> tag is used when to end a line, but not to start a new paragraph. The <br> tag forces a line break wherever you place it. The <br> tag is an empty tag. It has no closing tag. In HTML, the <br> tag has no end tag. In XHTML the <br> tag is written as <br />.

Horizontal Rule: The <hr> tag inserts a horizontal line in the Web page. The <hr> tag is an empty tag. It has no closing tag. In HTML the <hr> tag has no end tag. In XHTML the <hr> tag is written as <hr />.

Comments: The <!–> tag is used to insert a comment in the HTML source code. A comment will be ignored by the browser. You can use comments to explain the code, which can help during editing at a later date.

Text Format: It is not possible to pre-determine how the text is displayed in another browser. Some people have large computer displays, some have small. The text will be reformatted every time the user resizes his window. Never try to format the text in the HTML editor by adding empty lines and spaces to the text. HTML truncates blank spaces in the source file. Any number of spaces count as one. Further, a new line counts as one space. Table 8-3 is a list of common text formatting tags.

Tag	Description
<b>	Defines bold text
<big>	Defines big text
<em>	Defines emphasized text
<i>	Defines italic text
<small>	Defines small text
<sub>	Defines subscripted text
<sup>	Defines superscripted text
Table 8-3: Text Formatting Tags	

Unordered Lists: An unordered list is a list of items. The list items are marked with bullets (typically small black circles). An unordered list starts with the <ul> tag. Each list item starts with the <li> tag. Inside a list item there can be paragraphs, line breaks, images, links, other lists, etc. For instance, sample HTML list item statements are shown below.

```
<ul>
<li>Coffee</li>
<li>Milk</li></ul>
```

Ordered Lists: An ordered list is also a list of items. The list items are marked with numbers. An ordered list starts with the <ol> tag. Each list item starts with the <li> tag. Once again, inside a list item there can be paragraphs, line breaks, images, links, other lists, etc.

Image Element: Images in a Web page are displayed through the image <img> tag and the associated src attribute. The <img> tag is empty, which means that it contains attributes only and it has no closing tag. To display an image on a page, one needs to use the src attribute which is referred as "source". The value of the src attribute is the URL of the image you want to display on your page. The syntax of defining an image is <img src="url">. The URL points to the location where the image is stored. An image named "boat.gif" located in the directory "images" on "www.w3schools.com" has the URL http://www.w3schools.com/images/boat.gif.

The browser puts the image where the image tag occurs in the document. If you put an image tag between two paragraphs, the browser shows the first paragraph, then the image, and then the second paragraph.

Hyperlink Element: HTML uses an anchor <a> tag to hyperlink to another document on the Web. The hyperlink can point to any resource on the Web like a Web page, an image, a sound file, a movie, and so on. The <a> tag can also be utilized to link to other sections of an existing Web page. The syntax of creating an hyperlink is <a href="url">Text to be displayed</a>. The href attribute is used to enter the address of the document to link to, and the words between the open and close symbols of the anchor tag will display for the hyperlink in the Web page. For instance, the following syntax defines a link to W3Schools: <a href="http://www.w3schools.com/">Visit W3Schools!</a>

Table Element: Table consists of horizontal rows and vertical columns (like spreadsheets). The intersection of a row and a column is called a cell. HTML uses <table> tag pairs to define a table. A HTML table has two additional tags associated with it: <tr> for table row, and <td> for table data (i.e. information/content in a cell). Each row is enclosed within the <tr> tag pair. Each cell content is enclosed with the <td> cell pair. The following are the HTML table tags associated with a two-row, two-column table. Table layout associated with the table element syntax is shown below.

```
<table>
<tr>
<td> Row 1, Column 1</td>
<td> Row 1, Column 2</td> </tr>
<tr>
<td> Row 2, Column 1</td>
<td> Row 2, Column 2</td> </tr>
</table>
```

Most of the table appearance properties like background color, alignment, fonts, and so on can be set through their respective tags. However, there are few table properties outlined in Table 8-4 that need to be known for proper display of table contents.

Property	**Description**
Border	Specify the thickness of lines on the outside edge of the table.
Cell padding	Specify the distance between the cell's content and its border.
Cell spacing	Specify the thickness of the border between the cells.
Alignment	Aligns the content within the cell.

Table 8-4: HTML Table Properties

Section Elements: The <div> and <span> tags are used to define logical sections within a Web page. Such sectioning of a Web page is useful during HTML style definitions as well as document object model (DOM) manipulations.

The <div> tag is a container element that can hold related elements. It also defines a division or section of a Web page. There can be multiple DIV tags in a Web page, wherein each section associated with the tag can be separated through the ID attribute of the tag. For instance, the following Web page HTML contains <div> tag as a collection of <h1> and <p> tags.

```
<html>
<head>
<title>DOM list</title>
</head>
<body>
<div id="dContain">
<h1>This is a heading</h1>
<p>Sample DOM Paragraph</p> </div>
<h3>End of Page</h3>
</body>
</html>
```

HTML Styles: With HTML 4.01 all formatting can be moved out of the HTML document into a separate style sheet. When a browser reads a style sheet, it will format the document according to it. There are three ways of inserting a style sheet: (a) external style sheet - format the look of an entire Web site through one external file; (b) internal style sheet - separate styles for each page; and (c) inline styles - when a unique style is to be applied to a single occurrence of an element.

PL/SQL Web Toolkit

PL/SQL Web Toolkit utilizes the PL/SQL database language as a scripting language along with HTML to complete the composition of Web pages. These Web pages appear in the Web browser (on the client machine) as plain HTML pages with no special PL/SQL script tags. To enhance the utility of such Web pages in a Web browser, it is possible to include Javascript or another client-side scripting language.

PL/SQL Web Toolkit supports all browsers and browser levels equally. It makes network traffic efficient by minimizing the number of server round trips. Since PL/SQL is compiled and stored directly in the database, it has the distinct advantage of being fast. It does not require compilation or interpretation at runtime, and it interacts with the database server quickly. Further, when dealing with large volumes of data, having the logic within the database speeds up the processing and the generation of Web pages. Besides, it is also possible to utilize the security of the database for Web pages or applications.

The task of designing the layout of a Web page with regard to the HTML and database content can be quite complex and tedious. Often times in such cases one can lose focus of the database content, and instead, get bogged down with HTML layout specifications. Consequently, the focus in this chapter is on simple Web page layouts. Any HTML or Text editor can be utilized to complete the Web page layout.

A a Web application written with PL/SQL Web Toolkit is a set of stored procedures (referred to as *Web procedures*) that interact with Web browsers through HTTP. Web content with PL/SQL Web procedures utilizes the power and flexibility of database processing available through PL/SQL.

PL/SQL Web Toolkit is a collection of PL/SQL packages that allow a stored procedure to be called from the Web browser. One of the package in the toolkit is called HTP that generates HTML tags. A brief summary of some of the PL/SQL Web Toolkit packages is provided toward the end of the chapter. Within the HTP package there is a procedure called PRINT or PRN that can contain database data along with text and HTML tags. It outputs any value passed as a parameter. It will generate HTML tags as-is, non-standard HTML as-is, return value of functions, database variable value, or pass hard-coded text as-is to the generated HTML document. In this chapter HTP.PRINT procedure is utilized to generate Web procedures.
The syntax of htp.print is shown below in various forms:

- The syntax of htp.print to display text is htp.print('text').
- The syntax of htp.print to display html tags is htp.print('html-tag').
- The syntax of htp.print to display database variable value is: htp.print(data-variable).
- The syntax of htp.print to display html tags with database variable is: htp.print('<html-tag> '||data-variable||' ').

Examples of htp.print or htp.prn:

- htp.print('<html>') statement will output <html> tag.

- htp.print(value1) statement will output value of variable value1 (local or reference).
- htp.print('<tr><td>'||list_row.tenant_ss||'</td></tr>') statement will output html tags and database value of variable list_row.tenant_ss.

One of the benefits of having PL/SQL as a Web scripting language is the symmetry between the Web procedure and a regular procedure (with no htp statement) as far as database processing is concerned. What this means is that if a regular PL/SQL procedure with dbms_output statement run correctly then (a) the same procedure can be modified as a Web procedure with HTML layout htp statements, and (b) the Web procedure now will typically not generate database errors when viewed in the Web browser.

It is possible that the Web page may display a "page not found" message in the Web browser. One way to debug the reason for the message is to use the PL/SQL exception statement with sqlerrm function (as shown below) to display the Oracle error message.

```
exception
when others then
htp.prn(sqlerrm);
```

The following examples show the creation of Web pages with PL/SQL.

1. A Web procedure helloworld with no database content. The Web page displays "Helloworld from Oracle" text.

```
create or replace procedure helloworld as
begin
htp.print('<html><head>');
htp.print('<title>PL/SQL Web Toolkit</title></head><body>');
htp.print('<p>Helloworld from Oracle.</p></body></html>');
end;
```

2. Superflex Apartments database: A regular procedure sample_page1 with just the database processing shown first followed by its modification as a Web procedure sample_page1_prn. The Web page displays the auto_make and auto_model values for tenant_ss 173662690.

```
create or replace sample_page as
make_out tenant_auto.auto_make%type;
model_out tenant_auto.auto_model%type;
begin
select auto_make, auto_model
into make_out,model_out
from tenant_auto
where tenant_ss=173662690;
dbms_output.put_line('The automobile registered for Venessa Williams is '||make_out||' model
'||model_out);
end;
```

```
create or replace procedure sample_page1_prn as
make_out tenant_auto.auto_make%type;
model_out tenant_auto.auto_model%type;
begin
```

```
htp.prn('<html><body>');
select auto_make, auto_model
into make_out,model_out
from tenant_auto
where tenant_ss=173662690;
htp.prn(' The automobile registered for Venessa Williams is ');
htp.prn(make_out);
htp.prn(' model ');
htp.prn(model_out);
htp.prn('</body></html> ');
end;
```

3. Outdoor Clubs database: A regular procedure sample_page2 with just the database processing shown first followed by its modification as a Web procedure sample_page2_prn. The Web page displays how many credit card and check orders have been received.

```
create or replace procedure sample_page2 is
value1 number(2);
value2 number(2);
begin
select count(*)
into value1
from product_order
where payment_type = 'CC';
select count(*)
into value2
from product_order
where payment_type = 'Check';
dbms_output.put_line(' There are '||value1||' credit card orders. ');
dbms_output.put_line(' There are '||value2||' check orders. ');
exception
when others then
dbms_output.put_line(sqlerrm);
end;
```

```
create or replace procedure sample_page2_prn is
value1 number(2);
value2 number(2);
begin
select count(*)
into value1
from product_order
where payment_type = 'CC';
select count(*)
into value2
from product_order
where payment_type = 'Check';
htp.print('<!DOCTYPE HTML PUBLIC "-//W3C//DTD HTML 4.01 Transitional//EN">
<html><head><title>Outdoor Product Store</title></head><body>');
htp.print(' There are '||value1||' credit card orders. ');
htp.print(' There are '||value2||' check orders. ');
```

```
exception
when others then
htp.print(sqlerrm);
end;
```

HTML tables facilitate structured display of database information. To generate rows of database values an empty row <tr> tag pair should be utilized within a PL/SQL loop statement. In this case the htp.print statement to display database value can be placed inside an HTML table cell (which is represented by the <td> tag pair) within the empty row tag pair.

4. Superflex Apartments: The regular procedure tenant_list with just the database processing is shown first followed by its modification as a Web procedure tenant_list_prn.

```
create or replace procedure tenant_list as
begin
dbms_output.put_line('Tenant List');
dbms_output.put_line('Social Security'||' Name '||' Apartment');
for list_row in (select tenant_ss,tenant_name,apt_no from tenant,rental
where tenant.rental_no = rental.rental_no)
loop
dbms_output.put_line(list_row.tenant_ss||list_row.tenant_name||list_row.apt_no);
end loop;
end;
```

```
create or replace procedure tenant_list_prn as
begin
htp.prn('<!DOCTYPE HTML PUBLIC "-//W3C//DTD HTML 4.01 Transitional//EN">
<html><head><title>Tenant List</title></head><body>
<table border="0" cellpadding="1" cellspacing="1">
<tr><td></td><td><b>Tenant List</b></td><td></td></tr>
<tr><th>Social Security</th><th>Name</th><th>Apartment</th></tr>');
for list_row in (select tenant_ss,tenant_name,apt_no from tenant,rental
where tenant.rental_no = rental.rental_no)
loop
htp.prn('<tr><td>'||list_row.tenant_ss||'</td><td>'||list_row.tenant_name||'</td><td>'||li
st_row.apt_no||'</td></tr>');
end loop;
htp.prn('</table></body></html>');
end;
```

Access Web Page from Web Browser

The PL/SQL gateway enables a Web browser to access the PL/SQL Web page through an HTTP listener. The gateway is a platform to develop and deploy PL/SQL web applications. Web procedures are accessed from a Web browser through a database access descriptor (DAD). DAD is a mechanism that maps the URL to the correct database schema. All PL/SQL Web applications require a database access descriptor to facilitate their working. Essentially, access to any user's PL/SQL Web procedure is routed through the DAD. For example, if the PL/SQL Web procedures are stored in the server account "smiley," the DAD will forward the request from the Web server to this account.

The DAD is setup either with a specific username and password or no username/password. If there is no username assigned to a DAD, visitors to Web procedures will have to enter the database username/password of the account where the Web procedure is stored. However, if a DAD has been setup with an explicit username/password, then any user can access the account's Web pages. Also, a user wishing to access another user's PL/SQL Web application must receive SQL grant execute privileges for the application.

The database administrator account is needed to create the DAD through the create_dad procedure. The create_dad procedure requires two parameters – one for DAD name, and the other for an associated virtual path. For example in Oracle XE login with SYSTEM username and its password. Then enter the following PL/SQL anonymous block create a DAD named "classpsp" and its associated virtual path.

```
begin
DBMS_EPG.create_dad('classpsp','/classpsp/*');
end;
```

All three tiers of the Web architecture are involved while accessing the PSP. The communication between the components of the three-tier architecture towards the display of a PL/SQL server page is shown in Figure 8-4.

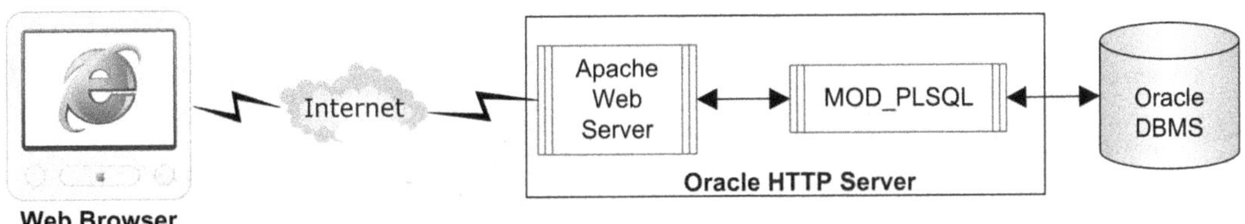

Figure 8-4: PL/SQL Web Toolkit Three-tier Architecture

The details of the interaction between the architecture components are as follows:

1. Web browser sends URL to the DNS server.
2. The DNS server converts the URL to its IP address and sends it back to the Web browser.
3. Using the IP address, the Web browser sends the request to the Apache Web Server within the Oracle HTTP server.
4. As the request is for a PL/SQL Web procedure, the Web server directs the request to the HTTP server module mod_plsql.
5. The mod_plsql module first parses the request and extracts the parameters/header information. Then it queries the database using the database access descriptor (DAD) in the URL address path.
6. The database executes the PL/SQL Web procedure, assembles the Web page, and sends it back to the HTTP server.
7. The HTTP server sends it back to the requesting Web browser.
8. The Web browser receives the Web pages and begins the request for additional files referred as embedded files. Embedded files are files like Javascript files, image files, etc., that are included in the Web page layout specification. These files are stored on the Web server, and accessed through the concept of virtual folders and access paths.

The URL syntax to access a PSP generated PL/SQL Web procedure is:

```
http://server-name[:port]/DAD/username.PLSQL-Web-procedure-name
```

where server-name is domain name, and port is the port number. Enter the port number if it is other than the default number 80. DAD is database access descriptor name, username is the account username which contains the PL/SQL Web procedure. PLSQL-Web-procedure-name is the na Web Forms me of the Web procedure in the account. The URL to view the Web procedure named sample_page1_prn in username cis52899 in Oracle XE is shown below. In the URL 127.0.0.1 is the localhost when accessing Oracle XE, 8080 is the default port, and classpsp is the DAD.

http://127.0.0.1:8080/classpsp/cis52899.sample_page1_prn

If the DAD was not explicitly created with a username, the browser will prompt for cis52899 username's password.

Web Forms

Web forms in Web pages are essentially utilized to capture user input and transmit it to the database server for processing. Typical forms on the Web include order forms, surveys, applications, or search criteria from a user. The database server processes the database using the data entered in the form and returns the results to the Web browser. A Web page can have multiple Web forms. Forms can also be positioned and mixed with the rest of the page content. Figure 8-5 shows the interaction between the Web browser and the database server with respect to Web form.

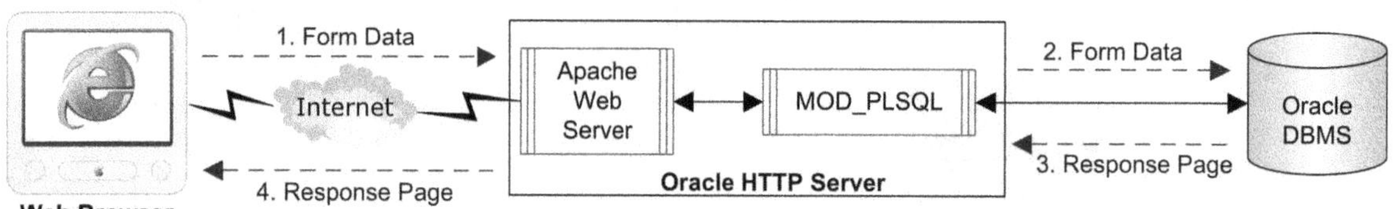

Figure 8-5: Web Form Interaction with Database Server

Each form is created with the <form> and </form> tag pair. When there can be many forms in a Web page, each form is contained in a separate <form> and </form> tag pair. However, forms cannot be nested within each other. The form tag has attributes that determine where the form data will be send, as well as other aspects of data submission. Table 8-5 gives the list of form attributes and their purpose.

Attribute	Description
action	Specification of the URL to which form data will be submitted.
method	Determines how form data will be submitted.
enctype	Specification of the format of the data being submitted.
target	Specifies the window in which any results returned from the server appears.
name	Define a name for the form.

Table 8-5: HTML Form tag attributes

The action attribute value names the URL where the form data is to be sent. If this attribute is excluded, the data is sent to the Web page URL that contains the form. The form input data is passed through the CGI mechanism. The method attribute provides the mechanism to transfer data. This attribute has two values – GET or POST. The default option is GET, which appends form data to the URL in the action attribute. In this case, the data values are passed as a query string of the URL, separated by "&" characters, with most non-alphanumeric characters in an encoded format (such as "%20" for a space). The POST option sends the form data separately from the action attribute URL. In this case, the data is passed directly and is not visible in the URL. The enctype attribute specifies the format of the data that is being submitted. The default value is application/x-www-form-urlencoded. The following Web form syntax defines an empty form.

```
<form action= "http://server-name/DAD/userid.home" name="Form1" method="POST">
</form>
```

The GET method format is more convenient for debugging, besides allowing visitors to pass exactly the same parameters when they return to the page through a bookmark. The URL in this case looks something like this:

http://server-name/DAD/userid.pspname?parmname1=value1&parmname2=value2

The POST method format allows a larger volume of parameter data, and is suitable for passing sensitive information that should not be displayed in the URL. (URLs linger on in the browser's history list and in the CGI variables that are passed to the next-visited page.) It is not practical to bookmark pages that are called this way.

Each form can consist of one or more form elements to pass input data to the database or display data from the database. Some of these form elements are text box, radio buttons, check box, drop-down list, scrolling list, and multi-line text area (shown in Figure 8-6). Forms can also contain push buttons to perform actions on data in form elements. Additionally, forms can also have hidden or password form elements.

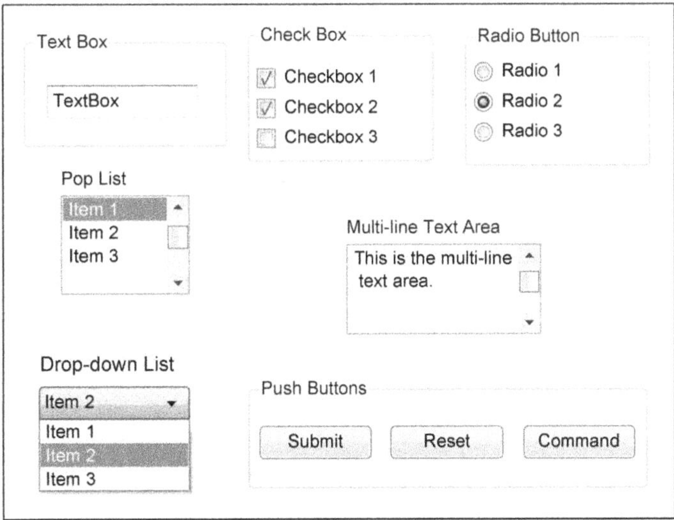

Figure 8-6: Web Form Elements

Text Box: Text box form element allows the user to enter information. The <input> tag is used for creating a text box. The attributes associated with the text box tag specification are shown in Table 8-6.

Attribute	Description
type	Type of Input. For text box the value is “text”.
name	Name for the text box.
value	Set an initial value.
maxlength	The maximum number of characters that can be entered.
size	Display width of the text box.
readonly	To make text box read only.
Table 8-6: Text box tag attributes	

The following HTML statement creates the text box as shown in Figure 8-6.

```
<input type=text name="text1" value="TextBox" size=25 maxlength=20>
```

Radio Button: Radio button form element show choices for selection. These buttons are part of a group. The <input> tag is also used for creating radio buttons where the type attribute has the value “radio.” All radio buttons in a group should have the same name attribute. The attributes associated with the radio button tag specification are shown in Table 8-7.

Attribute	Description
type	Type of Input having the value “radio”.
name	Name for the radio button.
value	Value of the radio button to be submitted.
checked	Initial value of the radio button. Only one radio button can be checked.
Table 8-7: Radio button tag attributes	

The following HTML statement creates three radio buttons as shown in Figure 8-6.

```
<input type=radio name="radio1" value="RadioValue 1">Radio 1
<input type=radio name="radio1" value="RadioValue 2" checked>Radio 2
<input type=radio name="radio1" value="RadioValue 3">Radio 3
```

Check Box: Check box form element allows users to include multiple values from a list of items. Check box can be set to yes (checked) or no (unchecked). The <input> tag is also used for creating check boxes where the type attribute has the value “checkbox.” Each check box can have different display label (Name) with associated value combination. However, like radio buttons, check boxes can also belong to a group by having the same name value, wherein multiple selections can be checked. The attributes associated with the check box tag specification are shown in Table 8-8.

Attribute	Description
type	Type of Input having the value “checkbox”.

name	Name for the check box.
value	Value of the check box to be submitted.
checked	Initial selection of the check box value.

Table 8-8: Check box tag attributes

The following HTML statement creates the three check boxes as shown in Figure 8-6.

```
<input type=checkbox name="checkbox1" value="CheckBox 1" checked> Checkbox 1
<input type=checkbox name="checkbox2" value="CheckBox 2" checked> Checkbox 2
<input type=checkbox name="checkbox3" value="CheckBox 3"> Checkbox 3
```

Selection List: Selection list form element shows a list of entries for selection. Each displayed entry has an associated value. The final value of the selection list is the value associated with the selected entry. Selection list can appear as a pop list or as a drop-down list. Depending on the number of items in the list, a selection list can also include a scroll bar. Selection lists use the <select> ... </select> tag pair to display list of values for user to choose from. The attributes associated with the selection list tag specification are shown in Table 8-9.

Attribute	Description
multiple	Specifies whether the user can select more than one item from the list.
name	Name for the selection list.
size	Specify how many lines of values will be displayed.

Table 8-9: Selection list tag attributes

There is an <option> tag inside the <select> tag pair to specify the items that will appear in the selection list. The attributes within the <option> tag pair are shown in Table 8-10.

Attribute	Description
label	Text to display in the selection list for list values.
value	Value of the text displayed in the list.
selected	Initial selection of a selection list value.

Table 8-10: Selection list OPTION tag attributes

The size attribute determines whether the selection list is a drop-down list or a pop list. If the SIZE attribute is excluded or set to one, then the selection list is a drop-down list. The following HTML statements create the selection list as shown in Figure 8-6. A pop list is created first followed by the drop-down list.

```
<select name="FormsComboBox2" size=5 >
    <option value="1" selected>Item 1</option>
    <option value="2">Item 2</option>
    <option value="3">Item 3</option>
```

```
</select>

<select name="FormsComboBox1" >
    <option value="1">Item 1</option>
    <option value="2" selected>Item 2</option>
    <option value="3">Item 3</option>
</select>
```

Multi-Line Text Area: Multi-line text area form element utilizes the <textarea> ... </textarea> tag pair to create an area for user to enter multiple lines of information. The attributes associated with the multiline text area tag specifications are shown in Table 8-11.

Attribute	Description
name	Name for the text area.
col	The number of columns to be displayed in the text area.
rows	The number of rows to be displayed in the text area.

Table 8-11: Multi-Line text area tag attributes

The following HTML statement creates the multi-line text area as shown in Figure 8-6.

```
<testarea name="FormsMultiLine1" rows=4 cols=14 >This is the multi-line text area.
</textarea>
```

Button: Button form element can be of different types to perform different form functions. A button of submit type will submit the data values in the form to a Web server. A button of reset type will reset the existing values in the form to the default values (set at the time of form loading). A button of command type will perform other functions as coded. The <input> tag is used for creating a button. The attributes associated with the button tag specification are shown in Table 8-12.

Attribute	Description
type	Type of Input.
name	Name for the button.
value	Display label on the button.

Table 8-12: Button tag attributes

The following HTML statement creates a submit button as shown in Figure 8-6.

```
<input type=submit name="FormsButton1" value="Submit">
```

The following HTML statement creates a reset button as shown in Figure 8-6.

```
<input type=reset name="FormsButton2" value="Reset">
```

The following HTML statement creates a command button as shown in Figure 8-6.

```
<input type=submit name="FormsButton3" value="Command">
```

It should be noted that unlike other HTML tags, the <input> tag is empty, it contains attributes only. Also, the <input> tag has no end tag. In XHTML the <input> tag must be properly closed like <input ... />.

Hidden: In form processing, when the Submit type button is pressed, the form element values are send to the database server. However, in some situations, additional data values may need to be passed to the database server. Hidden form element provides a way to pass data not in display in Web page or form.

Hidden form element values can either be static (fixed) values, input parameter values or variable values. To assign variable values to hidden form element, these variables must have their values set before the <FORM> tag is executed. The syntax of hidden form element is:

```
<input type=hidden name="hiddentext1" value="hiddenvalue">
```

Password: Password form element is like a text box where the entries are masked (shown as asterisks or circles). The syntax of password form element is:

```
<input type="password" name="pswd">
```

Input to Database Through Web Form

The following tutorial creates a two page Web site, with the home page having a Web form. The second page serves as the response page. In the database, both the Web pages are Web procedures that communicate with each other. Technically the Web procedure associated with the home page sends the form data to the Web procedure associated with the response page. The processing of the form data is done by the Web procedure associated with the response page.

The home page Web procedure is called "pay_rent_prn" while the response page Web procedure is called "rent_receipt_prn." The home page is used by tenants in the Superflex Apartment database to pay rent. The response page generates the rent receipt.

The home page Web form will have the following sequence of form elements corresponding to their respective attributes: "Rental Number" labeled text box, "Card Type" labeled radio buttons corresponding to the two payment_type attribute values, "Amount Charged" labeled text box, and a"Submit Payment" labeled button of submit type. The pay_rent_prn Web procedure is shown below.

```
create or replace procedure pay_rent_prn as
begin
htp.print('<!DOCTYPE HTML PUBLIC "-//W3C//DTD HTML 4.01 Transitional//EN">
<html><head><title>Pay Rent</title></head><body>
<p><b>Superflex Apartments</b></p>
<!-- Navigation Bar Links -->
<a href="pay_rent_prn">Pay Rent</a><br><hr /><br>
<p><b>Pay Rent</b><br />
(All entries have to be completed)</p>
```

```
<form action="rent_receipt_prn" method="post">
Rental Number: <input type="text" name="rental_no_text" value="" /> <br /><br />
Card Type: <input type="radio" name="cc_type_text" value="Visa"/> Visa
<input type="radio" name="cc_type_text" value="Mastercard"/> Mastercard <br /><br />
Amount Charged: <input type="text" name="invoice_due_text" value="" /><br /><br />
<input type="submit" name="FormsButton1" value="Submit Payment"/>
</form>
</body>
</html>');
end;
```

The response page (rent_receipt_prn) Web procedure processes the input data sent by the home page, and displays a rent receipt using HTML tables. The procedure first performs the SQL Insert operation on the rental_invoice table based on the data received from the home page through input parameters. The SQL queries thereafter are utilized to complete the receipt. These queries (i) fetch the new invoice_number attribute value from the rental_invoice_sequence sequence, and (ii) also fetch the tenant_name attribute value associated with the input rental_no attribute value. Once all the database information for displaying the receipt is available, the HTML table for rent receipt is completed wherein the database values are placed in the table.

To facilitate accuracy and a better understanding of the database processing involved in the Web page, a two step approach is outlined. The first step is to develop a PL/SQL procedure that concentrates on just the PL/SQL processing aspect of the Web page. In this case, the database values that will be displayed through the Web page are tested through the dbms_output statements. The PL/SQL procedure ch8_rent_receipt outlines the PL/SQL processing aspect of the Web page with the dbms_output statements showing the values that will be displayed as rent receipt. The input parameters of the procedure are named similar to the form element names in the home page (pay_rent_prn) procedure.

```
create or replace procedure ch8_rent_receipt (rental_no_text varchar2,
cc_type_text varchar2, invoice_due_text varchar2, formsbutton1 varchar2) is
tenant_name_text tenant.tenant_name%type;
invoice_no_text rental_invoice.invoice_no%type;
begin
insert into rental_invoice (invoice_no,invoice_date,invoice_due,cc_type,rental_no)
values(rental_invoice_sequence.nextval,sysdate,invoice_due_text,cc_type_text,rental_no_text);
commit;
select rental_invoice_sequence.currval into invoice_no_text from dual;
select tenant_name into tenant_name_text
from tenant
where rental_no = rental_no_text;
dbms_output.put_line('Tenant Name '||tenant_name_text);
dbms_output.put_line('Rental No '||rental_no_text);
dbms_output.put_line('Invoice No '||invoice_no_text);
dbms_output.put_line('Date '||sysdate);
end;
```

```
create or replace procedure rent_receipt_prn
(rental_no_text varchar2 default null, cc_type_text varchar2 default null, invoice_due_text
varchar2 default null, formsbutton1 varchar2 default null) as
tenant_name_text tenant.tenant_name%type;
```

```
invoice_no_text rental_invoice.invoice_no%type;
begin
htp.print('<!DOCTYPE HTML PUBLIC "-//W3C//DTD HTML 4.01 Transitional//EN">
<html> <head> <title>Rent Receipt</title> </head><body>
<p><b>Superflex Apartments</b></p>
<!-- Navigation Bar Links -->
<a href="pay_rent_prn">Pay Rent</a><br><hr /> <br> ');
insert into rental_invoice (invoice_no,invoice_date,invoice_due,cc_type,rental_no)
values(rental_invoice_sequence.nextval,sysdate,invoice_due_text,cc_type_text,rental_no_text);
commit;
select rental_invoice_sequence.currval into invoice_no_text from dual;
select tenant_name into tenant_name_text  from tenant where rental_no = rental_no_text;
htp.print('<table border="0" cellpadding="1" cellspacing="1" summary="">
<tr><td><b>Rent Receipt</b></td></tr>
<tr><td><i>Please print this receipt for your records.</i></td></tr>
<tr></tr>
<tr><td>Tenant Name:</td><td>'||tenant_name_text||'</td></tr>
<tr><td>Rental Number:</td><td>'||rental_no_text||'</td></tr>
<tr><td>Invoice Number:</td><td>'||invoice_no_text||'</td></tr>
<tr><td>Invoice Date:</td><td>'||sysdate||'</td></tr>
</table>
</body>
</html>');
end;
```

Web Forms with Database Values

Web forms are also utilized for the display of database content as well as their modifications. Form elements loaded with database values also serve as default values for such elements in the Web browser. Loading with database values in each form element is explained now.

Text Box: Loading of database values within a text box is done by assigning the PL/SQL Web Toolkit database value expression statement to the text box value attribute. For example, if variable_i is a PL/SQL variable, then the following syntax for the text box tag will display the value of this variable when the text box is loaded in Web browser.

```
<input type=text name="text1" value=" '||variable_i||' " size=25 maxlength=20>
```

Radio Button: A radio button aside from its assigned value, will either have a checked (or selected) display or an unchecked display. The settings for the checked or unchecked display is based on the presence or absence of checked attribute in the radio button tag. This is accomplished by embedding each radio button with an if/then PL/SQL statement inside the tag to set the checked attribute. For example, the following radio button tag syntax illustrates how the checked attribute for a radio button can be set if some PL/SQL logic condition is true. The result of PL/SQL statement processing provides the default setting for the radio button in the Web browser.

```
htp.print('<input type=radio name="radio1" value="RadioValue 2" ');
if ..condition.. then htp.print('checked'); end if;
htp.print(' >Radio 2 ');
```

Check Box: A check box aside from its assigned value, will either have a checked (or selected) display or an unchecked display. The settings for checked or unchecked display is based on the presence or absence of checked attribute in the check box tag. This is accomplished by embedding a check box with an an if/then PL/SQL statement inside the tag to set the checked attribute. For example, the following check box syntax illustrates how the checked attribute for a check box can be set if some PL/SQL logic condition is true.

```
htp.print('<input type=checkbox name="checkbox2" value="CheckBox 2" ');
if ..condition.. then htp.print('checked'); end if;
htp.print(' >Checkbox 2 ');
```

Selection List: Selection list appears in two styles – drop down menu list or pop list. The PL/SQL Web Toolkit statement to load database values for either style is similar. To populate a selection list with database values, position a PL/SQL cursor loop statement around the option tag, and then use toolkit expression statements for option tag label/value pair values. For example, the following syntax illustrates how a pop list can be populated with database values based on a cursor query.

```
htp.print('<select name="FormsComboBox2" size=5 > ');
for cursor_row in cursor_query loop
htp.print('<option value="'||cursor_row.attribute||'"><'||cursor_row.attribute||'></option>');
end loop; htp.print('</select>');
```

To generate a database generated selection list with default selected attribute, a PL/SQL if/then statement needs to be embedded in the option tag label/value pair values. For example, the following syntax illustrates how a pop list can be populated with database values wherein the default display value with selected attribute is based on some condition.

```
htp.print('<select name="FormsComboBox2" size=5 > ');
for cursor_row in cursor_name loop
    if cursor_row.attribute1 = value1 then
    htp.print('<option value=" '||cursor_row.attribute1||' >" selected>
    '||cursor_row.attribute2||' ></option>');
    else
    htp.print(' <option value=" 'cursor_row.attribute1||'"> '||cursor_row.attribute2||'</option>');
    end if;
    end loop;
htp.print('</select>');
```

Multi-line Text Area: The multi-line text area can display database information by having PL/SQL statements including toolkit expressions included directly within its content area.

Web Forms with Database Values Tutorial

The tutorial is based on Superflex Apartments database. It consists of three Web procedures/pages. The home page Web procedure named "tenant_intro_prn" displays a Web form with a drop down list box that displays all tenant names in the database along with their associated rental numbers. The user selects a tenant name from the drop-down list box, and the Web form button submits the selected rental number value to the second Web page. The home page source is shown below.

```
create or replace procedure tenant_intro_prn as
cursor rental_cursor is
```

```
select tenant_name,rental_no
from tenant;
rental_row rental_cursor%rowtype;
begin
htp.prn('<html> <head><title>Tenant Intro</title></head><body>
<p><b>Superflex Apartments</b></p> <a href="tenant_intro">Home</a><br><hr />
<form action="tenant_details_prn" method="post">
<p><b>Modify Rental</b></p>
Tenant Name: <select name="rental_no_text"> ');
for rental_row in rental_cursor loop
htp.prn('<option value="'||rental_row.rental_no||'">'||rental_row.tenant_name||'</option>');
end loop;
htp.prn('</select> <br /><br />
<input type="submit" name="FormsButton1" value="Modify Rental"/>
</form></body></html>');
end;
```

The second Web page procedure named "tenant_details_prn" displays a Web form with attribute values for two attributes associated with the rental (as submitted by the home page) – the Lease_type and apt_no attribute values. The user can change these attribute values in the Web form. The changes in the form values are then submitted by the form button to the third Web page. The second page source is shown below.

```
create or replace procedure tenant_details_prn (rental_no_text varchar2 default null,
formsbutton1 varchar2 default null) as
apt_no_text rental.apt_no%type; lease_type_text rental.lease_type%type;
begin
htp.prn('<html> <head> <title>Tenant Details</title></head><body>
<p><b>Superflex Apartments</b></p>
<a href="tenant_intro_prn">Home</a><br><hr />
<form action="tenant_details_thanks" method="post">
<p><b>Modify Rental</b></p>');
select lease_type,apt_no into lease_type_text,apt_no_text from rental where rental_no =
rental_no_text;
htp.prn('Rental Number: <input type="text" name="rental_no_text" value="'||rental_no_text||'"
/> <br /><br />');
htp.prn('Lease Type: <input type="radio" name="lease_type_text" value="One"');
if lease_type_text = 'One' then htp.prn('Checked'); end if;
htp.prn('/> One
<input type="radio" name="lease_type_text" value="Six" ');
if lease_type_text = 'Six' then htp.prn('Checked'); end if;
htp.prn('/> Six<br /><br />
Apartment Number: <input type="text" name="apt_no_text" value="'||apt_no_text||'" /> <br
/><br />
<input type="submit" name="FormsButton1" value="Modify"/>
</form></body></html>');
end;
```

The third Web page procedure named "Tenant_into_thanks" completes the update of the attribute values (as entered in the second Web page) and generate a completion message. The second page source is shown below.

```
create or replace procedure tenant_details_thanks_prn (rental_no_text varchar2 default null,
lease_type_text varchar2 default null, apt_no_text integer default null, formsbutton1 varchar2
default null) as
begin
update rental
set lease_type = lease_type_text,
apt_no = apt_no_text
where rental_no=rental_no_text;
commit;
htp.prn('<html><head><title>Tenant Details Thanks</title></head><body>
<p><b>Superflex Apartments</b></p>
<a href="tenant_intro_prn">Home</a><br><hr /><br>
<p>Updates Successful.</p></body></html>');
end;
```

Additional PL/SQL Web Toolkit Packages

Table 8-13 describes a sample of commonly used PL/SQL Web Toolkit packages. Oracle Application Express (APEX) platform and many enterprise applications utilize PL/SQL Web Toolkit.

Package	Description of Contents
HTF	Function versions of the procedures in the htp package. The function versions do not directly generate output in a Web page. Instead, they pass their output as return values to the statements that invoke them. Use these functions when you need to nest function calls.
HTP	Procedures that generate HTML tags. For instance, the procedure htp.anchor generates the HTML anchor tag <A>.
OWA_CACHE	Functions and procedures that enable the PL/SQL gateway cache feature to improve performance of your PL/SQL Web application.
OWA_COOKIE	Subprograms that send and retrieve HTTP cookies to and from a client Web browser.
OWA_IMAGE	Subprograms that obtain the coordinates where a user clicked an image.
OWA_OPT_LOCK	Subprograms that impose database optimistic locking strategies to prevent lost updates.
OWA_PATTERN	Subprograms that perform string matching and string manipulation with regular expressions.
OWA_SEC	Subprograms used by the PL/SQL gateway for authenticating requests.
OWA_UTIL	Dynamic SQL utilities, HTML utilities to retrieve the values of CGI environment variables and perform URL redirects.
WPG_DOCLOAD	Subprograms that download documents from a document repository that you define using the DAD configuration.

Table 8-13: Sample PL/SQL Web Toolkit Packages

Review Questions

1. How is a PL/SQL Web Toolkit page stored on Oracle database server? Explain.
2. What is the purpose of DAD?
3. Describe the different form elements.
4. Explain the two ways in which form data can be submitted.
5. What is the purpose of the action attribute in the <form> tag?
6. Explain the purpose of three types of form buttons.
7. Why multiple radio buttons are required for a value in a Web form.
8. What is the significance of the response page during input form processing?
9. Explain the purpose of hidden form element.
10. What is the approach to show the radio button for correct database value in Web browser?
11. What is the approach to show check box for correct database value in Web browser?

Review Exercises

1. A PL/SQL Web Toolkit page is a Web page which includes ___________ language statements.
2. The PL/SQL Web Toolkit page uses the PL/SQL language as a ________________ scripting language.
3. A PL/SQL Web Toolkit page is a PL/SQL ______________ in the database server.
4. The HTML tags in a PL/SQL Web Toolkit page are enclosed within the __________ package string within the database server.
5. The database access descriptor maps the _______________ to the correct database account/schema.
6. The ______________ of a PL/SQL Web Toolkit page based application must include the database access descriptor's name.
7. DAD in the following URL is ______________.
   http://www.studio.com/mywork/jack.getone
8. Web forms are used to capture user ______________ in a Web page.
9. The HTML tag to define a form is ______________.
10. The ______________ attribute specifies of the URL to which the form data will be submitted.
11. The ______________ attribute indicates how the form data will be submitted.
12. The two methods of submitting form data are _________ and ___________.
13. The form element where the user can enter information is ________________.
14. The form element that shows choices for selection is __________________.
15. Each choice is represented by a single ____________________.
16. The form element for selection list can appear as _______________ list.
17. A radio button label may be different from its assigned ____________.
18. A ______________ type of button submits the contents of the form to the Web server.
19. A ______________ type of button resets the existing values in the form to the default values.
20. During submission of form values to the database server, each form element name becomes a ______________ name in the response procedure.
21. A ______________ type of button submits the modified contents of the form to the Web server.
22. During submission of modified form values to the database server, each form element name becomes a ______________ name in the response procedure.

Problem Solving Exercises

8-1. Outdoor Clubs database: Create a Web site that provides membership in sporting clubs and order outdoor supplies. The home page is titled "Outdoor Activities." The other pages are titled "Join Club" and "Buy Supplies."

1. The Home page will have the following text: Outdoor activities can range from simple hiking to mountain climbing. Such activities require different equipments and supplies to enhance their enjoyment. We thank you for your visit. Please use the link buttons on the side to explore the site.
2. Create the following queries: (a) Compute the number of sporting clubs in the database, and (b) list the names of sporting clubs.
3. Use the queries created in requirement 2 to complete the following text for the Join Club page. In the Web page club_number1 will be a database value based on query (a) of requirement (2) above, and club_name1, club_name2, ... will be database values based on query (b) of requirement (2) above.

> Club Membership
>
> We offer membership to many existing sporting clubs. Currently there are club_number1 sporting clubs attached to this Site. The fee for membership is $50 per month. The listed sporting clubs are:
> 1. club_name1
> 2. club_name2
>
> We welcome new membership. Use the Apply button to join any club.

4. Create the following queries: (a) Compute the lowest price and the highest price of products available, and (b) list the names of products available.
5. Use the queries created in requirement 4 to complete the following text for the Buy Supplies page. In the Web page low_price1 and high_price1 will be a database values based on the low and high price of products in query (a) of requirement (4) above and product_name1, product_name2, ... will be database values based on query (b) of requirement (4) above .

> Order Supplies
>
> There are many outdoor supplies available. Prices for these supplies range from $ low_price1 to $ high_price1. The list of supplies are:
> - product_name1
> - product_name2
>
> . . .
>
> Please proceed with purchase when ready by using the Buy link button.

8-2. Superflex Apartments database: Create a Web page that displays apartments with pending complaints (use HTML table tag) . The Web page layout is shown below, with attributes from database in italics.

Pending Apartment Complaints			
Complaint#	Apartment#	Apartment Type	Description

complaint_no	*apt_no*	*(Apartment Description)*	*apt_complaint*

Create a PL/SQL procedure "w8_2_pending_complaints" that displays the data required for the table. The Apartment Type column should show description like Studio, One-Bedroom, and so on instead of numeric values. Use the procedure code to complete the Web page.

8-3. Superflex Apartments database: Create a Web page that displays a summary of rentals facilitated by staff (use HTML table tag). The Web page layout is shown below, with attributes and function value from database in italics.

Staff Rental Summary		
Staff Name	Position	Number of Rentals
first_name last_name	*position*	*staff_rental function value*

Create a PL/SQL procedure "w8_3_staff_rental_summary" that displays the data required for the table. Create a function staff_rental that gives a count of the number of rentals facilitated by a staff. Use the function value in Number of Rentals column. Use the procedure code to complete the Web page.

8-4. Superflex Apartment database: Create a Web page to display a list of apartments that have been rented by various staff (use HTML table tag). The Web page either displays for each staff either the apartment number or a message "No Apartment Rented" in case the staff has no associated rental. The Web page layout is shown below, with attributes from database in italics.

Staff Apartment Details
first_name last_name, position --------------------------------------- Apartment# {*apt_no* | No Apartment Rented}

Create a PL/SQL procedure "w8_4_staff_apartment_details" that displays the data required for the table. Use the procedure code to complete the Web page.

8-5. Outdoor Clubs database: Create a Web page that displays details on products that have been re-ordered so far (use HTML table tag). The Web page layout is shown below, with attributes and function value from database in italics.

Reorder List		
Product ID	Name	Re-ordered Status
product_id	*product_name*	*8_5_reord_status function value*

Create a PL/SQL procedure "w8_5_product_reorder_list" that displays the data required for the table. Create a boolean function w8_5_record_status that returns a value on whether a product has been re-ordered so far or not. The Re-ordered Status column will display a 'Yes' or 'No' value based on whether the product has been re-ordered or not. Save the program units in a script file. Use the procedure code to complete the Web page.

8-6. Outdoor Clubs database: Create a Web page which displays a product supplier list that counts the number of times a product has been ordered from a supplier (use HTML table tag). The Web page layout is shown below, with attributes and function value from database in italics.

Product Supplier Details	
supplier_id: name -----------------------------------	
Product Name	Times Ordered
product_name	*8_6_time_ord function value*

Create a PL/SQL procedure "w8_6_product_supplier_details" that displays the data required for the table. Create a function w8_6_time_ord that counts the number of times a product has been ordered from a given supplier. Use the function value in Times Ordered column. Save the program units in a script file. Use the procedure code to complete the Web page.

8-7. Outdoor Clubs database: Create a Web page which displays membership status list for customers who do not have club membership so far (use HTML table tag). The Web page layout is shown below, with attributes and function value from database in italics.

Non-Membership Status	
Customer Name	Membership Status
first_name last_name	*8_7_cust_status function value*

Create a PL/SQL procedure "w8_7_membership_status" that displays the data required for the table. Create a boolean function w8_7_cust_status that returns a value on whether a customer is a member of a mountain club. The Membership Status column will display a 'Yes' value (if membership exists) or 'No' value (if membership does not exist). Save the program units in a script file. Use the procedure code to complete the Web page.

8-8. Outdoor Clubs database: Create a Web site titled "Outdoor Product Reports" with three Web pages based on the previous problem solving exercises 8-5, 8-6, and 8-7. The home page is titled "Reordered List Web" and is based on 8-5. The second Web page is titled "Product Supplier List" based on 8-6, while the third Web page is titled "Non Membership List" based on 8-7. The banner for the Web site should be "Outdoor Product Reports." Create navigation links for each Web page.

Combine the three functions in a package w8_8_prod_rep_pkg. The procedures for the Web pages above should call their respective functions from the w8_8_prod_rep_pkg package. Save the package source as a script file.

8-9. Outdoor Clubs database: Create a two page Web site that allows users to join the various sporting clubs. The home page should display an input form for users to enter information for club membership. The response page should display a membership receipt for printing.

- The home page should be titled "Apply Membership." The response page should be titled "Membership Receipt." There should be only one navigation link titled after the Home page. The navigation URL should link to the home page. The banner for both the Web pages should be "Sporting Clubs."
- The form in the home page will have the following sequence of form elements corresponding to their respective attributes: Customer First Name text box, Customer Last Name text box, Street text box, City text box, Zip Code text box, State drop-down list, Phone text box, Sporting Clubs drop-down list, Membership Duration Clubs drop-down list box, and Payment Type radio buttons. Phone numbers should be entered a numbers only. The State drop-down list will have various state names as part of the label option tag attribute entry, while their corresponding short forms will be the value option tag attribute entry. The default state display name should be "Missouri." List at least 5 states. The Sporting Clubs drop-down list will have sporting club names for label option tag attribute entry, while their corresponding club_id attribute values will be the value option tag attribute entry. The default sporting club display is "Hillside Mountain Club." The Membership Duration drop-down list will have 2, 4, 5, and 12 for both the label and value option tag attributes entries. The default membership is for 4 months. The Payment Type radio buttons correspond to the two payment_type attribute values. The form will have a "Clear" labeled button of reset type, and a "Process Application" labeled button of submit type.
- The response page should display a receipt titled "Membership Receipt" followed by the text "Thank you for your membership. We appreciate your business" below the receipt content. The receipt will display the following data from the database: Membership ID, Membership Date, Duration, Customer ID, Customer Name, and Sporting Club name. The membership is $50 per month.
- Create a PL/SQL procedure "w8_9_membership_receipt" that completes the response page procedure processing. The procedure should complete the database processing required for the page and display the membership receipt values. Utilize the database table sequences to insert rows in respective tables. Save the procedure source as a script file. Use the procedure code to complete the Web page.

8-10. Outdoor Clubs database: Create a two page Web site that creates a new sporting club entry. The home Web page should display an form to enter information for the new club. The form in the home page will have the following sequence of form elements corresponding to their respective attributes: Club Name text box, Street text box, City text box, State text box, and Zip text box. The form will have a "Proceed" labeled button of submit type.

The response Web page should display a message after creating the new club successfully. The response page will display a text message "New Club club-name having ID club-id successfully created" where club-name and club-id entries are database values.

The home page should be titled "Input Club." The response page should be titled "Create Club." There should be only one navigation link titled after the home page. The navigation URL should link to the home page. The banner for both the Web pages should be "Sporting Clubs."

Create a procedure "w8_10_create_club" to complete the insertion of new club information in the sporting_clubs table. Utilize the database table sequences to insert rows in respective tables. The procedure should display the new club name as well as the generated club_id. Save the procedure source as a script file. Use the procedure code to complete the response Web page.

8-11. Superflex Apartments database: Create a two page Web site for tenants to pay rent. The home page Web form will have the following sequence of form elements corresponding to their respective attributes: Rental Number labeled text box, Card Type labeled radio buttons corresponding to the two payment_type attribute values, Amount Charged labeled text box, and a"Submit Payment" labeled button of submit type. The response page processes the input data sent by the home page, and displays a rent receipt using HTML tables or an error message. The error message "The amount entered is not correct! Please click Pay Rent to complete payment details!!" is displayed if the Amount Charged value in the Web form is not the same as apt_rent_amt attribute value. Rent receipt should consist of Tenant Name, Rental No, Invoice No and Date. Utilize the database table sequences to insert rows in respective tables.

The home page should be titled "Pay Rent2." The response page should be titled "Rent Receipt2." There should be only one navigation link titled after the Home page. The navigation URL should link to the home page. The banner for both the Web pages should be "Superflex Apartments."

Create a PL/SQL procedure to complete the response page procedure processing. The procedure should be named w8_11_rent_reciept. The procedure should either display the text message or complete the processing and display the rent receipt database values. Save the procedure source as a script file. Use the procedure code to complete the Web page.

8-12. Outdoor Clubs database: Create a three page Web site that allows users to modify details about products. The home page and is titled "Get Product." It will have a Web form with two elements: (a) a drop-down list that displays all product_name values in the database where the drop-down list option tag label/value attribute entries will correspond to product_name/product_id values in the database, and (b) a form button labeled "Get Details" that will submit the selected product name value to the second Web page.

The second Web page is titled "Modify Product." It will have a Web form that shows the attribute values in the database associated with the product_name selected in the first Web page. The form elements with attribute values are: (a) a text box that displays the current product_name attribute value, a text box that displays the current product's price attribute value, (b) a set of radio buttons for all the supplier_id attribute values with the correct supplier_id button checked for the associated product, (c) a text box that displays the current reorder_qty attribute value, and (d) a form button labeled "Modify" that will submit the form element values to the third Web page.

The third Web page is titled "Complete Product Change." The page will complete the update of the attribute values (as entered in the second Web page) in the relevant tables and generate a message "Update Successful."

There should be only one navigation link titled after the home page. The navigation URL should link to the home page. The banner for all the Web pages should be "Outdoor Product Update."

Create a PL/SQL procedure "w8_12_modify_product" that completes the processing of the second Web page. Use the dbms_output statements to display the form element database values. Save the procedure source as a script file. Use the procedure code to complete the Web page.

8-13. Outdoor Clubs database: Create a three page Web site that allows users to modify details about a sporting club. The home page and is titled "Get Club." It will have a Web form with the following form elements: (a) a drop-down list that displays all sporting club names in the database along with their associated club_id values, and (b) a form button labeled "Get Details" that will submit the selected sporting club name value to the second Web page. The drop-down list option tag label/value attribute entries will correspond to name/club_id values in the database. The user will select a sporting club name from the drop-down list, and the Web form button will submit the associated club_id value to the second Web page.

The second PSP page is titled "Modify Club." It will have a Web form that shows the attribute values in the database associated with the sporting club name selected in the first Web page. The form elements with attribute values are: (a) a text box that displays the current sporting club name attribute value, (b) a text box that displays the current sporting club's phone value, (c) a set of check boxes for all the club activity values wherein the correct activity check boxes are checked for the associated product, and (d) a form button labeled "Modify" that will submit the form element values to the third Web page.

The third PSP page is titled "Complete Club Change." The page will complete the update of the attribute values (as entered in the second Web page) in the relevant tables and generate a message "Update Successful." Update of club activity will be such that the unchecked activities will be deleted from the club_activity table, while the checked activities if not already existing will be added in the club_activity table.

There should be only one navigation link titled after the home page. The navigation URL should link to the home page. The banner for all the Web pages should be "Outdoor Club Update."

Create a PL/SQL procedure "w8_13_modify_club" that completes the processing of the second Web page. Use the dbms_output statements to display the form element database values. Save the procedure source as a script file. Create a PL/SQL procedure "w8_13_comp_club_change" that completes the processing of the third Web page. Use the dbms_output statements to display the form element database values. Save the procedure source as a script file. Use the procedure code to complete the Web pages.

8-14. Outdoor Clubs database: Create two page Web site that allows a user to create a new product order. The home page and is titled "Enter Order." It will have a Web form with the following form elements: (a) a drop-down list that displays all customer names (first_name last_name) in the database along with their associated customer_id values. The drop-down list option tag label/value attribute entries will correspond to customer first_name last_name/customer_id values in the database, (b) a drop-down list that displays all product_name in the database along with their associated product_id values. The drop-down list option tag label/value attribute entries will correspond to product_name/product_id values in the database, (c) a text box to enter quantity attribute value, (d) a set of radio buttons for the product_order payment_type attribute values, and (e) a form button labeled "Checkout" that will submit the form element values to the second Web page.

The second Web page is titled "Generate Order." The page will complete the generation of the new product order by inserting a row in product_order and order_details tables. The quantity_in_stock value for the product needs to be reduced by the quantity value of the product order. Add a $6 shipping and handling charge to the order amount. At the successful conclusion of the processing, the page will display a message "New product order

order-id for customer first-name last-name for amount total has been created." The message entries in italics are database values pertaining to the order.

There should be only one navigation link titled after the home page. The navigation URL should link to the home page. The banner for all the Web pages should be "Outdoor Club Update."

Create a PL/SQL procedure "w8_14_generate_order" that completes the processing of the second Web page. Use the dbms_output statements to display the message with database values. Save the procedure source as a script file. Use the procedure code to complete the Web page.

8-15. Outdoor Clubs database: Create a three page Web site that allows users to modify details about a customer along with the creation of a new club membership.The home page is titled "Enter Customer." It will have a Web form with the following form elements: (a) A text box to enter customer_id value, and (b) a form button labeled "Proceed" that will submit the entered customer_id to the second Web page.

The second Web page is titled "Modify Customer." The Web page will either display a message "Customer ID is not correct. Please go back and re-enter" when the customer_id entered in the home page is invalid or a Web form with another message at the top of the form. The Web form will show the attribute values in the database associated with the customer_id entered in the first Web page. The message displayed before the Web form is "Customer ID customer-id-text Details" where the customer-id-text is the value of customer_id entered in the first Web page. The form elements with attribute values are: (a) a text box that displays the current customer street attribute value, (b) a text box that displays the current customer city attribute value, (c) a text box that displays the current customer city attribute value, (d) a text box that displays the current customer state attribute value, (e) a text box that displays the current customer zip attribute value, (f) A drop-down list that displays all sporting club names in the database along with their associated club_id values wherein the drop-down list option tag label/value attribute entries will correspond to club name/club_id values in the database, (g) a set of radio buttons for all the club_membership duration attribute values wherein place a text beside the radio buttons stating "Membership Fee is $50 per month", (h) a set of radio buttons for all the club_membership payment_type attribute values, (i) a form button labeled "Modify" that will submit the form element values to the third Web page.

The third Web page is titled "Confirm Customer Change." The page will complete the update and insert operation for the attribute values (as entered in the second Web page) in the relevant tables and generate a message "Customer Update Successful." The Web page will process second Web page form data by first updating the customer table with the customer address entries, and secondly, the club_id, duration, and payment_type entries will be used to insert a new row in club_membership table.

There should be only one navigation link titled after the home page. The navigation URL should link to the home page. The banner for all the Web pages should be "Outdoor Anywhere."

Create a PL/SQL procedure "w8_15_modify_customer" that completes the processing of the second Web page. Use the dbms_output statements to display the form element database values. Save the procedure source as a script file. Use the procedure code to complete the Web page. Create a PL/SQL procedure "w8_15_confirm_club_change" that completes the processing of the third Web page. Use the dbms_output statements to display the form element database values. Save the procedure source as a script file. Use the procedure code to complete the Web pages.

Chapter 9. Business Logic with Database Design

Database design should not be limited to the modeling of business data but also include the development of business logic. Business logic from a database design perspective reflects the interaction of business activities with data through the medium of business rules. As business rules are data-centric, it is possible to encode the logic in the database in the form of stored program units. This can be expressed through one database program unit or split into multiple program units.

Since organizational activities are the source of data that is modeled and stored in the database, their business (operating) logic should also be part of database design. Just as database relationships express the use of data, similarly business rules that represent business logic guidelines also reflect the use of data. It is possible for business rules that represent business logic to also provide some clarity to the existing data model structure. In nutshell, business rules aside from identifying database structure also guide how the business process task is accomplished. As the database is shared across multiple applications and formats, it is essential that such business logic resides in the database (DBMS) to ensure that business rules are consistently enforced across all applications.

As business applications automate some or all of the business process activities, they can avail of such stored program units. When business logic is implemented in the database, the external application can focus on the user-interface, networking, and other aspects of the application, while leaving the database stored program units to complete the necessary database-related activity.

Chapter 3 showed how the business process model and business rules specifications can facilitate the modeling of organization data. This chapter focuses on how the business logic of a business process can be expressed through PL/SQL stored program units.

Business Logic

Business logic is the logic of how operational tasks are completed by the business process. This logic can range from how the activities in a business process are sequenced to how specific activities are completed. PL/SQL allows the development of business logic through stored program units. All enterprise systems irrespective of application language are essentially database-driven systems as they naturally thread business logic to reflect business operations. Just as any enterprise application reflects business working, business logic in the database should embody it more naturally.

One way to speed automation of a business process is to develop the business logic independent of user interface or application. As business logic interacts with business data, expressing it through stored program units in the database will (a) make it easily accessible to business applications, and (b) better shared and maintained. Besides as business activities change due to competitive pressures, associated stored program units can be modified or created without impacting the external application interface.

One way to develop business logic is to first identify business rules that involve data manipulation beyond data structure and secondly tie the business rules to activities to know the sequence of their implementation. The sequence of business rules occurrence ensures that business logic accurately reflects business operations.

For instance, Figure 9-1 is the high-level business logic of how a new apartment rental should be handled.

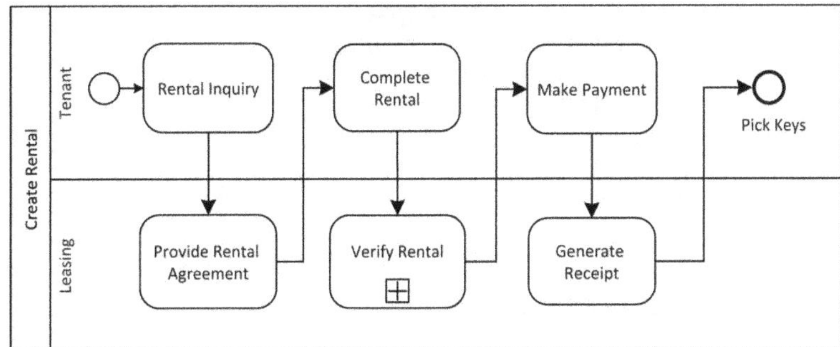

Figure 9-1: Create Rental Business Process Model

This diagram is similar to Figure 3-6 in chapter 3, except that a new symbol appears in Verify Rental activity. The symbol indicates that Verify Rental is a collapsed sub-process. Table 9-1 shows the business rules pertaining to the overall business process. These business rules are similar to Table 3-5 in chapter 3. Many of the business rules illustrate the use of data that is consequential to the business logic of Verify Rental activity.

Business Rules ID	**Business Rules Description**
BR-1	Terms tenant, rental relevant for business process.
BR-2	Only one tenant must sign a rental agreement to complete the rental process.
BR-3	Rental lease type can be monthly or yearly.
BR-4	A monthly rental lease is 10% more than the regular yearly apartment rent.
BR-5	Rental agreement payment will include the apartment deposit amount and first month rent.
BR-6	A rental agreement must have only one staff associated with it.
BR-7	Besides regular staff, even part-time staff can facilitate rental agreements.
BR-8	Every tenant automobile license plate number must be registered in the rental agreement.
BR-9	Every tenant is allowed free parking for one registered automobile.
BR-10	No apartment should be rented if there are complaints pending on the apartment.
BR-11	Apartment complaint status can be fixed, pending, or not determined.
BR-12	All tenants must have good credit scores.
BR-13	Tenant has to provide details on all persons staying in the apartment.

Table 9-1: Create Rental Business Process Business Rules

Additional business rules pertaining to use of data by other business process activities are shown below.

Business Rules ID	Business Rules Description	Business Process Activity
BR-25	Check tenant's identification and rental number.	Make Payment
BR-26	Tenant must pay one month rental and security deposit.	
BR-27	Process payment.	Generate Receipt
BR-28	Print payment receipt.	

Table 9-2: Additional Create Rental Business Process Business Rules

The details (business logic) of the expanded Verify Rental activity are shown in Figure 9-2. The diagram shows the business logic of how the apartment complex handles the verification of rental application. Since there are no sub-processes involved in the diagram, it is at the lowest level of detail with respect to Verify Rental business activity.

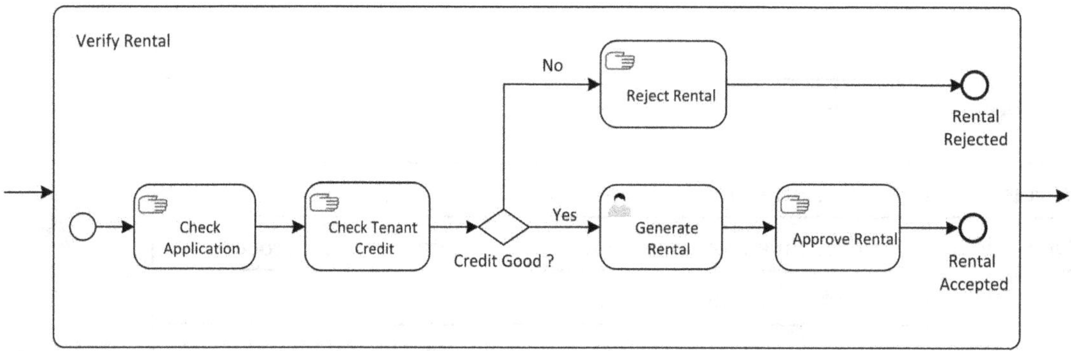

Figure 9-2: Verify Rental Business Logic

An expanded version of Verify Rental business logic with a short description and associated business rules is shown in Figure 9-3. Many of the activities are manual tasks, except Generate Rental. Generate Rental is a user task. This implies that a staff enters the tenant application details in the database, and the database generates a new rental number with an assigned apartment.

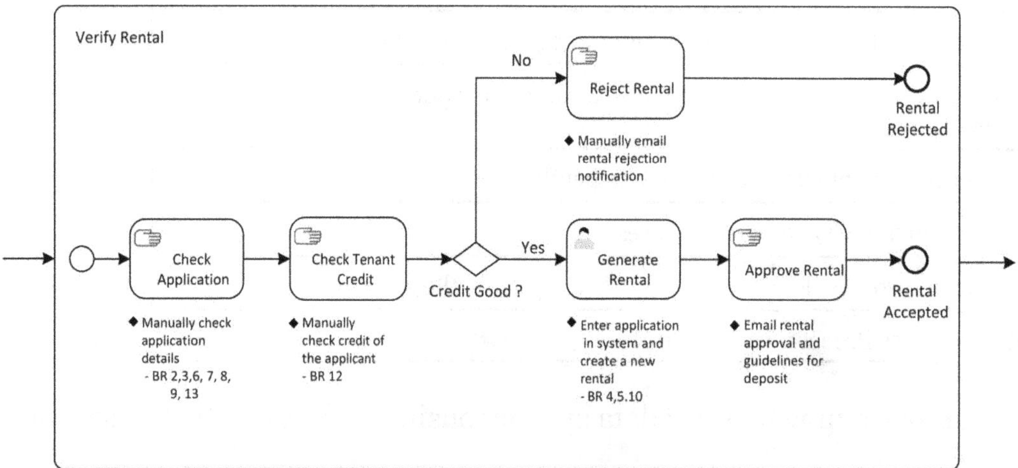

Figure 9-3: Verify Rental Business Logic with Business Rules

Due to the database-centric nature of the Generate Rental activity, a database program unit is created to complete the task. Figure 9-4 outlines the business logic of Generate Rental activity task. The logic utilizes SQL keywords to reflect the database aspect of the business logic.

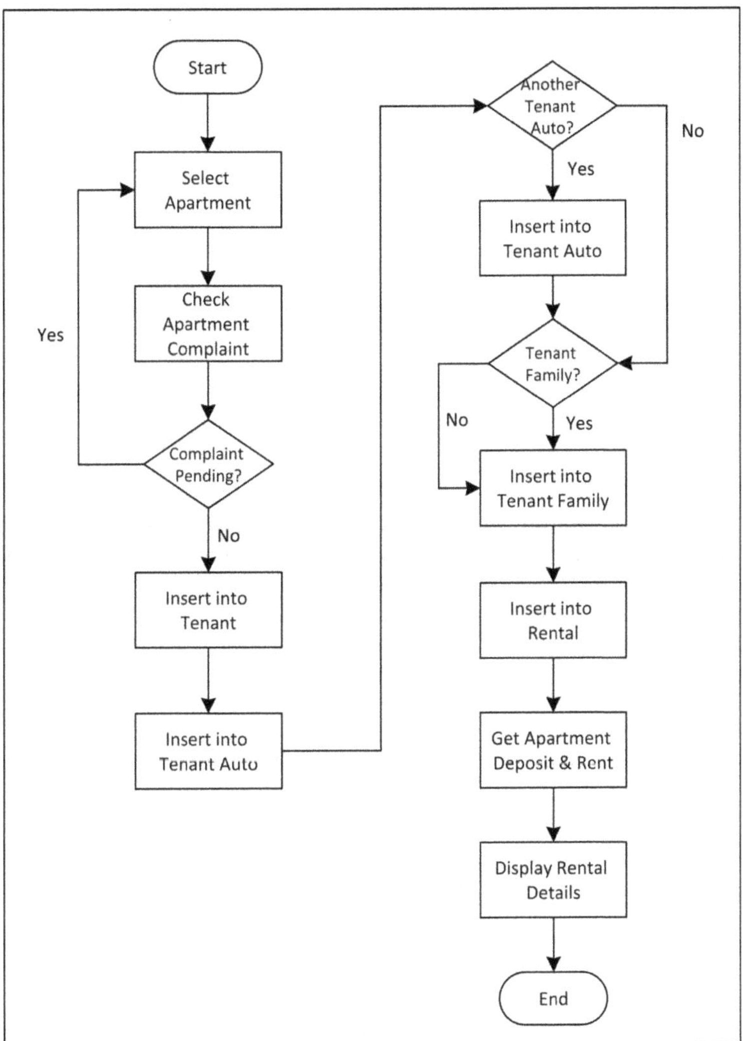

Figure 9-4: Database logic of Generate Rental activity task

Procedure create_rental along with functions assign_apartment and check_complaints below implements the logic of Figure 9-4. The procedure has input parameters for the corresponding entries in the rental application form. The dbms_output statements are utilized for checking the validity of the logic. It is possible for the dbms_output values to become output parameters if an external third party application was interacting with the procedure.

```
create or replace function assign_apartment return number as
cursor apt_cur is
select apt_no
from apartment
where apt_status = 'V';
apt_row apt_cur%rowtype;
apt_select apartment.apt_no%type;
begin
for apt_row in apt_cur
loop
    if not check_complaints(apt_row.apt_no) then
```

```
      apt_select := apt_row.apt_no;
      exit;
      end if;
end loop;
return apt_select;
end;

create or replace function check_complaints (apt_in number) return boolean as
status_ctr integer;
begin
select count(*)
into status_ctr
from complaints
where apt_no = apt_in
and status is null;
if status_ctr > 0 then
      return true;
else
      return false;
end if;
end;

create or replace procedure create_rental (tenant_ss_in int, tname varchar2, tdob varchar2, marital_in char,
w_phone varchar2, h_phone varchar2, emp varchar2, gender_in char, email_in varchar2, credit int,c_agency varchar2, lic_no
varchar2, a_make varchar2, a_model varchar2, a_year number, a_color varchar2,
f_ss_in int, f_name varchar2, spouse_in char, child_in char, f_gender char, fdob varchar2,
lic_no2 varchar2, a_make2 varchar2, a_model2 varchar2, a_year2 number, a_color2 varchar2,
rdate varchar2,ltype varchar2,lstart varchar2,staff_in varchar2) as
apt_select apartment.apt_no%type;
lend date;
new_rental_no rental.rental_no%type;
a_deposit apartment.apt_deposit_amt%type;
a_rent apartment.apt_rent_amt%type;
begin
apt_select := assign_apartment;
update apartment
set apt_status = 'R'
where apt_no = apt_select;
insert into tenant values
(tenant_ss_in,tname,to_date(tdob,'mm/dd/yyyy'),marital_in,w_phone,h_phone,emp,gender_in,email_in,credit,c_agenc
y,null);
insert into tenant_auto
values (tenant_ss_in,lic_no,a_make,a_model,a_year,a_color,0);
if lic_no2 is not null then
      insert into tenant_auto
      values (tenant_ss_in,lic_no2,a_make2,a_model2,a_year2,a_color2,45.5);
end if;
if f_ss_in is not null then
      insert into tenant_family
      values (tenant_ss_in, f_ss_in,f_name,spouse_in,child_in,f_gender,to_date(fdob,'mm/dd/yyyy'));
end if;
commit;
if ltype = 'One' then
      lend := add_months(to_date(lstart,'mm/dd/yy'),12);
end if;
if ltype = 'Six' then
      lend := add_months(to_date(lstart,'mm/dd/yy'),6);
end if;
insert into rental
values (rental_sequence.nextval,to_date(rdate,'mm/dd/yyyy'),'S',ltype,to_date(lstart,'mm/dd/yyyy'),lend,staff_in,apt_select);
new_rental_no := rental_sequence.currval;
```

```
select apt_deposit_amt,apt_rent_amt
into a_deposit,a_rent
from apartment
where apt_no = apt_select;
dbms_output.put_line('Rental No '||new_rental_no||' created');
dbms_output.put_line('Tenant Name '||tname);
dbms_output.put_line('Apartment Deposit '||a_deposit);
dbms_output.put_line('Apartment Rent '||a_rent);
end;
```

Sample Web Application

The following two Web pages illustrate the utilization of the database procedure create_rental to complete the Generate Rental activity task. The source utilizes PL/SQL Web Toolkit. The home page Web procedure is create_rental_web, while the second Web page is rental_web_confirm procedure. The rental_web_confirm procedure is an adaptation of create_rental procedure with Web extensions. The Web pages can be viewed through the PL/SQL Web Gateway setup.

```
create or replace procedure create_rental_web as
begin
htp.print('<!DOCTYPE HTML PUBLIC "-//W3C//DTD HTML 4.01 Transitional//EN">
<html>
<head>
<title>Superflex Apartment</title>
</head>
<body>
<p><b>Enter Rental Application Details</b></p>

<form action="rental_web_confirm" method="post">
<b>Tenant Details:</b><br /><br />
Tenant SS: <input type="text" name="tenant_ss_in" value=" " /> <br /><br />
Tenant Name: <input type="text" name="tname" value=" " /> <br /><br />
Tenant DOB: <input type="text" name="tdob" value=" " /> <br /><br />
Marital Status: Married <input type="radio" name="marital_in" value="M" />
Single <input type="radio" name="marital_in" value="S" /><br /><br />
Work Phone: <input type="text" name="w_phone" value=" " /> <br /><br />
Home Phone: <input type="text" name="h_phone" value=" " /> <br /><br />
Employer: <input type="text" name="emp" value=" " /> <br /><br />
Gender: Male <input type="radio" name="gender_in" value="M" />
Female <input type="radio" name="gender_in" value="F" /><br /><br />
Email: <input type="text" name="email_in" value=" " /> <br /><br />
Credit Score: <input type="text" name="credit" value=" " /> <br /><br />
Credit Agency: <input type="text" name="c_agency" value=" " /> <br /><br />

<b>Auto Details:</b> <br /><br />
License No: <input type="text" name="lic_no" value=" " /> <br /><br />
Auto Make: <input type="text" name="a_make" value=" " /> <br /><br />
Auto Model: <input type="text" name="a_model" value=" " /> <br /><br />
Auto Year: <input type="text" name="a_year" value=" " /> <br /><br />
Auto Color: <input type="text" name="a_color" value=" " /> <br /><br />

<b>Tenant Family:</b> <br /><br />
Family SS: <input type="text" name="f_ss_in" value=" " /> <br /><br />
Family Name: <input type="text" name="f_name" value=" " /> <br /><br />
Spouse: Yes <input type="radio" name="spouse_in" value="Y" />
No <input type="radio" name="spouse_in" value="N" /><br /><br />
Child: Yes <input type="radio" name="child_in" value="Y" />
No <input type="radio" name="child_in" value="N" /><br /><br />
Gender: Male <input type="radio" name="f_gender" value="M" />
```

```
Female <input type="radio" name="f_gender" value="F" /><br /><br />
Family DOB: <input type="text" name="fdob" value=" " /> <br /><br />

<b>Second Auto Details:</b> <br /><br />
License No: <input type="text" name="lic_no2" value=" " /> <br /><br />
Auto Make: <input type="text" name="a_make2" value=" " /> <br /><br />
Auto Model: <input type="text" name="a_model2" value=" " /> <br /><br />
Auto Year: <input type="text" name="a_year2" value=" " /> <br /><br />
Auto Color: <input type="text" name="a_color2" value=" " /> <br /><br />

<b>Rental Information:</b> <br /><br />
Rental Date: <input type="text" name="rdate" value=" " /> <br /><br />
Lease Type: <input type="text" name="ltype" value=" " /> <br /><br />
Lease Start: <input type="text" name="lstart" value=" " /> <br /><br />
Staff Number: <input type="text" name="staff_in" value=" " /> <br /><br />
<input type="submit" name="FormsButton1" value="Send"/>

</form>
<!-- End Page Content -->
</body>
</html>');
end;

create or replace procedure rental_web_confirm (tenant_ss_in int, tname varchar2, tdob varchar2, marital_in char,
w_phone varchar2, h_phone varchar2, emp varchar2, gender_in char, email_in varchar2, credit int,c_agency varchar2,
lic_no varchar2, a_make varchar2, a_model varchar2, a_year number, a_color varchar2,
f_ss_in int default null, f_name varchar2 default null, spouse_in char default null, child_in char default null,
f_gender char default null, fdob varchar2 default null,
lic_no2 varchar2 default null, a_make2 varchar2 default null, a_model2 varchar2 default null, a_year2 number default null,
a_color2 varchar2
default null,
rdate varchar2,ltype varchar2,lstart varchar2,staff_in varchar2, FormsButton1 varchar2) as
apt_select apartment.apt_no%type;
lend date;
new_rental_no rental.rental_no%type;
a_deposit apartment.apt_deposit_amt%type;
a_rent apartment.apt_rent_amt%type;
begin
apt_select := assign_apartment;
update apartment
set apt_status = 'R'
where apt_no = apt_select;
insert into tenant values
(tenant_ss_in,tname,to_date(tdob,'mm/dd/yyyy'),marital_in,w_phone,h_phone,emp,gender_in,email_in,credit,c_agenc
y,null);
insert into tenant_auto
values (tenant_ss_in,lic_no,a_make,a_model,a_year,a_color,0);
if lic_no2 is not null then
    insert into tenant_auto
    values (tenant_ss_in,lic_no2,a_make2,a_model2,a_year2,a_color2,45.5);
end if;
if f_ss_in is not null then
    insert into tenant_family
    values (tenant_ss_in, f_ss_in,f_name,spouse_in,child_in,f_gender,to_date(fdob,'mm/dd/yyyy'));
end if;
commit;
if ltype = 'One' then
    lend := add_months(to_date(lstart,'mm/dd/yy'),12);
end if;
if ltype = 'Six' then
    lend := add_months(to_date(lstart,'mm/dd/yy'),6);
```

```
end if;
dbms_output.put_line('lend '||lend);
insert into rental
values (rental_sequence.nextval,to_date(rdate,'mm/dd/yyyy'),'S',ltype,to_date(lstart,'mm/dd/yyyy'),lend,staff_in,apt_select);
new_rental_no := rental_sequence.currval;
select apt_deposit_amt,apt_rent_amt
into a_deposit,a_rent
from apartment
where apt_no = apt_select;
htp.print('<!DOCTYPE HTML PUBLIC "-//W3C//DTD HTML 4.01 Transitional//EN">
<html>
<head>
<title>Superflex Apartment</title>
</head>
<body>');
htp.print('Rental No '||new_rental_no||' created for Tenant Name '||tname);
htp.print('Apartment Deposit '||a_deposit||' and Apartment Rent '||a_rent);
exception
when others then
htp.print(sqlerrm);
end;
```

Review Questions

1. Describe the purpose of business logic?
2. Describe the role of stored program units in developing business logic?
3. Describe the role of business rules in business logic?

Review Exercises

1. Database design should not be limited to _______ of business data.
2. Business logic from a database design perspective reflects the _______ of business activities with data through the medium of ______ _______.
3. Business rules that represent business logic guidelines also reflect use of _____.
4. All enterprise systems irrespective of application language are essentially _________ systems.
5. One way to develop business logic is to identify business rules that involve data _______ manipulation beyond _____ structure.
6. The _______ of business rules occurrence ensures that business logic accurately reflects business operations.

Problem Solving Exercises

9-1. Extend chapter 3 problem 3-1 by developing the business logic of the restaurant service operations business process model in the form of PL/SQL stored program units. The business process model diagram and extended business rules list of the chapter 3 problem 3-1 is reproduced in Figure 9-5 and Table 9-3. Additional business rules BR-8, BR-9, and BR-10 have been added. Business logic should cover the activities of Check Table Availability, Make Menu Selection, Generate Bill and Make Payment.

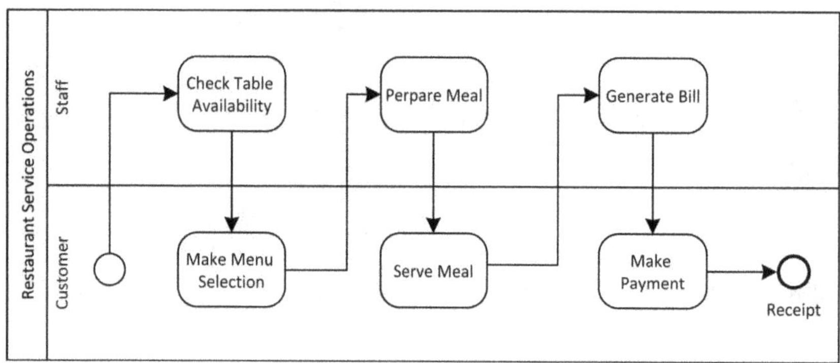

Figure 9-5: Restaurant Service Operation Business Process Model

Business Rules ID	Business Rules Description
BR-1	Terms Menu, SeatingTable, Booking, Server relevant for business process.
BR-2	A booking is taken care by one server. A server can attend to many bookings.
BR-3	It is possible for a server to have no bookings.
BR-4	Each booking is associated with at least one seatingtable.
BR-5	A seatingtable can service many bookings.
BR-6	Each booking is associated with one or more menu items.
BR-7	It is possible for a menu item to have not been ordered in any booking.
BR-8	It is possible to reserve more than one seatingtable for large booking party.
BR-9	Guests can pick multiple menu items from each menu category.
BR-10	A 10% gratuity added to each bill.

Table 9-3: Restaurant Service Operations Business Process Business Rules

Business term information that needs to be recorded (same as problem 3-1):

- Menu term information will consist of the following: MenuID, its Name, Description, Price, Ingredient, and IngredientQuantity. There can be many ingredients with specific quantities for each menu item. The ID of Menu is MenuID.
- SeatingTable term information will consist of the following: TableID and details like number of seats and location. The ID of seating table is TableID.
- Server term information will consist of the following: ServerID, FirstName, LastName. The ID of server is ServerID.
- Booking term information will consist of the following: BookingID, ServingDate, PartySize, GuestName, NumberOfAdults, NumberOfChildren. The ID of server is BookingID.

9-2. Extend chapter 3 problem 3-2 by developing the business logic of the lead to forecast business process model in the form of PL/SQL stored program units. The business process model diagram and extended business rules list of the chapter 3 problem 3-2 is reproduced in Figure 9-6 and Table 9-4. Additional business rules BR-8, BR-9, and BR-10 have been added. Business logic should cover all the activities.

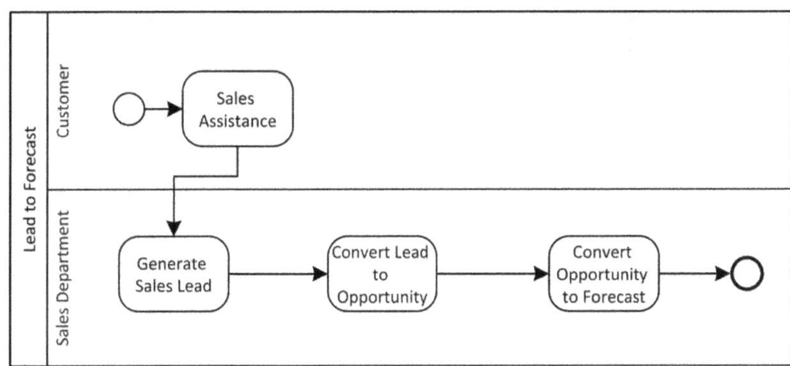

Figure 9-6: Lead to Forecast Business Process Model

Business Rules ID	Business Rules Description
BR-1	Terms SalesAgent, Customer, Product, SalesLead relevant for business process.
BR-2	SalesLead occurs when a customer requests the need for further assistance before placing an order.
BR-3	The salesagent records details about the customer and product.
BR-4	A customer can also be associated with multiple products.
BR-5	A product may not always have an interest from a customer.
BR-6	A salesaagent may initiate multiple salesleads.
BR-7	A customer can have multiple salesleads, while every saleslead must be associated with a customer.
BR-8	Every saleslead will have timeframe specification in the form of "soon or interest."
BR-9	Every saleslead that has timeframe of soon should have an MaturingPercent value.
BR-10	Saleslead from a customer must be aggregated continually and MaturingPercent opportunity ranked.
BR-11	Saleslead maturing within the incoming quarter should be part of salesforecast.

Table 9-4: Lead to Forecast Business Process Business Rules

Business term information that needs to be recorded (same as problem 3-2):

- SalesLead term information will consist of the following: SalesLeadID, LeadName, TimeFrame, LeadAmount, and MaturingPercent. The ID of SalesLead is SalesLeadID.
- Customer term information will consist of the following: CustomerID, Name, ContactType, ContactTitle, State, and Zip. The ID of Customer is CustomerID.
- Product term information will consist of the following: ProductID, Description, Price. The ID of Product is ProductID.
- SalesAgent term information will consist of the following: SalesAgentID, FirstName, LastName. The ID of SalesAgent is SalesAgentID.

9-3. Extend chapter 3 problem 3-3 by developing the business logic of the automobile rental web reservation business process model in the form of PL/SQL stored program units. The business process model diagram and business rules list of the chapter 3 problem 3-3 is reproduced in Figure 9-7 and Table 9-5. Business logic should cover all the activities.

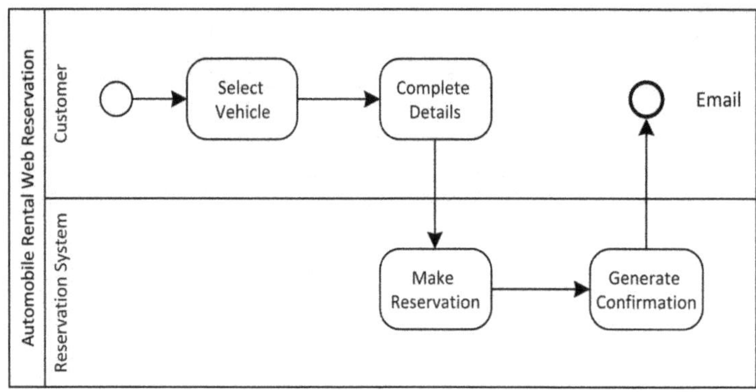

Figure 9-7: Automobile Rental Web Reservation Business Process Model

Business Rules ID	Business Rules Description
BR-1	Terms Customer Vehicle Rental relevant for business process.
BR-2	Only one vehicle per rental.
BR-3	Only one customer per rental.
BR-4	Repeat rental customers get 10% discount in Rental Amount.
BR-5	Rental vehicles must have less than 15000 miles.
BR-6	Rental vehicles with more than 10 minor dents are not allowed for future rentals.
BR-7	A vehicle can participate in many rentals.

Table 9-5: Automobile Rental Web Reservation Business Process Business Rules

Business term information that needs to be recorded (same as problem 3-3):

- Customer term information will consist of the following: CustomerNo, CustomerName, Street, City, State, Zip, Phone, Email. The ID of Customer is CustomerNo.
- Vehicle term information will consist of the following: VIN (Vehicle Identification Number), ModelYear, AutoMake, AutoModel, OdometerReading, MinorDents, MajorDents. The ID of Vehicle is VIN.
- Rental term information will consist the following: RentalNo, RentalDate, PickUp_City, DropOff_City, PickUp_Time, DropOff_Time, Navigation, SkiRack, Infant_Seat, Collison_Insurance, RentalAmount, Tax, RentalTotal. The ID of Rental is RentalNo.

9-4. Extend chapter 3 problem 3-4 by developing the business logic of the automobile rental business process model in the form of PL/SQL stored program units. The business process model diagram and business rules list of the chapter 3 problem 3-4 is reproduced in Figure 9-8 and Table 9-6. An additional business rule BR-12 has been added. Business logic should cover all the activities.

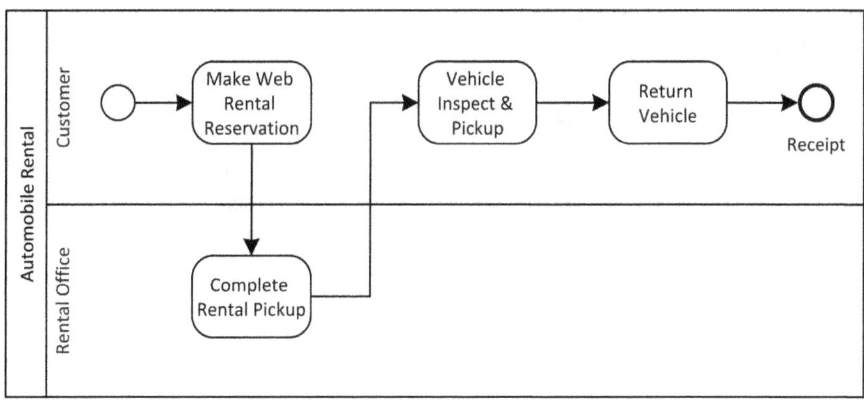

Figure 9-8: Automobile Rental Business Process Model

Business Rules ID	Business Rules Description
BR-1	Terms Registration, Vehicle, Rental, Location relevant for business process.
BR-2	A new customer first completes Web registration.
BR-3	A rental is always associated with a customer. The customer can visit the Web site again to make another reservation.
BR-4	The Web site generates a rental confirmation number with the Web rental rate.
BR-5	Every rental will have an assigned vehicle, but a vehicle may not be associated with a rental.
BR-6	A vehicle can be associated with many rentals over time.
BR-7	A rental is assigned to a location.
BR-8	A location may be taking care of multiple rentals.
BR-9	A vehicle may be stationed at multiple locations over time. A location can have multiple vehicles at its site.
BR-10	The vehicle rental rate is associated with the location where the vehicle is stationed.
BR-11	At the time of vehicle pickup, the StartOdometer reading is recorded as part of the rental. Also, at the conclusion of the rental, the EndOdometer reading is entered as part of the rental.
BR-12	Inspect vehicle on dents and scratches before pickup and match upon vehicle return.

Table 9-6: Automobile Rental Business Process Business Rules

Business term information that needs to be recorded (same as problem 3-4):

- Registration term information will consist of the following: RegistrationNo, FirstName, LastName, Address, Phone, and Email. The ID of Registration is RegistrationNo.
- Rental term information will consist of the following: ConfirmationNo, PickupDate, ReturnDate, WebRentalRate. The ID of Rental is ConfirmationNo.
- Vehicle term information will consist of the following: VIN, ModelYear, Odometer, Make, Type, and Model. The ID of Vehicle is VIN.

- Location term information will consist of the following: LocationID, State, City, LocationName. The ID of Location is LocationID.

9-5. Extend chapter 3 problem 3-5 by developing the business logic of nursing home admission business process model in the form of PL/SQL stored program units. The business process model diagram and business rules list of the chapter 3 problem 3-5 is reproduced in Figure 9-9 and Table 9-7. Additional business rules BR-8 and BR-9 have been added. Business logic should cover Register Patient, Patient Evaluation and Patient Billing activities.

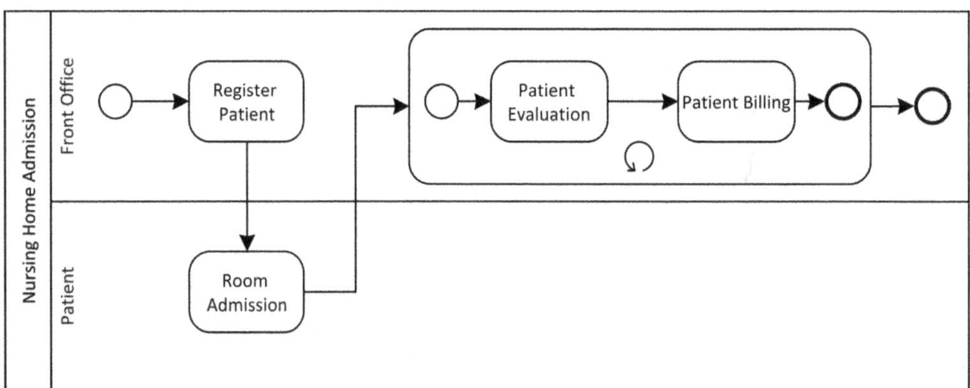

Figure 9-9: Nursing Home Admission Business Process Model

Business Rules ID	Business Rules Description
BR-1	Terms Family, Patient, Room, InsurancePolicy, InsuranceCo relevant for business process.
BR-2	Every patient is assigned a room. A patient can request a change to another room over time.
BR-3	A room will have only one patient at a time.
BR-4	Every patient must have some insurance policy.
BR-5	A patient can have multiple insurance policies.
BR-6	The nursing home may handle policies from different insurance companies (InsuranceCo term). Each patient insurance policy must belong to one of the associated insurance company.
BR-7	A patient can have multiple family members recorded. Also, a family can have multiple patients at the nursing home.
BR-8	Patients vitals in the form of blood pressure, temperature and medications are recorded everyday.
BR-9	Insurance is billed every month for patient medications.

Table 9-7: Nursing Home Admission Business Process Business Rules

Business term information that needs to be recorded (same as problem 3-5):

- Patient term information will consist of the following: PatientNo, FirstName, MiddleInitial, LastName, Phone, and Email. The ID of Patient is PatientNo.

- Room term information will consist of the following: RoomNo, TV, and Phone. The ID of Room is RoomNo.
- InsurancePolicy term information will consist of the following: PolicyNo, StartDate, EndDate, and PolicyDetails. The ID of InsurancePolicy is PolicyNo.
- InsuranceCo term information will consist of the following: CompanyID, Name, ContactPhone, ContactName, Address, and Email. The ID of InsuranceCo is CompanyID.
- Family term information will consist of the following: FamilyID, ContactName, PatientRelationship, Phone, Address, Email. The ID of Family is FamilyID.

9-6. Extend chapter 3 problem 3-6 by developing the business logic of automobile insurance claim business process model in the form of PL/SQL stored program units. The business process model diagram and business rules list of the chapter 3 problem 3-6 is reproduced in Figure 9-10 and Table 9-8. Additional business rules BR-8 and BR-9 have been added. Business logic should cover Check Policy, Assess Claim and Calculate Payment activities.

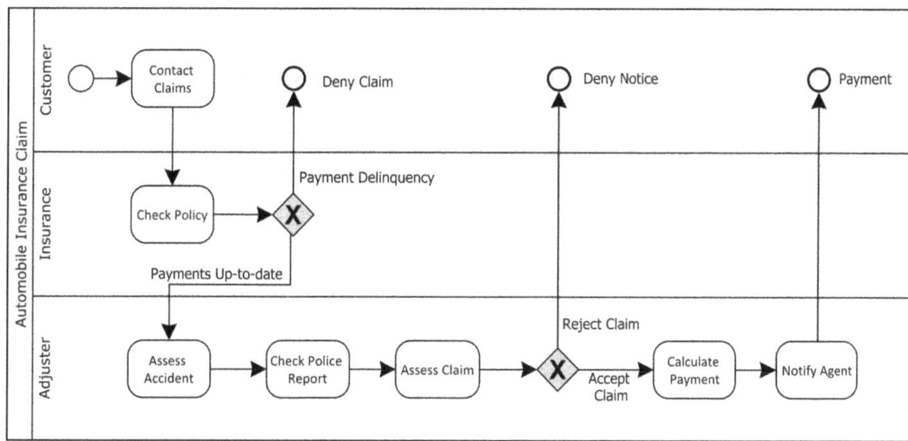

Figure 9-10: Automobile Insurance Claim Business Process Model

Business Rules ID	Business Rules Description
BR-1	Terms AutoPolicy, Claims, Agent, Adjustor relevant for business process.
BR-2	An auto policy may not have any claims in the beginning, but can have one or more claims over the life of the policy.
BR-3	An auto policy can include multiple vehicles.
BR-4	All auto policy payments are recorded.
BR-5	Only one agent must be associated with an auto policy.
BR-6	A claim must be handled by an adjustor. An adjustor may deal with many claims.
BR-7	A claim payment will incur a 10% rise in policy premium.
BR-8	Claims can be denied if policy payments are delinquent beyond 30 days.

Table 9-8: Automobile Insurance Claim Business Process Business Rules

Business term information that needs to be recorded (same as problem 3-6):

- AutoPolicy term information will consist of the following: PolicyNo, YearPremium, EffectiveDate, ExpirationDate. The ID of AutoPolicy is PolicyNo information.

- AutoPolicyPayments details associated with each AutoPolicy will consist of the following information: PaymentNo, PaymentDate, DueDate, AmountDue, AmountPaid. The ID of AutoPolicyPayments is PaymentNo.
- Vehicle details associated with each AutoPolicy will consist of the following information: VIN (Vehicle Identification Number), ModelYear, AutoMake, AutoModel, BodilyInjuryAmt, AutoDamageAmt, MedicalPaymentsAmt, and UninsuredMotoristsAmt. The ID of each Vehicle is VIN.
- Claims term information will consist the following: ClaimNo, ClaimDate, AmountClaimed, AccidentStreet, AccidentState, AccidentZip, AmountPaid, ClaimStatus, PoliceReportNote, PoliceTicket, PoliceBlame, AdjusterBlame, BodilyInjuryStatus, AutoDamageStatus, SettlementDate, and RepairEstimate. The ID of Claims is ClaimNo information.
- Agent term information will consist the following: AgentNo, AgencyName, Street, City, State, Zip, Phone, and Email. The ID of Agent is AgentNo.
- Adjuster term information will consist the following: AdjusterNo, AdjusterName, Street, City, State, Zip, Phone, and Email. The ID of Adjuster is AdjusterNo.

Appendix A. Superflex Apartment Database Tables

APARTMENT							
APT_NO	APT_TYPE	APT_STATUS	APT_UTILITY	FLOORING	BALCONY	APT_DEPOSIT_AMT	APT_RENT_AMT
100	0	R	Y	Carpet	N	200	300
101	0	R	N	Carpet	N	200	300
102	0	R	Y	Carpet	N	200	300
103	1	V	N	Carpet	N	300	400
104	1	R	Y	Carpet	N	300	400
200	2	V	Y	Hardwood	Y	400	500
201	2	R	Y	Carpet	N	400	500
202	3	V	Y	Hardwood	Y	500	700
203	3	R	Y	Hardwood	Y	500	700
* APT_NO is primary key							

STAFF							
STAFF_NO	FIRST_NAME	LAST_NAME	POSITION	STATUS	GENDER	DOB	SALARY
SA200	Joe	White	Assistant	T	M	7/8/1982	24000
SA210	Ann	Tremble	Assistant	T	F	6/12/1981	26000
SA220	Terry	Ford	Manager	R	M	10/20/1967	53000
SA230	Susan	Brandon	Supervisor	R	F	3/10/1977	46000
SA240	Julia	Roberts	Assistant	T	F	9/12/1982	28000
* STAFF_NO is primary key							

RENTAL							
RENTAL_NO	RENTAL_DATE	RENTAL_STATUS	LEASE_TYPE	LEASE_START	LEASE_END	STAFF_NO	APT_NO
100101	5/12/2016	O	One	6/1/2016	5/31/2017	SA200	201
100102	5/21/2016	O	Six	6/1/2016	11/30/2016	SA220	102
100103	10/12/2016	O	Six	11/1/2016	4/30/2017	SA240	203
100104	3/6/2017	O	One	4/1/2017	3/31/2018	SA210	101
100105	4/15/2017	O	One	5/1/2017	4/30/2018	SA220	104
100106	7/15/2017	S	One	8/1/2017	7/31/2018	SA200	100
* RENTAL_NO is primary key STAFF_NO is foreign key to STAFF table APT_NO is foreign key to APARTMENT table							

TENANT (Part I)						
TENANT_SS	TENANT_NAME	TENANT_DOB	MARITAL	WORK_PHONE	HOME_PHONE	EMPLOYER_NAME
123456789	Jack Robin	6/21/1960	M	4173452323	4175556565	Kraft Inc.
723556089	Mary Stackles	8/2/1980	S	4175453320	4176667565	Kraft Inc.
450452267	Ramu Reddy	4/11/1962	M	4178362323	4172220565	MSU
223056180	Marion Black	5/25/1981	S	4174257766	4176772364	MSU
173662690	Venessa Williams	3/12/1970	M	4175557878	4173362565	Kraft Inc.

* TENANT_SS is primary key

TENANT (Part II)				
TENANT_SS	EMAIL	CREDIT_SCORE	CREDIT_AGENCY	RENTAL_NO
123456789	jr252@gmail.com	650	Equifax	100101
723556089	ms432@outlook.com	675	Experian	100102
450452267	rred2@gmail.com	755	Equifax	100103
223056180	mblk34@gmail.com	720	Equifax	100104
173662690	ven567@outlook.com	740	Experian	100105
* TENANT_SS is primary key RENTAL_NO is foreign key to RENTAL table				

TENANT_AUTO						
TENANT_SS	LICENSE_NO	AUTO_MAKE	AUTO_MODEL	AUTO_YEAR	AUTO_COLOR	PARKING_FEE
123456789	SYK332	Ford	Taurus	1999	Red	0
123456789	TTS430	Volvo	GL 740	1990	Green	45.5
723556089	ABC260	Toyota	Lexus	2000	Maroon	0
450452267	LLT322	Honda	Accord	2001	Blue	0
450452267	KYK100	Toyota	Camry	1999	Black	45.5
223056180	FLT232	Honda	Civic	1999	Red	0
173662690	LLT668	Volvo	GL 980	2000	Velvet	0
* TENANT_SS, LICENSE_NO is primary key TENANT_SS is foreign key to TENANT table						

TENANT_FAMILY						
TENANT_SS	FAMILY_SS	NAME	SPOUSE	CHILD	GENDER	DOB
123456789	444663434	Kay Robin	Y	N	F	6/21/1965
450452267	222664343	Sarla Reddy	Y	N	F	6/11/1965
450452267	222663434	Anjali Reddy	N	Y	F	8/10/1990
173662690	111444663	Terry Williams	Y	N	F	3/21/1968
173662690	242446634	Tom Williams	N	Y	M	5/20/1991
* TENANT_SS, FAMILY_SS is primary key TENANT_SS is foreign key to TENANT table						

RENTAL_INVOICE						
INVOICE_NO	INVOICE_DATE	INVOICE_DUE	CC_NO	CC_TYPE	CC_EXP_DATE	RENTAL_NO
1000	5/12/2016	500	1234567890123460	visa	12/1/2019	100101
1001	6/30/2016	500	1234567890123460	visa	12/1/2019	100101
1002	7/30/2016	500	1234567890123460	visa	12/1/2019	100101
1003	8/30/2016	500	1234567890123460	visa	12/1/2019	100101
1004	9/30/2016	500	1234567890123460	mastercard	12/1/2019	100101
1005	10/30/2016	500	1234567890123460	mastercard	12/1/2019	100101
1006	11/30/2016	500	1234567890123460	visa	12/1/2019	100101
1007	12/30/2016	500	1234567890123460	visa	12/1/2019	100101
1008	1/30/2017	500	1234567890123460	visa	12/1/2019	100101
1009	5/21/2016	300	3343567890123460	mastercard	10/1/2020	100102

1010	6/30/2016	300	3343567890123460	mastercard	10/1/2020	100102
1011	7/30/2016	300	3343567890123460	mastercard	10/1/2020	100102
1012	8/30/2016	300	3343567890123460	mastercard	10/1/2020	100102
1013	9/30/2016	300	3343567890123460	mastercard	10/1/2020	100102
1014	10/30/2016	300	3343567890123460	mastercard	10/1/2020	100102
1015	11/30/2016	300	3343567890123460	mastercard	10/1/2020	100102
1016	10/12/2016	700	8654567890123300	discover	11/1/2020	100103
1017	11/30/2016	700	8654567890123300	discover	11/1/2020	100103
1018	3/6/2017	500	7766567890123200	visa	9/1/2019	100104
1019	4/30/2017	300	7766567890123200	visa	9/1/2019	100104
1020	5/30/2017	300	7766567890123200	visa	9/1/2019	100104
1021	6/30/2017	300	7766567890123200	visa	9/1/2019	100104
1022	7/30/2017	300	7766567890123200	visa	9/1/2019	100104
1023	4/15/2017	700	6599567890126210	visa	12/1/2021	100105
1024	5/30/2017	400	6599567890126210	visa	12/1/2021	100105
1025	6/30/2017	400	6599567890126210	discover	12/1/2020	100105
1026	7/30/2017	400	6599567890126210	discover	12/1/2020	100105

* INVOICE_NO is primary key
RENTAL_NO is foreign key to RENTAL table

COMPLAINTS						
COMPLAINT_NO	COMPLAINT_DATE	RENTAL_COMPLAINT	APT_COMPLAINT	RENTAL_NO	APT_NO	STATUS
10010	12/12/2017	kitchen sink clogged		100103	203	F
10011	8/17/2018	water heater not working		100105	104	F
10012	9/17/2018	room heater does not work		100105	104	
10013	9/17/2018		air conditioning not working		103	
10014	10/20/2018	car parking spots not clear		100103	203	
10015	11/8/2018	dryer not working		100104	101	F
10016	11/16/2018		washer not working		202	

* COMPLAINT_NO is primary key
RENTAL_NO is foreign key to RENTAL table
APT_NO is foreign key to APARTMENT table

CONTRACTOR (Part I)				
CONTRACTOR_ID	NAME	WORK_TYPE	STREET	CITY
C1011	Tony Home Repairs	Electric,Plumbing	727 W Sunshine Street	Springfield
C1012	Mr Fix It	Electric,Plumbing,Remodeling	102 S Cox Ave	Springfield
C1013	Sunny Home Solutions	Electric,Plumbing,Remodeling	2215 N Sexton Dr	Nixa
C1014	Affordable Repairs	Electric,Plumbing	115 W Oak Ave	Springdale

* CONTRACTOR_ID is primary key

CONTRACTOR (Part II)				
CONTRACTOR_ID	STATE	ZIP	EMAIL	PHONE
C1011	MO	65804	tony@gmail.com	4178829223
C1012	MO	65802	mrfixit@outlook.com	7611522515
C1013	MO	65714	sunny@gmail.com	4174251155

C1014	AR	72764	affordable@outlook.com	8629205252
* CONTRACTOR_ID is primary key				

WORKORDER (Part I)			
WORKORDER_NO	WORKORDER_DATE	WORK_DESC	WORK_TYPE
C101	12/13/2017	kitchen sink clogged	Plumbing
C102	8/18/2017	water heater not working	Plumbing
C103	9/20/2018	room heating does not work	Plumbing
C104	9/19/2018	air conditioning not working	Electric
C105	10/21/2018	car parking spots not clear - repaint parking	Remodeling
C106	11/11/2018	dryer not working - no drying	Electric
C107	11/17/2018	washer not working - regular setting does not work	Electric
* WORKORDER_NO is primary key COMPLAINT_NO is foreign key to COMPLAINTS table CONTRACTOR_ID is foreign key to CONTRACTOR table			

WORKORDER (Part II)			
WORKORDER_NO	TENANT_IN	COMPLAINT_NO	CONTRACTOR_ID
C101	Y	10010	C1011
C102	N	10011	C1012
C103	N	10012	C1011
C104	Y	10013	C1012
C105	N	10014	C1013
C106	Y	10015	C1011
C107	N	10016	C1014
* WORKORDER_NO is primary key COMPLAINT_NO is foreign key to COMPLAINTS table CONTRACTOR_ID is foreign key to CONTRACTOR table			

Appendix B. Superflex Apartment Database SQL Script

```
create table apartment
(apt_no number(3) constraint apartment_pk primary key,
apt_type number(1) constraint apartment_type_ck check ((apt_type = 0) or (apt_type = 1) or (apt_type = 2) or (apt_type
= 3)),
apt_status char(1) constraint apartment_status_ck check ((apt_status = 'R') or (apt_status = 'V')),
apt_utility char(1) constraint apartment_utility_ck check ((apt_utility = 'Y') or (apt_utility = 'N')),
flooring varchar2(10),
balcony char(1),
apt_deposit_amt number(3),
apt_rent_amt number(3));

create table staff
(staff_no varchar2(5) constraint staff_pk primary key,
first_name varchar2(15),
last_name varchar2(15),
position varchar2(12),
status char(1) constraint staff_status_ck check ((status='T') or (status='R')),
gender char(1),
dob date,
salary number(5));

create table rental
(rental_no number(6) constraint rental_pk primary key,
rental_date date constraint rental_date_nn NOT NULL,
rental_status char(1)constraint rental_status_ck check ((rental_status = 'S') or (rental_status = 'O')),
lease_type varchar2(3) default 'One' constraint lease_type_ck check ((lease_type = 'One') or (lease_type = 'Six')),
lease_start date,
lease_end date,
staff_no varchar2(5) constraint rental_apt_fk1 references staff,
apt_no number(3) constraint rental_apt_fk2 references apartment);

create table tenant
(tenant_ss number(9) constraint tenant_pk primary key,
tenant_name varchar2(25),
tenant_dob date,
marital char(1)constraint tenant_marital_ck check ((marital = 'M') or (marital = 'S')),
work_phone varchar2(10),
home_phone varchar2(10),
employer_name varchar2(25),
gender char(1) constraint tenant_gender_ck check ((gender = 'M') or (gender = 'F')),
email varchar2(50),
credit_score number(3),
credit_agency varchar2(15),
rental_no number(6) constraint tenant_rental_fk references rental);

create table tenant_auto
(tenant_ss number(9) constraint tenant_auto_fk references tenant,
license_no varchar2(6),
auto_make varchar2(15),
auto_model varchar2(15),
auto_year number(4),
auto_color varchar2(10),
parking_fee number(4,2),
constraint tenant_auto_pk primary key (tenant_ss,license_no));

create table tenant_family
(tenant_ss number(9) constraint tenant_family_fk references tenant,
```

```
family_ss number(9),
name varchar2(25),
spouse char(1) constraint family_spouse_ck check ((spouse = 'Y') or (spouse = 'N')),
child char(1) constraint family_child_ck check ((child = 'Y') or (child = 'N')),
gender char(1) constraint family_gender_ck check ((gender = 'M') or (gender = 'F')),
dob date,
constraint tenant_family_pk primary key(tenant_ss,family_ss));

create table rental_invoice
(invoice_no number(6) constraint rental_invoice_pk primary key,
invoice_date date,
invoice_due number(4),
cc_no number(16),
cc_type varchar2(10),
cc_exp_date date,
rental_no number(6) constraint rental_invoice_fk references rental);

create table complaints
(complaint_no number(6) constraint complaints_pk primary key,
complaint_date date,
rental_complaint varchar2(100),
apt_complaint varchar2(100),
rental_no number(6) constraint complaints_fk1 references rental,
apt_no number(3) constraint complaints_fk2 references apartment,
status char(1) constraint complaint_status_ck check ((status = 'F') or (status = 'P') or (status = NULL)));

create table contractor
(contractor_id varchar2(5) constraint contractor_pk primary key,
name varchar2(50),
work_type varchar2(50),
street varchar2(50),
city varchar2(15),
state char(2),
zip number(5),
email varchar2(50),
phone varchar2(10));

create table workorder
(workorder_no varchar2(4) constraint workorder_pk primary key,
workorder_date date,
work_desc varchar2(100),
work_type varchar2(15),
tenant_in char(1),
complaint_no number(6) constraint workorder_fk1 references complaints,
contractor_id varchar2(5) constraint workorder_fk2 references contractor);

create sequence apartment_sequence1
start with 100
nocache;

create sequence apartment_sequence2
start with 200
nocache;

create sequence staff_sequence
start with 200
increment by 10
nocache;

create sequence rental_sequence
start with 100101
```

```
nocache;

create sequence rental_invoice_sequence
start with 1000
nocache;

create sequence complaints_sequence
start with 10010
nocache;

create sequence contractor_sequence
start with 1011
nocache;

create sequence workorder_sequence
start with 101
nocache;

insert into apartment
values (apartment_sequence1.nextval,0,'R','Y','Carpet','N',200,300);
insert into apartment
values (apartment_sequence1.nextval,0,'R','N','Carpet','N',200,300);
insert into apartment
values (apartment_sequence1.nextval,0,'R','Y','Carpet','N',200,300);
insert into apartment
values (apartment_sequence1.nextval,1,'V','N','Carpet','N',300,400);
insert into apartment
values (apartment_sequence1.nextval,1,'R','Y','Carpet','N',300,400);

insert into apartment
values (apartment_sequence2.nextval,2,'V','Y','Hardwood','Y',400,500);
insert into apartment
values (apartment_sequence2.nextval,2,'R','Y','Carpet','N',400,500);
insert into apartment
values (apartment_sequence2.nextval,3,'V','Y','Hardwood','Y',500,700);
insert into apartment
values (apartment_sequence2.nextval,3,'R','Y','Hardwood','Y',500,700);

insert into staff
values('SA'||staff_sequence.nextval,'Joe','White','Assistant','T','M',to_date('7/8/82','mm/dd/yy'),24000);
insert into staff
values('SA'||staff_sequence.nextval,'Ann','Tremble','Assistant','T','F',to_date('6/12/81','mm/dd/yy'),26000);
insert into staff
values('SA'||staff_sequence.nextval,'Terry','Ford','Manager','R','M',to_date('10/20/67','mm/dd/yy'),53000);
insert into staff
values('SA'||staff_sequence.nextval,'Susan','Brandon','Supervisor','R','F',to_date('3/10/77','mm/dd/yy'),46000);
insert into staff
values('SA'||staff_sequence.nextval,'Julia','Roberts','Assistant','T','F',to_date('9/12/82','mm/dd/yy'),28000);

insert into rental values
(rental_sequence.nextval,to_date('05/12/2016','mm/dd/yyyy'),'O','One',to_date('6/1/2016','mm/dd/yyyy'),to_date('5/31/
2017','mm/dd/yyyy'),'SA200',201);
insert into rental values
(rental_sequence.nextval,to_date('05/21/2016','mm/dd/yyyy'),'O','Six',to_date('6/1/2016','mm/dd/yyyy'),to_date('11/30/
2016','mm/dd/yyyy'),'SA220',102);
insert into rental values
(rental_sequence.nextval,to_date('10/12/2016','mm/dd/yyyy'),'O','Six',to_date('11/1/2016','mm/dd/yyyy'),to_date('4/30/
2017','mm/dd/yyyy'),'SA240',203);
insert into rental values
(rental_sequence.nextval,to_date('03/6/2017','mm/dd/yyyy'),'O','One',to_date('4/1/2017','mm/dd/yyyy'),to_date('3/31/2
018','mm/dd/yyyy'),'SA210',101);
```

```
insert into rental values
(rental_sequence.nextval,to_date('4/15/2017','mm/dd/yyyy'),'O','One',to_date('5/1/2017','mm/dd/yyyy'),to_date('4/30/2
018','mm/dd/yyyy'),'SA220',104);
insert into rental values
(rental_sequence.nextval,to_date('7/15/2017','mm/dd/yyyy'),'S','One',to_date('8/1/2017','mm/dd/yyyy'),to_date('7/31/20
18','mm/dd/yyyy'),'SA200',100);

insert into tenant values
(123456789,'Jack Robin',to_date('6/21/1960','mm/dd/yyyy'),'M','4173452323','4175556565','Kraft
Inc.','M','jr252@gmail.com',650,'Equifax',100101);
insert into tenant values
(723556089,'Mary Stackles',to_date('8/2/1980','mm/dd/yyyy'),'S','4175453320','4176667565','Kraft
Inc.','F','ms432@outlook.com',675,'Experian',100102);
insert into tenant values
(450452267,'Ramu
Reddy',to_date('4/11/1962','mm/dd/yyyy'),'M','4178362323','4172220565','MSU','M','rred2@gmail.com',755,'Equifax',100
103);
insert into tenant values
(223056180,'Marion Black',to_date('5/25/1981','mm/dd/yyyy'),'S','4174257766', '4176772364',
'MSU','M','mblk34@gmail.com',720,'Equifax',100104);
insert into tenant values
(173662690,'Venessa Williams',to_date('3/12/1970','mm/dd/yyyy'),'M','4175557878', '4173362565','Kraft
Inc.','F','ven567@outlook.com',740,'Experian',100105);

insert into tenant_auto values
(123456789,'SYK332','Ford','Taurus',1999,'Red',0);
insert into tenant_auto values
(123456789,'TTS430','Volvo','GL 740',1990,'Green',45.50);
insert into tenant_auto values
(723556089,'ABC260','Toyota','Lexus',2000,'Maroon',0);
insert into tenant_auto values
(450452267,'LLT322','Honda','Accord',2001,'Blue',0);
insert into tenant_auto values
(450452267,'KYK100','Toyota','Camry',1999,'Black',45.50);
insert into tenant_auto values
(223056180,'FLT232','Honda','Civic',1999,'Red',0);
insert into tenant_auto values
(173662690,'LLT668','Volvo','GL 980',2000,'Velvet',0);

insert into tenant_family values
(123456789,444663434,'Kay Robin','Y','N','F',to_date('6/21/1965','mm/dd/yyyy'));
insert into tenant_family values
(450452267,222664343,'Sarla Reddy','Y','N','F',to_date('6/11/1965','mm/dd/yyyy'));
insert into tenant_family values
(450452267,222663434,'Anjali Reddy','N','Y','F',to_date('8/10/1990','mm/dd/yyyy'));
insert into tenant_family values
(173662690,111444663,'Terry Williams','Y','N','F',to_date('3/21/1968','mm/dd/yyyy'));
insert into tenant_family values
(173662690,242446634,'Tom Williams','N','Y','M',to_date('5/20/1991','mm/dd/yyyy'));

insert into rental_invoice values
(rental_invoice_sequence.nextval,to_date('5/12/2016','mm/dd/yyyy'),500,1234567890123456,'visa',to_date('12/19','mm/
yy'),100101);
insert into rental_invoice values
(rental_invoice_sequence.nextval,to_date('6/30/2016','mm/dd/yyyy'),500,1234567890123456,'visa',to_date('12/19','mm
/yy'),100101);
insert into rental_invoice values
(rental_invoice_sequence.nextval,to_date('7/30/2016','mm/dd/yyyy'),500,1234567890123456,'visa',to_date('12/19','mm
/yy'),100101);
insert into rental_invoice values
```

```
(rental_invoice_sequence.nextval,to_date('8/30/2016','mm/dd/yyyy'),500,1234567890123456,'visa',to_date('12/19','mm
/yy'),100101);
insert into rental_invoice values
(rental_invoice_sequence.nextval,to_date('9/30/2016','mm/dd/yyyy'),500,1234567890123456,'mastercard',to_date('12/1
9','mm/yy'),100101);
insert into rental_invoice values
(rental_invoice_sequence.nextval,to_date('10/30/2016','mm/dd/yyyy'),500,1234567890123456,'mastercard',to_date('12/
19','mm/yy'),100101);
insert into rental_invoice values
(rental_invoice_sequence.nextval,to_date('11/30/2016','mm/dd/yyyy'),500,1234567890123456,'visa',to_date('12/19','mm
/yy'),100101);
insert into rental_invoice values
(rental_invoice_sequence.nextval,to_date('12/30/2016','mm/dd/yyyy'),500,1234567890123456,'visa',to_date('12/19','m
m/yy'),100101);
insert into rental_invoice values
(rental_invoice_sequence.nextval,to_date('1/30/2017','mm/dd/yyyy'),500,1234567890123456,'visa',to_date('12/19','mm/
yy'),100101);

insert into rental_invoice values
(rental_invoice_sequence.nextval,to_date('5/21/2016','mm/dd/yyyy'),300,3343567890123456,'mastercard',to_date('10/2
0','mm/yy'),100102);
insert into rental_invoice values
(rental_invoice_sequence.nextval,to_date('6/30/2016','mm/dd/yyyy'),300,3343567890123456,'mastercard',to_date('10/
20','mm/yy'),100102);
insert into rental_invoice values
(rental_invoice_sequence.nextval,to_date('7/30/2016','mm/dd/yyyy'),300,3343567890123456,'mastercard',to_date('10/
20','mm/yy'),100102);
insert into rental_invoice values
(rental_invoice_sequence.nextval,to_date('8/30/2016','mm/dd/yyyy'),300,3343567890123456,'mastercard',to_date('10/
20','mm/yy'),100102);
insert into rental_invoice values
(rental_invoice_sequence.nextval,to_date('9/30/2016','mm/dd/yyyy'),300,3343567890123456,'mastercard',to_date('10/
20','mm/yy'),100102);
insert into rental_invoice values
(rental_invoice_sequence.nextval,to_date('10/30/2016','mm/dd/yyyy'),300,3343567890123456,'mastercard',to_date('10
/20','mm/yy'),100102);
insert into rental_invoice values
(rental_invoice_sequence.nextval,to_date('11/30/2016','mm/dd/yyyy'),300,3343567890123456,'mastercard',to_date('10/
20','mm/yy'),100102);

insert into rental_invoice values
(rental_invoice_sequence.nextval,to_date('10/12/2016','mm/dd/yyyy'),700,8654567890123296,'discover',to_date('11/20'
,'mm/yy'),100103);
insert into rental_invoice values
(rental_invoice_sequence.nextval,to_date('11/30/2016','mm/dd/yyyy'),700,8654567890123296,'discover',to_date('11/20'
,'mm/yy'),100103);

insert into rental_invoice values
(rental_invoice_sequence.nextval,to_date('3/6/2017','mm/dd/yyyy'),500,7766567890123203,'visa',to_date('09/19','mm/
yy'),100104);
insert into rental_invoice values
(rental_invoice_sequence.nextval,to_date('4/30/2017','mm/dd/yyyy'),300,7766567890123203,'visa',to_date('09/19','mm
/yy'),100104);
insert into rental_invoice values
(rental_invoice_sequence.nextval,to_date('5/30/2017','mm/dd/yyyy'),300,7766567890123203,'visa',to_date('09/19','mm
/yy'),100104);
insert into rental_invoice values
(rental_invoice_sequence.nextval,to_date('6/30/2017','mm/dd/yyyy'),300,7766567890123203,'visa',to_date('09/19','mm
/yy'),100104);
insert into rental_invoice values
```

```
(rental_invoice_sequence.nextval,to_date('7/30/2017','mm/dd/yyyy'),300,7766567890123203,'visa',to_date('09/19','mm
/yy'),100104);

insert into rental_invoice values
(rental_invoice_sequence.nextval,to_date('4/15/2017','mm/dd/yyyy'),700,6599567890126211,'visa',to_date('12/21','mm/
yy'),100105);
insert into rental_invoice values
(rental_invoice_sequence.nextval,to_date('5/30/2017','mm/dd/yyyy'),400,6599567890126211,'visa',to_date('12/21','mm/
yy'),100105);
insert into rental_invoice values
(rental_invoice_sequence.nextval,to_date('6/30/2017','mm/dd/yyyy'),400,6599567890126211,'discover',to_date('12/20','
mm/yy'),100105);
insert into rental_invoice values
(rental_invoice_sequence.nextval,to_date('7/30/2017','mm/dd/yyyy'),400,6599567890126211,'discover',to_date('12/20','
mm/yy'),100105);

insert into complaints values
(complaints_sequence.nextval,to_date('12/12/2017','mm/dd/yyyy'),'kitchen sink clogged',null,100103,203,'F');
insert into complaints values
(complaints_sequence.nextval,to_date('8/17/2018','mm/dd/yyyy'),'water heater not working',null,100105,104,'F');
insert into complaints values
(complaints_sequence.nextval,to_date('9/17/2018','mm/dd/yyyy'),'room heater does not work',null,100105,104,NULL);
insert into complaints values
(complaints_sequence.nextval,to_date('9/17/2018','mm/dd/yyyy'),null,'air conditioning not working',null,103,NULL);
insert into complaints values
(complaints_sequence.nextval,to_date('10/20/2018','mm/dd/yyyy'),'car parking spots not clear',null,100103,203,NULL);
insert into complaints values
(complaints_sequence.nextval,to_date('11/8/2018','mm/dd/yyyy'),'dryer not working',null,100104,101,'F');
insert into complaints values
(complaints_sequence.nextval,to_date('11/16/2018','mm/dd/yyyy'),null,'washer not working',null,202,NULL);

insert into contractor
values('C'||contractor_sequence.nextval,'Tony Home Repairs','Electric,Plumbing','727 W Sunshine
Street','Springfield','MO',65804,'tony@gmail.com','4178829223');
insert into contractor
values('C'||contractor_sequence.nextval,'Mr Fix It','Electric,Plumbing,Remodeling','102 S Cox
Ave','Springfield','MO',65802,'mrfixit@outlook.com','7611522515');
insert into contractor
values('C'||contractor_sequence.nextval,'Sunny Home Solutions','Electric,Plumbing,Remodeling','2215 N Sexton
Dr','Nixa','MO',65714,'sunny@gmail.com','4174251155');
insert into contractor
values('C'||contractor_sequence.nextval,'Affordable Repairs','Electric,Plumbing','115 W Oak
Ave','Springdale','AR',72764,'affordable@outlook.com','8629205252');

insert into workorder
values('C'||workorder_sequence.nextval,to_date('12/13/2017','mm/dd/yyyy'),'kitchen sink
clogged','Plumbing','Y',10010,'C1011');
insert into workorder
values('C'||workorder_sequence.nextval,to_date('8/18/2017','mm/dd/yyyy'),'water heater not
working','Plumbing','N',10011,'C1012');
insert into workorder
values('C'||workorder_sequence.nextval,to_date('9/20/2018','mm/dd/yyyy'),'room heating does not
work','Plumbing','N',10012,'C1011');
insert into workorder
values('C'||workorder_sequence.nextval,to_date('9/19/2018','mm/dd/yyyy'),'air conditioning not
working','Electric','Y',10013,'C1012');
insert into workorder
values('C'||workorder_sequence.nextval,to_date('10/21/2018','mm/dd/yyyy'),'car parking spots not clear - repaint
parking','Remodeling','N',10014,'C1013');
insert into workorder
```

```
values('C'||workorder_sequence.nextval,to_date('11/11/2018','mm/dd/yyyy'),'dryer not working - no
drying','Electric','Y',10015,'C1011');
insert into workorder
values('C'||workorder_sequence.nextval,to_date('11/17/2018','mm/dd/yyyy'),'washer not working - regular setting does
not work','Electric','N',10016,'C1014');

commit;
```

Appendix C. Outdoor Clubs & Product Database Tables

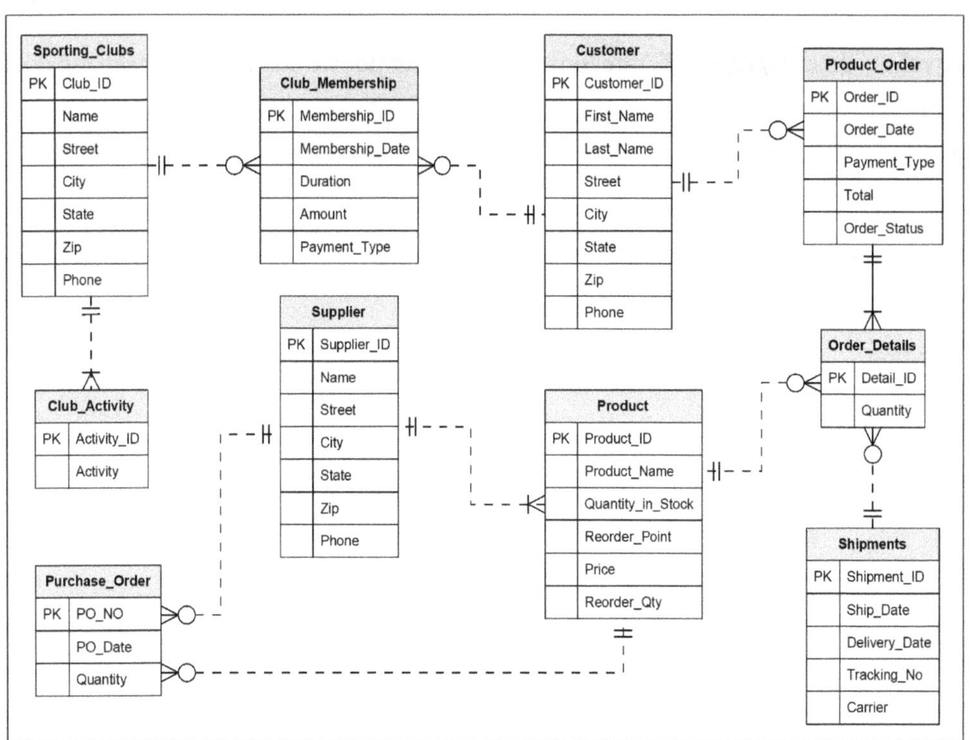

SPORTING_CLUBS						
CLUB_ID	NAME	STREET	CITY	STATE	ZIP	PHONE
100	Hillside Mountain Club	1 Winona St	Wichita	KS	34342	3163997676
110	Branson Climbing Club	2 Sherwood Dr.	Branson	MO	65670	4174485676
120	Cherokee Rafting Club	44 Kent Ave.	St. Charles	MO	66572	3147780870
130	White Plains Club	225 Tracy St.	New York	NY	13567	2126678090
* CLUB_ID is primary key						

CUSTOMER							
CUSTOMER_ID	FIRST_NAME	LAST_NAME	STREET	CITY	STATE	ZIP	PHONE
101	Jack	Russell	25 North Madison Ave.	Springfield	MO	65807	4178823434
102	Betty	Trumbell	550 South Court Dr.	St. Louis	MO	63140	3125556670
103	Anil	Kaul	400 South Circle St.	Kansas City	MO	64530	4316667070
104	Tom	Wiley	1500 North Grand St.	Springfield	MO	65810	4178825560
105	Sharon	Stone	200 West Wagner St.	Springfield	MO	65807	4176668890
* CUSTOMER_ID is primary key							

CLUB_MEMBERSHIP						
MEMBERSHIP _ID	MEMBERSHIP _DATE	DURATION	AMOUNT	PAYMENT _TYPE	CLUB_ID	CUSTOMER_I D
10010	12-JUN-20	4	200	CC	100	101
10020	15-JUN-20	2	100	Check	110	102
10030	21-JUN-20	5	250	Check	120	103
* MEMBERSHIP_ID is primary key CLUB_ID is foreign key to SPORTING_CLUBS table CUSTOMER_ID is foreign key to CUSTOMER table						

CLUB_ACTIVITY		
ACTIVITY_ID	CLUB_ID	ACTIVITY
500	100	Hiking
510	100	Climbing
520	100	Walking
530	110	Hiking
540	110	Climbing
550	110	Conservation
560	110	Walking
570	120	Conservation
580	120	Canoeing
590	130	Conservation
600	130	Canoeing
610	130	Walking
* ACTIVITY_ID primary key CLUB_ID foreign key		

PRODUCT						
PRODUCT _ID	PRODUCT_NAME	QUANTITY_ IN_STOCK	REORDER_ POINT	PRICE	SUPPLIER _ID	REORDER_QTY
10010	Beginner's Ski Boot	20	5	9.75	S500	25
10011	Intermediate Ski Boot	18	5	12.99	S500	20
10012	Pro Ski Boot	21	7	15.49	S510	25
10013	Beginner's Ski Pole	15	3	25.49	S500	20
10014	Intermediate Ski Pole	20	3	29.99	S520	22
10015	Pro Ski Pole	21	5	34.99	S530	25

10016	Road Bicycle	15	4	34.95	S520	18
10017	Mountain Bicycle	19	4	49.99	S520	20
10018	Tire Pump	8	2	7.99	S530	10
10019	Water Bottle	25	4	2.49	S510	25
10020	Bicycle Tires	30	5	4.99	S500	33
10021	Bicycle Helmet	23	6	10.95	S510	25

* PRODUCT_ID is primary key
SUPPLIER_ID is foreign key to SUPPLIER table

SUPPLIER

SUPPLIER_ID	NAME	STREET	CITY	STATE	ZIP	PHONE
S500	Hillside Ski	2717 S Western Ave	Los Angeles	CA	90006	7146654959
S510	Tiger Mountain	2600 S Vermont Ave	Los Angeles	CA	90006	7143327878
S520	Asha Outdoor	44 S. LaSalle St.	Chicago	IL	60603	3125554678
S530	Sheraton Recreation	225 Tracy St.	New York	NY	13567	2128889569

* SUPPLIER_ID is primary key

PRODUCT_ORDER

ORDER_ID	ORDER_DATE	PAYMENT_TYPE	TOTAL	CUSTOMER_ID	ORDER_STATUS
1001	27-MAY-20	CC	130.95	102	S
1002	28-MAY-20	CC	134.85	103	S
1003	28-MAY-20	Check	12.45	104	S
1004	05-JUN-20	CC	44.43	105	S
1005	06-JUN-20	Check	52.48	103	S
1006	08-JUN-20	CC	131.94	104	R

* ORDER_ID is primary key
CUSTOMER_ID is foreign key to CUSTOMER table
ORDER_STATUS values are R (received) or S (ship)

ORDER_DETAILS

DETAIL_ID	ORDER_ID	PRODUCT_ID	QUANTITY	SHIPMENT_ID
200	1001	10011	2	4501
201	1001	10015	3	4501
202	1002	10011	5	4502
203	1002	10016	2	4503

204	1003	10019	5	4504
205	1004	10018	3	4505
206	1004	10011	1	4505
207	1004	10019	3	4506
208	1005	10017	1	4507
209	1005	10019	1	4507
210	1005	10021	1	4507
211	1006	10012	4	
212	1006	10015	2	

* DETAIL_ID is primary key
ORDER_ID is foreign key to PRODUCT_ORDER table
PRODUCT_ID is foreign key to PRODUCT table
SHIPMENT_ID is foreign key to SHIPMENTS table

SHIPMENTS

SHIPMENT_ID	SHIP_DATE	DELIVERY_DATE	TRACKING_NO	CARRIER
4501	01-JUN-20	04-JUN-20	1z2356789046	UPS
4502	02-JUN-20	05-JUN-20	399040642570	FedEx
4503	03-JUN-20	06-JUN-20	456891278947	FedEx
4504	02-JUN-20	05-JUN-20	2z3567843971	UPS
4505	08-JUN-20	13-JUN-20	129986345612	USPS
4506	12-JUN-20	15-JUN-20	145456345619	USPS
4507	10-JUN-20	14-JUN-20	167896345621	USPS

* SHIPMENT_ID is primary key

PURCHASE_ORDER

PO_NO	PO_DATE	PRODUCT_ID	QUANTITY	SUPPLIER_ID
PO11	25-MAY-20	10011	20	S500
PO12	12-MAY-20	10015	25	S530
PO13	25-JUN-20	10011	20	S500
PO14	25-JUN-20	10018	10	S530
PO15	10-JUL-20	10015	25	S530
PO16	21-JUL-20	10019	25	S510

* PO_NO is primary key
PRODUCT_ID is foreign key to PRODUCT table
SUPPLIER_ID is foreign key to SUPPLIER table

Appendix D. Outdoor Clubs & Product Database SQL Script

```
create table sporting_clubs
(club_id number(3)constraint sporting_clubs_pk primary key,
name varchar2(30),
street varchar2(30),
city varchar2(15),
state char(2),
zip number(5),
phone varchar2(10));

create table club_activity
(activity_id integer constraint club_activity_pk primary key,
club_id number(3)constraint club_activity_fk references sporting_clubs,
activity varchar2(15));

create table supplier
(supplier_id varchar2(4) constraint supplier_pk primary key,
name varchar2(30),
street varchar2(30),
city varchar2(15),
state char(2),
zip number(5),
phone varchar2(10));

create table product
(product_id number(5) constraint product_pk primary key,
product_name varchar2(30),
quantity_in_stock number(3),
reorder_point number(2),
price number(5,2),
supplier_id varchar2(4) constraint product_fk references supplier,
reorder_qty number(2));

create table purchase_order
(po_no varchar2(4) constraint purchase_order_pk primary key,
po_date date,
product_id number(5) constraint purchase_order_fk1 references product,
quantity number(3),
supplier_id varchar2(4) constraint purchase_order_fk2 references supplier);

create table customer
(customer_id number(3) constraint customer_pk primary key,
first_name varchar2(10),
last_name varchar2(10),
street varchar2(30),
city varchar2(15),
state char(2)default 'MO',
zip number(5),
phone varchar2(10));

create table club_membership
(membership_id number(5) constraint club_membership_pk primary key,
membership_date date,
duration number(2),
amount number(4),
payment_type varchar2(5)constraint membership_payment_type_ck check ((payment_type = 'CC') or (payment_type =
'Check')),
club_id number(3) constraint club_membership_fk1 references sporting_clubs,
```

```
customer_id number(3) constraint club_membership_fk2 references customer);

create table product_order
(order_id number(4) constraint product_order_pk primary key,
order_date date,
payment_type varchar2(5) constraint prod_order_payment_type_ck check ((payment_type = 'CC') or (payment_type =
'Check')),
total number (6,2),
customer_id number(3) constraint product_order_fk1 references customer,
order_status char(1) constraint prod_order_ord_status_ck check ((order_status = 'S') or (order_status = 'R')));

create table shipments
(shipment_id integer constraint shipments_pk primary key,
ship_date date,
delivery_date date,
tracking_no varchar2(15),
carrier varchar2(10));

create table order_details
(detail_id integer constraint order_details_pk primary key,
order_id number(4),
product_id number(5),
quantity number(2),
shipment_id integer constraint order_details_fk3 references shipments,
constraint order_details_fk1 foreign key (order_id) references product_order,
constraint order_details_fk2 foreign key (product_id) references product);

create sequence club_sequence
start with 100
increment by 10
nocache;

insert into sporting_clubs
values(club_sequence.nextval, 'Hillside Mountain Club', '1 Winona St','Wichita','KS',34342,'3163997676');
insert into sporting_clubs
values(club_sequence.nextval, 'Branson Climbing Club', '2 Sherwood Dr.','Branson','MO',65670,'4174485676');
insert into sporting_clubs
values(club_sequence.nextval, 'Cherokee Rafting Club', '44 Kent Ave.','St. Charles','MO',66572,'3147780870');
insert into sporting_clubs
values(club_sequence.nextval, 'White Plains Club', '225 Tracy St.','New York','NY',13567,'2126678090');

create sequence act_sequence
start with 500
increment by 10
nocache;

insert into club_activity
values(act_sequence.nextval,100,'Hiking');
insert into club_activity
values(act_sequence.nextval,100,'Climbing');
insert into club_activity
values(act_sequence.nextval,100,'Walking');
insert into club_activity
values(act_sequence.nextval,110,'Hiking');
insert into club_activity
values(act_sequence.nextval,110,'Climbing');
insert into club_activity
values(act_sequence.nextval,110,'Conservation');
insert into club_activity
values(act_sequence.nextval,110,'Walking');
insert into club_activity
```

```
values(act_sequence.nextval,120,'Conservation');
insert into club_activity
values(act_sequence.nextval,120,'Canoeing');
insert into club_activity
values(act_sequence.nextval,130,'Conservation');
insert into club_activity
values(act_sequence.nextval,130,'Canoeing');
insert into club_activity
values(act_sequence.nextval,130,'Walking');

create sequence supplier_sequence
start with 500
increment by 10
nocache;

insert into supplier
values('S'||supplier_sequence.nextval,'Hillside Ski','2717 S. Western Ave.','Los Angeles','CA',90006,'7146654959');
insert into supplier
values('S'||supplier_sequence.nextval,'Tiger Mountain','2600 S. Vermont Ave.','Los Angeles','CA',90006,'7143327878');
insert into supplier
values('S'||supplier_sequence.nextval,'Asha Outdoor','44 S. LaSalle St.','Chicago','IL',60603,'3125554678');
insert into supplier
values('S'||supplier_sequence.nextval,'Sheraton Recreation','225 Tracy St.','New York','NY',13567,'2128889569');

create sequence product_id_sequence
start with 10010
increment by 1
nocache;

insert into product
values(product_id_sequence.nextval,'Beginner''s Ski Boot',20,5,9.75,'S500',25);
insert into product
values(product_id_sequence.nextval,'Intermediate Ski Boot',18,5,12.99,'S500',20);
insert into product
values(product_id_sequence.nextval,'Pro Ski Boot',21,7,15.49,'S510',25);
insert into product
values(product_id_sequence.nextval,'Beginner''s Ski Pole',15,3,25.49,'S500',20);
insert into product
values(product_id_sequence.nextval,'Intermediate Ski Pole',20,3,29.99,'S520',22);
insert into product
values(product_id_sequence.nextval,'Pro Ski Pole',21,5,34.99,'S530',25);
insert into product
values(product_id_sequence.nextval,'Road Bicycle',15,4,34.95,'S520',18);
insert into product
values(product_id_sequence.nextval,'Mountain Bicycle',19,4,49.99,'S520',20);
insert into product
values(product_id_sequence.nextval,'Tire Pump',8,2,7.99,'S530',10);
insert into product
values(product_id_sequence.nextval,'Water Bottle',25,4,2.49,'S510',25);
insert into product
values(product_id_sequence.nextval,'Bicycle Tires',30,5,4.99,'S500',33);
insert into product
values(product_id_sequence.nextval,'Bicycle Helmet',23,6,10.95,'S510',25);

create sequence po_sequence
start with 11
nocache;

insert into purchase_order
values('PO'||po_sequence.nextval,to_date('5/25/20','mm/dd/yy'),10011,20,'S500');
insert into purchase_order
```

```
values('PO'||po_sequence.nextval,to_date('5/12/20','mm/dd/yy'),10015,25,'S530');
insert into purchase_order
values('PO'||po_sequence.nextval,to_date('6/25/20','mm/dd/yy'),10011,20,'S500');
insert into purchase_order
values('PO'||po_sequence.nextval,to_date('6/15/20','mm/dd/yy'),10018,10,'S530');
insert into purchase_order
values('PO'||po_sequence.nextval,to_date('7/10/20','mm/dd/yy'),10015,25,'S530');
insert into purchase_order
values('PO'||po_sequence.nextval,to_date('7/25/20','mm/dd/yy'),10019,25,'S510');

create sequence customer_sequence
start with 101
nocache;

insert into customer
values(customer_sequence.nextval,'Jack','Russell','25 North Madison Ave.','Springfield','MO',65807,'4178823434');
insert into customer
values(customer_sequence.nextval,'Betty','Trumbell','550 South Court Dr.','St. Louis','MO',63140,'3125556670');
insert into customer
values(customer_sequence.nextval,'Anil','Kaul','400 South Circle St.','Kansas City','MO',64530,'4316667070');
insert into customer
values(customer_sequence.nextval,'Tom','Wiley','1500 North Grand St.','Springfield','MO',65810,'4178825560');
insert into customer
values(customer_sequence.nextval,'Sharon','Stone','200 West Wagner St.','Springfield','MO',65807,'4176668890');

create sequence membership_sequence
start with 10010
increment by 10
nocache;

insert into club_membership
values(membership_sequence.nextval,to_date('6/12/20','mm/dd/yy'),4,200,'CC',100,101);
insert into club_membership
values(membership_sequence.nextval,to_date('6/15/20','mm/dd/yy'),2,100,'Check',110,102);
insert into club_membership
values(membership_sequence.nextval,to_date('6/21/20','mm/dd/yy'),5,250,'Check',120,103);

create sequence product_order_sequence
start with 1001
nocache;

insert into product_order
values(product_order_sequence.nextval,to_date('5/27/20','mm/dd/yy'),'CC',134.95,102,'S');
insert into product_order
values(product_order_sequence.nextval,to_date('5/28/20','mm/dd/yy'),'CC',134.85,103,'S');
insert into product_order
values(product_order_sequence.nextval,to_date('5/28/20','mm/dd/yy'),'Check',12.45,104,'S');
insert into product_order
values(product_order_sequence.nextval,to_date('6/5/20','mm/dd/yy'),'CC',44.43,105,'S');
insert into product_order
values(product_order_sequence.nextval,to_date('6/6/20','mm/dd/yy'),'Check',52.48,103,'S');
insert into product_order
values(product_order_sequence.nextval,to_date('6/8/20','mm/dd/yy'),'CC',131.94,104,'R');

create sequence ship_sequence
start with 4501
nocache;

insert into shipments
values(ship_sequence.nextval,to_date('6/1/20','mm/dd/yy'),to_date('6/4/20','mm/dd/yy'),'1z2356789046','UPS');
insert into shipments
```

```
values(ship_sequence.nextval,to_date('6/2/20','mm/dd/yy'),to_date('6/5/20','mm/dd/yy'),'399040642570','FedEx');
insert into shipments
values(ship_sequence.nextval,to_date('6/3/20','mm/dd/yy'),to_date('6/6/20','mm/dd/yy'),'456891278947','FedEx');
insert into shipments
values(ship_sequence.nextval,to_date('6/2/20','mm/dd/yy'),to_date('6/5/20','mm/dd/yy'),'2z3567843971','UPS');
insert into shipments
values(ship_sequence.nextval,to_date('6/8/20','mm/dd/yy'),to_date('6/13/20','mm/dd/yy'),'129986345612','USPS');
insert into shipments
values(ship_sequence.nextval,to_date('6/12/20','mm/dd/yy'),to_date('6/15/20','mm/dd/yy'),'562356789354','USPS');
insert into shipments
values(ship_sequence.nextval,to_date('6/10/20','mm/dd/yy'),to_date('6/15/20','mm/dd/yy'),'816356782543','USPS');

create sequence det_sequence
start with 200
nocache;

insert into order_details values(det_sequence.nextval,1001,10011,2,4501);
insert into order_details values(det_sequence.nextval,1001,10015,3,4501);
insert into order_details values(det_sequence.nextval,1002,10011,5,4502);
insert into order_details values(det_sequence.nextval,1002,10016,2,4503);
insert into order_details values(det_sequence.nextval,1003,10019,5,4504);
insert into order_details values(det_sequence.nextval,1004,10018,3,4505);
insert into order_details values(det_sequence.nextval,1004,10011,1,4505);
insert into order_details values(det_sequence.nextval,1004,10019,3,4506);
insert into order_details values(det_sequence.nextval,1005,10017,1,4507);
insert into order_details values(det_sequence.nextval,1005,10019,1,4507);
insert into order_details values(det_sequence.nextval,1005,10021,1,4507);
insert into order_details values(det_sequence.nextval,1006,10012,4,null);
insert into order_details values(det_sequence.nextval,1006,10015,2,null);

commit;
```

Index

T

U

V

W

www.ingramcontent.com/pod-product-compliance
Lightning Source LLC
Chambersburg PA
CBHW060111090326
40690CB00064B/4865

* 9 7 9 8 7 2 0 6 6 0 0 3 1 *

Table of Contents

Chapter 1: Introduction to L5 Autonomous Vehicles

Definition and evolution of autonomous vehicles

The subchapter "Definition and evolution of autonomous vehicles" delves into the world of L5 autonomous vehicles, providing a comprehensive overview for professionals seeking to understand this cutting-edge technology. Autonomous vehicles, also known as self-driving cars, are vehicles capable of navigating and operating without human intervention. The evolution of autonomous vehicles has been a gradual process, with advancements in technology and artificial intelligence paving the way for fully autonomous driving capabilities.

The concept of autonomous vehicles dates back to the 1920s, with early experiments in driverless technology taking place in the decades that followed. However, it wasn't until recent years that significant progress was made in the development of L5 autonomous vehicles, which are vehicles capable of operating without any human intervention under all driving conditions. The evolution of autonomous vehicles has been driven by advancements in sensors, cameras, radar, and lidar technology, as well as improvements in artificial intelligence and machine learning algorithms.

As autonomous vehicles continue to evolve, safety features play a crucial role in ensuring the safe operation of these vehicles. L5 autonomous vehicles are equipped with a range of safety features, including collision avoidance systems, emergency braking, and advanced driver assistance systems. These safety features are designed to mitigate the risk of accidents and ensure the safety of passengers and pedestrians.

The legal implications of L5 autonomous vehicles are a complex and evolving area of law. Regulations surrounding autonomous vehicles vary from country to country, with many jurisdictions grappling with how to regulate this emerging technology. Liability issues, insurance requirements, and data privacy concerns are just a few of the legal considerations that must be addressed when it comes to autonomous vehicles.

In conclusion, the definition and evolution of autonomous vehicles are rapidly changing as technology continues to advance. Professionals in the field of autonomous vehicles must stay informed about the latest developments and regulations surrounding this technology to ensure its safe and successful integration into society. The future of autonomous vehicles holds great promise, with potential applications in a wide range of industries and the potential to revolutionize the way we think about transportation.

Levels of autonomy in vehicles

Autonomous vehicles are classified into different levels based on the extent to which they can operate without human intervention. These levels are defined by the Society of Automotive Engineers (SAE) and range from Level 0 to Level 5. Level 0 represents no automation, with the human driver having full control at all times. Level 5, on the other hand, represents full automation, with the vehicle capable of operating without any human input under all conditions.

In between these extremes are Levels 1 to 4, each representing increasing levels of automation. Level 1 vehicles have some automated features, such as adaptive cruise control or lane-keeping assist, but still require the human driver to be fully engaged and ready to take control at any time. Level 2 vehicles can handle some driving tasks, such as steering and acceleration, but still require the human driver to monitor the road and be ready to intervene if necessary.

Level 3 vehicles can operate autonomously under certain conditions, such as on highways, but still require the human driver to take over if the system encounters a situation it cannot handle. Level 4 vehicles can operate autonomously in specific areas or under specific conditions, such as in a geofenced area or in good weather conditions, without any human intervention. Finally, Level 5 vehicles are fully autonomous and can operate under all conditions without any human input.

Understanding the levels of autonomy in vehicles is crucial for professionals working in the field of autonomous vehicles, as it helps them understand the capabilities and limitations of different systems. It also helps them design and develop systems that are safe, reliable, and user-friendly. By knowing the different levels of autonomy, professionals can ensure that their systems meet the highest standards of safety and performance.

In addition to understanding the levels of autonomy in vehicles, professionals must also consider the legal implications of autonomous driving. As autonomous vehicles become more prevalent on the roads, lawmakers and regulators are grappling with how to ensure the safety and security of these vehicles. Professionals must stay up-to-date on the latest regulations and guidelines to ensure that their systems comply with all legal requirements.

Overall, understanding the levels of autonomy in vehicles is essential for professionals working in the field of autonomous vehicles. By knowing the different levels of autonomy and their implications, professionals can design, develop, and deploy systems that are safe, reliable, and user-friendly. This knowledge is crucial for ensuring the success of autonomous vehicles and for realizing their full potential in transforming the way we travel and commute.

Importance of L5 autonomous vehicles in the future

In the fast-evolving world of autonomous vehicles, L5 autonomous vehicles are considered to be the pinnacle of technological advancement. These vehicles are fully autonomous, meaning they can operate without any human intervention whatsoever. The importance of L5 autonomous vehicles in the future cannot be overstated, especially for professionals who are looking to stay ahead in the automotive industry.

One of the key benefits of L5 autonomous vehicles is their potential to drastically improve road safety. With advanced sensors and artificial intelligence, these vehicles can react to their surroundings with lightning-fast speed and precision, greatly reducing the likelihood of accidents caused by human error. This is a crucial consideration for professionals in the automotive industry, as safety features are always a top priority.

Another important aspect of L5 autonomous vehicles is the legal implications that come with their deployment. Professionals need to be well-versed in the current laws and regulations surrounding autonomous vehicles, as well as any potential changes that may be on the horizon. Understanding the legal landscape is essential for ensuring compliance and minimizing risks for both manufacturers and users of L5 autonomous vehicles.

Maintenance and repair of L5 autonomous vehicles is another key area of focus for professionals in the industry. These vehicles are equipped with complex systems that require specialized knowledge and tools for upkeep. Professionals must be prepared to handle any maintenance issues that may arise, as well as stay up-to-date on the latest repair techniques to keep L5 autonomous vehicles running smoothly.

Overall, the integration of L5 autonomous vehicles with smart cities is a crucial aspect of their future success. These vehicles have the potential to revolutionize urban transportation, reducing traffic congestion, emissions, and overall transportation costs. Professionals must understand the infrastructure requirements for L5 autonomous vehicles and work towards creating a seamless integration with existing city systems to maximize their benefits for society as a whole.

Chapter 2: Safety Features of L5 Autonomous Vehicles

Sensor technology used in L5 autonomous vehicles

In the realm of L5 autonomous vehicles, sensor technology plays a crucial role in ensuring the safety and efficiency of these advanced vehicles. L5 autonomous vehicles are the pinnacle of self-driving technology, capable of operating without any human intervention in all driving conditions and environments. To achieve this level of autonomy, these vehicles are equipped with an array of sensors that enable them to perceive their surroundings and make informed decisions in real-time.

One of the key sensor technologies used in L5 autonomous vehicles is LiDAR (Light Detection and Ranging). LiDAR sensors emit laser pulses to measure distances and create detailed 3D maps of the vehicle's surroundings. These high-resolution maps are essential for accurate localization and navigation, allowing the vehicle to precisely detect and avoid obstacles in its path. LiDAR sensors provide a comprehensive view of the vehicle's environment, even in challenging conditions such as low light or adverse weather.

Another crucial sensor technology used in L5 autonomous vehicles is radar. Radar sensors use radio waves to detect objects and measure their distance, speed, and direction of movement. Radar sensors are particularly useful for detecting objects at longer distances and in situations where visibility is limited, such as heavy rain or fog. By combining radar data with information from other sensors, L5 autonomous vehicles can build a comprehensive picture of their surroundings and make safe driving decisions.

Camera sensors are also an integral part of the sensor suite in L5 autonomous vehicles. Cameras capture high-resolution images and videos of the vehicle's environment, allowing it to recognize and interpret traffic signs, lane markings, and other visual cues. Advanced image processing algorithms enable the vehicle to identify and track objects, predict their movements, and make decisions based on visual information. Camera sensors are essential for tasks such as pedestrian detection, traffic light recognition, and lane keeping in autonomous driving scenarios.

In conclusion, sensor technology is a critical component of L5 autonomous vehicles, enabling them to perceive, interpret, and navigate their surroundings with a high degree of accuracy and reliability. LiDAR, radar, and camera sensors work together to provide a comprehensive view of the environment, allowing the vehicle to make informed decisions and ensure the safety of passengers and other road users. By leveraging the latest advancements in sensor technology, L5 autonomous vehicles are poised to revolutionize the future of transportation and usher in a new era of safe, efficient, and convenient mobility for all.

Collision avoidance systems

Collision avoidance systems are a crucial component of L5 autonomous vehicles, as they are designed to prevent accidents and ensure the safety of passengers, pedestrians, and other road users. These systems utilize a combination of sensors, cameras, radar, and lidar to detect potential obstacles in the vehicle's path and take evasive action if necessary. By constantly monitoring the vehicle's surroundings and reacting quickly to potential hazards, collision avoidance systems play a key role in reducing the risk of accidents and improving overall road safety.

One of the key features of collision avoidance systems in L5 autonomous vehicles is their ability to detect and respond to a wide range of potential hazards, including other vehicles, pedestrians, cyclists, and obstacles in the road. These systems use advanced algorithms to analyze sensor data in real-time and make split-second decisions about how to avoid a collision. For example, if a pedestrian suddenly steps into the road in front of the vehicle, the collision avoidance system may automatically apply the brakes or swerve to avoid a collision, potentially saving lives in the process.

In addition to detecting and avoiding potential collisions, collision avoidance systems in L5 autonomous vehicles also play a crucial role in improving traffic flow and reducing congestion on the roads. By reacting quickly to potential hazards and avoiding unnecessary stops and delays, these systems can help to keep traffic moving smoothly and efficiently, leading to a more pleasant driving experience for passengers and a reduction in overall travel times.

As L5 autonomous vehicles become more widespread, collision avoidance systems will play an increasingly important role in ensuring the safety and efficiency of our road networks. By incorporating the latest advances in sensor technology, artificial intelligence, and machine learning, these systems will continue to evolve and improve, making our roads safer for everyone. For professionals working in the field of autonomous vehicles, understanding the capabilities and limitations of collision avoidance systems is essential for designing and developing safe and reliable autonomous vehicles that can operate effectively in a wide range of real-world conditions.

Overall, collision avoidance systems are a critical safety feature of L5 autonomous vehicles that are designed to prevent accidents, improve traffic flow, and enhance overall road safety. By utilizing a combination of advanced sensors and intelligent algorithms, these systems can detect and respond to potential hazards in real-time, helping to avoid collisions and keep passengers and other road users safe. As autonomous vehicles become more prevalent on our roads, collision avoidance systems will continue to play a key role in ensuring the safety and efficiency of our transportation networks.

Emergency response protocols in autonomous vehicles

In the world of autonomous vehicles, safety is of utmost importance. With the rise of L5 autonomous vehicles, which are capable of fully autonomous operation in all driving scenarios, it is crucial to have robust emergency response protocols in place. These protocols are designed to ensure the safety of passengers, pedestrians, and other road users in the event of a system malfunction or unexpected situation.

One key aspect of emergency response protocols in autonomous vehicles is the ability to detect and respond to system failures in real-time. L5 autonomous vehicles are equipped with advanced sensors and AI algorithms that constantly monitor the vehicle's surroundings and internal systems. In the event of a malfunction, the vehicle must be able to quickly identify the issue and take appropriate action, such as safely pulling over to the side of the road or alerting emergency services.

Another important aspect of emergency response protocols is communication. L5 autonomous vehicles are capable of communicating with other vehicles, infrastructure, and emergency services in real-time. In the event of an emergency, the vehicle must be able to quickly and accurately convey information about its location, status, and any potential hazards to ensure a swift and coordinated response.

Furthermore, emergency response protocols in autonomous vehicles should also include fail-safe mechanisms to prevent accidents or mitigate their impact. For example, L5 autonomous vehicles can be programmed to prioritize the safety of passengers and pedestrians in emergency situations, such as by slowing down or coming to a complete stop to avoid a collision.

Overall, having robust emergency response protocols in place is essential for the safe and effective operation of L5 autonomous vehicles. By implementing these protocols, professionals can ensure that autonomous vehicles can respond to emergencies quickly, communicate effectively with other road users, and prioritize safety in all situations.

Chapter 3: Legal Implications of L5 Autonomous Vehicles

Regulations and standards for autonomous vehicles

Regulations and standards for autonomous vehicles play a crucial role in ensuring the safe and efficient operation of L5 autonomous vehicles. These regulations are put in place by government bodies to establish guidelines for the development, testing, and deployment of autonomous vehicles on public roads. For professionals in the autonomous vehicle industry, understanding these regulations is essential to ensure compliance and avoid potential legal issues.

One of the key regulations for autonomous vehicles is the Federal Motor Vehicle Safety Standards (FMVSS) set by the National Highway Traffic Safety Administration (NHTSA) in the United States. These standards cover a wide range of safety requirements, including crashworthiness, crash avoidance, and occupant protection. Autonomous vehicle manufacturers must demonstrate compliance with these standards before their vehicles can be approved for commercial use.

In addition to federal regulations, autonomous vehicles must also comply with state and local laws governing their operation. These laws may vary from state to state and can include requirements for vehicle registration, insurance, and licensing. It is important for professionals in the autonomous vehicle industry to stay informed about these regulations and ensure that their vehicles meet all necessary legal requirements.

Another important aspect of regulations for autonomous vehicles is cybersecurity. As autonomous vehicles rely on complex software systems to operate, they are vulnerable to cyber attacks that could compromise their safety and security. To address this issue, regulators are developing standards for cybersecurity in autonomous vehicles to protect against potential threats.

Overall, regulations and standards for autonomous vehicles are essential for ensuring the safe and responsible deployment of L5 autonomous vehicles. By following these guidelines, professionals in the autonomous vehicle industry can help to build public trust in this emerging technology and pave the way for its widespread adoption in the future.

Liability issues in accidents involving autonomous vehicles

Liability issues in accidents involving autonomous vehicles are a complex and evolving area of concern for professionals in the field of autonomous vehicles. As these vehicles become more prevalent on the roads, questions surrounding who is responsible in the event of an accident are becoming increasingly important to address. Unlike traditional vehicles where the driver is typically held liable, autonomous vehicles introduce a new layer of complexity due to the various parties involved in their operation and decision-making processes.

One of the key challenges in determining liability in accidents involving autonomous vehicles is the role of the vehicle's technology and software. In many cases, accidents involving autonomous vehicles can be attributed to errors in the vehicle's sensors, algorithms, or programming. This raises questions about whether the manufacturer, the software developer, or even the vehicle owner should be held responsible for any damages or injuries resulting from an accident.

Another factor to consider in liability issues involving autonomous vehicles is the role of the human operator, if there is one present. In some autonomous vehicles, there may still be a human driver who can take control in certain situations. This raises questions about whether the human operator should be held liable for accidents that occur while the vehicle is in autonomous mode, or if the responsibility should fall on the vehicle's technology and software.

Legal implications surrounding liability in accidents involving autonomous vehicles are still being developed and tested in real-world scenarios. As more accidents involving autonomous vehicles occur, legal experts are working to establish guidelines and regulations to determine liability and ensure that victims are fairly compensated. Professionals in the autonomous vehicle industry must stay informed on these legal developments to understand their responsibilities and obligations in the event of an accident.

Overall, the issue of liability in accidents involving autonomous vehicles is a complex and multifaceted area that requires careful consideration and ongoing research. Professionals working with L5 autonomous vehicles must be aware of the legal implications surrounding liability and be prepared to navigate these challenges as the technology continues to evolve. By staying informed and proactive in addressing liability issues, professionals can help ensure the safe and responsible integration of autonomous vehicles on our roads.

Privacy concerns with L5 autonomous vehicles

Privacy concerns with L5 autonomous vehicles have become a major topic of discussion as these vehicles become more prevalent on our roads. With the ability to collect vast amounts of data about passengers and their surroundings, there are valid concerns about how this data is being used and protected. Professionals in the field of autonomous vehicles need to be aware of these privacy concerns and take steps to address them in their designs and implementations.

One of the primary privacy concerns with L5 autonomous vehicles is the potential for data breaches. These vehicles are constantly collecting data about their surroundings, including information about pedestrians, other vehicles, and the environment. If this data were to fall into the wrong hands, it could have serious consequences for the individuals involved. Professionals working with L5 autonomous vehicles must ensure that robust cybersecurity measures are in place to protect this data from hackers and other malicious actors.

Another privacy concern with L5 autonomous vehicles is the potential for tracking and surveillance. With the ability to monitor passengers' movements and behaviors, there is a risk that this information could be used for invasive purposes. Professionals in the field must design their systems with privacy in mind, ensuring that passenger data is only used for its intended purpose and is not shared without consent.

Additionally, there are concerns about the sharing of data between autonomous vehicles and other connected devices. As these vehicles become more integrated with smart cities and other infrastructure, there is a risk that sensitive data could be shared without proper safeguards in place. Professionals must work to establish clear guidelines for data sharing and ensure that all parties involved are aware of the privacy implications.

Overall, privacy concerns with L5 autonomous vehicles are a complex and multifaceted issue that requires careful consideration and planning. Professionals in the field must be proactive in addressing these concerns to ensure that autonomous vehicles can be safely and ethically integrated into our society. By taking steps to protect passenger data and establish clear privacy guidelines, we can help ensure that autonomous vehicles are a positive force for change in our communities.

Chapter 4: Maintenance and Repair of L5 Autonomous Vehicles

Routine maintenance procedures for autonomous vehicles

In the world of autonomous vehicles, routine maintenance procedures are essential to ensure the safety and efficiency of these advanced machines. As professionals in the field of L5 autonomous vehicles, it is crucial to understand the maintenance requirements to keep these vehicles operating at their optimal level.

One important routine maintenance procedure for autonomous vehicles is regular software updates. Just like any other technology, autonomous vehicles require periodic updates to ensure they are running the latest software and algorithms. These updates often include bug fixes, performance enhancements, and new features that improve the vehicle's overall performance and safety.

In addition to software updates, autonomous vehicles also require regular inspections and maintenance checks. This includes checking the sensors, cameras, and other essential components to ensure they are functioning properly. Any issues should be addressed promptly to prevent potential safety hazards and malfunctions while on the road.

Another key aspect of routine maintenance for autonomous vehicles is data management. Autonomous vehicles generate a massive amount of data while in operation, which must be properly managed and analyzed to ensure the vehicle's performance and safety. Professionals must develop a robust data management system to store, analyze, and utilize this data effectively.

Lastly, routine maintenance procedures for autonomous vehicles should also include regular cleaning and upkeep of the vehicle's exterior and interior. This includes cleaning sensors, cameras, and other components to ensure they are free from dirt, debris, and other obstructions that could impair their functionality. By following these routine maintenance procedures, professionals can ensure that L5 autonomous vehicles operate safely and efficiently on the road.

Diagnostic tools and software for L5 vehicles

In the world of L5 autonomous vehicles, diagnostic tools and software play a crucial role in ensuring the safe and efficient operation of these advanced vehicles. These tools are essential for identifying and resolving any issues that may arise during the operation of L5 vehicles, allowing professionals to maintain the highest level of performance and safety.

One of the key diagnostic tools used for L5 vehicles is the onboard diagnostic system, which continuously monitors the vehicle's performance and communicates any issues to the driver or maintenance team. This system is equipped with sensors and software that can detect potential problems with the vehicle's sensors, cameras, radar, and other critical components, allowing for timely intervention and maintenance.

In addition to onboard diagnostic systems, professionals working with L5 vehicles also rely on advanced diagnostic software that can analyze data collected from the vehicle's sensors and systems. This software can identify patterns and trends in the vehicle's performance, helping professionals to predict and prevent potential issues before they occur. With the help of this software, professionals can optimize the performance of L5 vehicles and ensure their safe operation on the road.

Furthermore, diagnostic tools and software for L5 vehicles are designed to be user-friendly and accessible, allowing professionals to easily interpret and act upon the data collected. These tools often come with intuitive interfaces and detailed reports that provide valuable insights into the vehicle's performance, enabling professionals to make informed decisions about maintenance and repairs.

Overall, diagnostic tools and software are essential components of the comprehensive toolkit that professionals working with L5 vehicles need to have at their disposal. By leveraging these tools effectively, professionals can ensure the safe and efficient operation of L5 autonomous vehicles, ultimately contributing to the widespread adoption of this groundbreaking technology in various industries and sectors.

Training programs for maintenance technicians

In the world of L5 autonomous vehicles, maintenance technicians play a crucial role in ensuring that these cutting-edge vehicles operate efficiently and safely. Training programs for maintenance technicians are essential to equip them with the knowledge and skills needed to effectively maintain and repair L5 autonomous vehicles. These programs cover a wide range of topics, from understanding the complex technology behind autonomous vehicles to troubleshooting common issues that may arise during operation.

One key aspect of training programs for maintenance technicians is familiarizing them with the various sensors, cameras, and other advanced technologies that are used in L5 autonomous vehicles. Technicians need to understand how these components work together to enable the vehicle to navigate its surroundings and make decisions in real-time. Training programs often include hands-on experience with these technologies, allowing technicians to develop a deep understanding of how they function and how to diagnose and repair any issues that may arise.

In addition to technical knowledge, training programs for maintenance technicians also focus on safety protocols and best practices for working with L5 autonomous vehicles. Technicians need to be trained on how to safely access and service different components of the vehicle, as well as how to handle emergency situations that may arise during maintenance or repair. By following proper safety procedures, technicians can ensure that both themselves and the vehicle are protected from harm.

Another important aspect of training programs for maintenance technicians is teaching them how to effectively communicate with other members of the autonomous vehicle team. Technicians often work closely with engineers, software developers, and other professionals to diagnose and resolve issues with the vehicle. Training programs help technicians develop the communication skills needed to collaborate effectively with team members, ensuring that problems are addressed in a timely and efficient manner.

Overall, training programs for maintenance technicians are essential for ensuring the safe and efficient operation of L5 autonomous vehicles. By equipping technicians with the knowledge and skills needed to maintain and repair these advanced vehicles, training programs play a critical role in the success of autonomous vehicle technology. As the industry continues to evolve, ongoing training and education will be key to keeping maintenance technicians up-to-date on the latest advancements in autonomous vehicle technology.

Chapter 5: Infrastructure Requirements for L5 Autonomous Vehicles

Communication networks for autonomous vehicles

In the world of autonomous vehicles, communication networks play a crucial role in ensuring the safe and efficient operation of L5 autonomous vehicles. These networks enable vehicles to communicate with each other, with infrastructure such as traffic lights and road signs, and with centralized control systems. This seamless exchange of information allows autonomous vehicles to make split-second decisions based on real-time data, ultimately leading to smoother traffic flow and improved safety on the roads.

One key aspect of communication networks for autonomous vehicles is vehicle-to-vehicle (V2V) communication. This technology allows vehicles to share information such as speed, position, and direction with each other, enabling them to coordinate their movements and avoid collisions. By constantly updating each other on their intentions and actions, autonomous vehicles can navigate complex traffic situations with precision and confidence, reducing the risk of accidents caused by human error.

Another important component of communication networks for autonomous vehicles is vehicle-to-infrastructure (V2I) communication. This technology enables vehicles to connect with roadside sensors, traffic management systems, and other infrastructure elements to receive information about road conditions, traffic congestion, and other relevant data. By integrating this information into their decision-making processes, autonomous vehicles can optimize their routes, adjust their speeds, and avoid potential hazards, resulting in smoother and more efficient journeys for passengers and other road users.

Furthermore, communication networks for autonomous vehicles also include vehicle-to-cloud (V2C) communication, which allows vehicles to access data from centralized cloud-based platforms. This data can include maps, traffic updates, weather forecasts, and other relevant information that can help autonomous vehicles plan their routes and make informed decisions. By leveraging the power of the cloud, autonomous vehicles can tap into a vast array of resources to enhance their capabilities and provide a more seamless and enjoyable experience for passengers.

In conclusion, communication networks are the backbone of L5 autonomous vehicles, enabling them to interact with each other, with infrastructure, and with centralized control systems to navigate the roads safely and efficiently. By harnessing the power of V2V, V2I, and V2C communication technologies, autonomous vehicles can make split-second decisions based on real-time data, ultimately leading to smoother traffic flow, improved safety, and a better overall user experience. For professionals in the field of autonomous vehicles, understanding and optimizing these communication networks is essential for unlocking the full potential of L5 autonomous vehicles in the smart cities of the future.

Charging stations for electric autonomous vehicles

As the world transitions towards a future dominated by autonomous vehicles, the need for charging stations specifically designed for electric autonomous vehicles (AVs) is becoming increasingly apparent. These charging stations play a crucial role in ensuring that AVs have enough power to operate efficiently, thus enabling a seamless and sustainable transportation ecosystem. In this subchapter, we will explore the various aspects of charging stations for electric AVs, including their design, functionality, and importance in the broader context of AV infrastructure.

One of the key considerations when designing charging stations for electric AVs is their compatibility with different vehicle models and charging protocols. As the AV market continues to evolve, it is essential for charging stations to be able to accommodate a wide range of vehicles, each with its unique power requirements and charging capabilities. Additionally, the design of these stations should prioritize user-friendly interfaces and streamlined processes to make the charging experience as seamless as possible for AV operators.

In terms of functionality, charging stations for electric AVs should not only provide a reliable power source but also offer advanced features such as real-time monitoring, remote diagnostics, and predictive maintenance. These capabilities are essential for ensuring the optimal performance of AVs and minimizing downtime, thereby improving overall operational efficiency. Furthermore, integrating smart charging technologies can help optimize energy usage and reduce costs, making the transition to electric AVs more economically viable.

The importance of charging stations for electric AVs extends beyond simply providing power; they also play a vital role in supporting the growth of AV fleets and enabling the widespread adoption of autonomous transportation. By investing in a robust network of charging infrastructure, cities and municipalities can create an environment that is conducive to the deployment of AVs, thus paving the way for a more sustainable and efficient transportation system. Moreover, the availability of charging stations can incentivize individuals and businesses to switch to electric AVs, further reducing carbon emissions and promoting environmental sustainability.

In conclusion, charging stations for electric AVs are an integral component of the infrastructure required to support the widespread adoption of autonomous transportation. By designing these stations with compatibility, functionality, and scalability in mind, professionals can help facilitate the transition to electric AVs and create a more sustainable future for transportation. As the AV market continues to evolve, it is crucial for stakeholders to prioritize the development of charging infrastructure to ensure the seamless operation of electric AVs and maximize their potential benefits for society as a whole.

Road infrastructure upgrades for L5 vehicles

Road infrastructure upgrades are a crucial component of preparing for the widespread adoption of Level 5 autonomous vehicles. These vehicles, which are capable of navigating without any human intervention, require specific modifications to existing roads and infrastructure to ensure their safe and efficient operation. In this subchapter, we will explore the key upgrades that are needed to support the deployment of L5 vehicles on our roads.

One of the most important infrastructure upgrades for L5 vehicles is the implementation of dedicated lanes or corridors. These lanes would be reserved exclusively for autonomous vehicles, allowing them to travel without interference from human-driven vehicles. This would help to reduce the risk of accidents and improve the overall efficiency of the transportation system.

In addition to dedicated lanes, L5 vehicles also require advanced communication infrastructure to facilitate real-time data exchange between vehicles and the surrounding environment. This includes technologies such as vehicle-to-vehicle (V2V) and vehicle-to-infrastructure (V2I) communication systems, which enable vehicles to share information about their location, speed, and intended maneuvers. By implementing these systems, we can create a safer and more connected transportation network for autonomous vehicles.

Another critical infrastructure upgrade for L5 vehicles is the installation of sensors and other equipment along roads and highways. These sensors can help to provide valuable data to autonomous vehicles, such as road conditions, traffic patterns, and potential hazards. By leveraging this information, L5 vehicles can make more informed decisions and navigate complex environments with greater ease.

Overall, road infrastructure upgrades are essential for the successful deployment of Level 5 autonomous vehicles. By investing in dedicated lanes, advanced communication systems, and sensor technology, we can create a transportation network that is safe, efficient, and reliable for autonomous vehicles. As professionals in the field of autonomous vehicles, it is important to stay informed about these infrastructure upgrades and advocate for their implementation to support the future of autonomous transportation.

Chapter 6: User Experience Design for L5 Autonomous Vehicles

Interface design for autonomous vehicle control

Interface design for autonomous vehicle control is a crucial aspect of ensuring the safe and efficient operation of L5 autonomous vehicles. The interface serves as the primary means of communication between the vehicle and its passengers, as well as with external systems and infrastructure. In order to maximize the usability and effectiveness of the interface, designers must consider a range of factors, including user experience, safety, and functionality.

One key consideration in interface design for autonomous vehicle control is the need to provide clear and intuitive information to passengers. This includes real-time updates on the vehicle's location, speed, and upcoming maneuvers, as well as any potential hazards or obstacles in the road ahead. Designers must also consider the preferences and abilities of different users, including those with disabilities or special needs, to ensure that the interface is accessible to all.

Safety is another critical consideration in interface design for autonomous vehicle control. The interface must be designed to minimize distractions and reduce the likelihood of errors or accidents. This includes features such as voice commands, gesture controls, and tactile feedback to help users stay focused on the road and make informed decisions in real-time. Additionally, the interface should be designed to provide clear alerts and warnings in the event of emergencies or system failures.

Functionality is also a key aspect of interface design for autonomous vehicle control. The interface must be able to seamlessly integrate with the vehicle's sensors, cameras, and other onboard systems to provide accurate and reliable information to users. It must also be designed to adapt to changing conditions and user inputs, such as route changes or passenger requests, to ensure a smooth and efficient driving experience.

Overall, interface design for autonomous vehicle control is a complex and multifaceted process that requires careful consideration of user experience, safety, and functionality. By taking a holistic approach to design, professionals can create interfaces that enhance the overall performance and usability of L5 autonomous vehicles, while also ensuring the safety and well-being of passengers and other road users.

Passenger comfort features in L5 autonomous vehicles

Passenger comfort features are an essential aspect of L5 autonomous vehicles, ensuring that passengers have a pleasant and stress-free experience while traveling. These features are designed to provide a high level of comfort and convenience, making the journey as enjoyable as possible for passengers.

One of the key passenger comfort features in L5 autonomous vehicles is the interior design and layout. The interior of these vehicles is designed to maximize space and comfort, with plush seating, ample legroom, and ergonomic design elements. The seating arrangements are also flexible, allowing passengers to customize their seating preferences and adjust them to their liking. Additionally, the interior is equipped with advanced climate control systems to ensure a comfortable temperature for passengers at all times.

Another important passenger comfort feature in L5 autonomous vehicles is the entertainment and connectivity options. These vehicles are equipped with state-of-the-art entertainment systems, including high-definition screens, surround sound systems, and connectivity options for smartphones and other devices. Passengers can enjoy their favorite movies, music, and games during their journey, keeping them entertained and engaged throughout the ride.

In addition to entertainment features, L5 autonomous vehicles also offer advanced safety and convenience features to enhance passenger comfort. These vehicles are equipped with advanced driver assistance systems, such as lane-keeping assist, adaptive cruise control, and automatic emergency braking, to ensure a safe and smooth journey for passengers. Additionally, these vehicles are equipped with features such as automated parking assistance and remote vehicle monitoring, making it easy for passengers to navigate and manage their journey.

Overall, passenger comfort features in L5 autonomous vehicles are designed to provide a luxurious and convenient travel experience for passengers. These features are essential for ensuring that passengers feel relaxed, safe, and entertained during their journey, making L5 autonomous vehicles an ideal choice for professionals looking for a comprehensive and comfortable transportation option.

Personalization options for user preferences

In the realm of autonomous vehicles, personalization options for user preferences play a crucial role in enhancing the overall user experience. As professionals delve into the world of L5 autonomous vehicles, it is important to understand the various customization features available to cater to individual needs and preferences.

When it comes to personalization options for user preferences in L5 autonomous vehicles, there are a plethora of choices to consider. From adjusting seating positions and climate control settings to selecting preferred music playlists and entertainment options, the possibilities are endless. By allowing users to tailor their driving experience to their liking, autonomous vehicle manufacturers can create a more personalized and enjoyable journey for passengers.

One key aspect of personalization options for user preferences in L5 autonomous vehicles is the integration of voice recognition technology. This innovative feature enables passengers to control various aspects of the vehicle, such as navigation, entertainment, and climate control, simply by using voice commands. By incorporating voice recognition technology, autonomous vehicle manufacturers can offer a hands-free and seamless driving experience for users.

Another important consideration in personalization options for user preferences in L5 autonomous vehicles is the ability to store and recall individual user profiles. By saving personalized settings for each user, autonomous vehicles can automatically adjust preferences such as seat positions, mirror angles, and favorite destinations based on the user's profile. This level of customization not only enhances the convenience of using autonomous vehicles but also ensures a consistent and personalized experience for each user.

In conclusion, personalization options for user preferences are a crucial aspect of the user experience design for L5 autonomous vehicles. By offering a wide range of customization features, integrating voice recognition technology, and implementing user profile storage capabilities, autonomous vehicle manufacturers can create a truly personalized driving experience for users. As professionals explore the world of L5 autonomous vehicles, understanding and implementing these personalization options will be key to ensuring the success and widespread adoption of autonomous vehicles in the future.

Chapter 7: Integration of L5 Autonomous Vehicles with Smart Cities

Benefits of autonomous vehicles for smart city development

Autonomous vehicles have the potential to revolutionize the way we live and move within smart cities. One of the key benefits of autonomous vehicles for smart city development is increased efficiency in transportation. With autonomous vehicles, traffic flow can be optimized, reducing congestion and travel times. This can lead to a more streamlined and efficient transportation system, benefiting both residents and businesses in the city.

Another significant benefit of autonomous vehicles for smart city development is improved safety. Autonomous vehicles are equipped with advanced sensors and technology that allow them to detect and respond to potential hazards on the road. This can help reduce the number of accidents and fatalities on the road, making transportation safer for everyone in the city.

In addition to safety and efficiency, autonomous vehicles can also have a positive impact on the environment. By optimizing traffic flow and reducing congestion, autonomous vehicles can help reduce emissions and improve air quality in the city. This can have a significant impact on public health and the overall quality of life for residents in the city.

Furthermore, autonomous vehicles can also improve access to transportation for underserved communities in smart cities. By providing on-demand transportation services, autonomous vehicles can help bridge the gap in transportation access for those who may not have access to traditional modes of transportation. This can help create a more inclusive and equitable transportation system in the city.

Overall, the integration of autonomous vehicles into smart cities has the potential to transform the way we live, work, and move within urban environments. By harnessing the benefits of autonomous vehicles, smart cities can create a more efficient, safe, and sustainable transportation system that benefits all residents and businesses in the city.

Traffic management systems for autonomous vehicle integration

Traffic management systems are crucial for the successful integration of autonomous vehicles into our transportation networks. These systems play a vital role in ensuring the safe and efficient operation of self-driving cars on our roads. In this subchapter, we will explore the various traffic management systems that are being developed to support the integration of L5 autonomous vehicles.

One key aspect of traffic management systems for autonomous vehicles is the use of advanced sensors and communication technologies. These technologies allow autonomous vehicles to communicate with each other and with the infrastructure around them, enabling them to navigate complex traffic situations safely and efficiently. By leveraging real-time data and predictive analytics, traffic management systems can help optimize traffic flow and reduce congestion on our roads.

Another important component of traffic management systems for autonomous vehicles is the integration with smart cities. Smart cities are equipped with interconnected technologies that can communicate with autonomous vehicles to provide real-time traffic updates, optimize traffic signal timings, and even reroute vehicles to avoid congestion. By integrating autonomous vehicles with smart cities, we can create a more seamless and efficient transportation system for everyone.

Additionally, traffic management systems for autonomous vehicles must also take into account the legal and regulatory implications of self-driving cars. This includes ensuring that autonomous vehicles comply with local traffic laws, as well as developing new regulations to govern the operation of these vehicles on public roads. By working closely with policymakers and regulators, we can create a legal framework that supports the safe and widespread adoption of autonomous vehicles.

Overall, traffic management systems are essential for the successful integration of L5 autonomous vehicles into our transportation networks. By leveraging advanced sensors, communication technologies, and smart city infrastructure, we can create a safer, more efficient, and more sustainable transportation system for the future. Professionals in the field of autonomous vehicles must stay informed about the latest developments in traffic management systems to ensure the successful deployment of self-driving cars on our roads.

Data sharing and connectivity in smart cities

In the subchapter "Data sharing and connectivity in smart cities" of "The Ultimate Guide to L5 Autonomous Vehicles," we delve into the crucial aspects of how autonomous vehicles interact with the infrastructure of smart cities. One of the key components of a successful autonomous vehicle system is data sharing and connectivity. In smart cities, autonomous vehicles rely on real-time data from various sources such as traffic lights, road sensors, and other vehicles to navigate efficiently and safely.

Data sharing in smart cities is essential for autonomous vehicles to make informed decisions on the road. Through connectivity with infrastructure, autonomous vehicles can receive information about traffic conditions, road closures, and other relevant data that helps them optimize their routes and avoid congestion. This data exchange also allows for better coordination between autonomous vehicles and other vehicles on the road, leading to smoother traffic flow and improved safety.

Furthermore, connectivity in smart cities enables autonomous vehicles to communicate with each other and with the surrounding environment. This communication network, known as Vehicle-to-Everything (V2X) technology, allows autonomous vehicles to share information about their speed, direction, and behavior in real-time. This data exchange helps prevent accidents, reduce traffic congestion, and improve overall road safety.

In addition to enhancing safety and efficiency, data sharing and connectivity in smart cities also play a significant role in reducing environmental impact. By optimizing routes and minimizing idle time, autonomous vehicles can reduce fuel consumption and emissions, contributing to a greener and more sustainable urban environment. Furthermore, smart cities can use data from autonomous vehicles to analyze traffic patterns, identify areas of congestion, and implement strategies to reduce pollution and improve air quality.

Overall, data sharing and connectivity are crucial components of the integration of L5 autonomous vehicles with smart cities. Professionals in the field must understand the importance of these technologies to ensure the successful implementation and operation of autonomous vehicle systems in urban environments. By leveraging data sharing and connectivity, autonomous vehicles can revolutionize transportation, making our cities safer, more efficient, and environmentally friendly.

Chapter 8: Environmental Impact of L5 Autonomous Vehicles

Reduction of carbon emissions with autonomous vehicles

The reduction of carbon emissions with autonomous vehicles is a crucial topic that is gaining traction in the automotive industry. As the world continues to grapple with the effects of climate change, finding sustainable solutions to reduce carbon emissions has become a top priority for many professionals. L5 autonomous vehicles have the potential to play a significant role in this effort, thanks to their advanced technology and efficiency in transportation.

One of the key ways in which autonomous vehicles can help reduce carbon emissions is through their ability to optimize routes and driving patterns. By using advanced algorithms and real-time data, autonomous vehicles can choose the most fuel-efficient routes, avoid traffic congestion, and reduce unnecessary idling. This not only saves time for passengers but also minimizes the amount of harmful emissions released into the atmosphere.

Furthermore, autonomous vehicles are designed to be more energy-efficient than traditional vehicles. With features such as regenerative braking, electric powertrains, and lightweight materials, L5 autonomous vehicles can significantly reduce their carbon footprint compared to conventional cars. This is particularly important as the demand for transportation continues to grow, leading to increased emissions from vehicles on the road.

Another important aspect of reducing carbon emissions with autonomous vehicles is their potential for vehicle sharing and ride-hailing services. By promoting shared mobility and reducing the number of privately owned vehicles on the road, autonomous vehicles can help decrease overall emissions from transportation. This is especially beneficial in urban areas where congestion and pollution are major concerns.

In conclusion, the reduction of carbon emissions with autonomous vehicles is a multifaceted issue that requires collaboration between professionals in the automotive industry, policymakers, and environmental experts. By harnessing the power of L5 autonomous vehicles and implementing sustainable practices, we can work towards a cleaner and more efficient transportation system that benefits both the planet and its inhabitants. It is essential for professionals to stay informed and proactive in exploring the potential of autonomous vehicles in addressing environmental challenges and creating a greener future for generations to come.

Sustainable materials and energy sources for L5 vehicles

Sustainable materials and energy sources are crucial considerations for the development and operation of Level 5 (L5) autonomous vehicles. These vehicles are designed to operate without human intervention, relying solely on their sensors, cameras, and artificial intelligence to navigate the roads. As such, it is essential that the materials used in the construction of these vehicles are environmentally friendly and sustainable in order to minimize their impact on the planet.

One of the key considerations when it comes to sustainable materials for L5 vehicles is the use of recycled and recyclable materials in their construction. By using materials that can be easily recycled at the end of the vehicle's life cycle, manufacturers can reduce the amount of waste generated by these vehicles. Additionally, using recycled materials can help to lower the carbon footprint of L5 vehicles, making them a more environmentally friendly option for transportation.

In addition to using sustainable materials, L5 vehicles also need to rely on energy sources that are clean and renewable. This means that electric vehicles are the most popular choice for L5 autonomous vehicles, as they can be powered by electricity generated from renewable sources such as solar, wind, and hydroelectric power. By using electric vehicles, manufacturers can help to reduce the emissions of greenhouse gases and other pollutants associated with traditional gasoline-powered vehicles.

Furthermore, the use of renewable energy sources for charging L5 autonomous vehicles can help to reduce their overall environmental impact. By investing in solar panels or wind turbines to generate electricity for charging stations, manufacturers can ensure that the energy used to power these vehicles is clean and sustainable. This can help to further reduce the carbon footprint of L5 vehicles and make them a more environmentally friendly option for transportation.

Overall, the use of sustainable materials and energy sources is essential for the development and operation of Level 5 autonomous vehicles. By using recycled materials, electric vehicles, and renewable energy sources, manufacturers can help to minimize the environmental impact of these vehicles and make them a more sustainable option for transportation. Professionals in the field of autonomous vehicles should consider these factors when designing and implementing L5 vehicles in order to create a more sustainable future for transportation.

Impact on urban planning and green spaces

The introduction of L5 autonomous vehicles is set to have a significant impact on urban planning and green spaces. As cities continue to grow and expand, the need for efficient transportation solutions becomes increasingly important. L5 autonomous vehicles have the potential to revolutionize the way we think about urban planning, by reducing the need for parking spaces and creating more green spaces for pedestrians and cyclists.

One of the key benefits of L5 autonomous vehicles is their ability to reduce traffic congestion and improve the flow of traffic in urban areas. By utilizing advanced sensors and artificial intelligence, these vehicles can navigate through busy city streets with ease, reducing the need for large highways and interchanges. This will allow city planners to reevaluate existing infrastructure and create more pedestrian-friendly spaces, promoting a healthier and more sustainable urban environment.

Furthermore, L5 autonomous vehicles have the potential to transform the way we think about parking. With the ability to drop passengers off at their destination and then park themselves in designated areas, these vehicles will reduce the need for large parking lots and garages in urban areas. This will free up valuable space for green areas, parks, and other recreational facilities, creating a more livable and vibrant cityscape.

In addition to impacting urban planning, L5 autonomous vehicles will also have a positive effect on green spaces. By reducing the need for parking lots and garages, these vehicles will help to reduce the amount of impermeable surfaces in cities, allowing for more natural drainage and reducing the risk of flooding. This will not only improve the overall aesthetic of urban areas but also enhance the quality of life for residents by providing more opportunities for outdoor recreation and relaxation.

Overall, the introduction of L5 autonomous vehicles will have a profound impact on urban planning and green spaces. By reducing traffic congestion, reimagining parking solutions, and creating more green areas, these vehicles have the potential to transform the way we think about cities and create a more sustainable and livable urban environment. Professionals in the field of urban planning and transportation should be prepared to embrace these changes and work towards integrating L5 autonomous vehicles into their long-term planning strategies.

Chapter 9: Insurance Considerations for L5 Autonomous Vehicles

Insurance policies for autonomous vehicle owners

Insurance policies for autonomous vehicle owners are a crucial aspect of the autonomous vehicle industry. As professionals in the field of L5 autonomous vehicles, it is important to understand the various insurance options available to protect both the owners and users of these advanced vehicles. With the rise of autonomous technology, insurance companies have had to adapt their policies to account for the unique risks and liabilities associated with self-driving cars.

One key consideration for insurance policies for autonomous vehicle owners is the level of coverage needed. L5 autonomous vehicles are designed to operate without human intervention in all driving scenarios, which means that traditional insurance policies may not fully cover the risks associated with these vehicles. As such, owners may need to invest in specialized insurance policies that specifically cater to autonomous vehicles to ensure comprehensive coverage.

Another important aspect of insurance policies for autonomous vehicle owners is determining liability in the event of an accident. With autonomous vehicles, the lines of liability can become blurred, as the vehicle's software, the manufacturer, the owner, and other parties may all play a role in the accident. Insurance companies are working to develop policies that clearly outline liability in these situations to ensure that all parties are adequately protected.

In addition to liability coverage, insurance policies for autonomous vehicle owners may also include coverage for cybersecurity threats. As self-driving cars rely heavily on software and connectivity, they are vulnerable to cyber attacks that could compromise their safety and functionality. Insurance companies are beginning to offer policies that cover these risks, providing peace of mind to owners and users of autonomous vehicles.

Overall, insurance policies for autonomous vehicle owners are a complex and evolving aspect of the autonomous vehicle industry. As professionals in the field of L5 autonomous vehicles, it is important to stay informed about the latest insurance options and trends to ensure that owners and users are adequately protected. By understanding the unique risks and liabilities associated with autonomous vehicles, professionals can help shape the future of insurance policies for this groundbreaking technology.

Claims process for accidents involving autonomous vehicles

Accidents involving autonomous vehicles are a relatively new phenomenon, but they are becoming more common as the technology becomes more widespread. In this subchapter, we will discuss the claims process for accidents involving autonomous vehicles, including how it differs from traditional car accidents and what professionals need to know to navigate the complexities of these cases.

One of the key differences in the claims process for accidents involving autonomous vehicles is the role of the vehicle itself in the accident. In traditional car accidents, the driver is typically at fault, but in accidents involving autonomous vehicles, the technology and the manufacturer may also be liable. This can complicate the claims process and make it more difficult to determine who is responsible for the accident.

Another important factor to consider in the claims process for accidents involving autonomous vehicles is the issue of data collection. Autonomous vehicles are equipped with sensors and cameras that record data before, during, and after an accident. This data can be crucial in determining what caused the accident and who is at fault. Professionals working on these cases need to be familiar with how to access and analyze this data to build a strong case for their clients.

In addition to the technical aspects of the claims process, professionals also need to be aware of the legal implications of accidents involving autonomous vehicles. There are still many unanswered questions about how liability is determined in these cases and what standards should be applied. Professionals working on these cases need to stay up to date on the latest legal developments and be prepared to navigate the complexities of this emerging area of law.

Overall, the claims process for accidents involving autonomous vehicles is likely to be more complex and nuanced than traditional car accidents. Professionals working in this area need to have a deep understanding of the technology, the legal landscape, and the data involved in these cases to effectively represent their clients. By staying informed and being prepared for the unique challenges of these cases, professionals can ensure that they are able to provide the best possible representation for their clients in accidents involving autonomous vehicles.

Future trends in insurance for autonomous vehicles

As autonomous vehicles become more prevalent on the roads, the insurance industry is facing new challenges and opportunities. The future trends in insurance for autonomous vehicles are constantly evolving as technology advances and regulations change. In this subchapter, we will explore some of the key trends that professionals should be aware of in order to stay ahead in this rapidly changing landscape.

One of the most significant trends in insurance for autonomous vehicles is the shift from traditional auto insurance to product liability insurance. As autonomous vehicles take over more of the driving responsibilities from humans, the liability for accidents will increasingly fall on the manufacturers and developers of the technology. This shift will require insurance companies to adapt their policies and coverage options to account for the unique risks and responsibilities associated with autonomous vehicles.

Another important trend to watch is the development of usage-based insurance (UBI) for autonomous vehicles. UBI uses telematics data to track a driver's behavior and adjust their insurance premiums accordingly. With autonomous vehicles, this data can be used to assess the performance and safety of the vehicle itself, leading to more personalized and accurate insurance pricing. This trend could revolutionize the insurance industry by incentivizing safe driving behavior and rewarding responsible vehicle owners.

As autonomous vehicles become more integrated into smart cities and transportation networks, insurance companies will need to consider new factors when assessing risk and setting premiums. For example, insurance companies may need to take into account the cybersecurity measures and data privacy protections of autonomous vehicle systems, as well as the impact of vehicle-to-vehicle communication on accident rates. Professionals in the insurance industry will need to stay informed about these emerging trends and technologies in order to provide comprehensive coverage for autonomous vehicles.

In addition to these technological and regulatory trends, insurance professionals should also be aware of the ethical considerations surrounding autonomous vehicles. For example, who is responsible in the event of an accident caused by a self-driving car? How should insurance companies handle claims when the vehicle's programming is at fault? These questions raise complex ethical dilemmas that will require careful consideration and collaboration between insurance providers, manufacturers, and policymakers.

In conclusion, the future of insurance for autonomous vehicles is full of exciting opportunities and challenges for professionals in the industry. By staying informed about the latest trends in product liability insurance, UBI, smart city integration, and ethical considerations, insurance professionals can position themselves as leaders in this rapidly evolving field. As autonomous vehicles continue to revolutionize the way we think about transportation and mobility, the insurance industry must adapt and innovate in order to meet the needs of this new era of driverless technology.

Chapter 10: Ethical Considerations in Programming L5 Autonomous Vehicles

Ethical dilemmas in decision-making algorithms

In the rapidly evolving world of autonomous vehicles, ethical dilemmas in decision-making algorithms have become a hot topic of debate. As L5 autonomous vehicles become more advanced and prevalent on our roads, it is essential for professionals in the industry to understand and address these ethical considerations.

One of the primary ethical dilemmas in decision-making algorithms for L5 autonomous vehicles involves the infamous "trolley problem." This thought experiment poses a scenario in which a self-driving car must choose between hitting a group of pedestrians or swerving and potentially harming the car's occupants. How should the algorithm prioritize human lives in such a situation? This moral quandary raises questions about the value of different lives and the responsibility of programmers to make these life-and-death decisions.

Another ethical dilemma in decision-making algorithms for autonomous vehicles is the issue of bias. Algorithms are only as unbiased as the data they are trained on, which can lead to discriminatory outcomes. For example, if a self-driving car is more likely to detect and avoid white pedestrians than Black pedestrians, this can have serious consequences for road safety and social justice. Professionals must actively work to identify and mitigate these biases in their programming.

Furthermore, the issue of transparency and accountability is crucial in addressing ethical dilemmas in decision-making algorithms for L5 autonomous vehicles. Who is ultimately responsible for the decisions made by these algorithms? How can we ensure that these decisions are fair and just? Professionals must work to develop transparent systems that allow for accountability and oversight in the development and deployment of autonomous vehicles.

In conclusion, ethical considerations in programming L5 autonomous vehicles are complex and multifaceted. Professionals in the industry must grapple with difficult moral dilemmas, such as the trolley problem and bias in decision-making algorithms, while also prioritizing transparency and accountability. By addressing these ethical concerns head-on, we can ensure that autonomous vehicles are developed and deployed in a responsible and ethical manner.

Human behavior prediction and moral coding in L5 vehicles

Human behavior prediction and moral coding in L5 vehicles is a crucial aspect of autonomous vehicle technology that professionals need to understand. In order for L5 autonomous vehicles to operate safely and effectively, they must be able to predict and react to human behavior on the road. This includes anticipating the actions of other drivers, pedestrians, and cyclists in various scenarios. By incorporating advanced sensors, cameras, and artificial intelligence algorithms, L5 vehicles can analyze the environment in real-time and make split-second decisions to avoid accidents.

One of the key challenges in programming L5 vehicles is determining the ethical considerations that must be taken into account when making decisions on the road. For example, in a situation where a collision is unavoidable, the vehicle must be programmed to prioritize the safety of its occupants while also considering the well-being of others involved in the accident. This requires a complex moral coding system that takes into account various factors such as the age, gender, and health status of individuals in the vicinity.

In addition to predicting human behavior and implementing moral coding, L5 vehicles must also be designed to interact with other road users in a way that is safe and efficient. This includes communicating with pedestrians and cyclists through signals and gestures, as well as following traffic rules and regulations. User experience design plays a crucial role in ensuring that passengers feel comfortable and confident while riding in autonomous vehicles, which can help increase adoption rates and trust in the technology.

Furthermore, the integration of L5 vehicles with smart cities is essential for optimizing traffic flow and reducing congestion on the roads. By leveraging data from sensors and connected devices, autonomous vehicles can navigate through urban environments more efficiently and effectively. This integration also opens up opportunities for new transportation services and business models that can benefit both consumers and businesses.

Overall, human behavior prediction and moral coding are critical components of L5 autonomous vehicles that professionals must understand in order to develop and deploy this technology safely and responsibly. By addressing ethical considerations, designing user-friendly interfaces, and integrating with smart city infrastructure, L5 vehicles have the potential to revolutionize transportation and improve the quality of life for people around the world.

Transparency and accountability in autonomous vehicle programming

Transparency and accountability in autonomous vehicle programming are crucial aspects that must be carefully considered in the development and deployment of L5 autonomous vehicles. As these vehicles rely on complex algorithms and artificial intelligence to make split-second decisions on the road, it is essential that the programming behind these decisions is transparent to ensure accountability in case of accidents or malfunctions.

One of the key challenges in ensuring transparency in autonomous vehicle programming is the proprietary nature of the algorithms used by different companies. While companies may want to protect their intellectual property, there is a growing call for more transparency in the algorithms used in autonomous vehicles to ensure that they are safe and reliable. This transparency can also help regulators and policymakers understand how these vehicles operate and make informed decisions about their deployment.

Accountability in autonomous vehicle programming is equally important, as it determines who is responsible in case of accidents or failures. While developers and manufacturers may be held accountable for the design and programming of autonomous vehicles, there are also legal and ethical questions about the responsibilities of users, regulators, and other stakeholders. Clear guidelines and regulations are needed to ensure accountability and prevent potential legal disputes in the event of accidents or malfunctions.

To address these challenges, industry stakeholders are exploring ways to increase transparency and accountability in autonomous vehicle programming. This includes developing open-source platforms for sharing algorithms and data, creating industry standards for programming and testing autonomous vehicles, and establishing codes of conduct for developers and manufacturers. By working together to promote transparency and accountability, the industry can build trust among users, regulators, and the public, and ensure the safe and responsible deployment of L5 autonomous vehicles.

In conclusion, transparency and accountability in autonomous vehicle programming are essential for the safe and responsible deployment of L5 autonomous vehicles. By promoting transparency in algorithms and programming, and establishing clear guidelines for accountability, the industry can build trust among stakeholders and ensure the safe operation of autonomous vehicles on our roads. As professionals in the field of L5 autonomous vehicles, it is our responsibility to prioritize transparency and accountability in our programming practices to ensure the safety and reliability of these groundbreaking technologies.

Chapter 11: Use Cases and Applications of L5 Autonomous Vehicles in Different Industries

Transportation and logistics

Transportation and logistics play a crucial role in the development and implementation of L5 autonomous vehicles. These vehicles have the potential to revolutionize the way goods are transported and delivered, offering benefits such as increased efficiency, reduced costs, and improved safety. In this subchapter, we will explore the various aspects of transportation and logistics in relation to L5 autonomous vehicles, including the infrastructure requirements, user experience design, and integration with smart citics.

One of the key considerations when it comes to L5 autonomous vehicles is the infrastructure needed to support their operation. This includes not only the physical infrastructure such as roads and charging stations but also the digital infrastructure required for communication between vehicles and with other smart city systems. Ensuring that the necessary infrastructure is in place is essential for the successful deployment of L5 autonomous vehicles and maximizing their potential benefits.

User experience design is another important aspect to consider when it comes to L5 autonomous vehicles. Designing a seamless and intuitive user interface is critical for ensuring that passengers feel comfortable and safe while traveling in autonomous vehicles. This includes features such as easy-to-use controls, clear communication of the vehicle's actions, and the ability to quickly and easily override the autonomous system if necessary.

Integration with smart cities is another key area of focus when it comes to transportation and logistics for L5 autonomous vehicles. These vehicles have the potential to transform urban transportation systems by reducing congestion, improving traffic flow, and reducing emissions. By integrating L5 autonomous vehicles with smart city infrastructure such as traffic lights, sensors, and data analytics, cities can create a more efficient and sustainable transportation network.

In conclusion, transportation and logistics are critical components of the development and deployment of L5 autonomous vehicles. By addressing key considerations such as infrastructure requirements, user experience design, and integration with smart cities, professionals can help ensure the successful implementation of autonomous vehicles in the transportation industry. By understanding the unique challenges and opportunities presented by L5 autonomous vehicles, professionals can help shape the future of transportation and logistics for the better.

Healthcare and medical services

Healthcare and medical services are one of the most promising applications of L5 autonomous vehicles. These advanced vehicles have the potential to revolutionize the way medical professionals provide care to patients, improving efficiency, accessibility, and overall quality of healthcare services.

One of the key benefits of L5 autonomous vehicles in healthcare is the ability to provide on-demand medical transportation. Patients with mobility issues or those in remote areas can easily access healthcare facilities without the need for a driver. This can significantly reduce wait times for appointments and emergency services, ultimately saving lives in critical situations.

In addition to transportation, L5 autonomous vehicles can also be equipped with medical equipment and technology to provide mobile healthcare services. For example, an autonomous ambulance could be equipped with telemedicine capabilities, allowing medical professionals to remotely assess and treat patients in real-time while en route to the hospital. This can be especially beneficial in rural areas where access to healthcare services is limited.

Furthermore, these vehicles can be programmed to navigate traffic and road conditions more efficiently than human drivers, reducing the risk of accidents and improving overall safety for patients and medical professionals. With advanced safety features such as collision avoidance systems and real-time data analysis, L5 autonomous vehicles have the potential to significantly reduce medical errors and improve patient outcomes.

Overall, the integration of L5 autonomous vehicles in healthcare and medical services has the potential to transform the industry, making healthcare more accessible, efficient, and safe for everyone involved. As professionals in the field of autonomous vehicles, it is crucial to stay informed about the latest advancements and opportunities in this rapidly evolving sector to ensure that we are prepared to leverage this technology to its full potential in the healthcare industry.

Agriculture and farming

Agriculture and farming are industries that have seen significant advancements with the introduction of L5 autonomous vehicles. These vehicles have the potential to revolutionize the way crops are planted, monitored, and harvested. With their ability to operate without human intervention, L5 autonomous vehicles can increase efficiency and productivity in the agricultural sector.

One of the key benefits of using L5 autonomous vehicles in agriculture is their precision. These vehicles are equipped with advanced sensors and technology that allow them to navigate fields with accuracy and avoid obstacles. This precision not only increases the yield of crops but also reduces waste and environmental impact.

Safety is a major concern in the agricultural industry, and L5 autonomous vehicles can help improve safety for farmers and workers. By taking over tasks that are repetitive or dangerous, these vehicles can reduce the risk of accidents and injuries on the farm. Additionally, their ability to operate 24/7 without fatigue can help increase productivity and efficiency.

The legal implications of using L5 autonomous vehicles in agriculture are still being explored. Regulations around the use of autonomous vehicles on public roads may also apply to their use on farms. Farmers and agricultural companies will need to stay informed about any new laws or regulations that may impact their use of these vehicles.

In terms of maintenance and repair, L5 autonomous vehicles require specialized knowledge and expertise. Farmers will need to invest in training for their staff or work with external partners to ensure that their vehicles are properly maintained and serviced. Additionally, infrastructure requirements such as charging stations and storage facilities will need to be considered when integrating L5 autonomous vehicles into farming operations.

Retail and delivery services

In the world of L5 autonomous vehicles, retail and delivery services are experiencing a revolutionary transformation. With the ability to operate without human intervention, these vehicles are poised to revolutionize the way goods are transported and delivered to consumers. This subchapter will explore the various ways in which L5 autonomous vehicles are changing the landscape of retail and delivery services.

One of the key benefits of L5 autonomous vehicles in the retail and delivery sector is their ability to operate 24/7 without the need for breaks or rest periods. This means that retailers and delivery companies can significantly increase their efficiency and speed of service, leading to improved customer satisfaction and loyalty. Additionally, L5 autonomous vehicles can navigate through traffic and congestion more effectively than human drivers, further reducing delivery times and costs.

Safety is a top priority when it comes to autonomous vehicles, especially in the realm of retail and delivery services. L5 autonomous vehicles are equipped with advanced sensors and artificial intelligence systems that allow them to detect and avoid potential hazards on the road. These vehicles are programmed to prioritize safety above all else, ensuring that goods are delivered securely and without incident.

From a legal standpoint, the introduction of L5 autonomous vehicles in the retail and delivery sector raises a host of complex issues. Regulations surrounding autonomous vehicles vary from country to country, and it is crucial for businesses to stay informed and compliant with the latest laws and guidelines. Companies that operate L5 autonomous vehicles must also consider liability and insurance implications in the event of accidents or malfunctions.

In terms of maintenance and repair, L5 autonomous vehicles require specialized training and equipment to ensure they remain in optimal working condition. Regular software updates and maintenance checks are essential to prevent malfunctions and ensure the safety of both the vehicle and its cargo. Additionally, businesses must have contingency plans in place in case of technical failures or emergencies to minimize disruptions to their operations.

Entertainment and tourism industries

Entertainment and tourism industries are two sectors that are expected to be significantly impacted by the advent of L5 autonomous vehicles. These industries rely heavily on transportation to move people from one location to another, whether it be for a concert, theme park visit, or sightseeing tour. With the introduction of L5 autonomous vehicles, the entire experience for both entertainment and tourism activities is set to change dramatically.

One of the key benefits of L5 autonomous vehicles in the entertainment and tourism industries is the potential for increased safety. With fully autonomous vehicles, the risk of accidents caused by human error is significantly reduced, leading to a safer and more enjoyable experience for passengers. This increased safety factor is likely to attract more customers to entertainment venues and tourist destinations, as they can feel confident in the reliability of the transportation services provided.

In addition to safety, L5 autonomous vehicles also have the potential to revolutionize the user experience in the entertainment and tourism industries. Imagine a theme park where visitors can summon an autonomous vehicle to take them from one ride to the next, or a guided tour of a city where passengers can sit back and relax while the vehicle takes them to all the must-see sights. These types of experiences are made possible by the advanced technology and capabilities of L5 autonomous vehicles.

Furthermore, the integration of L5 autonomous vehicles with smart cities is expected to further enhance the entertainment and tourism experience. Smart city infrastructure can be leveraged to create seamless transportation networks that cater to the specific needs of entertainment and tourism activities. From designated pick-up and drop-off zones to optimized routes based on real-time traffic data, smart cities can play a crucial role in maximizing the efficiency and convenience of autonomous transportation services.

Overall, the entertainment and tourism industries stand to benefit greatly from the widespread adoption of L5 autonomous vehicles. From increased safety and improved user experiences to enhanced integration with smart city infrastructure, the possibilities for innovation and transformation are endless. Professionals in these industries should stay informed and prepared for the inevitable changes that will come with the rise of autonomous transportation.

www.ingramcontent.com/pod-product-compliance
Lightning Source LLC
Chambersburg PA
CBHW060111090326
40690CB00064B/5229

* 9 7 9 8 3 2 8 3 4 2 5 6 8 *

Excel Guide for Absolute Beginners: Shortcuts, Formulas, and Charts

Purpose of This Guide

This guide is designed for absolute beginners who are looking to understand and effectively use Microsoft Excel. Whether you're a student, a senior, or someone new to this spreadsheet application, you'll find the information presented here invaluable for enhancing your productivity and understanding of Excel.

What to Expect

Readers can expect a comprehensive introduction to Excel, focusing on fundamental aspects such as:

- **Basic Excel Interface and Layout: Understanding the Excel window, including the Ribbon, formula bar, and worksheet area.**
- **Essential Shortcuts: Learning keyboard shortcuts that save time and streamline workflow.**
- **Introduction to Formulas: Discovering the basic formulas that form the backbone of Excel's calculation capabilities.**
- **Creating Charts: Learning how to create various types of charts for data visualization.**

What You Will Learn

- **Data Management: How to organize and maintain data efficiently using Excel's structured grid layout.**
- **Basic Calculations: Performing simple mathematical operations with built-in formulas.**
- **Data Visualization: Creating visual representations of data through charts and graphs to enhance understanding and presentation.**
- **Advanced Techniques: An introduction to more sophisticated features such as conditional formatting, data validation, and PivotTables.**

How to Use This Guide

This guide serves as a stepping stone for anyone looking to develop their Excel skills. By following the instructions and examples provided:

- **Increase Efficiency: Use shortcuts and basic formulas to perform tasks more quickly and accurately.**
- **Enhance Data Analysis: Learn to visualize data trends and patterns effectively with charts.**
- **Improve Decision-Making: Utilize Excel's analytical tools to make informed decisions based on data insights.**

This guide encourages exploration and practice, allowing you to build confidence and proficiency with Excel. As you grow more comfortable with its features, you'll find new ways to leverage Excel's capabilities to meet your specific needs, whether for personal, educational, or professional purposes.

Excel is a powerful tool that can help you organize data, perform calculations, and create visual representations of information. Whether you're a student, a senior, or someone new to Excel, this guide will introduce you to essential shortcuts, basic formulas, and popular charts to enhance your productivity and understanding.

The Evolution and Purpose of Excel

Excel, developed by Microsoft, was first introduced to the public in 1985. It was crafted as a robust spreadsheet application aimed at simplifying the management and analysis of complex data. Initially, Excel emerged to compete with other spreadsheet software like Lotus 1-2-3, but it quickly gained traction thanks to its intuitive interface and powerful features.

Key Purposes of Excel

Excel was created to fulfill several important functions:

1. **Data Organization and Management:**
   Excel offers a structured grid layout, making it simple to organize, store, and manage extensive data sets. The arrangement of rows and columns facilitates systematic data entry and retrieval.
2. **Mathematical and Statistical Calculations:**
   With a wide range of built-in functions and formulas, Excel enables users to execute complex mathematical and statistical calculations effortlessly. This capability is vital in areas such as finance, engineering, and research, where accuracy is essential.

3. **Data Visualization:**
   Excel's charting tools allow users to convert raw data into visual formats like charts and graphs. These visual representations enhance the interpretation of data trends and patterns, making them invaluable for presentations and reports.
4. **Data Analysis and Decision Making:**
   The application supports data analysis through features like PivotTables, which assist in summarizing and exploring large data sets. Excel also provides tools for trend analysis, forecasting, and scenario planning, empowering users to make informed decisions.
5. **Automation of Repetitive Tasks:**
   By utilizing macros, Excel enables users to automate repetitive tasks, saving time and minimizing errors. This feature is particularly useful for tasks that require consistent operations.

Excel continues to evolve, with Microsoft frequently updating its features and functions to meet the changing demands of its users. Today, it is widely utilized across various sectors, including business, education, and personal finance, showcasing its versatility and significance in data management and analysis.

Excel's development and adaptation over time have made it an essential tool in the digital era. As technology progresses, Excel integrates with other Microsoft products and services, enhancing its utility and accessibility. For example, its integration with cloud services like OneDrive allows for real-time collaboration, enabling teams to work together on data projects from different locations. Furthermore, Excel's compatibility with other Microsoft applications like Word and PowerPoint streamlines workflows and enriches presentations, making data more dynamic and engaging.

The versatility of Excel makes it a crucial tool for users of all expertise levels. From managing personal budgets to executing sophisticated financial models, Excel's adaptability is apparent in its widespread use across various fields. In education, it aids students and educators in managing grades and analyzing academic data effectively. In business, it supports financial analysis, project management, and inventory tracking. In scientific research, Excel assists in data collection and statistical analysis, proving invaluable in deriving meaningful conclusions from experimental data.

Additionally, Excel boasts a vast and active user community that offers a wealth of resources for learning and troubleshooting. Online forums, tutorials, and courses are readily available, providing support and guidance for both beginners and advanced users. This community-driven support network ensures that users can continuously improve their skills and stay informed about new features and techniques.

In summary, Excel's transformation from a basic spreadsheet application to a comprehensive data management tool highlights its importance in today's digital landscape. Its ability to adapt and evolve alongside technological advancements guarantees its relevance for anyone looking to organize, analyze, and visualize data efficiently. Whether you are a novice exploring its foundational features or an experienced user utilizing its advanced functionalities, Excel presents endless opportunities for innovation and productivity.

Excel's ongoing evolution exemplifies its enduring significance and adaptability in an ever-changing technological landscape. As new features are introduced, they often focus on enhancing efficiency, improving user experience, and fostering collaborative work environments. The integration of artificial intelligence, for instance, is paving the way for smarter data insights, allowing users to uncover trends and patterns with greater ease and accuracy.

For those embarking on their Excel journey, the abundance of resources available makes it easier than ever to achieve proficiency. From online video tutorials to interactive courses, users can access a plethora of tools designed to accelerate learning and mastery. Meanwhile, advanced users can explore more sophisticated functionalities, such as Power Query for data transformation or Power Pivot for advanced data modeling, both of which expand Excel's capabilities beyond traditional spreadsheet functions.

As Excel continues to integrate with emerging technologies like machine learning and predictive analytics, its role in data-driven decision-making becomes increasingly significant. These innovations empower businesses to optimize their operations and provide individuals with the tools needed to make informed choices, whether in personal finance or academic research.

Looking forward, Excel's journey will likely include further integration with cutting-edge technologies and an increased emphasis on automation and predictive capabilities. This evolution ensures that Excel remains not just a data management tool, but a comprehensive platform for innovation and strategic planning.

Ultimately, the combination of simplicity and power in Excel allows it to cater to a diverse audience, making it an essential tool in both professional and personal contexts. Whether entering data, crafting dynamic reports, or conducting intricate analyses, Excel is equipped to handle the task, enhancing the efficiency and effectiveness of your data management efforts.

Introduction to Excel for Absolute Beginners

Excel is a versatile spreadsheet application that can handle everything from simple lists to complex data analysis. Its capabilities make it an essential tool for students, professionals, and anyone who needs to manage data efficiently. This introductory guide aims to familiarize you with the basic concepts and functionalities of Excel to help you get started on your journey to becoming an Excel adept.

Understanding Excel's Potential

Excel is much more than just a grid of rows and columns. It's a dynamic platform for:

- **Data Management: Organize and maintain your data efficiently.**
- **Calculations: Perform mathematical operations using formulas and functions.**
- **Data Visualization: Create charts and graphs to visualize your data.**
- **Data Analysis: Analyze trends, patterns, and relationships within your data.**

Whether you're managing a budget, tracking a project, or analyzing sales data, Excel offers tools that can make your tasks more manageable.

Basic Features and Layout

The Excel interface is designed to be intuitive, with several key components:

- **Cell: The basic unit of Excel where data is entered. Each cell is identified by a column letter and row number (e.g., A1, B2).**
- **Workbook: The entire Excel file containing one or more worksheets.**
- **Worksheet: An individual spreadsheet within a workbook.**
- **Ribbon: The toolbar at the top of Excel, containing tabs like Home, Insert, and Formulas with various tools and commands.**

Getting Started with Excel

1. **Open Excel: Launch the Excel application. You can start with a blank workbook or choose from a variety of templates.**
2. **Enter Data: Click on a cell and type your data. Press Enter to move to the next cell.**
3. **Save Your Workbook: Click on the Save icon or use the shortcut Ctrl + S. Choose a file name and location for your workbook.**

Common Excel Tasks for Beginners

- **Creating Lists: Use Excel to keep track of tasks or items. Each row can represent a different entry, and you can use columns for specific details (e.g., due dates, statuses).**
- **Budgeting: Track income and expenses using Excel's formulas to calculate totals and balances.**
- **Scheduling: Organize appointments and deadlines using Excel's calendar templates or create your own schedule from scratch.**

By understanding these basics and practicing regularly, you'll quickly gain confidence in using Excel. Remember, the key to mastering Excel is exploration and practice. As you become more comfortable, you'll find new ways to leverage Excel's capabilities to suit your specific needs. Enjoy discovering the endless possibilities Excel has to offer!

With just a bit of practice, you'll find that Excel can streamline many of your data-related tasks, making it easier to manage information and draw insights.

Getting Started

Before diving into shortcuts and formulas, it's important to familiarize yourself with the Excel interface. Take some time to explore the Ribbon, where you'll find tabs like Home, Insert, and Formulas, each containing groups of related commands. This will help you navigate Excel more smoothly as you begin to work.

Tips for Beginners

1. **Explore the Ribbon**: Familiarize yourself with the different tabs and tools available in Excel. This will help you quickly find the functions you need.
2. **Use Templates**: Excel offers a variety of templates for budgeting, scheduling, and more. These can be a great starting point for new users.
3. **Practice Regularly**: Like any skill, proficiency in Excel comes with practice. Try creating simple spreadsheets to build your confidence.
4. **Seek Help**: Don't hesitate to use the Help feature or search online for tutorials if you get stuck. There are countless resources available to assist you.

Understanding the Excel Interface

As you start your Excel journey, understanding the interface is crucial for maximizing your efficiency and productivity. The Excel window is divided into several key components:

- **Title Bar**: Displays the name of your workbook.
- **Ribbon**: The main toolbar that houses all the tabs, such as Home, Insert, Data, and Review. Each tab contains groups of related commands.
- **Formula Bar**: Shows the contents of the active cell and allows you to enter or edit data and formulas.
- **Worksheet Area**: The grid where you input and manipulate your data, consisting of rows and columns that form cells.
- **Status Bar**: Provides information about the current mode (e.g., Ready, Edit) and can display quick calculations of selected data.

Creating Your First Spreadsheet

1. **Open Excel**: Launch the application and choose 'Blank Workbook' to start fresh.
2. **Enter Data**: Click on a cell and begin typing to input your data. Press Enter to move to the next cell.
3. **Save Your Work**: Regularly save your work by clicking the Save icon or using Ctrl + S to prevent data loss.

Basic Operations

- **Adding Rows/Columns**: Right-click on a row number or column letter and select 'Insert' to add new rows or columns.
- **Deleting Rows/Columns**: Right-click and choose 'Delete' to remove any unwanted rows or columns.
- **Adjusting Column Width/Row Height**: Double-click the boundary between column letters or row numbers for automatic adjustment, or click and drag to manually resize.

By becoming comfortable with these basics, you'll lay a strong foundation for more advanced Excel skills. Remember to explore and experiment, as hands-on practice is the best way to learn and grow your capabilities in Excel. Enjoy your journey to mastering Excel!

Advanced Techniques for Excel Users

Once you're comfortable with the basics, it's time to explore some advanced techniques that can further enhance your Excel productivity and analytical capabilities.

Conditional Formatting

- **Purpose**: Highlights cells with specific criteria, making it easier to spot trends and outliers.
- **How to Use**: Go to the Home tab, click on 'Conditional Formatting', and select a rule type. Customize the criteria and formatting to suit your needs.

Data Validation

- **Purpose**: Controls the type of data or values users can enter into a cell.
- **How to Use**: Select the cells you want to apply data validation to, go to the Data tab, click 'Data Validation', and set your criteria.

Pivot Tables

- **Purpose**: Summarizes, analyzes, explores, and presents summary data.
- **How to Create**:
  a. Select your data range.
  b. Go to the Insert tab.
  c. Click 'PivotTable'.
  d. Choose where you want the PivotTable to be placed and click 'OK'.
  e. Drag fields to Rows, Columns, and Values to organize your data.

VLOOKUP and HLOOKUP

- **Purpose**: Searches for a value in a table and returns a corresponding value from another column (VLOOKUP) or row (HLOOKUP).
- **Syntax**:
  - **VLOOKUP**: =VLOOKUP(lookup_value, table_array, col_index_num, [range_lookup])
  - **HLOOKUP**: =HLOOKUP(lookup_value, table_array, row_index_num, [range_lookup])
- **Example**: =VLOOKUP("Product A", A2:C10, 2, FALSE) searches for "Product A" in the first column of the range A2:C10 and returns the value in the second column of the matched row.

Macros

- **Purpose**: Automates repetitive tasks by recording actions that can be played back later.
- **How to Record**:
  a. Go to the View tab.
  b. Click 'Macros', then 'Record Macro'.
  c. Perform the tasks you want to automate.
  d. Click 'Stop Recording' when finished.

By incorporating these advanced techniques into your Excel toolkit, you'll be able to tackle more complex data challenges with confidence and efficiency. Keep exploring and practicing, and you'll soon become an Excel power user! Happy data crunching!

Essential Excel Shortcuts

Learning keyboard shortcuts can greatly increase your efficiency when working in Excel. Here are some of the most important shortcuts for beginners:

Navigation Shortcuts

- **Arrow Keys**: Move one cell up, down, left, or right.
- **Ctrl + Arrow Key**: Move to the edge of the current data region.
- **Home**: Move to the beginning of the row.
- **Ctrl + Home**: Move to the beginning of the worksheet.
- **Ctrl + End**: Move to the last cell with data.
- **Page Up/Page Down**: Move one screen up or down within the worksheet.
- **Alt + Page Up/Page Down**: Move one screen to the left or right.

Data Entry Shortcuts

- **Tab**: Move one cell to the right in a worksheet.
- **Shift + Tab**: Move one cell to the left in a worksheet.
- **Enter**: Move one cell down in a selection.
- **Shift + Enter**: Move one cell up in a selection.

Mastering these navigation shortcuts will make it easier to move around your data efficiently, allowing you to focus more on analysis and insights rather than the mechanics of data entry.

Selection Shortcuts

- **Shift + Arrow Key**: Select adjacent cells.
- **Ctrl + Shift + Arrow Key**: Select a range of cells in the direction of the arrow.
- **Ctrl + A**: Select the entire worksheet.

Editing Shortcuts

- **Ctrl + C**: Copy selected cells.
- **Ctrl + V**: Paste copied cells.
- **Ctrl + X**: Cut selected cells.
- **Ctrl + Z**: Undo the last action.
- **Ctrl + Y**: Redo the last action.

Formatting Shortcuts

- **Ctrl + B**: Bold text.
- **Ctrl + I**: Italicize text.
- **Ctrl + U**: Underline text
- **Ctrl + 1**: Open the Format Cells dialog box.
- **Ctrl + Shift + $**: Apply currency format.
- **Ctrl + Shift + %**: Apply percentage format.

These shortcuts will help you quickly format your spreadsheet, making it easier to read and present your data professionally. By mastering these selection, editing, and formatting shortcuts, you will streamline your workflow and enhance your efficiency in Excel. Remember, practice makes perfect, so don't hesitate to apply these shortcuts as you work on your spreadsheets. Happy Excel mastering!

Introduction to Basic Formulas in Excel

Formulas are the backbone of Excel's powerful calculation capabilities, enabling you to perform everything from simple arithmetic to complex analyses. Understanding and utilizing formulas is essential for anyone looking to harness the full potential of Excel. This section will guide you through the basics of formulas, illustrating how they work and how you can start using them in your spreadsheets.

What Are Excel Formulas?

Excel formulas are expressions that calculate the value of a cell. They can be used to perform a variety of tasks, such as adding numbers, finding averages, or even making logical decisions based on specific criteria. Formulas always start with an equal sign (=) and can include numbers, cell references, operators (like +, -, *, /), and built-in functions.

How Do Excel Formulas Work?

When you enter a formula into a cell, Excel evaluates it and displays the result in that cell. If your formula includes cell references, Excel will use the values from those cells in the calculation. This allows formulas to be dynamic; if the values in the referenced cells change, the formula's result updates automatically.

Starting with Basic Formulas

To begin using formulas in Excel, follow these simple steps:

1. **Select a Cell: Click on the cell where you want the formula result to appear.**
2. **Enter the Equal Sign: Type = to signal the start of your formula.**
3. **Input Your Formula: Type the formula using numbers, cell references, operators, and functions as needed. For example, to sum values in cells A1 and A2, you would type =A1 + A2.**
4. **Press Enter: Once your formula is complete, press Enter to display the result in the selected cell.**

Illustration: Simple Formula Example

Imagine you have a small table of sales data and you want to calculate the total sales for the first two days. Here's how you would use a formula:

Day	Sales
Day 1	150
Day 2	200

1. **Select Cell C1: Where you want the total sales.**
2. **Enter the Formula: Type =B2 + B3.**
3. **Press Enter: The result, 350, will appear in cell C1.**

	A	B	C
1	Day	Sales	350
2	Day 1	150	
3	Day 2	200	

This simple example demonstrates how easy it is to start using formulas in Excel. With practice, you can move on to more complex formulas that incorporate functions and logical operations.

Key Points to Remember

- **Always start formulas with an equal sign =.**
- **Use cell references to make formulas dynamic and responsive to changes in your data.**
- **Explore built-in functions to expand your formula capabilities.**

By mastering these basic concepts, you'll be well on your way to using Excel more effectively for data analysis and management. As you become more comfortable, don't hesitate to experiment with different functions and scenarios to see how formulas can simplify your tasks. Happy calculating!

Formulas are at the heart of Excel's calculation capabilities. Here are some basic formulas that beginners should know:

SUM

- **Purpose**: Adds up a range of numbers.
- **Syntax**: =SUM(number1, [number2], ...)
- **Example**: =SUM(A1:A10) adds all the numbers from cells A1 to A10

	A
1	5
2	47
3	8
4	9
5	2.3
6	4.5
7	21
8	1.99
9	2.88
10	2.77
SUM	104.44

AVERAGE

- **Purpose**: Calculates the average of a range of numbers.
- **Syntax**: =AVERAGE(number1, [number2], ...)
- **Example**: =AVERAGE(A1:A10) calculates the average of numbers from cells A1 to A10

	A
1	5
2	47
3	8
4	9
5	2.3
6	4.5
7	21
8	1.99
9	2.88
10	2.77
AVERAGE	10.44

COUNT

- **Purpose**: Counts the number of cells that contain numbers.
- **Syntax**: =COUNT(value1, [value2], ...)
- **Example**: =COUNT(A1:A10) counts the number of cells containing numbers in the range A1 to A10.

	A
1	5
2	47
3	8
4	9
5	2.3
6	4.5
7	21
8	1.99
9	2.88
10	2.77
COUNT	10

IF

- **Purpose**: Performs a logical test and returns one value for a TRUE result, and another for a FALSE result.
- **Syntax**: =IF(logical_test, value_if_true, value_if_false)
- **Example**: =IF(A1>10, "High", "Low") returns "High" if the value in A1 is greater than 10, otherwise returns "Low".

	A	B
1	5	Low
2	47	High
3	8	Low
4	9	Low
5	2.3	Low
6	4.5	Low
7	21	High
8	1.99	Low
9	2.88	Low
10	2.77	Low

MIN and MAX

- **MIN**
  - **Purpose**: Finds the smallest number in a set of values.
  - **Syntax**: =MIN(number1, [number2], ...)
  - **Example**: =MIN(A1:A10) returns the smallest number in the range A1 to A10.

	A
1	5
2	47
3	8
4	9
5	2.3
6	4.5
7	21
8	1.99
9	2.88
10	2.77
MIN	1.99

- **MAX**
  - **Purpose**: Finds the largest number in a set of values.
  - **Syntax**: =MAX(number1, [number2], ...)
  - **Example**: =MAX(A1:A10) returns the largest number in the range A1 to A10.

	A
1	5
2	47
3	8
4	9
5	2.3
6	4.5
7	21
8	1.99
9	2.88
10	2.77
MAX	47

CONCATENATE

- **Purpose**: Joins two or more strings together.
- **Syntax**: =CONCATENATE(text1, [text2], ...)
- **Example**: =CONCATENATE(A1, " ", A2) combines the text from cells A1 and A2 with a space in between.

	A
1	Hello
2	World
CONCATENATE	Hello
	World

ROUND

- **Purpose**: Rounds a number to a specified number of digits.
- **Syntax**: =ROUND(number, num_digits)
- **Example**: =ROUND(A1, 2) rounds the number in cell A1 to two decimal places.

	A
1	5.482
ROUND	5.48

TODAY and NOW

- **TODAY**
  - **Purpose**: Returns the current date.
  - **Syntax**: =TODAY()
  - **Example**: =TODAY() displays the current date.

Today	4/3/2025

- **NOW**
  - **Purpose**: Returns the current date and time.
  - **Syntax**: =NOW()
  - **Example**: =NOW() displays the current date and time.

NOW	4/3/2025

These basic formulas will serve as the building blocks for more complex calculations as you become more proficient with Excel. Practice using them in various scenarios to see how they can simplify your data management and analysis tasks. Happy calculating!

To use formulas in Excel like a pro, start by familiarizing yourself with essential functions such as SUM, AVERAGE, VLOOKUP, and IF. Mastering these will provide a solid foundation for more complex calculations. Additionally, use named ranges to make your formulas easier to read and manage, and take advantage of Excel's built-in formula auditing tools to trace and troubleshoot errors. Remember to use absolute and relative references appropriately; absolute references (A1) are crucial when applying the same formula across different cells. Lastly, explore Excel's array formulas and functions like INDEX and MATCH for more advanced data manipulation. Practice regularly, and don't hesitate to explore online resources and Excel communities for tips and tricks.

Popular Charts and How to Create Them

Charts are a great way to visualize data. Here are some of the most popular types and how to create them:

Column Chart

- **Purpose**: Compares values across categories.
- **How to Create**:
  a. Select the data range.
  b. Go to the **Insert** tab.
  c. Click **Insert Column Chart** and choose a style.

Line Chart

- **Purpose**: Displays trends over time.
- **How to Create**:
  a. Select the data range.
  b. Go to the **Insert** tab.
  c. Click **Insert Line Chart** and choose a style.

Pie Chart

- **Purpose**: Shows proportions of a whole.
- **How to Create**:
  a. Select the data range.
  b. Go to the **Insert** tab.
  c. Click **Insert Pie Chart** and choose a style.

Bar Chart

- **Purpose**: Compares values across categories, similar to a column chart but horizontal.
- **How to Create**:
  a. Select the data range.
  b. Go to the **Insert** tab.
  c. Click **Insert Bar Chart** and choose a style.

Scatter Plot

- **Purpose**: Shows the relationship between two sets of data.
- **How to Create**:
  a. Select the data range.
  b. Go to the **Insert** tab.
  c. Click **Insert Scatter (X, Y) Chart** and choose a style.

Advanced Charting Techniques

As you become more comfortable with Excel, you can explore advanced charting techniques to enhance your data visualization:

- **Combo Charts**
  - **Purpose**: Combine different types of charts to compare datasets with varying scales.
  - **How to Create**: Select your data, go to the **Insert** tab, click **Insert Combo Chart**, and choose a suitable combination.
- **Sparklines**
  - **Purpose**: Insert small, simple charts within cells to provide a quick visual summary.
  - **How to Insert**: Select the cell where you want the sparkline, go to the **Insert** tab, click **Line**, **Column**, or **Win/Loss** under Sparklines.

- **Trendlines**
  - **Purpose**: Add a trendline to chart data to highlight trends.
  - **How to Add**: Click on your chart, go to the **Chart Design** tab, click **Add Chart Element**, and then **Trendline**.
- **Chart Templates**
  - **Purpose**: Save a chart format as a template for future use.
  - **How to Save**: Right-click on your chart, choose **Save as Template**, and follow the prompts.

Basic Examples of Using Charts in Excel

Charts are a powerful way to visually communicate data insights. Below are some basic examples of how to use charts in Excel, along with example tables and descriptions of how to create corresponding charts.

Example 1: Sales Performance Over Time

Data Table: Monthly Sales

Month	Sales ($)
January	5,000
February	6,500
March	7,000
April	5,500
May	8,000
June	7,500

Chart Type: Line Chart

- **Purpose: To display sales trends over time.**
- **How to Create:**
  a. **Select the data range (A1:B7).**
  b. **Go to the Insert tab.**
  c. **Click Insert Line Chart and choose a style.**

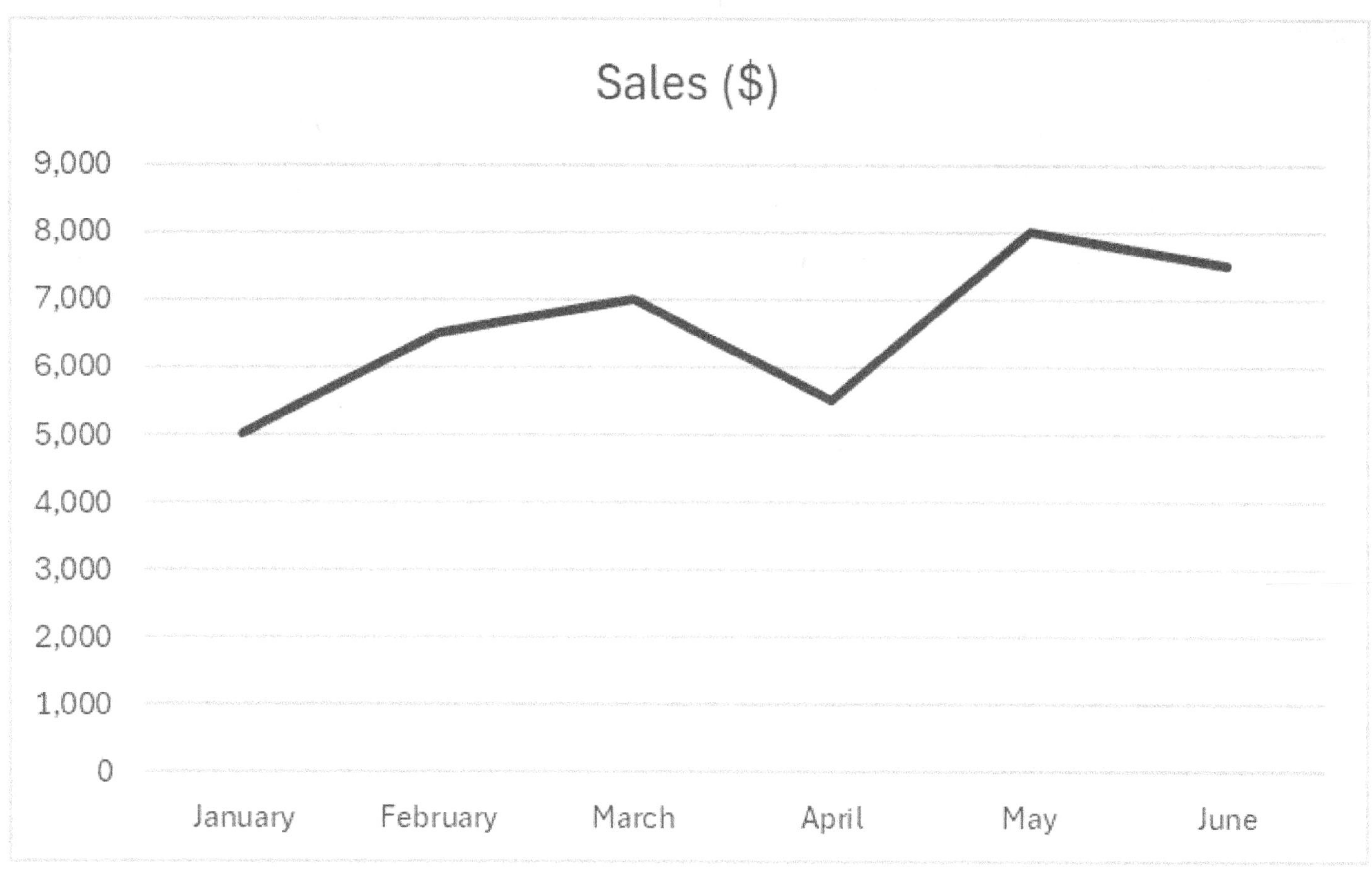

This line chart will show the sales performance from January to June, allowing you to quickly identify trends and patterns.

Example 2: Departmental Budget Allocation

Data Table: Budget Allocation

Department	Budget (%)
Marketing	30
Research	25
Development	20
Operations	15
HR	10

Chart Type: Pie Chart

- **Purpose: To illustrate the proportion of the total budget allocated to each department.**
- **How to Create:**
  a. **Select the data range (A1:B6).**
  b. **Go to the Insert tab.**
  c. **Click Insert Pie Chart and choose a style.**

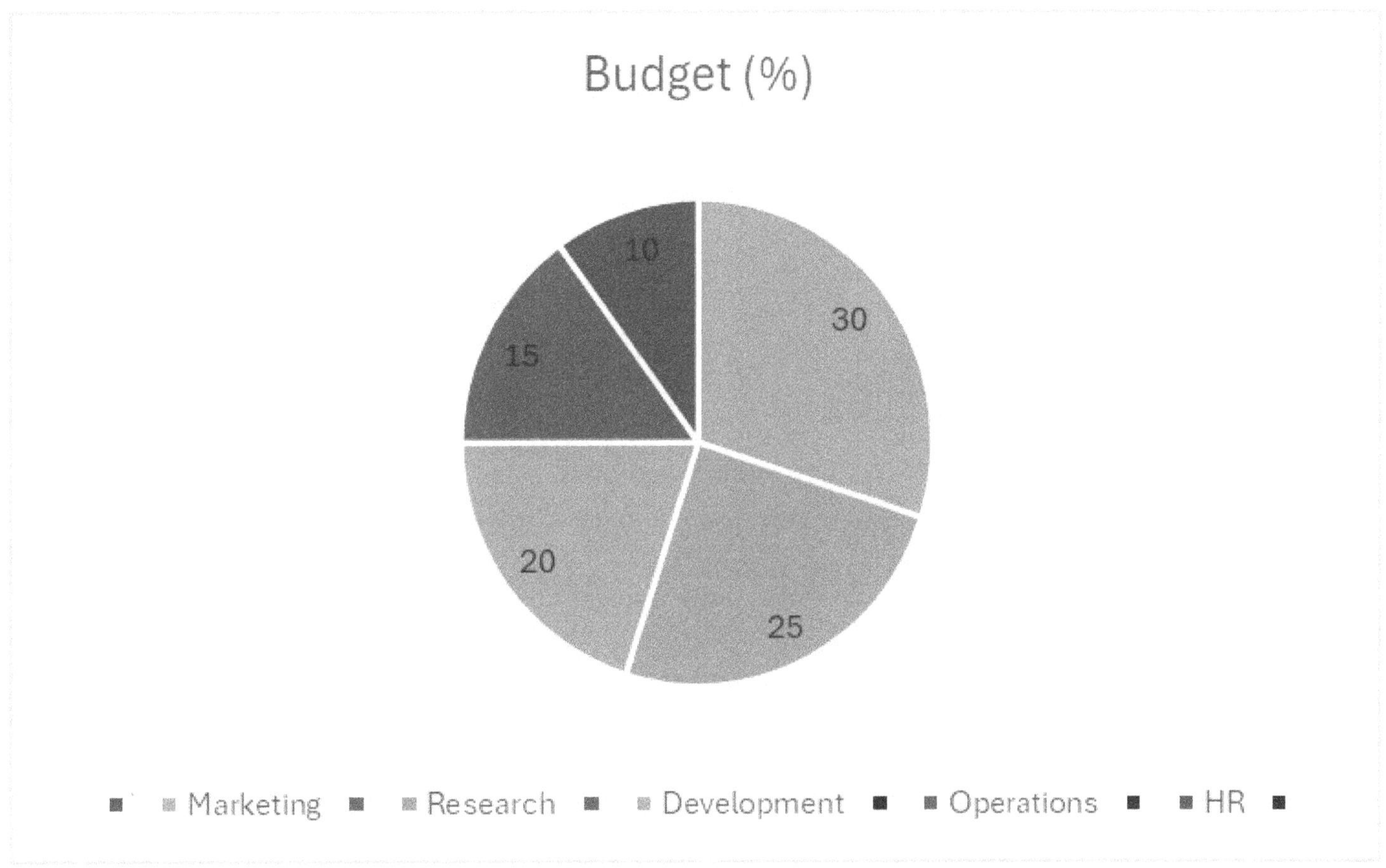

This pie chart will visually represent the budget distribution among the departments, making it easy to see which department receives the most funding.

Example 3: Product Comparison

Data Table: Product Sales

Product	Q1 Sales	Q2 Sales
Product A	2,000	2,500
Product B	3,000	3,500
Product C	1,500	1,800

Chart Type: Column Chart

- **Purpose: To compare sales figures between different products over two quarters.**
- **How to Create:**
  a. **Select the data range (A1:C4).**
  b. **Go to the Insert tab.**
  c. **Click Insert Column Chart and choose a style**

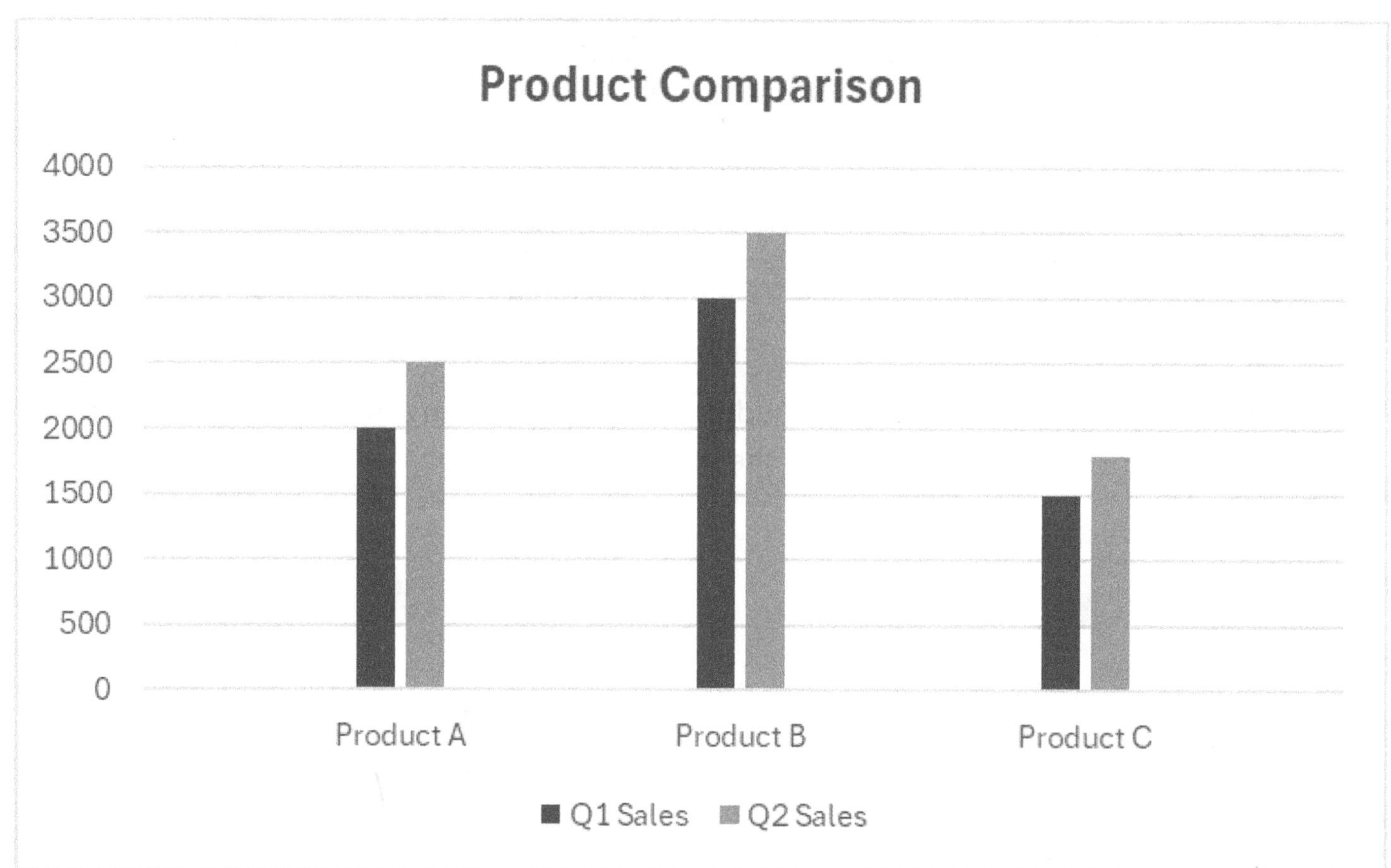

This column chart allows you to compare the sales performance of each product across the two quarters, highlighting which products are performing better.

Example 4: Correlation Between Variables

Data Table: Study Hours vs Test Scores

Study Hours	Test Score
2	70
4	75
6	85
8	90
10	95

Chart Type: Scatter Plot

- **Purpose: To examine the relationship between study hours and test scores.**
- **How to Create:**
  a. **Select the data range (A1:B6).**
  b. **Go to the Insert tab.**
  c. **Click Insert Scatter (X, Y) Chart and choose a style.**

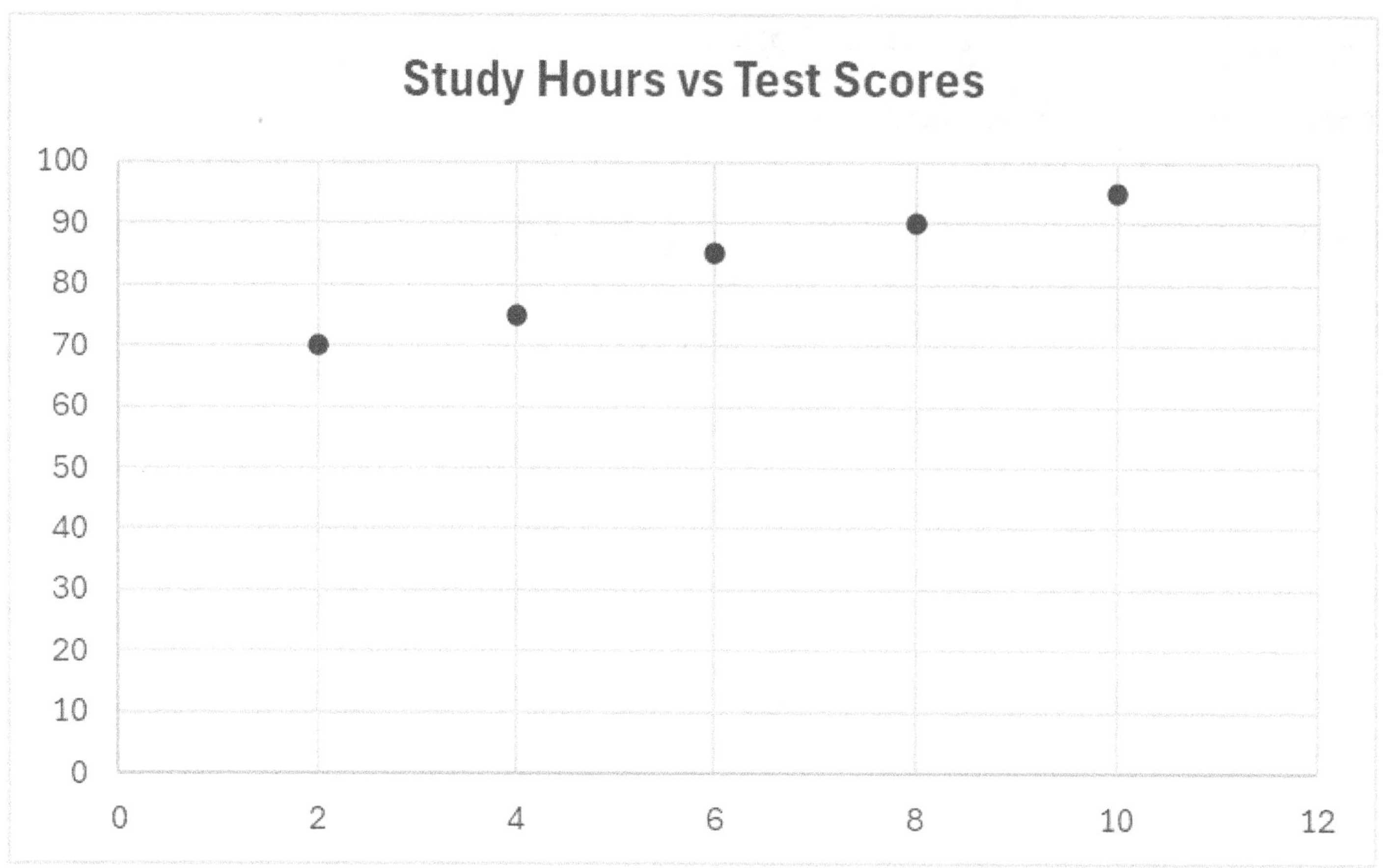

This scatter plot will help visualize the correlation between the number of hours spent studying and the resulting test scores, indicating any positive or negative trends.

By using these examples, you'll be able to create simple yet effective charts that provide clear insights into your data, enhancing your ability to communicate information efficiently.

www.ingramcontent.com/pod-product-compliance
Lightning Source LLC
Chambersburg PA
CBHW060111090326
40690CB00064B/5230
* 9 7 9 8 3 1 6 6 1 2 4 5 1 *